HUMILITY

THE VIRTUES: MULTIDISCIPLINARY PERSPECTIVES

Series Editors

Nancy E. Snow

Professor of Philosophy and Director of the Institute for the Study of Human Flourishing, University of Oklahoma

Darcia Narvaez

Professor of Psychology, University of Notre Dame

Published

Justice

Edited by Mark LeBar

Humility

Edited by Jennifer Cole Wright

Forthcoming

Sustainability

Edited by Jason Kawall

Honesty, Integrity, and Truth-Seeking

Edited by Christian B. Miller and Ryan West

HUMILITY

Edited by Jennifer Cole Wright

THE VIRTUES

OXFORD
UNIVERSITY PRESS

OXFORD
UNIVERSITY PRESS

Oxford University Press is a department of the University of Oxford. It furthers the University's objective of excellence in research, scholarship, and education by publishing worldwide. Oxford is a registered trade mark of Oxford University Press in the UK and certain other countries.

Published in the United States of America by Oxford University Press
198 Madison Avenue, New York, NY 10016, United States of America.

Library of Congress Cataloging-in-Publication Data
Names: Wright, Jennifer Cole, editor.
Title: Humility / edited by Jennifer Cole Wright.
Description: New York : Oxford University Press, 2019. |
Includes bibliographical references and index. |
Identifiers: LCCN 2018056207 (print) | LCCN 2019017002 (ebook) |
ISBN 9780190864910 (Online content) | ISBN 9780190864897 (updf) |
ISBN 9780190864903 (epub) | ISBN 9780190864873 (cloth : alk. paper) |
ISBN 9780190864880 (pbk. : alk. paper)
Subjects: LCSH: Humility.
Classification: LCC BJ1533.H93 (ebook) | LCC BJ1533.H93 H86 2019 (print) |
DDC 179/.9—dc23
LC record available at https://lccn.loc.gov/2018056207

1 3 5 7 9 8 6 4 2

Paperback printed by Marquis, Canada
Hardback printed by Bridgeport National Bindery, Inc., United States of America

CONTENTS

PART III
INTELLECTUAL HUMILITY

SERIES EDITORS' FOREWORD

This series is a product of a long partnership between the series editors on a topic of mutual interest: virtue. Typically, having a virtue is being disposed to have certain kinds of perceptions, thoughts, motives, emotions, and ways one is inclined to act. We firmly believe that the study of virtue itself, as well as the study of individual virtues, is greatly enhanced by taking multiple disciplinary perspectives. This is not to deny the value of studying virtue from within single disciplines but is, instead, to urge scholars to take a broader outlook—to look beyond the bounds of their own disciplines and explore what other academic fields have to offer.

The challenges to moving outside of one's disciplinary perspective are daunting. For one thing, seasoned academics are immersed in the language and methods of their own disciplines and often find those of others alien and confusing. For another, academics often feel unqualified simply to dip into the writings of another discipline and are not confident that reading and studying fields other than their own will repay the time and effort. The upshot is the impression that academics from different disciplines are talking at cross-purposes, even when they're discussing such important topics as justice, generosity, or other virtues.

We certainly recognize the challenge of cross-disciplinary work and have experienced it ourselves. Nevertheless, we believe there is much to be learned from cross-disciplinary interaction—from serious attempts made by academics of different disciplines to engage with each other's work around issues of importance. One area in which serious cross-disciplinary engagement has been lacking is the study of specific virtues. This series seeks to remedy that deficiency through fifteen books in which practitioners of different disciplines write about single virtues or clusters of virtues. In each volume of the series, editors seek to show the unity of writings by identifying common themes, threads, and ideas. In each volume, too, we have sought to include a "wild card" discipline—a discipline that perhaps one would not expect to see included in a collection of essays on a particular virtue. We do this for two reasons: first, so that readers will not tire of seeing the "usual suspects" of disciplines consulted for work on specific virtues; and second, so that readers will be surprised, enlightened, and consistently challenged to expand their horizons of thinking about virtue.

We regard the audience for this series as practitioners of many academic disciplines who are interested in the topic of virtue and in broadening and deepening their understanding of specific virtues. The series will be also accessible to academics who have not previously studied virtue. Volumes such as those included in this series help provide resources for the work of the scholar who desires to know the literature on a virtue in a field different from her own. Those trained in philosophy, for example, often do not know where to look to find material of interest in psychology or anthropology, and vice versa. The volumes in this series, while not promising to provide a comprehensive overview of work on a virtue in a specific field, should nonetheless be informative to any academic who wishes to learn about virtue from a variety of disciplinary perspectives.

Nancy E. Snow
Professor of Philosophy and Director of the Institute of Human Flourishing
University of Oklahoma

Darcia Narvaez
Professor of Psychology
University of Notre Dame

CONTRIBUTOR BIOGRAPHIES

Antonio Argandoña is Emeritus Professor of Economics and of Business Ethics, and holds the "la Caixa" Chair of Corporate Social Responsibility and Corporate Governance at IESE Business School. He is the author of numerous books and articles on economic and business ethics, corporate social responsibility, corporate governance, monetary and international economics. His recent publications on ethics and business have been published in *Journal of Business Ethics, Impresa Progetto. Electronic Journal of Management, Handbook on the Economics of Reciprocity and Social Enterprise, Journal of Business Ethics, La persona al centro del Magistero sociale della Chiesa, The Future of Leadership Development, Journal of Business Ethics, Rethinking Business Management. Examining the Foundations of Business Education,* and *Moral Foundations of Management Knowledge.*

Michael W. Austin is Professor of Philosophy at Eastern Kentucky University. His research and teaching focuses on subjects in ethics and philosophy of religion. He has published on issues in family ethics, sports ethics, virtue ethics, and on religious pluralism. His current research focuses on the nature of virtues and their relevance for practical ethics, with a focus on the virtue of humility. He is the author or editor of 10 books, including *Conceptions of Parenthood* (Ashgate, 2007); *Being Good: Christian Virtues for Everyday Life* (Eerdmans, 2012); and *The Olympics and Philosophy* (University Press of Kentucky, 2012). His most recent book is an anthology entitled *Virtues in Action: New Essays in Applied Virtue Ethics* (Palgrave Macmillan, 2013). In his other life, he is a husband, father, and soccer coach.

Chloe C. Banker received her BA in Psychology and Neuroscience at Duke University and is currently a law student at the University of Southern California.

David J. Bobb is president of the Bill of Rights Institute, in Arlington, Virginia. He earned a PhD in political science from Boston College.

Don E. Davis, PhD, is Associate Professor of Psychology at the Georgia State University. His research interests include humility and related virtues (e.g., gratitude and forgiveness) and spirituality and its intersection with other identities.

Kay de Vries is Deputy Head of School and Head of Centre for Health Research at the School of Health Sciences, University of Brighton, UK. She is an active researcher in the areas of end of life, old age, and dementia care, in acute, community, and care home environments and has conducted research in the UK and in New Zealand. She has developed and led a number of postgraduate programs and supervised a large number of MSc and PhD students. Recent research has focused on the experiences of caregivers of people with dementia. She is particularly interested in aspects of caregiving and dementia in relation to bereavement and loss, and in virtue ethics with a focus on humility and generosity. Kay is predominantly a qualitative researcher and has expertise in all qualitative research methodologies but is also experienced in using mixed-methods approaches. She has a strong network of collaborators within her research field, both nationally and internationally. Kay holds three research affiliate positions: Associate Professor with the University of Washington, Seattle; Senior Research fellow with Association for Dementia Studies, University of Worcester, UK; and Research Associate with Victoria University of Wellington, New Zealand.

Megan C. Haggard is Assistant Professor of Psychology at Francis Marion University in Florence, South Carolina, USA. She completed her Master's and doctoral studies at Baylor University and a post-doctoral fellowship at the Institute for the Study of Human Flourishing at the University of Oklahoma. Her research interests include the intellectual virtues and their related cognitive, emotional, and behavioral outcomes, as well as the intersection of morality, gender, and religion/spirituality.

Joshua N. Hook is Associate Professor of Counseling Psychology at the University of North Texas. He is also a licensed Clinical Psychologist in the state of Texas. His research interests focus on humility, religion/spirituality and multicultural counseling. He is co-editor of the forthcoming *Handbook of Humility.* He also blogs regularly about personal and spiritual growth at www.JoshuaNHook.com.

Pelin Kesebir is a social psychologist currently employed as an assistant scientist at the Center for Healthy Minds at the University of Wisconsin-Madison. She received her PhD from the University of Illinois at Urbana-Champaign in 2009 and has worked as a postdoctoral research associate at the University of Colorado, Colorado Springs, until 2014. Her main research interests revolve around the study of happiness and virtue. The goal of her research is to gain insights into the bidirectional relationship between virtue and happiness while discovering ways to encourage "virtuous cycles" in people. She is also interested in existential psychology, particularly in how the human awareness of mortality affects various psychological dynamics. Combining positive psychology and existential psychology, Pelin has studied how virtues, such as humility, can buffer the destructive effects of death anxiety and induce existential well-being.

Mark R. Leary is Garonzik Professor of Psychology and Neuroscience at Duke University, where he is Director of the Interdisciplinary Behavioral Research Center. Dr. Leary's research and writing has centered on social motivation and emotion, with an emphasis on people's concerns with interpersonal evaluation and the negative effects of excessive self-preoccupation. He has published 13 books and more than 200 scholarly articles and chapters on topics such as self-presentation, self-preoccupation, social emotions, interpersonal rejection, and self-esteem. His books include: *Interpersonal Rejection, The Social Psychology of Emotional and Behavioral Problems, Self-Presentation, Handbook of Self and Identity, Handbook of Individual Differences in Social Behavior, Handbook of Hypo-egoic Processes,* and *The Curse of the Self.* Dr. Leary was editor of *Personality and Social Psychology Review,* founding editor of *Self and Identity,* and President of the Society for Personality and Social Psychology. He is a fellow of the American Psychological Association, the Association for Psychological Science, and the Society for Personality and Social Psychology. He was the recipient of the 2011 Lifetime Career Award from the International Society for Self and Identity and the recipient of the 2015 Scientific Impact Award from the Society for Experimental Social Psychology.

Alan Morinis is Dean and Founder of the Mussar Institute (www.mussarinstitute.org) and is an active interpreter of the Jewish spiritual tradition of Mussar. Born and raised in a culturally Jewish but non-observant home, he studied social anthropology at Oxford University on a Rhodes Scholarship, earning his DPhil degree on the topic of Hindu pilgrimage. He is the author of *Pilgrimage in the Hindu Tradition* (Oxford University Press, 1984) and editor of several other volumes on global pilgrimage traditions. He has also produced feature films, television dramas, and documentaries, as well as taught at several universities. His journey to discover the Mussar teachings is recorded in *Climbing Jacob's Ladder* (Trumpeter, 2002). He is also the author of a guide to Mussar practice, *Everyday Holiness: The Jewish Spiritual Path of Mussar* (Trumpeter, 2007), *Every Day, Holy Day* (Trumpeter, 2010), and *With Heart in Mind* (Trumpeter, 2014). He now regularly gives lectures and workshops in Mussar thought and practice. The Mussar Institute offers courses and training in Mussar in dozens of cities to thousands of people annually.

David K. Mosher is a doctoral student studying counseling psychology at the University of North Texas. His research interests include religion, spirituality, and positive psychology, with an emphasis on the study of virtues such as humility and forgiveness in a religious/spiritual context.

Darcia Narvaez is Professor of Psychology at the University of Notre Dame. She brings evolutionary theory, neurobiology, and positive psychology to considerations of well-being, morality, and wisdom across the lifespan, including early life, childhood, and adulthood and in multiple contexts (parenting, schooling). She has published over 120 articles and chapters and is author or editor of 13 books including *Moral Development in the Professions; Postconventional Moral Thinking; Moral Development, Self and Identity; Personality, Identity and Character; Evolution, Early Experience and Human Development; Ancestral Landscapes in Human Evolution: Culture,*

Childrearing and Social Wellbeing; Neurobiology and the Development of Human Morality: Evolution, Culture and Wisdom; Embodied Morality: Protectionism, Engagement and Imagination; Contexts for Young Child Flourishing: Evolution, Family and Society. She is a fellow of the American Psychological Association. She is Executive Editor of the *Journal of Moral Education*. She also writes a popular blog for *Psychology Today* ("Moral Landscapes").

C. Thi Nguyen is Assistant Professor of Philosophy at Utah Valley University. His primary areas of research are moral epistemology and aesthetic epistemology, including topics such as the importance of disagreement, trust, expertise, and intellectual autonomy. His dissertation was "An Ethics of Uncertainty," which argued that the existence of moral disagreement was a basis for moral humility and self-doubt. He also works in the philosophy of games, focusing on questions of moral and aesthetic value of games. He is a founding editor at the new *Journal of the Philosophy of Games*, the founder of the North American Philosophy of Games Working Group, and on the steering committee of the Philosophy of Computer Games Conference. In a previous life, he was a food writer for the *Los Angeles Times*, trying to convince people of the value of taco trucks, Koreatown noodle shops, and back-alley oyster shacks.

Robert C. Roberts is Distinguished Professor of Ethics, Emeritus, at Baylor University and Chair in Ethics and Emotion Theory at the Jubilee Centre, the University of Birmingham. His most recent book is *Emotions in the Moral Life* (2013). For the past year and a half, he has worked mostly on the concept of humility and related concepts, and he is a recipient, with Michael Spezio, of a grant from the Self, Motivation, and Virtue project at the Institute for the Study of Human Flourishing at the University of Oklahoma and the Templeton Religion Trust for a study of Humility in Loving Encounter.

Michael Spezio is Associate Professor of Psychology and Neuroscience at Scripps College in Claremont, CA, and a Visiting Researcher with the Valuation in the Human Brain Group at the Institute for Systems Neuroscience of the University Medical Center in Hamburg-Eppendorf, Hamburg, Germany. He works in the areas of affective, social, and decision-valuation neuroscience and heads the Laboratory for Inquiry into Valuation and Emotion (LIVE) at Scripps College. His peer-reviewed neuroscience publications have appeared in the *Proceedings of the National Academy of Sciences*; the *Journal of Neuroscience; Social, Cognitive, and Affective Neuroscience*; and *Neuropsychologia*. He co-edited the *Routledge Companion to Religion and Science* (2012) and the interdisciplinary volume *Theology and the Science of Moral Action: Virtue Ethics, Exemplarity, and Cognitive Neuroscience* (Routledge, 2012). He is a co-editor of the journal *Philosophy, Theology, and the Sciences* (Mohr Siebeck) and was the neuroscience editor for the journal *Religion, Brain, and Behavior* (Taylor & Francis). His work in the areas of social, affective, and decision-valuation neuroscience has over 1500 citations. His research concerning the bases of exemplary love, compassion, and care is part of the HABITVS Project (Humane Archetypes: Biology, Intersubjectivity, and Transcendence in Virtue Science).

Daryl R. Van Tongeren, Ph.D., is an Associate Professor of Psychology at Hope College. His research focuses on social psychological approaches to meaning, religion, and virtues.

Erik J. Wielenberg is Professor of Philosophy at DePauw University in Greencastle, Indiana. He works primarily in ethics and the philosophy of religion and is particularly interested in ethics in a secular context. He earned his PhD in philosophy at the University of Massachusetts at Amherst in 2000, where he wrote a dissertation on virtue under the direction of Fred Feldman. As a graduate student he spent a year as a Visiting Graduate fellow at the Center for Philosophy of Religion at the University of Notre Dame; more recently (2014–2015) he was a visiting fellow at the Centre for Ethics, Philosophy, and Public Affairs at the University of St. Andrews. While there, he spent a lot of time thinking about (and trying to acquire) humility. He is the author of *Value and Virtue in a Godless Universe* (Chicago University Press, 2005); *God and the Reach of Reason: C.S. Lewis, David Hume, and Bertrand Russell* (Chicago University Press, 2007); and *Robust Ethics: The Metaphysics and Epistemology of Godless Normative Realism* (Oxford University Press, 2014).

Everett L. Worthington, Jr. is Commonwealth Professor Emeritus at Virginia Commonwealth University, working from the Department of Psychology. In 2018-9, he is Distinguished Visiting Scholar at Wheaton College (Illinois). He studies positive psychology, especially forgiveness and humility, and religion and spirituality.

Jennifer Cole Wright is Associate Professor of Psychology at the College of Charleston, as well as Affiliate Member of the Philosophy Department and Environmental and Sustainability Studies Program. She is also currently a *Sustainability and Social Justice* faculty fellow with the Honors College. Her area of research is moral development (at both the individual and community level) and moral psychology more generally. She studies virtues such as humility, meta-ethical pluralism, the relationship between moral values and tolerance for divergent attitudes, behaviors, and practices, the influence of "liberal vs. conservative" mindsets on moral judgments, and young children's early socio-moral development. She co-edited, with Hagop Sarkissian, *Advances in Experimental Moral Psychology* (Bloomsbury Publishing) and edited an interdisciplinary volume on *Humility* (Oxford Press). She is currently co-authoring *Understanding*

Virtue: Theory and Measurement with Nancy Snow and Michael Warren (Oxford Press). Her research articles appear in a diverse range of psychology and philosophy journals, including *Cognition, Self & Identity, Journal of Moral Philosophy, Journal of Moral Education, Philosophical Psychology, Journal of Cognition and Culture, Personality & Individual Differences, Journal of Experimental Social Psychology, Mind & Language, Personality & Social Psychology Bulletin, Social Development,* and *Merrill-Palmer Quarterly.*

HUMILITY

Introduction

JENNIFER COLE WRIGHT

This volume is part of a multidisciplinary series, The Virtues, edited by Nancy E. Snow. The aim of the series is to showcase scholarly work on specific virtues or clusters of virtues from a variety of disciplines. Humility, the topic of this volume, is explored from a variety of philosophical and psychological perspectives, as well as in specific contexts such as hospice care, business management, competitive contexts, and political history.

Moral humility is a virtue with a long and checkered history. Its benefits and pitfalls (indeed, even its status as a virtue) have been hotly debated over the centuries by philosophers and theologians. Recently, there has been a renewed interest in moral humility, as well as the controversies surrounding it, which has led to new attempts to conceptualize it as a virtue and locate it and its importance within the larger context of our lives.

Examples of these efforts can be found in this volume. Indeed, the overarching aim of this volume is to provide a multidimensional, genuinely interdisciplinary perspective on humility that secures its place among the virtues and highlights its significance and value within a variety of life domains.

Part I explores several accounts of moral humility, each providing a different way to conceptualize humility as a moral virtue. Part II explores moral humility as a virtue in the context of our daily lives—what roles it plays (e.g., in fostering happiness and managing unhealthy pride) and where it can most readily be found and/or cultivated (e.g., in contexts of "deep caring" with others).

Although much of this book is dedicated to humility as a moral virtue, it would be remiss to not also touch upon (albeit too briefly) humility as an intellectual virtue—a virtue that has been much discussed of late in both virtue epistemology and psychology. Part III of this volume will do just that.

Not surprisingly, these parts do not represent hard boundaries, and there will be a fair degree of overlap between them. We hope that the approaches featured in this volume will give some indication of the depth and vigor of recent thinking about humility. Though common themes pervade the chapters, conceptual issues about humility remain far from settled, and empirical work on humility is growing. The complexity of humility and the scope of its applicability in our lives remain lively topics for further research.

HUMILITY AS A MORAL VIRTUE

When we consider humility as a moral virtue, several important questions arise. The chapters in this part work hard to address these questions, including, first and foremost, what is the nature of humility, and why should it be considered a moral virtue? They also address questions about the relationship between humility and other virtues, as well as other desirable features of human life, such as loving relationships. They explore the relationship between humility and pride—can and should the two coexist? And they consider the problem of humility, greatness, and leadership—can people who are highly skilled, talented, and accomplished, and/or in a leadership role, be humble? Finally, several authors explore the question of how humility is best cultivated.

The first two chapters, by Alan Morinis and Erik Wielenberg, introduce a religious conception of moral humility and a secular conception. **Chapter 1,** "Occupying Your Rightful Space" by Alan Morinis, explores the nature of humility (*anavah*) from within the Jewish tradition of self-development known as Mussar. According to the Mussar tradition, humility develops through our aspiration to be faithful servants of God, setting aside our selfish personal aspirations so that we can serve the needs of others, in allegiance with the divine. One becomes a "nothing" through which God's will can be done—a process that requires an extensive personal transformation to overcome our natural self-importance and self-orientation. This makes humility, Morinis argues, virtue's "foundation stone" (p. 26), upon which all other virtues depend (a theme that will come up again in my chapter).

One might worry that Morinis's account advocates servility, meekness, and passivity—a criticism leveled against the dominant Christian view of humility by philosophers like Hume and Nietzsche (as discussed in Wielenberg's chapter). Yet, according to Morinis, this is not the case. Indeed, in the Mussar tradition Moses is held up as one of the great exemplars of humility—raising the question of the relationship among greatness, leadership, and humility that emerges in several chapters in this volume. Instead, the key to humility for the Mussar is learning to *occupy your rightful space,* whether that space be physical, emotional, verbal, financial, or some other form. The Mussar ideal is to learn to take up exactly the amount of space that is necessary—even when that space, as in the case of Moses, is fairly large—to fulfill one's mission of service in life, not more or less. His point is that occupying less than the appropriate space (as in the form of self-denigration) is as much a defect in one's humility as the opposite. Humility promotes and requires an inner dignity, one that allows us to recognize and value our worth so that we can stand strong in the face of whatever trials and tribulations may come our way. This highlights the importance of an appropriate level of pride in the healthy expression of humility—a view shared by many of the authors in this volume.

While Erik Wielenberg in chapter 2, "Secular Humility," agrees with Morinis that humility has historically been viewed as an important virtue in prominent monotheistic religions, he argues that there is a virtue meriting the title of humility that can be disentangled from religious trappings, rendering it purely secular. For Wielenberg, humility resides in two things. First, it resides in the secularized recognition and acceptance of three fundamental universal limitations—limitations we all experience because of our humanness: *helplessness, fallibility,* and *moral frailty*. That is, our ultimate *helplessness* in the face of forces beyond our understanding and control; our *fallibility* (i.e., our vulnerability to ignorance and error; and our *moral frailty* (replacing a more theistic notion of sin), which requires us to acknowledge our moral imperfection and our daily battles with weakness and vice. Second, while in Morinis's theistic account of humility, we are humbled before God, in Wielenberg's account of secular humility, we are humbled instead before our *relative insignificance*, our small place within a much larger awe-inspiring universe.

Wielenberg argues that the combination of these two—the recognition and acceptance of our universal limitations and of our relative insignificance—generates humility insofar as it creates a resistance to arrogance and excessive pride and guards against feelings of entitlement, of deserving more than others, as well as jealousy and envy. It also promotes open-mindedness and feelings of gratitude, respect, forgiveness, and appreciation for others, since we recognize our fates as bound up together with them. It helps break down the barriers between "us" and "them," so we can see our moral differences as largely a function of our human limitations rather than indicators of goodness and evil.

But what if your "place" in the larger scheme of things is truly greater than someone else's? This once again raises the question of greatness and humility—can someone who is truly outstanding be humble? Agreeing with Morinis, Wielenberg argues that, yes, people who are truly outstanding can possess humility, and they can do so while remaining fully cognizant of their value, objectively speaking. Indeed, he argues that they may even overestimate, to some degree, their value (e.g., overestimating their capacities, strengths, and skills relative to their competition) and yet remain humble—as long as they recognize their universal limitations and maintain an appreciation for the fact that they are only a part (even if a potentially important part) of the larger scheme of things.

Chapter 3, "A Critical Examination and Reconceptualization of Humility," by Mark Leary and Chloe Banker, takes a different approach to humility. They start by reviewing the common features of most psychological accounts of humility, noting that such accounts (including some in this volume) commonly include features such as accurate self-knowledge, awareness of one's limitations, modest self-presentation, and other-oriented interpersonal orientation as critical components of their accounts. Yet, each of these, Leary and Banker argue, are problematic as reliable and valid indicators of humility for reasons they cogently articulate in their chapter.

What, then, is the core ingredient—the necessary and sufficient attribute—of humility, the one thing that would meaningfully separate a humble response from a nonhumble response and a humble person from a nonhumble person? Leary and Banker argue that the core of humility is the understanding and acceptance that no matter the greatness of our personal accomplishments or positive characteristics, no one is fundamentally more special than anyone else because of them. Nor should anyone be viewed or treated as more special, especially outside the domain of their accomplishments or characteristics (but also to some degree within it).

Some—famous actors, athletes, business tycoons, and other public figures—seem to think that because they are particularly good in one arena, they are entitled to receive special treatment (extra attention, respect, and deference) from everyone else, wherever they go. Others, on the other hand, while certainly cognizant of their arena of excellence, do not expect this, and may even shy away from it. Here, Leary and Banker agree with Wielenberg that even if your estimation of your excellence is somewhat inflated, as long as it is not accompanied by this sense of entitlement to special treatment, you can still possess the virtue of humility.

Leary and Banker provide some preliminary evidence of this core, showing that 70% of the variance in people's attributions of humility was predicted by the degree to which they viewed a person as thinking she should receive special treatment, feels entitled to special treatment all the time, and thinks she is a special person. What is more, those people's humility (measured by the brief state humility scale) predicted their attitudes about their own specialness and entitlement to special treatment—the higher they were in state humility, the less they viewed themselves as special or entitled to special treatment for their skills, talents, and accomplishments.

In chapter 4, "A Relational Humility Framework: Perceptions of Humility in Relational Contexts," David Mosher, Joshua Hook, Don Davis, Daryl Van Tongeren, and Everett Worthington introduce a new model of humility. According to this model, humility is fundamentally *relational,* in the sense that it is best estimated through certain judgments those in relation to a person make about her. Or, as they argue, a person's humility is best estimated "by aggregating estimates from several relationships, at different times, and from diverse perspectives" (p. 93). The relevant judgments pertain to the person's self-knowledge (whether she has an accurate view of herself), her other-oriented consideration for their welfare, and the degree to which her interpersonal behaviors are considered "socially pleasing" (p. 94)—i.e., marked by a lack of self-aggrandizing attitudes or emotions (such as pretentiousness or superiority). Thus, according to these authors, humility has an essentially *relational* function: people's attributions of humility to a particular person function as an estimate of how they are likely to be treated while in a relationship with her.

Additionally, they propose (and provide evidence) that humility governs and facilitates many forms of internal processes, other-oriented emotions, and social behaviors. Specifically, they view humility as a powerful relational buffer and support system, especially under times of stress and hardship. When situations arise that "tempt, test, or strain one's ego" (p. 96), a humble person is able to maintain her other-oriented stance, promote positive emotions in herself and others, and thereby deepen her relationships. In this way, humility facilitates the forming—and strengthening—of social bonds (i.e., social bonds hypothesis). Relatedly, humility serves as a sort of social lubricant (i.e., social oil hypothesis) that prevents relationships from being damaged by stressful events that would otherwise cause harm—e.g., conflict, suffering, grief, and other negative life events.

They conclude by examining these dual roles of humility in several specific contexts where difficult situations and relational stresses are likely to arise: marriages and family relationships, cross-cultural engagement, and businesses/organizations (also discussed in Austin's and Argandoña's chapters). Across all three contexts, they illustrate how relational humility predicts more positive short-term and long-term outcomes. Based on these findings, they recommend infusing humility into these areas, in particular through the education and training of professionals who are likely to cross paths with people in these contexts, especially during difficult times (e.g., counselors, therapists, doctors, consultants, and teachers).

In chapter 5, "Humility in Four Forms: Intrapersonal, Interpersonal, Community and Ecological," Darcia Narvaez also discusses relational humility, providing a developmental perspective on how it is embodied in our neurobiological systems. According to Narvaez, humility requires people to be neurobiologically "balanced" and healthy, able to approach uncertain and stressful situations calmly and with compassion (a view echoed by Mosher, et al.), and thus unlikely to become "socially threat reactive" (p. 121)—i.e., perceiving others as a threat—in challenging social encounters.

As a developmental process, humility is fostered and shaped through our daily interactions, where we encounter other-oriented care, respect, and concern, both as the receiver and the giver. Ideally, according to Narvaez, children are born into "evolved nests" where they are appropriately nurtured by responsive caregivers, their needs met in a respectful and loving fashion by a range of family and community members, thereby allowing them to develop secure emotional attachments (see also Kesebir, this volume). Under these conditions, humility naturally develops as a multilayered virtue, encompassing intra- and interpersonal, community, and ecological concerns, and relationships.

Here, Narvaez introduces a new aspect of humility—our connection to the larger living world around us. While other authors emphasize the importance of recognizing one's place in the grander scheme of things, Narvaez takes it a step further by illuminating one way in which humility connects us to that larger frame, highlighting our interconnectedness with and interdependence on other living beings, and on the natural world that sustains us.

She contrasts two worldviews: the first considers the universe to be sacred, unified, and living, where we are bound together by a sacred moral code; the second sees the universe as fragmented and amoral, largely filled with non-living matter to use as a resource for our benefit, with objects we can own and other living beings we can dominate. The former worldview, Narvaez argues, is cultivated and reinforced through a "humble" upbringing, while the latter is fostered through the sort of upbringing modern humans are more likely to undergo—where children are exposed to toxic levels of stress across multiple dimensions (e.g., home, school, community, media), and parents are unsupported in their efforts to create evolved nests for their children. Such upbringings create people with "rigid, brittle, self-protective orientations" (p. 127) that chronically activate the brain's survival systems, resulting in hypervigilance, hyperactive stress responses, and feelings of deep alienation from and suspicion toward oneself, others, and the living world.

In chapter 6, "Humility as a Foundational Virtue," I also strive to locate the core of humility but end up in a different place than Leary and Banker. I argue that the need for humility arises from a universally experienced feature of our psychology—phenomenologically speaking, we experience ourselves as the center of the universe. This experience naturally gives rise to a "centeredness" that strongly orients us toward our own internal states. We experience our needs and interests as most important, and our values, beliefs, and commitments as more true and worthy of pursuit than others. Thus, it feels normal and unproblematic to privilege and prioritize ourselves. Yet, the ethical life requires that we transcend this, at least to some degree. And this, I argue, is where humility is vital, because at its core humility is an *epistemically* and *ethically aligned state of awareness*; a state of awareness that is free of the epistemic and ethical biases normally generated by our centeredness. This frees us up to directly engage with reality and experience the world as it really is and to find our place within the vast interconnected web of other morally relevant living beings, whose needs, interests, values, and goals are as valuable and as worthy of consideration and concern as our own.

I also argue that much of what other authors have located within the concept of humility—accurate self-knowledge, awareness of limitations, modest self-presentation, occupying rightful space, a lack of entitlement and feeling that one deserves special treatment, an appreciation for the objective value in the world, and so on—follow naturally from this epistemically and ethically aligned state of awareness. Indeed, echoing Morinis, I argue that humility is a foundational virtue, one necessary for the full development and exercise of other virtues, and maturely virtuous character.

In closing, I consider various methods for cultivating humility, highlighting the importance of several contributions to this volume, such as the argument for secure attachment and other positive early life experiences and practices (Kesebir and Narvaez), as well as the need to expose ourselves to "deep caregiving" situations, where we encounter our own finitude, fragility, and helplessness in the unalterable and unavoidable vulnerability and suffering of others (Roberts and Spezio; de Vries). Finally, in line with Wielenberg and Narvaez, I emphasize the importance of awe-inspiring experiences, ideally through spending time in relationship with the natural world.

MORAL HUMILITY IN OUR LIVES

Starting this part, in chapter 7, "Humility: The Soil in Which Happiness Grows," Pelin Kesebir moves us in a somewhat different direction, discussing humility as an approach to one's self, others, and life in general that is most conducive to enduring happiness. She argues that humility—which she defines as "an ability to see oneself in true perspective and be at peace with it" (p. 177)—is vital to our lives because it fosters stable happiness, in the sense of enduring mental and emotional health.

It does so, according to Kesebir, in a number of ways. First, it facilitates healthy relationships with our selves. As many other authors have argued, people possessing humility see themselves for who they are, harboring neither feelings of "entitled" superiority, nor inferiority. They have developed a "deeply secure self" (p. 184)—i.e., a firm, secure, and serene sense of self-worth and appropriate (or "optimal") self-esteem. This stabilizes the self against ego-threats and fosters a more "selfless" psychological functioning made up of reduced levels of self-preoccupation (e.g., hypo-egoic states; see also Leary and Banker).

Second, humility facilitates a healthy relationship with reality, insofar as it fosters (echoing previous authors) a "true perspective" (p. 186) of how and where we fit into the grander scheme of things, defusing any sense of specialness or entitlement. People possessing humility honestly look at reality because they feel able to deal with whatever they see. They can take responsibility, as appropriate, for both good and bad outcomes. Here, Kesebir reinforces the idea that humility protects against narcissistic entitlement and the expectation of "specialness" that leads to the presumptive and disrespectful treatment of others.

And finally, echoing Mosher et al.'s chapter on "Relational Humility," Kesebir argues that humility facilitates healthy relationships with others by protecting against the interpersonal friction created by selfishness, arrogance, entitlement, and other nonhumble qualities people can possess. Here she reminds us that previous research has found a strong connection between humility and helpfulness, generosity, gratitude, and forgiveness, as well as empathy and compassion.

In closing, Kesebir discusses the cultivation of humility. In line with Narvaez, she discusses the importance of secure attachment, as well as early exposure to exemplars of humility, along with various practices (e.g., mindfulness and meditative exercises) that are known to lower self-centeredness and promote humility-related virtues, such as compassion, gratitude, respect, and egalitarianism.

In chapter 8, "Self-Other Concept in Humble Love as Exemplified by Long-Term Members of L'Arche," Robert Roberts and Michael Spezio discuss the virtue of humility within the context of L'Arche communities, which began in a single home in 1964 and now boast 150 around the world. These are communities composed of people with varying intellectual disabilities (referred to as the "Core Members") along with non-disabled "Assistants." Rather than assuming a caregiver/care-receiver hierarchical approach often found in facilities that house and/or support people with disabilities, people in the L'Arche communities live together as equals and friends. By doing so, they achieve a deep capacity for love and humility, cherishing one another and acting in service of one another's good. The humility (or, as Roberts and Spezio call it, "humble love") found in these communities highlights the absence of several vices commonly found in society and in our everyday relationships: distorted agency (e.g., selfish ambition), empty self-display (e.g., vanity), corrupt entitlement (e.g., arrogance), invidious comparison (e.g., self-righteousness, envy), and tribal superiority (e.g., racism). Through sharing their lives with the Core Members, the Assistants learn to disentangle the fundamental value and worth of a person from what she is able to do or accomplish. This allows them the courage to open themselves to both giving and receiving love and friendship, and the self-discipline to dive into lovingly serve the needs of the community, creating a bi-directional communion reminiscent of Narvaez's discussion of the "evolved nest." In this way, L'Arche communities allow people to protect and heal themselves from the "Normal"—i.e., the toxic worldview that promotes selfishness, domination, and competition (again, see Narvaez)—and shed the vices they came in with that block them from deeply experiencing love and humility.

One important contribution of this chapter is the discussion of the relationship between humility and love, or *agapê*—the feeling of kinship and neighbor-love that leads you to care for the well-being of another, even a complete stranger, for *their own sake,* rather than your own. Combined with humility, humble love rejoices in the well-being of others and in their excellence (rather than feeling threatened by or in competition with it). As other authors have stated, humility requires an appreciation for the objective value of others, as well as for the excellence they generate and contribute to the world. With humble love this appreciation becomes something more—a celebration.

Along a similar vein, in chapter 9, "Humility and Helplessness in the Realization of Limitations within Hospice," Kay de Vries discusses humility within the context of hospice care. De Vries argues that the hospice environment is one that naturally cultivates and requires humility because it is within this sacred "liminal" space that we encounter ourselves and others in our true state of weakness; we must face the unresolvable and unconquerable limitations of being human (something other authors in this volume have also highlighted as essential to humility). While this weakness may be encountered elsewhere, the hospice environment creates a unique opportunity: by accompanying and assisting others on the journey toward death, we experience the powerlessness and helplessness of being unable to save the sick or change the fate of the dying. We must instead become immersed in the deeply humbling tasks of caring, easing suffering, and holding the space for death to occur with dignity and respect.

De Vries argues that medical environments often foster inequality and a hierarchical dominance relationship between the caregiver and the patient, as doctors and nurses are perceived as the "specialists" with the all the power, knowledge, and control. Hospice, on the other hand, has the power to transform this purely clinical environment into a sacred one—one in which both caregiver and patient are confronted with, and humbled by, the great mysteries of life and death. The extreme weakness and suffering often encountered in the hospice environment strips away the nonessential features of our lives, relationships, and self-narratives, leaving only that which resides at the core.

De Vries also observes that while caregivers within hospice are often deeply humble—and humbled by their experiences—they are also largely unaware of their humility. This highlights a potentially paradoxical quality of humility (and moral virtues generally)—is self-awareness of the possession of such virtues necessary for their possession or even desirable? Either way, de Vries argues, most hospice caregivers do not think about humility; rather, they simply see what is to be done and do it, thereby embodying the ideal of "selfless service." She remarks that, as with other humble people, they "have their feet planted firmly on the earth and go about their lives in a steady level-headed way" (p. 237). Also echoing several authors, she emphasizes the relational and collective nature of humility, something that nurtures social bonds and creates a sense of "deep collegiality" within groups.

Chapter 10, by Michael Austin, turns to the subject of "Humility in Competitive Contexts." In line with other authors, Austin defines humility as both proper self-assessment and self-lowering other-centeredness (i.e., the ability to put the interests of others ahead of one's own, when appropriate). Echoing Narvaez and I, he argues that this extends beyond the realm of human beings to encompass other nonhuman animals and the natural world. In addition, he argues that humility involves an accurate recognition and appreciation for objective value (in the forms of truth, beauty, and goodness) in the world, regardless of how it came to be or who created it. While not emphasized as much in other chapters, this is viewed as central in other accounts of humility (see, for example, Kupfer, 2003).

Austin points out that these characteristics of humility make it an apt trait for competitive contexts (contexts where we pursue excellence and objective value), even though historically it has been largely dismissed from this arena. It promotes a lack of insecurity about how others view us, and therefore a willingness to be vulnerable, freeing us up to take risks and to try new things, even when failure is possible or even likely. He addresses the worry that there is a conflict between humility and competition—that humility makes us less competitive, since to be competitive is to be generally hostile toward (or at least unconcerned about) the interests of others. Here, he argues that, ideally speaking, competitiveness (i.e., proper ambition) is made up of the desire to *do well,* not to do *better than others.* Thus, the possibility of losing or placing second is not harmful to our self-worth; our value as persons is not tied to what we have done or accomplished. We are free to pursue excellence for its own sake. This relates back to appreciating objective value in the world—a competitive person is humble to the degree that they appreciate excellence wherever they encounter it, whether it be in themselves or others. This makes humility not antithetical to but actually good for competition, because it fuels our collective fire to seek greater heights, to achieve our best, not for our sake, but for the sake of bringing objective value into the world.

Austin discusses humility in the competitive contexts of sports, academia, and business, which meshes well with chapter 11, "Humility and Decision-Making in Companies" by Antonio Argandoña. Argandoña discusses humility in businesses—in particular, in those who occupy positions of authority in them—explaining the critical role it plays in appropriately motivating employees and gaining their voluntary participation (which often includes coordinating with others) in the firm's activities, aligning them with the well-being of the firm, seen as a human community. According to Argandoña, managers' responsibilities go beyond their own advancement and achievement because they "encompass the firm's mission, organization, structure, and culture" (p. 278). It is up to them to create an environment that promotes and accommodates ethical behavior and prosocial interaction (e.g., teamwork) in the firm, meanwhile discouraging the opposite.

Argandoña defines humility as a "strength of character" associated with temperance—and, as such, he sees it as moderating our natural instincts to put ourselves first, to seek status and superiority. He explores humility along four dimensions (intellectual, emotional, motivational, and behavioral), arguing that humble managers possess realistic and objective self-knowledge, the desire to continue to gain knowledge and recognize their defects and errors, to seek objective information about their environments, and to appreciate any limitations imposed upon them by those environments. They also possess and display an openness to others (without feelings of superiority or inferiority), as well as the desire to behave in ways that promote virtue development, and excellence more generally, in their firm. Such managers genuinely care about the well-being of the members of their firm and seek opportunities to actively contribute to their advancement and development, both as employees within the firm and as persons. Contrary to what some may think, Argandoña argues that such caring is not only good for the firm's employees but also good for the firm (and the achievement of its goals).

He also addresses the question of how humility can be cultivated, in this case, within the context of managing a business firm. He emphasizes the importance of developing the habit of virtue, voluntarily seeking out constructively critical input from the other members of the firm (regardless of their position) and creating a safe environment for such open exchange, as well as engaging in active and uncompromising self-examination and reflection, which includes openly acknowledging and "owning" our mistakes when they are made known to us.

Part II ends with chapter 12, "Frederick Douglass and the Power of Humility," by David Bobb, in which he discusses the role of humility in the life of Frederick Douglas, a 19th-century ex-slave and abolitionist. He argues that humility played a crucial role in not only Douglas's fight for his ultimate freedom from slavery but also his rise into the public life as a well-known orator and advocate for the abolishment of slavery (through which he would eventually become a friend and inspiration to Abraham Lincoln).

Bobb confronts the difficult question of the appropriateness of humility within the context of oppression, where possessing humility is seen as a potential barrier to rising up and confronting social injustice. He argues (and Wielenberg agrees) that there is a critical difference between *humiliation*—such as the humiliation that Douglas was forced to repeatedly experience as a slave—and *humility*. Consistently with the views of other contributors to this volume, Bobb locates that difference in the healthy pride that accompanies humility—a sense of internal dignity and worth that defies the self-denigration and devaluing typically associated with externally imposed humiliation. This means that, contrary to being a barrier, insofar as humility naturally coexists with an appropriate level of pride, it promotes our ability to combat oppressive practices and stand up for our rights and the rights of others.

Indeed, Bobb argues that humility not only opens the door for confronting our oppressors with compassion and grace—providing the intellectual, moral, and physical resistance necessary to fight for our dignity and freedom—but it also fosters a sense of hope for a better future. According to Bobb, it was humility that allowed Douglas to not only forgive his former owner, Hugh Auld, but to also embrace the United States as a nation worth fighting for. His pride and humility gave him the courage to become not only a voice against slavery but also a voice for a future in which his fellow countrymen could embrace the greatness of their nation, understanding that greatness is founded on a commitment to the equal and fair treatment of all people.

HUMILITY AS AN INTELLECTUAL VIRTUE

As noted, humility is not only considered a moral virtue, it has more recently been recognized as an intellectual virtue. Chapter 13, "Self-Trust and Epistemic Humility," by C. Thi Nguyen engages with intellectual (or what he calls "epistemic") humility through a puzzle: the puzzle created by the fact that certain intellectual domains (i.e., the moral, aesthetic, and religious domains) appear to require a special kind of intellectual autonomy—i.e., they require we think for ourselves and not simply believe on the basis of the testimony of others. This is a puzzle because it requires we ignore our fallibility and proneness to error. Normally an epistemic practice that required us to ignore our fallibility and proneness to error would be frowned upon. Yet, certain domains are "peculiar," insofar as they require that we think for ourselves (or self-legislate). As Nguyen notes, while there is "nothing wrong with unquestioningly following my doctor's orders" (p. 326) without understanding why, it would be morally problematic to, for example, unquestionably not harm others simply because we had been told not to, even if it was by a moral authority. After all, as moral agents, we must be able to grasp the grounds for our own moral beliefs, and forming moral beliefs (and/or making moral decisions) solely on the basis of others' testimony does not incorporate that "grasping." This leads to demand for "radical intellectual self-sufficiency" (p. 328) in these domains.

Luckily, Nguyen thinks we can solve the puzzle. To do so, he argues we need only recognize that because of our epistemic similarity with other human beings (our epistemic peers), the epistemic basis for our own self-trust—which justifies us having and trusting our own beliefs, despite evidence of our fallibility and proneness to error—can (and should) be extended to the trusting of others; even (if not especially) in the "peculiar" domains. What is more, he argues, intellectual (epistemic) humility requires us to weigh disagreeing testimony of our epistemic peers alongside our own, thereby allowing it to appropriately decrease our confidence in the relevant beliefs that we hold.

Nguyen considers—and rejects—arguments for both epistemic nihilism (abandoning all claims to knowledge) and dogmatism (trusting only one's own epistemic authority). And finally, he argues that while the move he makes from self-trust to trusting our epistemic peers defuses the need for radical self-sufficiency, it is nonetheless consistent with the demand for intellectual autonomy, since discovering and taking into appropriate consideration others' disagreement is an important part of thinking for ourselves.

In our last chapter, 14, "Understanding Humility as Intellectual Virtue and Measuring It as Psychological Trait," Megan Haggard argues that intellectual humility should be considered a psychological "trait" and be measured accordingly. Unfortunately, as Haggard explains, there is substantial disagreement in the field about what that means and how it should be approached. Some have adopted the data-driven "factor-analytic" approach to traits (e.g., Values in Action; Peterson and Seligman, 2004), while others have relied on a top-down, theory-guided approach. Some have viewed intellectual humility as a single trait (Whitcomb et al., 2015), others as part of a constellation of distinct qualities—e.g., Roberts and Woods (2003, 2007) view intellectual humility as a conglomeration of low concern for intellectual status, an intrinsic desire for knowledge and truth, low intellectual domination, and a lack of unwarranted intellectual claims. There is also disagreement about the relationship between humility and intellectual arrogance. If intellectual arrogance is the inclination to regard one's beliefs as true because they are your own, is humility simply the disinclination to do so? Haggard thinks not, citing Gregg and Mahadevan (2014)'s definition of intellectual humility as "due deference to an epistemic principle that one subjectively regards as having legitimate authority" (p. 357).

In the end, Haggard argues for an account of intellectual humility as an Aristotelian "golden mean" between intellectual arrogance (deficiency) and intellectual servility (excess) that results in people being able to "own" (i.e., accept and not feel threatened by) their intellectual limitations, while at the same time desiring to improve them, which is grounded in and driven by a general appreciation for and desire to seek the truth. In support of this "limitations-owning" approach to humility (see Whitcomb et al., 2015), Haggard presents research suggesting that intellectually humble people (as measured by her limitations-owning intellectual humility scale) demonstrate more careful and open-minded thinking styles and thereby create more receptive, open intellectual environments for others. In line with other authors in this volume, Haggard argues that possessing intellectual humility does not result in a complete lack of concern for one's level of knowledge, skills, or abilities—nor for one's career. After all, our careers are often the means through which we accomplish good in the world, such as a professor who actively cultivates a love of wisdom in her students. Instead, once again, proper intellectual humility is accompanied by an appropriate level of intellectual pride.

CONCLUSION

Though humility is conceptualized somewhat differently across the chapters in this volume, there is nonetheless widespread agreement on several things. First, the authors agree that humility is not only a virtue but also an important—perhaps even foundational—one, with applicability across a wide range of human experiences and endeavors. Moral humility powerfully impacts our relationship to reality, to ourselves, to other human beings (both those with whom we are in relationship and those with whom we are not), to other living creatures, and to the natural world. Intellectual humility generates epistemic responsibility, both individually and collectively—keeping us open to new ideas, willing to embrace our weaknesses and limitations, and able to give disagreeing voices their appropriate weight. Second, contributors maintain that humility is consistent with (and contributes to) appropriate, healthy pride. And third, they believe that cultivating humility makes us better humans, more open, compassionate, loving, and willing to be vulnerable—but also more willing to take risks, challenge ourselves, and do what must be done for others in their hour of need.

We now turn to more in-depth explorations of this complex and fascinating virtue.

REFERENCES

Gregg, A. P., and N. Mahadevan. 2014. "Intellectual arrogance and intellectual humility: An evolutionary-epistemological account." *Journal of Psychology and Theology*, 42(1), 7–18.

Kupfer, J. 2003. "The moral perspective of humility." *Pacific Philosophical Quarterly*, *84*(3), 249. doi:10.1111/1468-0114.00172.

Peterson, C., and M. E. P. Seligman. 2004. *Character Strengths and Virtues: A Handbook and Classification*. Washington, DC; New York: American Psychological Association.

Roberts, R. C., and W. J. Wood. 2003. "Humility and epistemic goods." In *Intellectual Virtue: Perspectives from Ethics and Epistemology*, edited by L. Zagzebski and M. DePaul, 257–279. New York: Oxford University Press.

Roberts, R. C., and W. J. Wood. 2007. *Intellectual Virtues: An Essay in Regulative Epistemology*. New York: Clarendon Press: Oxford University Press.

Whitcomb, D., H. Battaly, J. Baehr, and D. Howard-Snyder. 2015. "Intellectual humility: Owning our limitations." *Philosophy and Phenomenological Research*, 94(3), 509–539. https://doi.org/10.1111/phpr.12228.

PART I

CONCEPTUALIZING HUMILITY

Chapter 1

Occupying Your Rightful Space

ALAN MORINIS

INTRODUCTION

When focusing on the trait of humility from a Jewish perspective, we encounter something typical of Jewish thought: there are a variety of perspectives on the topic. My grounding is within the Jewish tradition of virtues and virtue cultivation called Mussar, which has an 1,100-year history, dating back to 10th-century Babylonia. Mussar gained its greatest presence in the Jewish world in 19th-century eastern Europe, when it blossomed into what became known as the "Mussar movement" (Etkes, 1993).

Three schools of Mussar developed within that movement, and my teacher is in the lineage called Novarodok, where the students were known for their great humility (Levin, 1996). To reach such levels, it is reported that they would sit in the study hall for an extended period each morning, rocking back and forth, chanting the Yiddish phrase, "*Ich been ein gornisht*" which translates as "I am a nothing."

One morning, a new student arrived at the yeshiva, and, upon entering the study hall, was surprised to find hundreds of students chanting over and over, "I am a nothing. I am a nothing." He did what any new student would do: he took a seat, and joined in rocking back and forth, chanting, "I am a nothing; I am a nothing." Before too long, the student seated beside him turned to him and said: "Not so fast! I was here an entire year before I became a nothing!"

It's a joke, of course, but it makes sense only within the frameworks of virtue cultivation that have evolved in the Jewish context. Humility has been given a primary place in the Jewish appreciation for the inner life, and as far back as the 11th century, Rabbi Bahya ibn Paquda devoted an entire chapter of his *Duties of the Heart/Chovot HaLevavot* (Paquda, 1996), one of the primary Mussar texts, to the question: "Does humility depend on the other virtues, or do the virtues depend on humility?" He answered squarely that humility is the foundation stone upon which all virtue depends, based on the principle that the proper role to which a human being should aspire is to be a servant of God, and humility is the defining feature of the faithful servant who sets aside all personal aspirations and shapes himself in order to serve a master.

This same notion that all inner qualities depend on and reflect the state of one's humility is stated even more clearly in the 16th-century Mussar text *Orchot Tzaddikim/Ways of the Righteous* in the chapter "The Gate of Humility" where the author tells us that "humility is the root [quality] of Divine service" (Anonymous, 1995, 57).

The joke about being "a nothing" also reveals an understanding that humility does not come naturally to most human beings and needs to be cultivated. In the words of Rabbi Moshe Chaim Luzzatto, in his work *Mesillat Yesharim/Path of the Just*. Another of the pillars of the Mussar tradition, he states:

> Since it is a person's nature to swell with self-importance, it is difficult to root out this inclination at its source. It is only through outward actions, which are under his control, that he can affect

> his inner self, . . . that is, he should seek devices by which to counteract his nature and its inclination until he is victorious over them. (Luzzatto, 1996, 301)

There are several terms in Hebrew for humility, but the one that is most common and that translates most accurately the English word "humility" is *anavah.*[1] Probing the conceptual category captured by this term requires that we start where most Jewish thought begins, which is with the Torah, the Five Books of Moses. In the book of Numbers (12:3) we read the verse:

> Now the man Moses was more humble [*anav me'od*] than any other person on the face of the earth.

This depiction of the national leader Moses as the most humble of all people calls into question any preconceptions we might have had that humility is synonymous with meekness, passivity, or diffidence, as is generally held.[2]

Biblical stories about Moses further emphasize that his humility does not coincide with general notions that equate humility with subservience, passivity, and timidity. In the first incident recorded in the Bible that tells of Moses's adult life, he aggressively defends a Jewish slave by slaying the oppressive Egyptian taskmaster (Exodus 2:11). He repeatedly confronted the Pharaoh in his quest to win the people freedom, he fought a war against Amalek, and he stood up time and again to castigate members of his own people, such as Korach and the spies.

Scripture reports that Moses was anything but diffident in his dealings with other people. Perhaps, then Moses may have been identified as such a paragon of humility because he willingly submitted to God and God's will. In fact, what we read in the Torah also contradicts any notion that humility inherently involves submission to a higher power.

In the first instance of encounter between God and Moses, when God calls to Moses from the burning bush and directs him to return to Egypt to lead the Jewish people from slavery to freedom (Exodus 3:2), Moses balks at accepting the mission he is being assigned. Then in a later incident, after the Israelites built the golden calf (Exodus 32:4), when God expresses the wish to destroy the entire people and start anew from Moses, Moses stands up and openly argues with God (32:11–12):

> But Moses implored the Lord his God, and said, "O Lord, why does Your wrath burn hot against Your people, whom You brought out of the land of Egypt with great power and with a mighty hand? Why should the Egyptians say, 'It was with evil intent that He brought them out to kill them in the mountains, and to consume them from the face of the earth'? Turn from Your fierce wrath; change Your mind and do not bring disaster on Your people."

Moses is judged humble, but clearly that cannot be because he meekly submits himself, neither to other people nor to God's will. As if the character of Moses is not evidence enough that the concept of humility in Jewish thought is not consistent with general notions linking humility to subservience or submission, there are teachings that identify the paragon of humility as being none other than God. Humility is found to be a characteristic of the One Above in the creation story itself, where the biblical verse reads: "Let us make man in our image" (Genesis 1:26). Judaism is nothing if not zealously monotheistic, and so the rabbis who have interpreted the Torah have been very challenged by this verse. They wonder, who is this plural "us" that is about to create people? The primary medieval commentator,

Rashi,[3] interprets this plural pronoun as referring to God and the angels. Before creating humanity, God discussed the plan with the angels. Rashi finds a pointed lesson in humility here, saying, "From here we learn the humility of the Holy Blessed One. Since man was to be created in the likeness of the angels, and they would envy him, God consulted them [the angels]."

Rashi continues: "Even though the angels did not help in the making of the first human and this verse gives heretics a basis for rebelling, the Torah would not be stopped from teaching decency and humility—that the great should take counsel and ask permission from the small."

God is accorded the quality of humility for having the consideration to consult with the angels about the creation of humanity, to forestall their envy. We can see even more easily in this example that there is nothing here that equates humility to meekness or diffidence or any other timid, shrinking, unassertive quality. While praising humility, the Mussar teachers even warned against timidity. Rabbi Yechezkiel Levenstein, the storied Mussar supervisor in the Mir yeshiva in the mid-20th century, considered the timid person to be one who acts from weakness, whereas the truly humble person is of strong character, like Moses (Feuer, 1989, 45).

HUMILITY AS OCCUPYING RIGHTFUL SPACE

Though the biblical examples of the humility of Moses and God are remarkable and point to a distinctive view of humility in Jewish thought, and they may succeed in freeing the notion from certain other concepts often held to be synonymous, they do not provide us with enough clarity to develop a clear definition of what is involved in humility, as conceived in the Jewish world. To frame such a definition, we have to turn to rabbinic thought, which we find in the Talmud, where the character traits of humility and arrogance are dealt with at length.

One primary source that helps us in this regard is found in the Babylonian Talmud in Tractate Berachot (6b), where we read the dictum:

> Anyone who sets for himself a particular place to pray in the synagogue, the God of Abraham stands in his aid, and when he dies, people say of him, "This was a humble person [*anav*]."

There is a lot that could be unpacked from this teaching, but the one piece I want to focus on is the notion of setting oneself a particular place to pray in the synagogue as a qualification for humility. We might have thought that the humble person would endeavor to occupy the most insignificant and minimal place in a public gathering, but this source teaches otherwise. The humble person is not one who occupies the least possible space, but rather one who occupies his or her *own* space.

We see that definition being reinforced by a case brought by the Talmud in which someone failed to occupy sufficient space. This is the story of Rabbi Zechariah ben Avkulas.

The passage in the Babylonian Talmud (Gittin 55b–56a) begins: "The humility [*anivut*] of Rabbi Zechariah son of Avkulas caused the destruction of our House in Jerusalem." The house in question is the Temple, and its destruction was a cataclysmic event in Jewish history that is still mourned today. But how could a virtue like humility cause so terrible a catastrophe, and what did Zechariah son of Avkulas do to earn such condemnation?

To understand, we have to enter the story a little earlier. A man named Bar Kamtza was mistakenly invited to the banquet of his enemy. Seeing him at the party, the host tried to throw him out, but Bar Kamtza pleaded with the host not to shame him by publicly removing him from the room. Many prominent rabbis were present and did not intercede, and ultimately, Bar Kamtza was grabbed and thrown out into the street.

The humiliated Bar Kamtza sought revenge. He went to the Roman rulers to claim that the Jews were rebelling. He told them that this could be proven if the Roman leadership sent a sacrifice to the Temple. Normally, such a sacrifice would be offered up by the Jews as a token of goodwill toward Rome. However, Bar Kamtza caused a minor blemish on the animal that he knew would cause the rabbis to refuse the offering.[4] This refusal would be "proof" that the Jews were in rebellion against Rome.

When the sacrifice was brought before the rabbis in the Temple, they of course noticed the hidden blemish, and they understood immediately what was going on. One suggested that they offer the sacrifice anyway to forestall the appearance of rebellion. Rabbi Zechariah ben Avkulas, however, argued that if they did that, people could draw the incorrect conclusion that it was permitted to offer blemished sacrifices.

The rabbis then suggested another solution to their dilemma, which was to have Bar Kamtza killed. To this Rabbi Zechariah ben Avkulas also responded, saying, "If we do so, people will incorrectly think that those who inflict blemishes on sacrificial animals are put to death."

Rabbi Zechariah was unwilling to accept either course of action, and in consequence Bar Kamtza succeeded in his plan. The sacrifice was denied, and the Romans took this as proof that the Jews were in rebellion. They attacked and ultimately destroyed the Temple. The Talmud concludes that "the humility of Zechariah ben Avkulas caused the loss of our House, the burning of our sanctuary, and our exile from the land."

We gain insight into the Jewish view of humility by analyzing what Zechariah ben Avkulas did in this story that could be identified as humble. This question has troubled Talmud commentators through the centuries, and the answer that most ascribe to is that he exhibited what could be called an excess of that trait by shrinking from the task he had been handed. He held the fate of the Temple and his people in his hands, yet he seemed to say, "Who am I to make such unprecedented decisions that will potentially mislead the people as to the law?" This was humility taken to an extreme and hence to the point of defect. The Mussar teachers understood this to be a general principle of the inner life: even the best of traits taken to an extreme becomes tainted. Generosity is good but taken to an extreme can spoil a child or create co-dependence. Patience is a praiseworthy trait but in an exaggerated form can undermine initiative and responsibility. And while humility is good, it is not a virtue if a person sees themselves as so insignificant that they demur from their human tasks. The rabbis praised Moses for his humility that was accompanied by appropriate action, and in calling the Zechariah ben Avkulas's failure to act "humble," they are cautioning that this virtue ceases to be a virtue when it is practiced in an extreme form that undermines personal agency and gives rise to negative consequences.

To explain this in terms we introduced in the discussion of the Talmud's teaching about one who sits in the same place in the synagogue as humble, we can say that Zechariah ben Avkulas was humble to excess because he did not occupy the space of others, and he stood aside from occupying the place he was called upon to take up.

A similar criticism was leveled against King Saul when he failed to eradicate the Amalekites. The prophet Samuel challenged him, saying: "Though you may have appeared small in your own eyes, did you not become head of the tribes of Israel, and the Lord anointed you king over Israel?" (1 Samuel 15:17). The criticism is that King Saul, like Zechariah ben Avkulas, shrank from the task he had been handed because he had a diminished view of himself: both were small in their own eyes. Whereas being "small in one's own eyes" actually conforms to the contempory and Christian-derived definition of humility,[5] in the Jewish view, proper humility does not involve self-negation to the extreme; rather, from these several sources we can synthesize a distinctive Jewish definition that characterizes humility as "occupying one's rightful space." The story of the man in the synagogue refers to actual physical space. When he says that this seat is mine, he is also saying that the other seat is not mine. By making a set place, he is also giving space to others.

But from the stories of Zecharia ben Avkulus and King Saul, we can see that the notion of "space" involved here can be a metaphor for responsibility, and, indeed, the space that defines humility can be in any realm in which a person interacts, be that emotional, financial, verbal, and so on.

This definition is confirmed by looking at Jewish teachings that deal with what we might think of as the opposite of humility, which is arrogance, or *ga'avah* in Hebrew. The rabbis of the Talmud equate this extreme manifestation of egotism to idol worship, which is one of the cardinal sins of Judaism. The concept is that when one puts oneself at the center of one's life, as the arrogant person does, one takes over the space reserved for the divine, hence the analogy of worshipping idols as opposed to the true God. To put it in the words of the relatively recent Mussar teacher, Rabbi Avraham Grodzensky (1883–1944), "An arrogant person in essence wants to replace God on the throne of dominion."[6]

That the arrogant person occupies more than his or her rightful space is confirmed in the dictum brought in the Talmud (Sotah 5a) in the name of God, "I and the arrogant one cannot abide in the same world." Here, too, we find a reference that can be related to occupying space, and arrogance is presented as an appetite for more space than is appropriate to the person, since no one has the right to try to displace God from the world. The exemplars of this trait in Jewish thought are the Pharaoh, the self-proclaimed man-god of Egypt, and

Haman in the Purim story,[7] whose undoing was his obsession over the one person in the whole city who would not bow down to him. The arrogance (i.e., lack of humility) on the part of both of these characters is rooted in their attempt to occupy vastly more than their rightful space.

HUMILITY AS A TRAIT

The Mussar teachers graph all inner traits on a range of four qualities: two that represent opposing extremes of that trait as well as two that describe and position moderate, or central, manifestations. In the case of humility, it is situated as one moderate point on a range of traits that all relate to a person's sense of ego, as seen in figure 1.1.

This continuum gives graphic representation to the way in which the Mussar teachers define virtue in this realm, which is not as a single inner quality but as a swath of inner territory that encompasses and is defined by both pride and humility. As we will see later, the Mussar teachers categorize humility that is devoid of self-esteem as defective.

Figure 1.1 also shows us that a statement I just made calling arrogance the opposite of humility is actually not true to the Mussar concept. Arrogance sits at an extreme point on the range but not so humility. There is an extreme beyond humility where we find a self-deprecating view of oneself as nothing or less than nothing. One's rightful space can and does vary depending on the context: the policeman who has every right to direct traffic at the intersection has no business doing the same in the doctor's office where she is a patient.

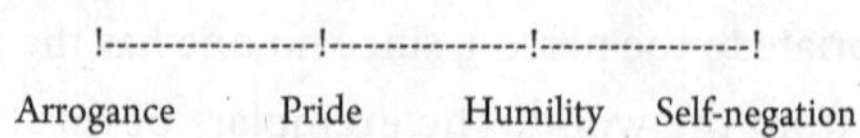

Figure 1.1. The Trait-Range for Humility

Regardless of context, ideal behavior always falls to the middle range that encompasses a measure of self-esteem or pride *along with* humility, while avoiding both the extremes of arrogance (occupying too much space) or self-negation (not occupying one's own appropriate space).

Understanding that humility relates to how much space one occupies is easier to grasp in theory than it is to apply in practice. There may be clues in the moment that can be read—perhaps other people push back when someone arrogates more to themselves than is appropriate, or they express frustration with, or even make demands on, a person who is not stepping up to occupy the space that would be ideal for them in a situation—but it usually comes clearest to us in hindsight. Over time, what we learn in hindsight can be applied with foresight, and behavior can change. Indeed, recalibrating inner traits in the pursuit of virtue is a key part of the Mussar discipline, though beyond the scope of this current chapter.

Though he occupied a lot of space in his environment, Moses was judged humble because doing so was entirely appropriate for him in his context. Rabbi Zecharia ben Avkulas and King Saul, in contrast, did not attain humility because they veered into self-negation when they failed to take up the space that they ought to have occupied. The Pharaoh and Haman are reviled for occupying more space than was their rightful allotment.

We seem to have identified a consistent and practically applicable definition of humility from Jewish sources, but before we can ratify this view of humility, we have to consider a challenge that comes from Maimonides. The Rambam,[8] as he is known in Jewish literature, was the 12th-century Jewish philosopher who is a point of reference for most things Jewish. Regarding all the inner traits, Rambam says (*Hilchot De'ot* 1:4 cited in Kravitz and Olitzky, 1995, 270) that a person should follow the "path of the middle" and not incline toward one extreme or the other. With regard to two traits, however, this rule does not apply, the two being arrogance and anger. Rambam (2:3) writes that in the case of those two qualities, one is actually prohibited from conducting oneself in the manner of the middle path. Rather than be arrogant, one must go to the opposite extreme and be not only humble (*anav*), but rather as lowly of spirit (*sh'fal ru'ach*), which is an extreme manifestation of humility. He writes:

> There are some dispositions in regard to which it is forbidden merely to keep to the middle path. They must be shunned to the extreme. Such a disposition is arrogance. The right way in this regard is not to be merely humble [*anav*] alone, but that he shall be lowly of spirit [*sh'fal ruach*] to the utmost. (Twersky, 1972, 54)

It would seems from this that Rambam advocates a definition of humility other than the one I have constructed, calling on us to cultivate an extreme of self-denial of personal worth. Someone characterized by *sh'fal ruach* goes beyond the trait of *anavah* by seeing himself as insignificant and weak in relation to others.

Yet in the next chapter of the same work (2:2), Rambam qualifies his advocacy of extreme humility. He says that one who comes to awareness of a tendency to be arrogant

> should degrade himself greatly. He should sit in the least honorable seat and wear worn-out clothes that shame their wearer. He should do the above and the like until the arrogance is uprooted from him. Such people may then return to the middle path, which is the proper one, and continue in it for the rest of their lives.

What is revealed here is that the practice of an extreme form of egolessness is not being presented as a virtuous way of living but rather as a practice one takes on for a limited period of time to counter a tendency to arrogance. He is identifying a practical path, not presenting a different definition of humility. Rambam's thought owed a great deal to Aristotle and his position on extreme humility as a practice but not a persisting ideal. It is reminiscent of Aristotle's analogy in book II of the *Nicomachean Ethics* where he says that to attain virtue:

> And then we must bend ourselves in the opposite direction; for by keeping well away from error we shall fall into the middle course, as we straighten a bent stick by bending it the other way. (Aristotle, 1886, 56)

This strong pull away from arrogance eventually helps us achieve the more moderate state of humility as well as its counterpart of self-esteem.

This is exactly what we found the yeshiva students doing when they chanted their phrase, "I am a nothing." That was not meant to be their enduring view of themselves. Rather, this is a practice to recalibrate the inner trait of arrogance back to the middle range, at which point the practice should be abandoned because it will have done its work.

That humility does not lie at the extreme of the range of ego traits finds support in the Babylonian Talmud (Sotah 5a) where we read: "Rebbi Chiya bar Ashi said in the name of Rav: 'A student of the sages must have an eighth of an eighth of pride.'"

If humility were defined as an extreme on the range of ego traits, why would a spiritual aspirant tolerate any amount of pride? An answer is provided by Rabbi Yitzchak Reitbord of Vilna,[9] who probes a midrash, the classical collection homiletic teachings of the Sages on the Torah. The midrash in question (Leviticus Rabbah 13) says that when God was preparing to give the Torah, all the mountains vied for the honor of having the Torah given on them. "I am the highest mountain," said one. "I am the steepest," said another. One by one, they all stated their claim. In the end, God chose Mount Sinai not because it was the tallest or the grandest but because it was the most humble of the mountains.

Based on this midrash Rabbi Reitbord asks a question. If arrogance is so reviled and if humility is meant to be taken to the extreme, why did God give the Torah on any mountain at all? Shouldn't it have been given in a lowly plain or valley? It must be that while arrogance is to be shunned, a moderate degree of pride—represented in the symbol of a low mountain, but still a mountain—is correct inner calibration for a spiritual aspirant.

Indeed, the sage Rava is quoted in the same section of the Talmud (Sotah 5a) as saying: "[A student of the Sages] who possesses [haughtiness of spirit] deserves excommunication. And if he does not possess it, he deserves excommunication."

This enigmatic teaching addresses the problem of extreme tendencies. Not only is there great spiritual danger in an overinflated ego, there is just as much spiritual danger in being devoid of self-esteem. A person who lacks self-esteem is at the least overlooking or denying the implication of the biblical creation story, which invests worth in every human being in virtue of being created in the divine image (Genesis 1:26).

CONCLUDING THOUGHTS

I will close with the words of Rabbi Abraham Isaac Kook (1865–1935), the first Ashkenazi chief rabbi of Israel, who wrote: "Humility is associated with spiritual perfection. When humility effects depression it is defective, when it is genuine it inspires joy, courage, and inner dignity" (Kook, 1966, 174). His thought is in line with the Mussar sources that associate humility with healthy self-esteem (Krumbein,

2005).[10] The commonly held notion that humility entails focusing on one's deficiencies reflects (and, indeed, fosters) lack of self-esteem, which, in turn, leads to a false sense of worthlessness, and that is what is ultimately depressing. Being humble doesn't mean being nobody: it just means being no more nor less of a somebody than you ought to be.

That quality of inner dignity that Rav Kook associates with humility is what grounds the appropriate expression of the trait firmly in the middle range, not at the extreme. That virtuous territory is defined not as a midpoint but as a range that includes both self-esteem and humility and that shuns arrogance and self-negation. Behavior that displays virtuous humility will vary with the context, but in all cases reflects a person's occupying a rightful space within that context, appropriate to one's unique soul and responsibilities, and eschewing the extremes at either end of the range.

NOTES

1. From the Hebrew root *ayin-nun-vav*.
2. According to the thesaurus, synonyms for "humble" include timid, meek, diffident, submissive, sheepish, docile, lowly, and servile.
3. Rabbi Shlomo Yitzchaki (1040–1105), known by the acronym "Rashi," was a French rabbi who authored a comprehensive commentary on the Talmud and commentary on the written Torah.
4. Exodus 12:5: "The animals you choose must be year-old males without blemish." There are traditions that say that Bar Kamtza made a blemish to the eye of the animal because the rabbis had seen Bar Kamtza being humiliated and had not interceded. Others say the blemish was to the ear because the rabbis heard what was going on and did not speak up.
5. As, for example, Charles Hodges's commentary to Acts 20:18–19: "All Christian graces are products of truth. So humility is the state of mind which the truth concerning our character and relations ought to produce. It includes . . . a sense of insignificance, because we are both absolutely and relatively insignificant. We are as nothing before God, in the universe, in the hierarchy of intelligences, in the millions of mankind. We are insignificant in capacity, learning, influence,

and power, compared to thousands of our predecessors and contemporaries. Humility is not only the consciousness of this insignificance, but the recognition and acknowledgment of it, and acquiescence in it" (18:224).

6. Quoted in http://asimplejew.blogspot.ca/2007/11/.
7. In the Book of Esther.
8. An acronym for Rabbi Moshe Ben Maimon. His perspective on the inner traits was heavily influenced by the philosophy of Aristotle.
9. *Koheles Yitzchak*, Parshas Yisro.
10. See a clear example in Elyakim Krumbein, *Musar for Moderns*, p. 31, in which he develops the argument to a conclusion that is graphed as "humility = self-esteem." The argument is made there as elsewhere in the Mussar literature that lack of self-esteem not only creates a sense of unworthiness in a person, it can also be the source of arrogance, which can be understood as a person's efforts to assert in behavior what is lacking in inner feeling.

REFERENCES

Anonymous. 1995. *Orchot Tzaddikim*. Translated by Shraga Silverstein. Jerusalem and New York: Feldheim.

Aristotle. *Nicomachean Ethics*. 1886. Translated by F. H. Peters. London: Keegan Paul, Trench.

Etkes, Immanuel. 1993. *Rabbi Israel Salanter and the Mussar Movement*. Philadelphia and Jerusalem: Jewish Publication Society.

Feuer, Avrohom Chaim. 1989. *A Letter for the Ages*. Brooklyn: Mesorah.

Hodge, Charles. 1879. *Conference Papers: Or Analyses of Discourses, Doctrinal and Practical*. New York: Charles Scribner's Sons.

Kook, Avraham Isaac. 1966 *The Moral Principles*. Translated by Ben Zion Bokser. New York and Toronto: Paulist Press.

Kravitz, Leonard, and Kerry Olitzky. 1995. *The Journey of the Soul*. Northvale, NJ, and London: Aronson.

Krumbein, Elyakim. 2005. *Musar for Moderns*. Jersey City: KTAV.

Levin, Meir. 1996. *Novarodock: A Movement that Lived in Struggle and Its Unique Approach to the Problems of Man*. Northvale, NJ: Jason Aronson.

Luzzatto, Moshe Chaim. 1966. *Path of the Just*. Translated by Shraga Silverstein. New York and Jerusalem: Feldheim.

Paquda, Bahya ibn. 1996. *Duties of the Heart*. Translated by Daniel Haberman. Jerusalem and New York: Feldheim.

Twersky, Isidore (ed.). 1972. *A Maimonides Reader*. Springfield, NJ: Behrman House.

Chapter 2

Secular Humility

ERIK J. WIELENBERG

INTRODUCTION

If there is no God, should we be humble? If so, what form should our humility take? Humility is prized as a central virtue in prominent monotheistic religions, but its status outside of such traditions is contested. Humility is prominently absent from the list of Aristotelian virtues; in its place is *megalopsychia*—"high-mindedness" or "greatness of soul"—a virtue that deals with tracking how much honor and respect one deserves from others—and with taking steps to ensure that one is appropriately honored by others. Aristotle's high-minded person correctly sees himself as superior to the "common run" of people and is justified in looking down on them (Aristotle, 2000, 4.3). Hume includes humility in his famous list of "monkish virtues" that are really vices because they tend to produce negative effects. Specifically, they "stupefy the understanding and harden the heart, obscure the fancy and sour the temper" ([1751] 2006, 73). And Nietzsche sees humility as "anxious lowliness" that is perhaps suitable for ordinary people (the herd) but should be replaced by "self-reverence" in "higher men" (Leiter, 2015, 97–100; see also Nietzsche, [1887] 1998, 27).[1]

I hold that there is a character trait that (a) merits the title "secular humility," (b) is a virtue, (c) has some important similarities with Christian humility, and (d) requires neither *belief* in anything like the God of Judaism, Christianity, or Islam nor the *existence* of such a deity.[2] In this chapter I describe secular humility and make the case that it is a virtue. I begin with a brief overview of humility in Christian thought and explain secular humility and some of its benefits. Next, I explain how an outstanding, high-achieving, self-confident person can possess secular humility, and I then answer two objections. Finally, I put some flesh on the bones of my account of secular humility by considering a real-life example of secular humility.

CHRISTIAN HUMILITY

Traditional Christian thought identifies the first sin as pride: Lucifer's refusal to accept his assigned place in the cosmic hierarchy led to a failed rebellion against divine rule and to the Fall of man. Humility, pride's antidote, is a central virtue in Christian thought. Aquinas identifies the core of humility as recognizing and accepting one's place in the universe (1947, II-II, Q. 161). "Humility" derives from the Latin word *humilus*, meaning on the ground or from humus (earth). The humble recognize and accept both their lowly status in the cosmic order and the tremendous gap between themselves and God. In Christian thought we are not only from the earth; our nature is also corrupted by sin as a result of the Fall. Accordingly, some Christian thinkers suggest that the humble, recognizing their own true nature, take a dim view of themselves. Bernard of Clairvaux ([1124] 1987) characterizes humility as "the virtue by which a man recognizes his own unworthiness because he really knows himself" (103) as well as "contempt of one's own worth" (112).

Our corrupted nature makes humility crucial because of its connection with obedience. God knows what is truly best for us, yet our sinful nature inclines us away from what God commands of us. Humility promotes obedience, which in turn leads to morally right action and genuine happiness. That is why Augustine describes obedience as "the mother and guardian of all other virtues in a rational creature" (1988, 607). Thus, Christian thought places humility at the foundation of human goodness and happiness (see Trakakis, 2014, 85). But what might humility look like outside of a Christian framework?

SECULAR HUMILITY

Aquinas, Clairvaux, and others hold that humility has a *cognitive foundation*. They see the heart of humility as recognition of (i) one's possession of certain flaws or limitations shared by all human beings and (ii) one's relative insignificance in comparison with some aspect of reality. On the Christian account, (i) = one's sinful nature and (ii) = one's relative insignificance in comparison with God. I agree that humility has a cognitive foundation, but the heart of secular humility cannot consist of the Christian versions of (i) and (ii). Accordingly, I shall identify secular versions of (i) and (ii) that can ground secular humility and describe the benefits of secular humility to support my contention that it is a virtue.

Universal Limitations

We are heavily influenced by factors outside of our control. Whereas the God of traditional theism is subject to no external forces and creates whatever natural forces exist, we find ourselves thrown into the universe in a time, place, and circumstances entirely not of our choosing and have our character and our lives shaped by forces over which we have little or no control. Call this universal human limitation *helplessness*. In a humble person, recognition of one's helplessness inhibits excessive pride in one's excellences and accomplishments (see Kupfer, 2003, 252–253 and Wielenberg, 2005, 110) and guards against emotions that are serious threats to social harmony. Misplaced pride can lead to an unwarranted belief that one deserves special treatment from others; when such special treatment is not forthcoming, indignation and anger can result (see Lewis [1942] 2002, 122).[3]

Confucian thought is particularly alert to the threat posed to social harmony by misplaced pride. Confucianism emphasizes the importance of humility because "harmony is the highest ideal for Confucianism as a whole" (Li, 2006, 588). This harmony encompasses both interpersonal social harmony and intrapersonal psychological harmony (Angle, 2009, 65–66). Misplaced pride, jealousy, and frustration threaten both sorts of harmony. Chenyang Li suggests that precisely because there is no God in the Confucian universe "there is no order or natural law from God" and hence "the world has to generate an order of its own" (2006, 594). *The Analects of Confucius* begins with the assertion that going unacknowledged by others without harboring frustration is the mark of a *junzi*—an exemplary or virtuous person (*Analects* 1.1). A later passage tells the story of Meng Zhifan, who stayed with the rearguard during a retreat (a particularly dangerous place to be) and afterward offered the following explanation: "It was not that I dared to take up the rear; only that my horse could not be roused" (*Analects* 6.15). Meng characterizes his actions so that the ultimate responsibility for his position at the rear does not lie with him. Of course, Meng's account is false: it was his brave character and not his horse's laziness that placed him among the rearguard. But someone like Meng could truthfully exhibit secular humility by saying, for example: "I am just lucky to have enough courage to join the rearguard."

Recognition of our helplessness may also lead to the gratitude and respect for parents and ancestors that is emphasized in Confucian thought (see, e.g., Chong, 2007, 76, 110), for they have had tremendous influence over many of the factors that have shaped us (see Kupfer, 2003, 260–261).[4] Secular humility, then, is conducive to harmony within individuals and society as well as gratitude toward parents, ancestors, and social institutions.

A second important limitation of human beings is that we are inescapably subject to ignorance and error. Whatever knowledge we possess is unavoidably incomplete and we are incorrigible mistake-makers; this ignorance and fallibility extends in sometimes surprising ways to our knowledge of ourselves (see, e.g., Wilson, 2002; Cassam, 2014). Call this limitation *fallibility*. Humble people, recognizing their own fallibility, are disposed to take the possibility that they are mistaken to be a live option (at least when it comes to difficult or contentious questions), and to be open to the views of others. As emphasized in Confucian thought, even the wisest human being has something to learn from the most foolish (see, e.g., Klancer, 2012, 668). Recognition of our fallibility, like recognition of our helplessness, promotes social harmony by forestalling obnoxious intellectual arrogance; it also promotes a kind of open-mindedness conducive to the acquisition of knowledge (see Damon and Colby, 2015, ch. 5). As psychologists June Tangney and Debra Mashek write, "the key elements of true humility" include "an ability to acknowledge one's mistakes and limitations" and "a corresponding openness to new ideas and advice" (2002, 161).

A third important limitation is that we are inevitably morally imperfect.[5] Recognizing one's moral imperfection is the secular version of recognizing one's sinfulness. Kant ([1797] 1996) discusses the importance of comparing one's conduct with the requirements of the categorical imperative (rather than with the conduct of one's fellow flawed human beings) and noting the respects in which one's actions fall short of what the moral law requires (187; see also Grenberg, 2005). Similarly, "Confucius maintains that even someone with the highest virtue of humanity is [morally] fallible" (May, 2007, 209; see also Angle, 2009, 85). Call this limitation *moral frailty*. Recognition of moral frailty motivates a humble person to strive continuously to do better morally, thereby avoiding a sort of moral complacency (Newman, 1982). It also helps protect against wrongdoing by working against a tendency to overestimate one's own moral excellence. Psychological research into the influence of situational factors on behavior illustrates the dangers of overestimating one's own moral character (see, e.g., Zimbardo, 2007, 211).[6]

Recognition of one's moral frailty can also promote social harmony by promoting forgiveness. Writing in a Christian context, Bernard of Clairvaux claims that recognition of one's own sinfulness removes an obstacle to compassion for one's fellow sinners ([1124] 1987, 111). Psychological research supports Clairvaux's position. Exline et al. (2008) found that people show greater forgiveness toward wrongdoers to the extent that they can recall or envision themselves committing similar offenses. They claim that "[s]eeing the similarities between oneself and an offender" is conducive to humility and humility works against "a self-righteous, judgmental mindset that distances the perpetrator from the victim" (2008, 496; see also Worthington, 2007, 33).

Human nature includes a well-documented tendency toward "in-group, out-group" thinking (see, e.g., Brown, 1991, 138–139; de Waal, 2006, 53). Such thinking involves positing a moral boundary between us and them. We in the in-group are superior to those in the out-group, and hence we are morally entitled to things that they are not. In the extreme case, only we in the in-group are fully human (see, e.g., Smith, 2011). In narcissism, the in-group shrinks to one, consisting of an individual who, in their mind, possesses unique rights and entitlements and is particularly sensitive to perceived slights (Worthington, 2007, 55–57; see also Kupfer. 2003, 261–263). Such narcissists are especially disruptive of social harmony. Recognition of our own helplessness, fallibility, and moral frailty works against such problematic in-group/out-group thinking by reminding us that we all share the same (flawed) human nature.

In fact, a truly humble person's recognition of herself as a member of a species subject to helplessness, fallibility, and moral frailty will be accompanied by a tendency toward a "relatively low-self focus" or "forgetting of the self" (Tangney and Mashek, 2002, 161; see also Snow, 1995). J. L. A. Garcia writes that a humble person has a "stable, deep-seated, and restrained disposition to play down in her own thinking, self-concept, and feelings—and therein to de-center, to (place in the) background, (not to stress, focus on, make much of, relish, or delight in)" her excellences and achievements (2006, 418; see also Lewis [1952] 2002, 128). There is empirical evidence that such decrease in self-focus benefits its possessor. Tangney points out that "[c]linicians have long noted the links between excessive self-focus and a broad range of psychological symptoms, including anxiety, depression, social phobias and so on" (2009, 488). Additionally, decreased self-focus leaves more room for noticing the needs and accomplishments of others and is linked with gratitude (see Kruse et al., 2014).[7]

Relative Insignificance

From a theistic perspective we ought to be humbled before God; with God out of the picture, before what may we humble ourselves? Lisa Gerber thinks there are many features of the natural world that are up to the task (see also Worthington, 2007, 41–43). Gerber sees a connection between humility and awe, declaring that "humility needs a reality greater than ourselves; a reality that inspires awe" (2002, 43). On her view, the natural world is brimming with suitable awe-inspiring entities, ranging from the sprouting of a bean to the Grand Canyon (2002, 43–45).[8] Comparing ourselves with the natural world can highlight our relative spatial and temporal tininess. Nature is filled with entities far vaster than us that have existed since long before humans were around and will exist long after humans are gone. We can also be humbled by the power of certain natural phenomena—e.g., a roaring waterfall or the centuries-old larger-than-earth storm that constitutes Jupiter's great red spot. One worry here is that fully grasping our insignificance in relation to the universe in its entirety leads to despair—a thought exploited to comic effect by Douglas Adams's fictional Total Perspective Vortex.[9] But notice that I have spoken only of *relative* insignificance. The point of seeing ourselves in a broader perspective or context is to put things into the *proper* perspective—to see the *relative* importance and value of various things, to see oneself "in proper perspective against bigger and grander things" (Worthington, 2007, 49; see also Damon and Colby, 2015, 139–141). In doing this, we do not come to see ourselves as without value; instead, we see ourselves as one valuable thing in a universe filled with value.

As Gerber's remarks about the connection between humility and awe suggest, a person with secular humility will be disposed to engage in awe-inducing activity and reflection. Positive psychologists have identified a number of benefits associated with the feeling of awe, which they define as "the emotion that arises when one encounters something so strikingly vast that it provokes a need to update one's mental schemas" (Rudd, Vohs, and Aaker, 2012, 1130; see also Shiota, Keltner, and Mossman, 2007; and Keltner and Haidt, 2003, 304). Typical elicitors of awe so-defined are "information-rich stimuli, particularly panoramic nature views and novel art and music" (Shiota, Keltner, and Mossman, 2007, 950). Rudd, Vohs, and Aaker (2012) found that experiencing awe increases the amount of time that one feels is available to oneself, which in turn promotes patience, willingness to donate one's time, and a tendency to prefer experiential goods (e.g., vacations) over material ones (that last tendency is in turn positively correlated with life satisfaction). Shiota, Keltner, and Mossman (2007) found that people who are awe prone are more comfortable with ambiguity and open to revising their beliefs and are more inclined to see themselves as part of a greater whole (see also van Cappellen and Saroglou, 2012). Similarly, Piff et al. found that "awe leads to more prosocial tendencies [like generosity and helpfulness] by broadening the individual's perspective to include entities vaster and more powerful than oneself and diminishing the salience of the individual self" (2015, 896–897). Finally, there is some evidence that awe meshes particularly well with *secular* humility. Gottlieb, Lombrozo, and Keltner found that people who are more prone to experiencing awe are "less likely to accept scientifically-unwarranted teleological explanations of the natural world" (including creationism) and "are more likely to explain significant life events by appeal to luck and chance" (2015, 4).

I propose, then, the following account of secular humility:

> S has *secular humility* to the degree that
> (i) S recognizes that she shares with all humans the important limitations of helplessness, fallibility, and moral frailty; (ii) S recognizes her relative insignificance in the grand scheme of things; and (iii) in virtue of (i) and (ii), S is (a) resistant to misplaced pride in her excellences and achievements, envy, and indignation at being slighted by others and (b) disposed toward forgiveness, gratitude, open-mindedness, low self-focus, and feelings of awe.[10]

There may seem to be some tension between the first two conditions, which involve recognizing certain facts about oneself, and the disposition toward low self-focus in condition (iii.b). However, the tension is merely apparent. A person's degree of self-focus has to do with how much time she spends *consciously* thinking about herself. But we can recognize and be emotionally responsive to various facts about ourselves without spending a lot of time consciously thinking about those facts. For example, each of us has internalized various physical facts about ourselves—our approximate height, size, strength, various athletic skills, and so on—and each of us acts in accordance with our recognition of such facts without spending much time consciously thinking about them. Similarly, a person with secular humility has internalized her limitations and relative insignificance and these things permeate her emotional life without her spending much time dwelling consciously on them.

SECULAR HUMILITY AND SELF-KNOWLEDGE

Can someone who is so truly outstanding that they are superior to most human beings—particularly in the moral domain—possess the virtue of humility (see, e.g., Statman, 1992 and Hare, 1996)? It seems that a truly amazing person has nothing to be humble about—but if humility really is a virtue, then it is a trait that everyone ought to have. The challenge is to explain how a person can be both outstanding and humble. One approach has it that the humble person is someone disposed to underestimate her own worth and accomplishments (Driver, 1989 and 2001). But this approach allows for the possibility of a humble braggart, as an amazing person might underestimate herself and yet take excessive pride in and brag excessively about the excellences and accomplishments she does recognize in herself (see Richards, 1988; Wielenberg, 2005, 105–106; and Garcia, 2006). An alternative approach has it that a humble person has an accurate assessment of her own worth and accomplishments and the capacity to resist various sorts of temptations to overestimate such worth and accomplishments (see, e.g., Richards, 1988 and Flanagan, 1990). But the humble braggart problem afflicts the accurate assessment account as well: an amazing person might accurately assess herself and be immune to all temptations to overestimate herself and yet loudly tout her worth and accomplishments whenever possible.[11]

Notice that overestimating oneself in some ways is compatible with possessing certain types of humility. A person might overestimate herself as an athlete and a scholar and yet recognize her sinful nature and her lowliness in comparison with God and so possess Christian humility while at the same time possessing a somewhat inflated view of herself. That suggests that what is central to humility is not having an overall accurate view of oneself but rather recognizing the presence of specific limitations in oneself. A person might overestimate herself as an athlete and a scholar and yet fully recognize her own helplessness, fallibility, and moral frailty as well as her relative insignificance in the grand scheme of things. Such a person would thereby possess secular humility while at the same time possessing a somewhat inflated view of herself. As long as this inflated view of oneself exists in the context of the cognitive and emotional components of secular humility discussed above, genuine humility will be present. Recognizing that one's excellences are largely due to factors beyond one's control should forestall bragging about such excellences—even if one overestimates them. Therefore, my account of secular humility implies that an outstanding person can be humble while at the same time excluding the possibility of a humble braggart.

TWO OBJECTIONS

The claim that humility is a virtue we ought to strive for is among the moral claims that Nietzsche sees as a threat to the existence of "higher men." Nietzsche's higher man reveres himself "as one might a God" (Leiter, 2015, 97). In Nietzsche's view, this "fundamental certainty about oneself and one's values (that often strikes others as hubris)" is a characteristic that lends itself "to *artistic* and *creative* work" (Leiter, 2015, 98). Brian Leiter discusses the case of Beethoven, who wrote in a letter: "The devil take you. I refuse to hear anything about your whole moral outlook. *Power* is the moral principle of those who excel others, and it is also mine" (quoted in Leiter, 2015, 98). According to the Nietzsche-inspired *creativity argument*, secular humility inhibits creativity whereas Nietzschean self-reverence promotes it. Because creative work is so valuable, self-reverence should be pursued (at least among the creative) rather than secular humility. A second challenge arises from the thought that humility on the part of those subject to oppression and exploitation functions as an obstacle to overcoming that oppression and may even promote self-hatred and servility (see, e.g., Tessman, 2005, 64–65). According to this *oppression argument*, those subject to oppression should not possess secular humility, a result that threatens secular humility's claim to be a genuine virtue.[12] It seems to me that work in contemporary psychology suggests how to answer these challenges. Consider the creativity argument first. Psychologists have devoted considerable effort to identifying personality traits associated with creativity. While the picture is complicated, it appears that the currently available evidence does not support the claim that secular humility inhibits creativity whereas self-reverence promotes it.[13] While some studies find positive correlations between narcissism and creativity (e.g., Raskin, 1980 and Solomon, 1985), more recent work speaks against the Nietzschean view rather than for it. Damian and Robins

(2013) investigated the relationship between creative achievement and two kinds of pride—*authentic* pride and *hubristic* pride. To feel authentic pride is to feel proud about a concrete personal achievement resulting from "internal, unstable, and specific causes"—e.g., "I won because I practiced before the game." To feel hubristic pride, by contrast, is to feel proud about oneself "in a global sense"—e.g., "I won because I am always good at everything" (Damian and Robins, 2013, 157). Authentic pride is tied to specific acts, whereas hubristic pride "arises from a self-evaluation of 'being'" (Carver, Sinclair, and Johnson 2010, 698). Damian and Robins found that the disposition toward authentic pride is positively correlated with creative achievement whereas the disposition toward hubristic pride is not (2013, 158). The disposition toward hubristic pride seems to correspond at least roughly with Nietzschean self-reverence and to conflict with secular humility whereas there is no conflict between secular humility and the disposition toward authentic pride, since one can feel proud about particular accomplishments while still possessing the intellectual and emotional dispositions that constitute secular humility as I've defined it here.[14] So there is little reason to accept the creativity argument's premise that secular humility inhibits creativity.[15]

The distinction between authentic and hubristic pride also reveals where the oppression argument goes wrong. The disposition toward authentic pride is correlated with conscientiousness, self-control, a "sense of purpose in life" and "the tendency to respond to losses in life by moving on to new goals" (Carver, Sinclair, and Johnson, 2010, 702)—attributes that aid rather than hinder those seeking to overcome oppression. Some psychologists suggest that authentic pride is the "affective core" of healthy self-esteem associated with successful interpersonal functioning whereas hubristic pride is the core of narcissistic self-aggrandizement associated with interpersonal difficulty (Tracy et al., 2009; see also Tracy and Robins, 2007). Secular humility is compatible with a tendency toward authentic pride, which is associated with achievement and successful interpersonal functioning. Contrary to the central premise of the oppression argument, secular humility does not engender self-hatred or servility.

This completes my theoretical discussion of secular humility. In the next section I flesh out the preceding theoretical discussion with a real-life example.[16]

THE CASE OF PAT TILLMAN

Pat Tillman is well-known in the United States as a professional football player who decided shortly after the terrorist attacks of September 11, 2001, to put his career in the National Football League (NFL) on hold to serve in the US military and was killed in a friendly-fire incident in Afghanistan. Tillman seems to have instantiated at least some of the central elements of secular humility while at the same time possessing a high degree of self-confidence. Consideration of Tillman will not only shed light on the nature of secular humility; it will also help us see how this sort of humility can coexist with self-confidence. In April 2002, after Tillman had played for the NFL's Arizona Cardinals for four seasons, the Cardinals offered Tillman a three-year $3.6 million contract.[17] In May, Tillman declined the Cardinals' offer and enlisted in the US Army. In a journal entry about this decision, Tillman wrote that in light of the 9/11 attacks and subsequent events, his football career seemed "shallow and insignificant" and that the path he had been following was "no longer important" (Krakauer, 2009, 138). Particularly relevant here is Tillman's secularity. According to Jon Krakauer, Tillman "was agnostic, perhaps even an atheist" but believed "in the transcendent importance of continually striving to better oneself—intellectually, morally, and physically" (2009, 116). While serving in Iraq, Tillman wrote in his journal that he was confident that "nothing" awaited him after death (2009, 314), and he requested that no chaplain or minister officiate at any memorial services held for him in the event of his death (2009, 315).[18] When Tillman signed up for three years in the army, he gave up a life of wealth, comfort, and star status in exchange for the modest pay, discomfort, and low status of a new recruit. He quite literally humbled himself. He declined all requests to be interviewed about his decision and did not try to use his fame as a football player to secure special treatment. Another new recruit whom Tillman befriended during basic training reported that Tillman never mentioned that he was a professional football player (Krakauer, 2009, 146). Tillman's journals and the reports of those who knew him support Kraukauer's contention that Tillman was committed to continual self-improvement. He regularly engaged in critical self-examination, generating brutally honest assessments of his strengths and weaknesses as a football player, soldier, and leader. Krakauer reports that Tillman "spoke self-deprecatingly about his intelligence" and was "bracingly open-minded" (2009, 115). This open-mindedness led Tillman to read widely and to pursue a master's degree in history while he was a professional football player. A fellow soldier commented that Tillman "didn't go around beating his chest" and "would talk to these goofy, scrawny-looking privates and treat them as equals" (Krakauer, 2009, 163). The same soldier reports that Tillman "was nonjudgmental" and "was interested even in the most idiotic person in the group. . . . Pat would always start out by giving them the benefit of the doubt" (Krakauer, 2009, 213). Tillman exemplifies recognition of fallibility and the associated Confucian willingness to learn from everyone.

Tillman's journal entries indicate that he agonized over leaving behind his new wife upon enlistment; he writes of "strong feelings of guilt and pain for all I'm putting her through" (Krakauer, 2009, 160). Tillman struggled to do what was right while at the same time recognizing his own moral shortcomings, thus recognizing what above I called "moral frailty." One particularly powerful journal entry illustrates this aspect of Tillman's character as well as hinting at his recognition of helplessness (as characterized above):

> What kind of man will I become? Will people see me as an honest man, hardworking man, family man, a good man? Can I become the man I envision? Is vision and follow-through enough? How important is talent & blind luck? . . . There are no true answers, just shades of grey, coincidence, and circumstance. (Krakauer, 2009, 151)

So far I have connected Tillman with the first cognitive element of secular humility—the recognition of helplessness, fallibility, and moral frailty. What of the other cognitive element—recognition of one's relative insignificance? The best evidence that Tillman possessed this aspect of secular humility lies in his decision to leave the NFL. A document that Tillman wrote in April 2002 outlines his reasons for that decision. The document includes a lengthy account of the many attractions of continuing his NFL career, followed by this paragraph:

> However, it is not enough. For much of my life I've tried to follow a path I believed important. Sports embodied many of the qualities I deem meaningful: courage, toughness, strength, etc., while at the same time, the attention I received reinforced its seeming importance. . . . However, these last few years, and especially after recent events, I've come to appreciate just how shallow and insignificant my role is. I'm no longer satisfied with the path I've been following . . . it's no longer important. (Krakauer, 2009, 138)

In the earlier discussion of recognizing one's relative insignificance, I emphasized that the point of such recognition is to see the relative importance and value of things. Whether or not we agree with Tillman that his joining the military was the morally right thing to do, we can agree with him that doing what is morally right is more important than pursuing a life of comfort, wealth, and shallowness. Tillman possessed enough of the cognitive elements of secular humility to make him significantly resistant to excessive pride in his accomplishments as well as to envy and indignation at being slighted by others. I earlier noted his open-mindedness; there are indications of low self-focus as well. The same college friend I quoted earlier reports that Tillman was "down-to-earth" and "was interested in other people and remembered things about them" and that "he didn't like to talk about himself that much" (Krakauer, 2009, 65).[19] Similarly, a new recruit in Tillman's platoon in Afghanistan reports that Tillman stood out from the other veteran soldiers (Tillman had already served in Iraq) in that he would talk to you like a human being: "A lot of the Rangers were cocky and arrogant and muscle-bound. They treated the new guys like shit. Pat was never like that. He was always polite. He was a genuinely nice guy" (Krakauer, 2009, 225).

Krakauer identifies "unwavering self-confidence" as one of Tillman's defining traits (2009, 4); he also likens Tillman to Nietzsche's higher man (2009, 343–344). The keys to resolving any apparent tension between these claims by Krakauer and my claim that Tillman instantiates secular humility are (a) the distinction discussed earlier between authentic and hubristic pride and (b) the related distinction between self-confidence and self-reverence. Tillman certainly had (warranted) confidence in (some of) his abilities; however, as I noted earlier, his journal entries contain plenty of self-criticism. He seems to have been disposed toward authentic pride rather than hubristic pride. Krakauer reports that Tillman "claimed that his academic success in college came from hard work rather than brainpower" (2009, 115). And his most common response to the various setbacks he recorded in his journals was to "just keep working" (Krakauer, 2009, 103, 147). This is what self-assurance looks like in the context of secular humility. Tillman shows that secular humility can coexist with self-assurance, drive, and achievement. He is neither Nietzsche's self-worshipping higher man nor his bland and vapid "last man" who has created a world in which "all human excellence and creativity is gone" and is left with little to do but blink (Leiter 2015, 22); he is something better.[20]

NOTES

1. For a list of similarities between Aristotelian *megalopsychia* and Nietzsche's higher men, see Leiter 2015, 97, note 8. The differing status of humility in religious and secular moral thought is also reflected in a 2004 study that found a positive correlation between religiosity and holding a positive view of humility (Exline and Geyer, 2004).
2. Secular humility as I understand it does not require religious belief, but it is, as far as I can see, compatible with such belief. Consequently, secular humility is for nonbelievers but not only for them; it is a virtue that is available to believers and nonbelievers alike.
3. In the penultimate section of the paper, I discuss a distinction between *authentic* and *hubristic* pride; when I speak of pride here I mean hubristic pride.
4. The gratitude described here makes sense only if, despite the tremendous influence of factors beyond our control, there is nevertheless a place for free action in our lives (and our ancestors' lives). While I believe that to be the case, a proper discussion of it lies outside the scope of the present paper.
5. Philippa Foot relates the story of the old priest who, when asked what he had learned after many years of hearing confessions, replied: "There are no grown-ups" (2001, 108).
6. Tony Milligan provides an interesting example of this danger from Iris Murdoch's novel *The Bell*; see Milligan, 2007, 223.
7. For a helpful discussion of the many conceptions of gratitude in play in psychology (and philosophy), see Gulliford, Morgan, and Kristjansson, 2013.
8. Brymer and Oades (2009) argue that participation in extreme sports can also induce humility.

9. "When you are put into the Vortex you are given just one momentary glimpse of the entire unimaginable infinity of creation, and somewhere in it there's a tiny little speck, a microscopic dot on a microscopic dot, which says, 'You are here.'" (Adams, 1981, 70).
10. I do not claim that the presence of conditions (i) and (ii) inevitably lead to (iii); as Garrard and McNaughton (unpublished) note, there are many possible emotional responses to recognitions of the sort involved in conditions (i) and (ii). Secular humility has a cognitive *foundation* but also includes emotional dispositions that are appropriate responses to the humility's cognitive foundation but are not guaranteed by that foundation.
11. G. Alex Sinha distinguishes private and public components of humility, identifying the essence of the former as the disposition to be motivated by an awareness that ego often drives us to overestimate our merits to guard against such overestimation and the latter as the disposition to be motivated by concern for others' feelings to refrain from claiming credit that one wants to claim (2012, 260–261). But Sinha's "public humility" seems to be a type of politeness toward others rather than humility. And Sinha's account of private humility cannot solve the amazing-yet-humble puzzle on its own: an amazing person might be strongly motivated to guard against overestimating herself and yet be a braggart.
12. Thanks to Diane Fruchtman for pressing this sort of worry.
13. One reason for the complexity is the existence of "literally hundreds of different tests assessing various aspects of creativity" (Kyaga, 2015, 65).
14. Milligan (2007) similarly argues that humility is compatible with what he calls "recognition pride," which bears some similarity with authentic pride.
15. Also relevant here is Gusewell and Ruch's finding of a correlation between awe and "love of learning, creativity, and curiosity" (2012, 231).
16. For additional relevant real-life exemplars of some aspects of secular humility, see Damon and Colby, 2015, ch. 5.
17. The Cardinals used their final pick of the 1998 NFL draft to select Tillman despite that he was widely considered to be too small to succeed in the NFL. He did succeed, however; after his second season with the Cardinals another team offered him a five-year $9.6 million contract, which Tillman declined out of loyalty to the Cardinals (Krakauer, 2009, 113).
18. That request was not honored.
19. The documentary film *The Tillman Story* includes a clip of a young Tillman after a football game being pressed by a reporter to take some credit for the team's victory. Like Meng Zhifan refusing to take credit for staying with the rearguard during the retreat, Tillman responds to the reporter by praising the coaching staff.
20. I presented earlier versions of this chapter to audiences at the C. S. Lewis Society at Oxford University, the Jubilee Centre for Character and Virtues

at the University of Birmingham, DePauw University, and the University of Oklahoma. I thank my audiences on those occasions for their very helpful feedback. Much of the work on this chapter was completed with the support of a Sabbatical Leave from DePauw University.

REFERENCES

Adams, Douglas. 1981. *The Restaurant at the End of the Universe*. New York: Ballantine Books.

Ames, Roger. 1999. *Analects of Confucius: A Philosophical Translation*. New York: Ballantine Books.

Angle, Stephen C. 2009. *Sagehood: The Contemporary Significance of Neo-Confucian Philosophy*. Oxford: Oxford University Press.

Aquinas, Thomas. 1947. *Summa Theologica*. New York: Benziger Brothers.

Aristotle. 2000. *Nicomachean Ethics*. Translated by Roger Crisp. Cambridge: Cambridge University Press.

Augustine. 1998. *The City of God against the Pagans*. Edited by R. W. Dyson. Cambridge: Cambridge University Press.

Brown, Donald. 1991. *Human Universals*. Philadelphia: Temple University Press.

Brymer, E., and L. G. Oades., 2009. "Extreme sports: A positive transformation in courage and humility." *Journal of Humanistic Psychology* 49, 1, 114–126.

Carver, C. S., S. Sinclair, and S. L. Johnson. 2010. "Authentic and hubristic pride: Differential relations to aspects of goal regulation, affect, and self-control." *Journal of Research in Personality*, 44, 698–703.

Cassam, Quassim. 2014. *Self-knowledge for Humans*. Oxford: Oxford University Press.

Chong, Kim-chong. 2007. *Early Confucian Ethics*. New York: Carus.

Clairvaux, Bernard of. (1124) 1987. "On the steps of humility and pride." In *Bernard of Clairvaux: Selected Works*, translated by G. R. Evans. New York: Paulist Press, 99–144.

Damian, R. I., and R. W Robins. 2013. "Aristotle's virtue or Dante's deadliest sin? The influence of authentic and hubristic pride on creative achievement." *Learning and Individual Differences*, *26*, 156–160.

Damon, William, and Anne Colby. 2015. *The Power of Ideals: The Real Story of Moral Choice*. Oxford: Oxford University Press.

De Waal, Frans. 2006. *Primates and Philosophers: How Morality Evolved*. Princeton, NJ: Princeton University Press.

Driver, Julia. 1989. "The virtues of ignorance." *Journal of Philosophy*, *86*, 373–384.

Driver, Julia. 2001. *Uneasy Virtue*. Cambridge: Cambridge University Press.

Exline, J. J., R. F. Baumeister, A. L. Zell, A. J. Kraft, and C. V. O. Witvliet. 2008. "Not so innocent: Does seeing one's own capability for wrongdoing predict forgiveness?" *Journal of Personality and Social Psychology, 94*, 3, 495–515.

Exline, J. J., and R. W. Geyer. 2004. "Perceptions of humility: A preliminary study." *Self and Identity*, 3, 95–114.

Flanagan, Owen. 1990. "Virtue and ignorance." *Journal of Philosophy, 87*, 420–428.

Foot, Philippa. 2001. *Natural Goodness*. Oxford: Oxford University Press.

Furnham, A., D. J. Hughes, and E. Marshall. 2013. "Creativity, OCD, Narcissism and the big five." *Thinking Skills and Creativity*,10, 91–98.

Garcia, J. L. A. 2006. "Being unimpressed with ourselves: Reconceiving humility." *Philosophia, 34*, 417–435.

Garrard, Eve, and David McNaughton. "Humility: From sacred virtue to secular vice?" Unpublished manuscript.

Gerber, Lisa. 2002. "Standing humbly before nature." *Ethics and the Environment, 7*, 1, 39–53.

Grenberg, Jeanine. 2005. *Kant and the Ethics of Humility: A Story of Dependence, Corruption and Virtue*. Cambridge: Cambridge University Press.

Gulliford, L., B. Morgan, and K. Kristjansson. 2013. "Recent work on the concept of gratitude in philosophy and psychology." *Journal of Value Inquiry, 47*, 3, 285–317.

Gusewell, A., and W. Ruch. 2012. "Are only emotional strengths emotional? character strengths and dispositions to positive emotions." *Applied Psychology: Health and Well-Being*, 4, 2, 218–239.

Hare, Stephen. 1996. "The paradox of moral humility." *American Philosophical Quarterly*, 33, 2, 235–241.

Hume, David. (1751) 2006. *An Enquiry Concerning the Principles of Morals: A Critical Edition*. Oxford: Oxford University Press.

Kant, Immanuel. (1797) 1996. *The Metaphysics of Morals*. Translated by Mary Gregor. Cambridge: Cambridge University Press.

Keltner, D., and J. Haidt. 2003. "Approaching awe, a moral, spiritual, and aesthetic emotion." *Cognition and Emotion, 17*, 2, 297–314.

Klancer, Catherine Hudak. 2012. "How opposites (should) attract: Humility as a virtue for the strong." *Heythrop Journal*, 662–677.

Krakauer, Jon. 2009. *Where Men Win Glory: The Odyssey of Pat Tillman*. New York: Anchor Books.

Kruse, E., J. Chancellor, P. M. Ruberton, and S. Lyubomirsky. 2014. "An upward spiral between gratitude and humility." *Social Psychological and Personality Science*, 5, 7, 805–814.

Kupfer, Joseph. 2003. "The moral perspective of humility." *Pacific Philosophical Quarterly*, 84, 249–269.

Kyaga, Simon. 2015. *Creativity and Mental Illness: The Mad Genius in Question*. New York: Palgrave Macmillan.

Leiter, Brian. 2015. *Nietzsche on Morality*. New York: Routledge.
Lewis, C. S. (1942) 1996. *The Screwtape Letters*. New York: Simon and Schuster.
Lewis, C. S. (1942) 2002. *Mere Christianity*. New York: HarperCollins.
Li, Chenyang. 2006. "The Confucian ideal of harmony." *Philosophy East & West, 56*, 4, 583–603.
Milligan, Tony. 2007. "Murdochian humility." *Religious Studies, 43*, 2, 217–228.
Newman, Jay. 1982. "Humility and self-realization." *The Journal of Value Inquiry, 16*, 275–285.
Nietzsche, Friedrich. (1887) 1998. *On the Genealogy of Morality: A Polemic*. Translated by M. Clark and A. J. Swanson. Indianapolis: Hackett.
Piff, P. K., P. Dietze, M. Feinberg, D. M. Stancato, and D. Keltner. 2015. "Awe, the small self, and prosocial behavior." *Journal of Personality and Social Psychology, 108*, 6, 883–899.
Raskin, Robert N. 1980. "Narcissism and creativity: Are they related?" *Psychological Reports, 46*, 1, 55–60.
Richards, Norvin. 1988. "Is humility a virtue?" *American Philosophical Quarterly, 25*, 3, 253–259.
Rudd, M., K. D. Vohs, and J. Aaker. 2012. "Awe expands people's perception of time, alters decision making, and enhances well-being." *Psychological Science, 23*, 10, 1130–1136.
Shiota, M. N., D. Keltner, and A. Mossman. 2007. "The nature of awe: Elicitors, appraisals, and effects on self-concept." *Cognition and Emotion, 21*, 5, 944–963.
Sinha, G. Alex. 2012. "Modernizing the virtue of humility." *Australasian Journal of Philosophy, 90*, 2, 259–274.
Smith, David Livingstone. 2011. *Less than Human: Why We Demean, Enslave, and Exterminate Others*. New York: St. Martin's Press.
Snow, Nancy E. 1995. "Humility." *Journal of Value, 29*, 203–216.
Solomon, Robert. 1985. "Creativity and normal narcissism." *Journal of Creative Behavior, 19*, 1, 47–55.
Statman, Daniel. 1992. "Modesty, pride, and realistic self-assessment." *Philosophical Quarterly, 42*, 169, 420–438.
Tangney, June Price. 2009. "Humility." In *Oxford Handbook of Positive Psychology*, edited by Shane Lopez and C. R. Snyder, 2nd ed., 483–490. New York: Oxford University Press.
Tangney, June Price, and Debra J. Mashek. 2002. "In search of the moral person: Do you have to feel really bad to be good?" In *Handbook of Experimental Existential Psychology*, edited by Jeff Greenberg, Sander Leon Koole, and Thomas A. Pyszczynski, 156–166. New York: Guilford Press.
Tessman, Lisa. 2005. *Burdened Virtues: Virtue Ethics for Liberatory Struggles*. Oxford: Oxford University Press.

Tracy, J. L., J. T. Chang, R. W. Robins, and K. H. Trzesniewski. 2009. "Authentic and hubristic pride: The affective core of self-esteem and narcissism." *Self and Identity*, *8*, 196–213.

Tracy, J. L., and R. W. Robins. 2007. "The psychological structure of pride: a tale of two facets." *Journal of Personality and Social Psychology*, 92, 3, 506–525.

Trakakis, N. N. 2014. "The paradox of humility and dogmatism." In *Skeptical Theism: New Essays*, edited by Trent Dougherty and Justin P. McBrayer, 85–100. Oxford: Oxford University Press.

Van Cappellen, Patty, and Saroglou, Vassilis. 2012. "Awe Activates Religious and Spiritual Feelings and Behavioral Intentions", *Psychology of Religion and Spirituality* 4:3: 223–236.

Wielenberg, Erik J. 2005. *Value and Virtue in a Godless Universe*. Cambridge: Cambridge University Press.

Wilson, Timothy. 2002. *Strangers to Ourselves: Discovering the Adaptive Unconscious*. Cambridge, MA: Harvard University Press.

Worthington, Everett L., Jr. 2007. *Humility: The Quiet Virtue*. West Conshohocken, PA: Templeton Foundation Press.

Zimbardo, Philip. 2007. *The Lucifer Effect*. New York: Random House.

Chapter 3

A Critical Examination and Reconceptualization of Humility

MARK R. LEARY AND CHLOE C. BANKER

INTRODUCTION

Although psychologists have been interested for many years in phenomena associated with low humility—such as egotism, self-enhancement, narcissism, and dogmatism—humility itself did not begin to receive concerted research attention until quite recently. Fueled by growing interest in positive aspects of human nature, work on humility has gone from virtually nonexistent to a cottage industry in the past 10 years. In that time, efforts have been made to identify the central features of humility, describe the characteristics and behaviors of people who are low and high in humility, develop valid measures, and understand how humility plays out in a number of contexts, such as in close relationships, leadership, persuasion, and religious practice (for reviews, see Davis et al., 2017; Exline, 2008; Hill and Laney, 2016; Worthington, Davis, and Hook, 2017; Worthington et al., 2016).

Progress has been made in each of these areas, yet the study of humility remains fragmented and beset by controversy. Within psychology, three areas are particularly problematic. First, although research has identified personality characteristics, self-views, and behaviors that characterize people who are high in humility, we lack consensus regarding which of these features should be viewed as necessary and sufficient to identify someone as high in humility and which should be considered as correlates, manifestations, or implications of humility. Currently, most conceptualizations of humility involve a list of associated features without identifying its psychological core.

Second, although most researchers assume that humility involves both intrapersonal and interpersonal features (e.g., Davis et al., 2011; Farrell et al., 2015), we lack an integrative model that clearly explains how the intrapersonal aspects of humility relate to its behavioral manifestations. Why do the characteristic patterns of beliefs, self-views, and motives that characterize humility lead humble people to behave as they do?

Third, lack of clarity and coherence in the conceptualization of humility has impeded the development of theoretically grounded and psychometrically sound measures. Although some measures have been based on explicit and precise psychological conceptualizations, many were based on lay views of humility that may or may not have psychological coherence.

The goal of this chapter is to take a step forward in the study of humility by critically examining current approaches, offering an integrative novel conceptualization that avoids the problems with existing models, and exploring the interpersonal nature of humility through this lens. Much of what we will say is not entirely new, having been hinted at by previous writers. Yet, we believe that previous conceptualizations and operationalizations have overlooked the key feature of humility in favor of less central or nondiagnostic elements. By taking a critical look at existing views and highlighting themes that have only been hinted at in previous work, we hope to provide a basis for improved measurement and research.

CONCEPTUALIZATIONS OF HUMILITY

Much has been written about the characteristics of people who are high versus low in humility, and many studies have examined psychological and social correlates of humility. In identifying the features of humility, most writers have suggested a set of interrelated characteristics, often on the basis of lay assumptions about humble people. For example, writers have suggested that people who are higher in humility focus less on themselves, have more accurate self-views, are less defensive, behave in more generous ways, feel more connected to other people, appreciate other people's strengths, are kinder and more forgiving, and are not as concerned with impressing other people (e.g., Exline and Hill, 2012; Farrell et al., 2015; LaBouff et al., 2012; Tangney, 2002, 2009; Wang, Edwards, and Hill, 2017; Worthington, 2007).

On average, these descriptions are probably correct. Yet, simply identifying characteristics on which humble and nonhumble people tend to differ is only an initial step in developing an understanding of the psychology of humility. The scientific study of any phenomenon requires going beyond a description of its features to a precise and specific conceptualization that identifies the necessary and sufficient features that allow us to unambiguously measure the construct and to distinguish it from related phenomena. Without a precise, psychologically-sound conceptualization, we cannot separate core features of a construct from correlated characteristics, develop viable measures, or offer explanations regarding why the phenomenon operates as it does.

At present, most efforts to conceptualize humility involve a laundry list of ways in which people who are low versus high in humility probably differ. However, as we will explain, few, if any, of these characteristics can be regarded as defining, essential features of humility that unambiguously indicate whether someone is or is not actually humble.

Commonly Specified Features of Humility

Most definitions of humility conceptualize humility in terms of a small number of defining characteristics. For example, Tangney (2002, 2009) specified six core features of humility: (1) accurate assessment of oneself, (2) acknowledgement of one's limitations and mistakes, (3) openness to other perceptions and ideas, (4) viewing one's accomplishments and abilities in perspective, (5) lower self-focus, and (6) appreciating other people and things. Similarly, Worthington (2007) suggested that humility is reflected by traits such as being other-oriented, prosocial, altruistic, modest, willing to accept both strengths and weaknesses, and the absence of thoughts or behaviors that reflect being prideful, arrogant, or entitled. Despite differences across the myriad descriptions in the literature, most writers have mentioned one or more of four central themes.

Accurate Self-Views

Most theorists stress that humble people perceive and evaluate themselves accurately. This consideration is intended to convey that humble people do not overestimate their positive characteristics, distinguish humble people from those who underestimate their positive attributes due to unrealistically negative self-images or lack of self-insight, and counter the popular assumption that humble people view their positive characteristics less favorably than is the case.

However, if perceiving and evaluating oneself accurately is a defining feature of humility, then all indications suggest that there are no humble people. Virtually every study ever conducted on the accuracy of people's self-views shows that people's beliefs about themselves are highly suspect. Not only do people show pervasive biases to view themselves much more favorably than they should (Alicke and Sedikides, 2009; Dunning, 2005), but people also simply do not have access to the self-relevant information and social comparisons necessary to form and maintain an accurate self-image (Wilson and Dunn, 2004). Certainly, people have insight into where they stand on certain dimensions, but due to inadequate information, the impact of nonconscious processes of which they are not aware, attributional errors, and motivated biases, no one—absolutely no one—has an accurate view of their abilities, personalities, and other characteristics.

In light of this, the accuracy of people's self-views cannot be a criterion for conceptualizing and identifying humility. One could argue that the accuracy requirement might be salvaged by specifying an upper bound to the allowable errors or degree of inaccuracy in people's self-beliefs, or by considering errors arising from self-enhancing biases but not those due to lack of knowledge or insight. However, we can see no basis for making either of these determinations or ways of assessing them.

Fortunately, accuracy of self-views does not appear to be a valid indicator of humility anyway. Imagine two equally accomplished people, both of whom have perfectly accurate views of their exceptional abilities and accomplishments. Despite the fact that they differ neither in their accomplishments nor in the accuracy of their judgments of their accomplishments and characteristics, they still might differ markedly in humility. One person might be notably low in humility, reveling in his or her achievements, constantly bringing attention to them, and expecting approbation and special treatment. The other person might take those same achievements in stride, being disinterested in receiving attention or recognition, or being treated as special. In this example, accuracy of self-views does not distinguish a highly arrogant person from a highly humble one.

Or, consider two people who, if such things could be assessed, stand at the 95th percentile (Person A) and 90th percentile (Person B) on some important attribute, but both believe that they rank at the 90th percentile. Person A views his (inaccurate) 90th percentile standing as no big deal in the grand scheme of things, whereas Person B views his (accurate) 90th rank as a cause for attention, approbation, and special treatment by other people. Person A would seem to be more humble than Person B even though Person B's self-view is accurate and Person A's is not. As these examples show, accuracy of self-views does not seem to be a valid or useful indicator of humility.

Awareness of One's Limitations

Closely related to the notion that humble people have accurate self-views is the idea that they are aware of and acknowledge their limitations (e.g., Chancellor and Lyubomirsky, 2013; Sezer, Gino, and Norton, 2018; Tangney, 2009). Some theorists go further to say that humble people are not only aware of their limitations but "own" them as well (Whitcomb et al., 2016). Owning a limitation seems to go beyond merely recognizing that one has a limitation or weakness to embracing it as a part of oneself.

The conceptual problems with this provision are essentially the same as requiring accuracy as a criterion. Perhaps somebody, somewhere, is aware of all of his or her limitations, but, like accuracy, full awareness of one's limitations is an unattainable standard. Furthermore, everyday judgments of humility do not appear to require this. People seem to view others as humble with no consideration whatsoever of whether they acknowledge their many limitations. We suspect that humble people probably do recognize more of their limitations than less humble people do, but this seems to be an associated feature of humility rather than a defining characteristic, and humility can be reliability identified without this provision.

Modest Self-Presentation

Humility tends to be associated with modest self-presentations, and highly humble people do not appear to be as motivated to convey enhanced images of themselves to other people as less humble people (Davis et al., 2011; Davis et al., 2016; Worthington et al., 2016). The question is whether people's social behavior should be regarded as a defining characteristic of humility, or whether humility should be regarded as an intrapersonal characteristic for which modesty is one of its behavioral correlates. Other theorists have wrestled with the question of whether humility should be regarded as intrapersonal or interpersonal concept, but their conclusions differ (Davis et al., 2013; Kruse et al., 2017).

Specifying particular behaviors as defining features of a psychological construct has two drawbacks. First, the relationships between beliefs, attitudes, and self-views on the one hand and behaviors on the other are notoriously complex and often weak. Thus, unless a construct can be conceptualized as inherently behavioral (such as bullying or impulsivity), specifying behavioral criteria for a psychological construct runs the risk of failing to detect intrapersonal characteristics that people may not display or may try to conceal. For example, one would not want to require behavioral manifestations for definitions of prejudice, anxiety, or mindfulness because people may sometimes be prejudiced, anxious, or mindful without showing it, or, conversely, they might appear to be prejudiced, anxious, or mindful when, in fact, they are not. Similarly, humility may not always manifest in behavior, and seemingly modest behavior may not reflect psychological humility.

Other-Oriented Interpersonal Orientation

Finally, many writers have specified that humility involves an other-oriented interpersonal stance, and some regard other-focus as a central feature of humility (Davis et al., 2017; Nadelhoffer and Wright, 2017; Wang et al., 2017). Empirically, highly humble people are, in fact, more oriented toward other people than less humble people are (Exline and Hill, 2012; Kruse et al., 2014). However, the relationship between other-orientation and humility is probably not strong enough to regard it as a criterion for humility, and being focused on other people is associated with many constructs in addition to humility.

Imagine a person who, based on all other evidence, would be regarded as high in humility according to common conceptualizations: he or she has a reasonably accurate self-image, is more aware of his or her limitations than most people are, does not regard him- or herself more favorably than the facts support, has a modest self-presentation, and so on. But the person is also not particularly oriented toward other people, scoring only average on measures of empathy, generosity, agreeableness, willingness to compromise, and other indications of being oriented toward other people. This person is by no means self-focused, selfish, or mean; he or she is simply average in the degree to which he or she is oriented toward other people. Even so, based on the person's other characteristics, it would seem odd to conclude that this person is not humble, and, in fact, that would be true even if he or she were largely indifferent toward other people. Certainly, humility correlates with psychological and behavioral manifestations of a prosocial orientation that includes acceptance of other people and an appreciation of others' strengths. But, in our view, other-orientation should not be regarded as an indicator, much less a defining feature, of humility (Schrader and Tangney, forthcoming).

Some conceptualizations suggest that humility involves a high focus on other people paired with a low degree of self-focus (Kruse et al., 2017; Nadelhoffer and Wright, 2017; Tong et al., 2016; Van Tongeren et al., 2017), but specifying this combination of self- and other-focus is problematic for the same reason. Moreover, there are many manifestations of low self-focus and high other-focus that do not involve humility (low selfishness, for example), so simply falling into the low self-focus, high other-focus quadrant does not necessarily indicate high humility. "Self-focus" and "other-focus" are far too broad and multidimensional as psychological constructs to be useful without much greater specificity. (Wright et al. [2018] offer one approach to specifying the precise nature of the self- and other-focus that characterizes humility.) Again, we do not question that highly humble people are less focused on themselves and more focused on others than less humble people are, but using this criterion alone cannot distinguish humble from nonhumble people with an acceptable degree of accuracy.

Traits and States

Aside from the fact that most conceptualizations of humility focus on this small set of themes, most reflect an effort to distinguish people who tend to be humble from those who aren't. Yet, a viable conceptualization of humility must also account for *state* humility—humility manifested in a particular situation at a particular time (Chancellor and Lyubomirsky, 2013; Kruse et al., 2017; Stellar et al., 2018). Although trait and state humility correlate (Kruse et al., 2017), people who are not characteristically high in trait humility might occasionally manifest state humility, and people who are typically high in trait humility may occasionally react in nonhumble ways. Given that trait humility is essentially the degree to which people display state humility across situations and time, the same conceptualization must apply to both constructs.

Yet, many features highlighted by existing conceptualizations of trait humility are not helpful when characterizing state humility because they refer to people's general views and behaviors rather than to their reactions in a particular situation. For example, people may respond with great humility in a particular situation even though their self-views tend to be inaccurate and they do not usually recognize their limitations. A viable conceptualization of humility must be useful in characterizing specific instances of low and high humility as well as identifying individual differences in how humble people tend to be overall. Yet no existing conceptualization of trait humility converts easily to an analysis of state humility.

SEARCHING FOR THE CORE OF HUMILITY

As we have shown, many of the features that appear in existing conceptualizations of humility may describe differences between humble and nonhumble people on average, but they do not seem to identify the fundamental feature that distinguishes people who are and are not humble or allow unambiguous identification of humble versus nonhumble people. What's the central ingredient—the necessary and sufficient attribute—that defines humility? To say it differently, what one thing would we want to know about someone that would provide the strongest, most valid indicator that he or she is responding in a humble fashion (state humility) or is generally a humble person (trait humility)?

The conceptualization we propose here is that, at its core, humility involves a person's recognition that, however great one's personal accomplishments or positive characteristics may be, one is not fundamentally a more special person because of them and, thus, should not be viewed or treated as special outside the domain of one's accomplishments or characteristics (and sometimes even within it). In our view, all the recognized features of both state and trait humility are either antecedents of the simple recognition that one's accomplishments and positive characteristics do not entitle one to be treated special overall or are psychological or behavioral manifestations of that recognition.

In contexts that operate as meritocracies, people who are good at something or who possess exceptional characteristics are entitled to preferential treatment within the domain of their expertise and accomplishments. The best athletes should get more playing time, the best employees should receive larger salaries, the best actors should win more awards, and so on. In general, norms often specify that people who accomplish and contribute the most may deserve additional recognition, respect, or deference in contexts in which their accomplishments and positive characteristics are relevant. Believing that one deserves to be treated as different or special in such contexts is normal and appropriate.

Yet, people sometimes believe that their accomplishments and positive characteristics entitle them to special treatment not only in the domain in which they excel but also more generally. Nonhumble people expect, and may feel entitled to, extra attention, deference, respect, and special treatment in contexts that lie outside the domain of their excellence. Some outstanding athletes, actors, scientists, businesspeople, philanthropists, teachers, public figures, and seemingly ordinary people expect attention, deference, and special treatment wherever they go. This expectation that one should be treated special overall—outside the domains in which norms specify that special treatment may be appropriate—is the hallmark of low humility.

In contrast, the humble response is to recognize one's accomplishments and positive characteristics, and perhaps even to feel good about them, but to think that they should make little, if any, difference in how one should be treated outside of the relevant domain. In fact, the greatest signs of humility occur when people forgo special treatment even when their accomplishments or characteristics are relevant. For example, on the day that he was inaugurated as pope in 2013, Pope Francis was widely praised for his humility when he stopped by his hotel to pay the bill and pick up his luggage himself. Presumably, Francis didn't regard becoming pope as entitling him to special treatment in contexts having nothing to do with his new role. Furthermore, humble people appear to be relatively unperturbed, and perhaps even gracious, in situations in which they do not receive special recognition or treatment that they might, in fact, deserve.

Importantly, this conceptualization of humility does not emphasize the importance of accurate self-views, thereby avoiding the problem described earlier regarding the fact that people's self-views are notoriously inaccurate. No matter what one's self-views are—and even when they are normatively inflated—not regarding oneself as special or entitled to special treatment remains the hallmark of humility.

A few previous writers have hinted at the importance of this consideration. For example, several authors have suggested that humble people keep their accomplishments "in perspective," implying that they do not make a big deal out of them (Tangney, 2009). Along these lines, Kruse et al. (2017) included items on their scale that express this notion (e.g., "I feel that I do not deserve more respect than other people)." (Respect is only one form of special treatment to which nonhumble people may feel entitled). Empirically, humility correlates negatively with general entitlement and with narcissism, which of course is characterized by entitlement and superiority (Chancellor and Lyubomirsky, 2013; Kruse et al., 2017).

Similarly, Kupfer (2003) proposed four dimensions of a "moral perspective" that can lead people to remain humble even while demonstrating excellence in a particular domain. These dimensions—such as recognizing the degree to which one's accomplishments depend on other people and fortuitous circumstances, and realizing that one fails to exhibit the highest levels of moral behavior—essentially chip away at one's sense of being special overall.

Preliminary Evidence

In preparation for writing this chapter, we conducted two small studies to examine the viability of this conceptualization of humility. One study examined whether people's judgments of others' humility were associated with the degree to which they believe that the person feels entitled to special treatment. The second study examined the link between people's own expectations of special treatment and their humility with respect to a personal accomplishment or characteristic. Although conceptualizations in scientific psychology should decidedly not be based on laypeople's conceptions of psychological constructs (we wouldn't want to base a measure of psychopathy on the public's beliefs about psychopathic people, for example), we thought it would be informative to know whether the degree to which people expect to be treated special enters into people's judgments of humility in themselves and others.

Inferences about Others' Humility

In the first study, we randomly assigned 200 adult participants to think of a person whom they considered to be either humble or not humble. After participants identified a humble or nonhumble person, they rated the person on attributes that previous theory and research suggested should be related to humility, plus items that tapped into the notion that humble people do not expect to be treated as if they're special.

A regression analysis showed that participants' ratings on three items that reflected the degree to which the person (1) thinks that he or she should be treated special, (2) feels entitled to special treatment all the time, and (3) thinks he or she is a special person accounted for 69.9% of the variance in ratings of humility. With variance due to those three ratings removed, three other items also contributed to variance in humility ratings: has an accurate view of his strengths, is self-centered, and is concerned about other people. Thus, accuracy of self-views, self-centeredness, and other-orientation also play a role in people's perceptions of humility as others have suggested, but perceiving that another person does not expect to be treated special is a very important consideration.

Predictors of Humility

In a second study, 200 adult participants completed the Brief State Humility Scale but answered the items with respect to how they usually are. Then, they described a personal accomplishment or positive characteristic that they were particularly pleased about and answered questions about it. Humility scores were strongly predicted by participants' ratings of the degree to which they agreed that "This characteristic or accomplishment makes me a more special person than I would be if I did not have it," "People should treat me differently because I have this characteristic or accomplishment," and "People should give me special treatment because I have this characteristic or accomplishment." The wording of these items does not allow us to discern whether the special treatment in question is in an area in which one's characteristic or accomplishment is relevant, but they nonetheless show that people who score higher in humility indicate a lower sense of deserving to be treated special. In addition, humility was predicted weakly by participants' ratings of how good the accomplishment or characteristics makes them feel about themselves and believing that their personal characteristic or accomplishment was better than the characteristics and accomplishments of other people.

These findings do not, by themselves, necessarily indicate that humility is fundamentally about expecting to be treated special or that our conceptualization is correct. As noted, laypeople's assumptions about constructs may or may not reflect a viable psychological conceptualization. But, these pilot studies are consistent with the notion that expecting to be treated special may be a central feature of humility and that low humility goes beyond simply viewing oneself positively to broadly expecting to be treated special.

HUMILITY AND INTERPERSONAL BEHAVIOR

All theorists agree that humility is associated with an array of prosocial behaviors, and studies support this link. For example, trait humility is associated with gratitude (Kruse et al., 2014), generosity (Exline and Hill, 2012), willingness to help others (LaBouff et al., 2012), empathy (Kruse et al., 2017), forgiveness (Wang et al., 2017), and success in working and communicating with others (Peters, Rowatt, and Johnson, 2011). In close relationships, humble people display greater skill at conflict resolution and are more likely to make sacrifices for others (Farrell et al., 2015), and they display more trust, greater cooperation, and less defensiveness (Wang et al., 2017). Not surprisingly, humility is highly correlated with relationship satisfaction and relationship quality (Peters et al., 2011; Wang et al., 2017). Humility is clearly associated with an array of positive qualities and behaviors that help explain why humility is so highly admired (Worthington, 2007). However, most conceptualizations of humility do not provide a clear and direct explanation for why the features of humility they identify (such as having accurate self-views or low self-focus) lead to these sorts of interpersonal behaviors and outcomes.

In our view, the proximal psychological cause of the undesirable social behaviors exhibited by people low in humility is simply the unwarranted expectation that one's accomplishments and positive characteristics entitle one to be treated special overall. The central problem with low humility is not that people think that they are better than others; if arrogant people kept their beliefs to themselves no one would be the wiser. Rather, it's the fact that people low in humility expect others to treat them special. In essence, people low in humility try to reap social benefits that they don't deserve, and their sense of entitlement leads them to behave in self-centered ways that disadvantage other people. Even when people's positive self-views are entirely accurate, always expecting to be treated special often imposes on or disadvantages other people.

In contrast, people who do not put themselves above others, expect preferential treatment, or think they are entitled to a disproportionate share of material and interpersonal spoils are more likely to treat others in an egalitarian, respectful, and fair manner. Such behaviors then have positive downstream consequences such as positive interpersonal interactions, stronger social connections, and the enhanced well-being of those with whom they interact. Viewed in this way, it is easy to see why humility is often considered to be a virtue.

But what about the negative characteristics that have sometimes been associated with humility, such as submissiveness, shame, and feelings of insignificance? Based on laypeople's views of humility, Weidman, Cheng, and Tracy (2018) concluded that humility has two distinct forms, which they called appreciative and self-abasing humility. Appreciative humility is a highly positive reaction that occurs after success and achievement, while self-abasement involves shame, low self-esteem, and submissiveness following failure. Yet, the fact that laypeople use "humility" in two distinct ways in no way indicates the existence of a single psychological reaction with two variants. Interestingly, though, what both types of humility identified by Weidman et al. have in common is the conviction that one is not special.

PSYCHOLOGICAL UNDERPINNINGS OF LOW AND HIGH HUMILITY

Our conceptualization of humility also offers insights into factors that increase and decrease humility by affecting the degree to which people believe that their accomplishments and positive characteristics merit special treatment by others. In this section, we speculate regarding four sets of factors.

Explicit Beliefs Regarding Specialness and Entitlement

Some humble people may have a conscious, explicit belief that they are an ordinary sort of person who, despite their accomplishments and positive characteristics, is no more special than anyone else. For some people, this belief may be rooted in a foundational worldview that everyone is fundamentally equal. For example, believing that everyone is equal in the sight of God or believing that all people are expressions of the same underlying essence (consciousness, the Tao, God, or whatever) may lead certain people to respond humbly. Along these lines, humility seems to be associated with the perception that one is connected to aspects of a larger whole (McFarland, Webb, and Brown, 2012; Tangney, 2002; Worthington, 2007).

Similarly, certain cultural norms and religious teachings may discourage the belief that one is better than other people and stigmatize behaviors that convey that one is better or more important than others. Perhaps that is why those who are religious tend to report higher humility and place greater importance on humility than non-religious people do (Van Tongeren et al., 2017).

The belief that one is not entitled to be treated better than others might also arise from explicit instruction from parents or others who try to teach a child that he or she is fundamentally no more special than anyone else and, thus, not entitled to be treated special. Conversely, parents who overvalue their children, seeing them as decidedly special individuals, may promote the sort of narcissistic mindset that undermines humility (Brummelman et al., 2015).

Attributional Overgeneralization

A second route to low versus high humility may lie in the ways in which people draw inferences about themselves from their own behavior. Just as people draw inferences about other people based on the others' behavior (Gilbert and Malone, 1995), they also draw inferences about themselves, generalizing from specific actions and outcomes to correspondent inferences about their abilities, personality traits, and other characteristics. So, for example, students may generalize getting good grades to the trait of being intelligent, and people who have experienced a few failed relationships may infer that they are unlovable.

People's correspondent inferences differ along a continuum of generalization and abstraction. At the lowest level, no generalization whatsoever occurs—the person simply recognizes that he or she behaved or performed in some particular way. Often, though, people generalize from their actions or outcomes to inferences about their personal characteristics. A student who generally does well on math tests might go beyond the recognition that "I did well on this test" to infer "I'm good at math" or "I'm a good student" or, more broadly, "I'm really smart." Of course, people are not particularly even-handed in these inferences, being more likely to draw inferences about themselves from desirable than undesirable behaviors.

Overgeneralizing from particular accomplishments or characteristic to broad inferences about oneself might increase the likelihood that people will conclude that other people should regard and treat them as special. General and broad positive attributes are arguably more laudable than the specific actions on which they are based. For example, concluding that one is an exceptional "athlete" is more noteworthy than the more specific and accurate observation that one is good at softball, swimming fast, or kicking a football. Thus, people who tend to generalize specific accomplishments or characteristics to broad self-relevant beliefs should be likely to be low in humility. The relationship between attributional generalization and low humility is likely to be bidirectional: a tendency to generalize from specific attributes to broad self-relevant beliefs may promote low humility, and being low in humility may lead people to overgeneralize in these ways.

Minimal Self-Enhancement

As we noted, most conceptualizations of humility emphasize that humble people are less self-enhancing and more accurate in their self-views and that they recognize their weaknesses and limitations. Of course, lower self-enhancement is associated with humility, but we do not think it lies at the core of humility. Rather, having more accurate, less self-enhancing views of oneself is associated with humility because people with less aggrandizing self-beliefs are less likely to think they should be treated special.

To put it another way, the more positively people perceive themselves, the more they might reasonably conclude that they are entitled to special attention, respect, deference, and other desirable outcomes. As a result, people with particularly inflated self-views are more inclined to expect special treatment than people with less inflated views, accounting for the relationship between self-aggrandizement and humility.

Hypo-egoic Characteristics

People generally operate in a rather egoic mindset in the sense that they are excessively preoccupied with themselves even when they don't need to be, often with undesirable psychological and interpersonal consequences (Leary, 2004). Presumably, people are very unlikely to display humility when they are in an egoic mindset, and people who are more prone to egoicism are less likely to be humble.

However, when people are being less egoic, they should be more likely to respond in a humble fashion, and most theorists agree that humility arises predominantly, or maybe only, when people are less self-focused than they typically are (e.g., Kruse et al., 2014; Nadelhoffer and Wright, forthcoming). Hypo-egoic states are characterized by four interrelated features, each of which should increase the likelihood of humility (Leary et al., 2016). First, in a hypo-egoic mindset, people's thoughts and feelings primarily involve the immediate situation rather than the past or future. Being present-focused attenuates the degree to which people think about past accomplishments or personal characteristics that are not relevant in the current context. Second, when operating in a hypo-egoic mindset, people introspect less than they usually do, attending to their experiences without extensively thinking about, evaluating, or talking to themselves about them. Put simply, people in a hypo-egoic state are less focused on their feelings, goals, characteristics, and thoughts about themselves.

Third, people in a hypo-egoic mindset tend to think about themselves in concrete rather than abstract ways, and their construals, interpretations, and evaluations of themselves are concrete rather than abstract or symbolic. As a result, people may evaluate what they are doing at the moment without generalizing their evaluations to broader judgments of their ability or personality. Fourth, people in a hypo-egoic mindset think less about how they are being perceived and evaluated by other people than they typically do. Of course, people must be attuned to others' perceptions and evaluations of them in order to function effectively, but those concerns are attenuated when people are hypo-egoic.

These four hypo-egoic features may naturally lower the degree to which people expect other people to view and treat them as special. As a result, people are more likely to display humility when they are focused on the present situation, are not introspecting, think about themselves in concrete rather than abstract terms (so they are less likely to generalize specific actions and achievements to abstract, global self-views), and are less concerned about other people's evaluations of them.

Linking humility to hypo-egoic processes helps explain why humility tends to be associated with many of the characteristics with which it is related, such as non-defensiveness, forgiveness, generosity, a lower concern with others' evaluations, awe, and so on. Although some writers have suggested that humility causes these kinds of reactions (Exline and Hill, 2012; Kruse et al., 2014; Tong et al., 2016), we believe that, like humility, each of these various prosocial responses is facilitated when people are in a hypo-egoic state (Leary et al., 2016). All of these reactions, including humility, are far less likely when people are being egoic.

If so, the kinds of situations in which people display humility are likely to be those in which people are in a hypo-egoic mindset. And, the reasons that some people are dispositionally more humble than other people likely lie in psychological characteristics that predispose people to process information and respond hypo-egoically (see Leary, Brown, and Diebels, 2016). This hypo-egoic perspective provides an integrative framework for understanding and testing the situational and dispositional antecedents of state and trait humility. At an even deeper psychological level than consciously articulated beliefs about one's specialness or about how one should be treated, certain psychological characteristics may predispose some people to respond in more humble ways.

HUMILITY AND HUMAN NATURE

In considering the origins of humility, the question arises of whether the psychological characteristics that predispose people to be humble are an inherent aspect of human nature. That is, are people are naturally predisposed to be humble (and their intrinsic humility is undermined by external forces) or are they predisposed to be nonhumble (and humility requires a conscious effort to resist one's egoic impulses)? This is a complex question because pervasive human tendencies are a function not only of evolved predispositions (i.e., human nature) but also of the context in which those tendencies play out. Yet, we can begin to examine this question by considering the natural history of humility. This is a highly speculative exercise without a clear resolution, but it demonstrates the way in which such a question can be approached.

Humility would not have become possible until our prehuman ancestors acquired a sophisticated ability for symbolic self-relevant thought that allowed them to consider whether they should be treated special because of their attributes or accomplishments. (It makes no sense to consider whether an animal without the capacity for self-relevant thought is responding in a humble fashion.) Although anthropologists do not know for certain when symbolic self-reflection first arose, no evidence of it appears in the archeological record until less than 100,000 years ago, a quite recent date in the span of human evolution (Leary and Buttermore, 2003). In any case, humility is not even remotely relevant for understanding human behavior during most of human evolution.

For most of the species' prehistory, our prehuman and human ancestors lived in small, highly mobile groups that survived by hunting, gathering, and scavenging. Analyses of similar hunter-gatherer groups over the past 100 years reveal that such groups tend to be highly egalitarian, with a high level of cooperation and non-contingent sharing within the clan (Martin et al., 2016). Although individuals may be recognized for their contributions to the group (the best hunters may be granted more influence over group decisions, for example), status differences are minimized and group members have equal access to the group's resources. And, because one's value to a small nomadic group is obvious to everyone, opportunities for self-aggrandizement are limited, and bragging and self-enhancement are strongly discouraged, if not scorned (Boehm, 2012). Indeed, Martin et al. (2016) made the case that social relations during Paleolithic times were far more hypo-egoic compared to today. If so, at the time that *Homo sapiens* acquired the ability for symbolic self-thought, individuals probably would not have entertained the notion that they should be treated special as a person.

However, with the agricultural revolution, approximately 12,000 years ago, people began to settle into stable communities. As civilizations arose and people began to accumulate land and possessions, people found themselves living under conditions that promoted greater egoicism than in hunter-gatherer groups (Martin et al., 2016). Communities grew larger, social relationships became less communal, interactions became increasingly role based, and people often had to prove their value to those who did not know them well. Under these conditions, self-aggrandizement and efforts to be perceived and treated as special emerged as interpersonal tactics.

Evidence does not indicate which of these responses, if either, is the default. As highly social animals, human beings have the capacity to adapt their behavior in ways that conform to group norms and help them achieve their goals. During the Paleolithic period, people may have behaved "humbly" because doing so was more functional in hunter-gatherer groups than egoic entitlement, but with changes in social circumstances that occurred with the agricultural revolution, people began to seek opportunities to be treated as special. We have little basis for concluding whether humility is or is not an inherent part of human nature, though the evidence suggests that *a lack of* humility (in the form of egoic entitlement) is something that would have only become advantageous fairly recently in our evolution, after the development of stable civilizations.

CONCLUSIONS

Our central thesis is that humility fundamentally involves people's expectations regarding how they should be treated by virtue of having accomplished particular things or possessing particular desirable characteristics. Believing that one's accomplishments and positive characteristics entitle one to special treatment overall constitute a low degree of humility regardless of whether people's self-beliefs are accurate.

This conceptual approach has implications for both research and measurement. First, according to the model, the cognitive and behavioral features of humility that have been identified previously can be viewed as antecedents of people's expectations about how they should be treated by others due to their accomplishments or characteristics, manifestations of such expectations, or co-effects of other processes that promote a hypo-egoic orientation more generally. This framework provides a model for identifying and testing the features of humility with greater precision and specificity than has been done up until now.

In addition, the model offers new directions for measurement. As many writers have noted, measuring humility via self-report is problematic because humble people might be disinclined to rate themselves as exceptionally humble, and some of the central features of humility that have been discussed, such as accuracy of one's self-views or recognizing one's limitations, are impossible to assess through direct self-report (e.g., Rowatt et al., 2006; Davis, Worthington, and Hook, 2010). In contrast, assessing the degree to which people think that their accomplishments and positive characteristics entitle them to special treatment by others seems a relatively straightforward affair, one that we are currently exploring. No matter how people rate themselves, not expecting to be treated as broadly special because of one's perceived accomplishments and characteristics would provide strong evidence of humility. In contrast, thinking that others should treat one special overall because of one's exceptional achievements or attributes would, in our view, be prima facie evidence of low humility.

REFERENCES

Alicke, M, and C. Sedikides. 2009 "Self-enhancement and self-protection: What they are and what they do." *European Review of Social Psychology, 20*, 1–48.

Boehm, C. 2012 *Moral Origins: The Evolution of Virtue, Altruism, and Shame*. New York: Basic Books.

Brummelman, E., S. Thomaes, S. A. Nelemans, B. Orobio de Castro, G. Overbeek, and B. J. Bushman. 2015. "Origins of narcissism in children." *Proceedings of the National Academy of Sciences of the United States of America, 112*, 3659–3662.

Chancellor, J., and S. Lyubomirsky. 2013. "Humble beginnings: Current trends, state perspectives, and hallmarks of humility." *Social and Personality Psychology Compass*, 7(11), 819–833.

Davis, D. E., J. N. Hook, R. Mcannally-Linz, E. Choe, and V. Placeres. 2017. "Humility, religion, and spirituality: A review of the literature." *Psychology of Religion and Spirituality*, 9(3), 242–253.

Davis, D. E., J. N. Hook, E. L. Worthington, D. R. Van Tongeren, A. L. Gartner, D. J. Jennings, and R. A. Emmons. 2011. "Relational humility: Conceptualizing and measuring humility as a personality judgment." *Journal of Personality Assessment, 93*(3), 225–234.

Davis, D. E., S. E. Mcelroy, et al. 2016. "Is modesty a subdomain of humility?" *Journal of Positive Psychology, 11*(4), 439–446.

Davis, D. E., E. L. Worthington, and J. N. Hook. 2010. "Humility: Review of measurement strategies and conceptualization as personality judgment." *Journal of Positive Psychology, 5*(4), 243–252.

Davis, D. E., E. L. Worthington, Jr., J. N. Hook, R. Emmons, P. C. Hill, R. A. Bollinger, and D. Van Tongeren. 2013. "Humility and the development and repair of social bonds: Two longitudinal studies." *Self and Identity, 12*, 58–77.

Dunning, D. 2005 *Self-Insight: Roadblocks and Detours to Knowing Thyself.* New York: Psychology Press.

Exline, J. J. 2008 "Taming the wild ego: The challenge of humility." In *Transcending Self-Interest: Psychological Explorations of the Quiet Ego*, edited by H. A. Wayment and J. J. Bauer, 53–62. Washington, DC: American Psychological Association.

Exline, J. J., and P. C. Hill. 2012. "Humility: A consistent and robust predictor of generosity." *Journal of Positive Psychology, 7*(3), 208–218.

Farrell, J. E., J. N., Hook, M. Ramos, D. E. Davis, D. R. Tongeren, and J. M. Ruiz. 2015. "Humility and relationship outcomes in couples: The mediating role of commitment." *Couple and Family Psychology: Research and Practice, 4*(1), 14–26.

Gilbert, D. T., and P. S. Malone. 1995. "The correspondence bias." *Psychological Bulletin, 117*, 21–38.

Hill, P. C., and E. K. Laney. 2016. "Beyond self-interest: Humility and the quieted self." In *Oxford Handbook of Hypo-egoic Phenomena*, edited by M. R. Leary and K. W. Brown, 243–269. New York: Oxford University Press.

Krause, N. 2016 "Assessing the relationships among wisdom, humility, and life satisfaction." *Journal of Adult Development, 23*(3), 140–149.

Kruse, E., J. Chancellor, and S. Lyubomirsky. 2017 "State humility: Measurement, conceptual validation, and intrapersonal processes." *Self and Identity, 16*(4), 399–438.

Kruse, E., J. Chancellor, P. M. Ruberton, and S. Lyubomirsky. 2014. "An upward spiral between gratitude and humility." *Social Psychological and Personality Science, 5*(7), 805–814.

Kupfer, J. 2003. "The moral perspective of humility." *Pacific Philosophical Quarterly, 84*, 249–269.

LaBouff, J. P., W. C. Rowatt, M. K. Johnson, J. Tsang, and G. McCullough Willerton. 2012. "Humble persons are more helpful than less humble persons: Evidence from three studies." *Journal of Positive Psychology, 7*, 16–29.

Leary, M. R. 2004. *The Curse of the Self: Self-Awareness, Egotism, and the Quality of Human Life.* New York: Oxford University Press.

Leary, M. R., W. K. Brown, and K. J. Diebels. 2016. "Dispositional hypo-egoicism: Insights into the hypo-egoic person." In *Oxford Handbook of*

Hypo-egoic Phenomena, edited by K. W. Brown and M. R. Leary, 297–311. New York: Oxford University Press.

Leary, M. R., and N. R. Buttermore. 2003. "The evolution of the human self: Tracing the natural history of self-awareness." *Journal for the Theory of Social Behavior*, 33, 365–404.

Leary, M. R., K. J. Diebels, K. P. Jongman-Sereno, and A. Hawkins. 2016. "Perspectives on hypo-egoic phenomena from social and personality psychology." In *Oxford Handbook of Hypo-egoic Phenomena*, edited by K. W. Brown and M. R. Leary, 47–61. New York: Oxford University Press.

Martin. L. L., A. Kulkarni, W. C. Anderson, M. A. Sanders, J. A. Newbold, and J. Knowles. 2016. "Hypo-egoicism and cultural evolution." In *Oxford Handbook of Hypo-egoic Phenomena*, edited by K. W. Brown and M. R. Leary, 63–77. New York: Oxford University Press

McFarland, S., M. Webb, and D. Brown. 2012. "All humanity is my ingroup: A measure and studies of identification with all humanity." *Journal of Personality and Social Psychology, 103*, 830–853.

Nadelhoffer, T., and J. C. Wright. Forthcoming. "The twin dimensions of the virtue of humility: Low self-focus and high other focus. In *Moral Psychology*, edited by W. Sinnott-Armstrong and C. Miller. Vol. 5. Boston: MIT Press.

Peters, A. S., W. C. Rowatt, and M. K. Johnson. 2011. "Associations between dispositional humility and social relationship quality." *Psychology*, 2(3), 155–161.

Rowatt, W. C., C. Powers, V. Targhetta, J. Comer, S. Kennedy, and J. Labouff. 2006. "Development and initial validation of an implicit measure of humility relative to arrogance." *Journal of Positive Psychology, 1*(4), 198–211.

Schrader, S. W., and J. P. Tangney. Forthcoming. "Assessing humility is a humbling experience: Commentary on Nadelhoffer and Wright." In *Moral Psychology*, edited by W. Sinnott-Armstrong and C. Miller. Vol. 5. Boston: MIT Press.

Sezer, I., Gino, O., and M. I. Norton. 2017. "Humblebragging: A distinct—and ineffective—self-presentation strategy." *Journal of Personality and Social Psychology, 114*, 52–74.

Stellar, J. E., A. Gordon, C. L. Anderson, P. K. Piff, G. D. McNeil, and D. Keltner. 2018. "Awe and humility." *Journal of Personality and Social Psychology, 114*, 258–269.

Tangney, J. P. 2000. "Humility: Theoretical perspectives, empirical findings and directions for future research." *Journal of Social and Clinical Psychology, 19*, 70–82.

Tangney, J. P. 2009. "Humility." In *Oxford Handbook of Positive Psychology*, edited by C. R. Snyder and S. J. Lopez, 2nd ed., 483–490. New York: Oxford University Press.

Tong, E. M., K. W. Tan, A. A. Chor, E. P. Koh, J. S. Lee, and R. W. Tan. 2016. "Humility facilitates higher self-control." *Journal of Experimental Social Psychology, 62*, 30–39.

Van Tongeren, D. R., D. E. Davis, J. N. Hook, W. Rowatt, and E. J. Worthington. 2017. "Religious differences in reporting and expressing humility." *Psychology of Religion and Spirituality*, advance online publication. http://dx.doi.org/10.1037/rel0000118.

Wang, F., K. J. Edwards, and P. C. Hill. 2017. "Humility as a relational virtue: Establishing trust, empowering repair, and building marital well-being." *Journal of Psychology and Christianity*, *36*(2), 168–179.

Weidman, A. C., J. T. Cheng, and J. L. Tracy. 2018. "The psychological structure of humility." *Journal of Personality and Social Psychology*, *114*, 153–178.

Whitcomb, D., H. Battaly, J. Baehr, and D. Howard-Snyder. 2015. "Intellectual humility: Owning our limitations." *Philosophy and Phenomenological Research*, *94*(3), 509–539.

Wilson, T. D., and E. Dunn. 2004. "Self-knowledge: Its limits, value, and potential for improvement." *Annual Review of Psychology*, *55*, 493–518.

Worthington, E. L. 2007. *Humility: The Quiet Virtue*. West Conshohocken, PA: Templeton Foundation Press.

Worthington E. L., Jr., D. E. Davis, and J. N. Hook, eds. 2017. *Handbook of Humility: Theory, Research, and Applications*. New York: Routledge.

Worthington, E. L., Jr., L. Goldstein, B. Cork, B. J. Griffin, R. C. Garthe, C. R. Lavelock, D. E. Davis, J. N. Hook, and D. R. Van Tongeren. Forthcoming. "Humility: A qualitative review of definitions, theory, concept, and research support for seven hypotheses." In *The Oxford Handbook of Positive Psychology*, edited by L. Edwards and S. Marques. 3rd ed. New York: Oxford University Press.

Wright, J. C., T. Nadelhoffer, L. T. Ross, and W. Sinnott-Armstrong. 2018. "Be it ever so humble: Proposing a dual-dimension account and measurement of humility." *Self and Identity*, *17*, 92–125.

Wright, J. C., T. Nadelhoffer, T. Perini, A. Langville, M. Echols, and K. Venezia. 2016. "The psychological significance of humility." *Journal of Positive Psychology*, *12*(1), 3–12.

Chapter 4

A Relational Humility Framework

Perceptions of Humility in Relational Contexts

DAVID K. MOSHER, JOSHUA N. HOOK,
DON E. DAVIS, DARYL R. VAN TONGEREN,
AND EVERETT L. WORTHINGTON JR.[1]

INTRODUCTION

In the field of psychology, the study of virtues increased with the rise of the positive psychology movement (Lopez and Snyder, 2009; Seligman and Csikszentmihalyi, 2000). Although research on many character strengths and virtues (e.g., forgiveness, gratitude, hope) flourished, the study of humility lagged due to difficulties measuring (Tangney, 2009) and defining the construct (see Davis, Worthington, and Hook, 2010, for a review). Regarding measurement, researchers were concerned about methodological problems, such as socially desirability bias and the paradox of self-reporting humility (Chancellor and Lyubomirsky, 2013). Namely, humbler people might underestimate their humility, and less humble people might overestimate their humility, which could attenuate the validity of self-reports (Davis et al., 2013). Regarding definitions, humility research was impeded by difficulties in agreeing on a consensus definition of humility and in parsing out what makes humility distinct from virtues like modesty, respect, and empathy (Davis et al., 2010).

To deal with these challenges, new strategies and theories were formulated to vitalize humility research and allow researchers to better understand the virtue of humility. One model that gained momentum was a relational humility model. *Relational humility* is defined as an observer's judgment that a target person within a particular relationship demonstrates (a) an accurate view of himself or herself, (b) an other-oriented stance that considers the welfare of the other, and (c) interpersonal behaviors marked by a lack of superiority (e.g., expressions of modesty; Davis et al., 2011).

Relational humility theory draws from prior research of personality judgments (see Funder, 1995). It uses an other-report measurement strategy by asking an informant who is already in a relationship with the target individual to rate that person's humility (Davis et al., 2011). Humility as a trait can be estimated by aggregating estimates from several relationships, at different times, and from diverse perspectives (e.g., self-report, other-report, observation of behavior). It is important to study humility in relational contexts that make humility difficult or in situations that strain a person's ego, such as receiving honor or recognition, participating in hierarchical roles, or experiencing relational conflicts (Davis et al., 2011; Davis et al., 2013). Thus, it is human nature to find staying humble more difficult in contexts that promote one to inflate their sense of self (e.g., receiving an award), view others as "lesser" (e.g., CEO executive interacting with a company intern), or contexts where one perceives a threat to their personal character (e.g., relational conflict with spouse). However, research reveals that humility has much to offer humanity as a pathway to enhancing relationships and an effective means of navigating differences or conflicts. This chapter focuses on the core tenets of the relational humility model, the benefits of humility in relationships, and also reviews humility research in various relational contexts where it might be difficult to practice humility.

CORE TENETS OF RELATIONAL HUMILITY

Our relational humility model suggests that people judge humility in others so they can predict how they are likely to be treated while in a relationship with that person. Thus, the crux of humility judgments involves inferring that another person (a) has an accurate view of self and (b) is other-oriented rather than self-focused. People regularly adjust their humility judgments based on relevant behaviors, such as observing a target person's ability to cultivate positive, other-oriented emotions and regulate self-focused emotions in modest and socially pleasing ways (Davis et al., 2010). We propose humility may act as a foundational virtue that encompasses, governs, and facilitates many forms of internal processes, other-oriented emotions, and behaviors. For example, a spouse might judge their partner's humility by their partner's language, behavior, or characteristics that exemplify other-oriented emotions (e.g., empathy, compassion, gratitude) and their partner's ability to regulate self-focused emotions (e.g., pretentiousness, arrogance, or superiority). Hence, a benefit of holding high degrees of relational humility would be that it leads to positive evaluations of oneself that then propel one's partner to seek a deeper connection (see Farrell et al., 2015).

In contrast, a spouse that perceives the partner to express self-focused emotions (e.g., pride, contempt, shame) in a socially offensive manner may perceive their partner as selfish or disrespectful, which could then cause the spouse to become anxious and view the partner as less humble. Thus a core tenet of relational humility theory is that perceiving others as humble invites the person to move closer toward that person, but negative perceptions of humility signal the person to be cautious and create distance from that self-focused other. This is the crux for why humility is beneficial for humans, and it builds upon a large body of evidence that demonstrates how it is in human nature to seek close, supportive connections with other human beings (Bowlby, 1977). In fact, isolation for human beings has been found to be more dangerous for health than smoking (House, Landis, and Umberson, 1988). Hence, evaluating humility is crucial for developing strong connections with others and this is done by assessing relevant cognitive, behavioral, and emotional markers within oneself, in the target person, and within others who know that target person (Davis et al., 2013). Subsequently, diagnostic information is gathered from multiple sources to predict how likely the target person will be humble. Gathering information from multiple external sources is important because a target may be perceived as demonstrating differing levels of humility in various relational contexts. For example, an individual could be perceived as a humble employee or work supervisor but an arrogant spouse or parent. Indeed, humility is theorized to play a critical role in the human emotional experience by affecting interpersonal processes (Kruse, Chancellor, and Lyubomirsky, 2017), and these interpersonal processes can look very different depending on the relationship or social context. In essence, a relational humility model helps one understand how humility affects relationships in various contexts by using an individual's subjective judgment of a target person's humility.

Another core tenet of a relational humility model is that situations that strain the ego are methodologically advantageous opportunities to accurately judge humility (Davis et al., 2010). Some contexts that make humility especially difficult to practice include (a) receiving honor or recognition, (b) being in a hierarchical relationship, or (c) experiencing conflict. Across each situation, there is potential for relational conflict, as jealousy, anxiety, or contempt threaten to destabilize the relationship. For example, employees may compete with one another to receive a reward or honor from their company, which could create conflict and tempt the winner to bolster their ego by expressing pride or even gloating. Such emotional expression could lead to dissention among coworkers and to instability. However, humility could buffer a relationship from such negative emotions during these situations and even strengthen the relationship as a result. When situations arise that tempt, test, or strain one's ego, a person with humility may maintain an other-oriented stance, promote positive emotions in others, and deepen their relationships.

SOCIAL BONDS HYPOTHESIS

One of the core hypotheses of a relational humility model is the *social bonds hypothesis*: that humility helps form, maintain, and strengthen social bonds (Davis et al., 2013; Davis et al., 2011). The social bonds hypothesis draws on theories of altruism. Social bonds allow people to not only act in their own interests but also to react to the needs of others as if they were as important as their own needs. Of course, such relationships could lead to exploitation if not precisely regulated, thus humility judgments are theorized to regulate the strength of social bonds. Namely, to the extent one perceives a relationship partner to be humble, the person is willing to trust that the humble partner will act in ways that feel safe, providing a platform for enhanced social connection.

For that reason, humility helps form social bonds. When people see evidence of humility in another person, it makes it easier to maintain or even deepen commitment (i.e., a psychological proxy for the strength of the social bond) within that relationship. Humility has also been shown to be associated with greater relationship quality (Farrell et al., 2015; Peters, Rowatt, and Johnson, 2011). Also, a study of romantic relationships found that potential dating partners who were perceived to be humble were rated more favorably and more attractive than dating partners perceived to be less humble or arrogant (Van Tongeren, Davis, and Hook, 2014). Furthermore, a sample of adults in an exclusive romantic relationship had greater relationship satisfaction and a stronger social bond when they perceived their partners to be humble, with an accurate view of self being the most important component in predicting relational satisfaction (Dwiwardani et al., 2017). This was true even after controlling for other personal virtues (e.g., gratitude) and commitment to the relationship (Dwiwardani et al., 2017). In addition, Holden et al. (2014) found romantic partners high in honesty-humility were less likely to be manipulative, deceptive, or exploitative of romantic partners. Together, these studies highlight some benefits of humility in forming long-lasting and satisfying relationships with others.

SOCIAL OIL HYPOTHESIS

A second core hypothesis of the relational humility model is the *social oil hypothesis,* which states that humility is especially crucial in preventing relationships from being damaged due to events that put a strain on social relationships, such as competitive behaviors, conflict, suffering, loss, grief, tension, and negative life events. Specifically, people, businesses, or groups competing over limited resources or vying for stability in stressful times could see strains in relationships from the wear-and-tear of stress or negative effects of competitive behaviors. For instance, couples transitioning into parenthood could experience tension over sleep, energy, or family roles that would benefit the individual, which could lead to the common occurrence of deterioration in relationship satisfaction often seen during this time period (Fillo et al., 2015). However, the social oil hypothesis theorizes humility would buffer against relationship deterioration during this stressful transition or minimize the negative effects of stress over a lengthy period of time (Davis et al., 2017).

One example that highlights the social oil hypothesis emerges in studies looking at business companies who had high performance that extended beyond the leader's incumbency (Collins, 2001). In his book, *Good to Great,* Collins (2001) found that extraordinary leaders displayed an uncanny combination of competitiveness and drive, as well as humility. One way to understand this finding is that being driven often causes a wake of negative interpersonal consequences, but humility gives leaders an advantage because it mitigates this potential for relational wear and tear. Similarly, another study found evidence for the social oil hypothesis in that health-care managers high in narcissism were less effective as leaders and had employees with lower job engagement and performance; however, these associations were buffered when the leader was perceived as more humble (Owens, Wallace, and Waldman, 2015).

A second example of the social oil hypothesis involves the role of humility in the context of adversity and struggle. In a longitudinal study, researchers examined couples during the often stressful transition to parenthood (Ripley et al., 2016). Higher levels of relational humility predicted lower levels of stress initially and over time, thus allowing the social bond to endure when under duress (Ripley et al., 2016). In this study, humility promoted more positive social support in the couple by helping partners maintain an other-oriented stance, which helped reduce perceived stress in the parents who were coping with the high demands of raising a newborn (Ripley et al., 2016). Davis et al. (2013) explored how humility affected small groups of college students that underwent three tasks designed to challenge humility. They found that trait humility ratings from other-report measures predicted greater group status and acceptance than other students who were rated as having lower levels of humility. Both research studies support the idea that, even when facing stress and adversity, humility is associated with stronger relationships.

Finally, humility also helps repair social bonds when they have been damaged by conflict. All relationships involve some conflict, and it is not just the degree of conflict, but rather how well conflict is managed that influences the quality of a relationship (Thomas, 1992; Moore, 2014). Humility is theorized to promote effective behaviors during and after conflict. For example, humble people ought to maintain a strong respect for the needs and interests of others during conflict and quickly acknowledge mistakes and seek to repair damaged caused by offenses. A longitudinal study examined individuals who had been recently hurt within a romantic relationship and found that perceiving the offender as humbler predicted greater forgiveness (Davis et al., 2013). This study corroborated several cross-sectional studies that found a positive relationship between relational humility and forgiveness (see Davis et al., 2010; Davis et al., 2011).

RESEARCH ON HUMILITY IN RELATIONSHIPS

Our relational humility theory views humility in the context of a relationship because the characteristics of the relationship may be crucial to how a person might interact based on situational cues, relationship factors, or roles in the relationship. For instance, individuals may be less humble in relationships in which they are not strongly invested but display high levels of humility in relationships that are viewed as more personally central or important. Although humility is a virtue likely to enhance all social relations, the context could alter how people present themselves to others. Thus, we briefly review the literature on humility in different relational contexts.

Couples, Families, and Social Relationships

Social relationships characterized by high levels of humility often have a more positive relationship quality (Peters, Rowat, and Johnson, 2011). Human beings are relational creatures (Gergen, 2009), and prosocial behavior that is prompted by humility can help individuals form strong friendships in social relationship contexts (Çardak, 2013). Humility is viewed as a collaborative, growth-oriented approach in relationships that leads people to respect and learn from each other (Wallace and Louden, 1994), thus adding to the greater quality of the relationship. For instance, humility can deepen family relationships by acknowledging one's own fallibility, which can lead to forgiveness and restoration (Worthington, 1998). Thus, in this familial context, humility could help parent-child relationships by facilitating forgiveness and helping foster a strong family bond. Furthermore, humility has been linked to couples being more likely to weigh the costs of vengeful behaviors before making a decision to get even with their romantic partner (Sheppard and Boon, 2012). Humility is beneficial in promoting forgiveness in romantic relationship contexts as well, in part by increasing one's commitment to their relationship partner (e.g., Farrell et al., 2015). Also, humble people have been found to be more compassionate and thus more likely to help others by lending support in ways that enrich the relationship (Krause and Hayward, 2015). It also appears that the compassion and acknowledgement of one's strengths and weaknesses seen in humble people can also extend toward themselves and promote self-forgiveness (Krause, 2015). Broadly speaking, the research indicates strong support for the role of humility in deepening and enriching social bonds in couples, families, and social relationships.

In a couple or martial relational context, communication and listening are important aspects of the relationship, but it is theorized that romantic relationships and marriages only truly thrive when partners invest more into the social bond of the relationship by being other-oriented rather than investing in their own individual happiness (Hargrave, 2000). For example, partners in a couple often feel competition with one another if each individual focuses on their own needs. However, humility shifts the focus to the togetherness, or the "us-ness" (e.g., the transformation of motivation), of the relationship, hence shifting the focus to meeting one's partner's needs (Hargrave, 2000). Drawing form interdependence theory (see Kelly and Thibaut, 1978), relationship researchers term this the *transformation of motivation,* in which people shift from prioritizing their selfish motives (i.e., the given outcome) to prioritizing the relationship (i.e., the effective outcome) (Yovetich and Rusbult, 1994). Indeed, this was found in a study where humility was associated with greater forgiveness of a relational offense (Van Tongeren et al., 2014). Similarly, humility was linked to positive relationship outcomes (e.g., greater relationship satisfaction, greater forgiveness of partner), and this association was partially mediated by the commitment to the relationship or commitment to togetherness (Farrell et al., 2015). Given these studies follow the social bonds and social oil hypotheses, humility could be especially important in marital contexts in which couples are regularly struggling for power or feel as though they are competing, or for couples that want to develop a greater sense of intimacy and satisfaction to their relationship.

Also, attachment styles (e.g., secure, preoccupied, dismissing) can play a major role in how couples interact, and there is some evidence that humility may develop from a secure attachment. Dwiwardani et al. (2014) theorized that securely attached individuals with a positive internal view of themselves and others would have an increased sense of security to operate from, allowing them to accurately assess their strengths and limitations non-defensively. Attachment styles are not always of proximal influence on behavior, but they can greatly influence the interactional patterns and communications of individuals (Ryan, Brown, and Creswell, 2007), which could affect a person's perceptions of a target person's humility. Indeed, attachment styles are often triggered or activated in couples when one partner feels stressed, tired, or hurt. Partners with an insecure attachment (e.g., anxious preoccupied, dismissing) may struggle with humility and act dismissively, condescendingly, or self-focused (Dwiwardani et al., 2014). Hence, humility may be expressed differently depending on the context of a person's attachment style and whether any antecedent triggers the individual's secure or insecure attachment style. All these examples help highlight the social bonds hypothesis in that humility helps individuals develop, maintain, strengthen, and repair relational bonds to the people who are closest to them.

Moreover, humility is good for human beings in the sense that human beings thrive when they find deep connection and emotional engagement with other people (Yalom, 1995). What we know from humility research is that, while difficult to maintain, humility is a way of being with others that strengthens the social ties that bind humanity together. Indeed, many psychologists have theorized that most, if not all, psychological problems can be translated into interpersonal difficulties or maladaptive interpersonal patterns (Hopwood et al., 2013). Clearly, humility in relationships has the potential to (a) strengthen social bonds, (b) reduce conflict and expedite relational repair to maintain social bonds, and (c) help cultivate a flourishing life that is full of meaningful, enriched relationships.

Cultural Differences

A second context that could raise unique challenges in relationships is dealing with cultural differences because individuals and groups can be highly invested in their own cultural worldview, beliefs, and values (Hook et al., 2017). You could conceptualize ethnocentrism (e.g., viewing one's culture as superior compared with others) as being a common response in humanity or even a base level of human nature. Thus, trying to infuse humility into relationships where cultural differences are present can be very difficult. Indeed, cross-cultural research supports this idea that culture and conflict are inextricably linked (Berry, 2002). Cultural factors that could bring about conflict include a wide range of contexts (e.g., politics, religion, and race). Thus, humility can be essential in buffering against ruptures in relationships or by successfully working through cultural conflicts. For example, Van Tongeren et al. (2016) provided experimental and correlational evidence in a series of studies that humility was associated with positive attitudes toward others with different religious beliefs, and humble individuals held less aggressive intentions toward religious outgroup members that criticized the participant's beliefs. Moreover, implicitly priming participants with humility decreased aggressive behavior toward the offending outgroup member, suggesting a causal link between humility and reduced defensiveness. Also, Hook et al. (2015) found that participants were more likely to forgive a religious leader who had hurt them when the religious leader was humble about their religious beliefs and values. Religious leaders in particular may struggle with humility in religious/spiritual contexts because they are often placed in hierarchical roles and may struggle to be humble toward others (Hook et al., 2015). However, humility in this context could help strengthen the relationships between the religious leader and their religious community, as well as repair relationships and promote forgiveness.

Some important ways people assess humility in others in cultural contexts may include (a) how well the target person knows themselves, (b) whether the target person desires a mutual partnership characterized by respect, and (c) whether the target person is open to new information and is invested in learning more (Foronda et al., 2016). For instance, in cross-cultural contexts, people may judge another's humility in part by assessing how the other person makes them feel, such as feeling like the target person respects their culture, does not make assumptions about them, and feels like an equal. Also, when making humility judgments, people may evaluate the emotions in the target person, such as whether the target person has a good self-awareness of biases, lacks a sense of superiority or ethnocentrism, or has a genuine curiosity of wanting to know and understand their culture.

However, it is important to note that not all cultures value humility equally. For instance, one study found humility in leaders was more strongly valued in Asian cultures than in European cultures (Mittal and Dorfman, 2012). Therefore, due to differences in how cultures interpret and value humility in certain contexts, conflict could ensue when an individual expects and appreciates humility but engages in a cross-cultural dialogue with another person who does not value humility or even sees humility as a weakness.

In a broader sense, helping professions, such as doctors, social workers, and counselors, are treating an increasingly diverse population, and humility has been shown to play a pivotal role in developing positive relationships with positive outcomes in cultural contexts (see Mosher et al. 2017, for a review). For instance, counselors who were humble toward their client's culture were found to have stronger working alliances, better therapeutic outcomes, and their humility buffered against negative therapeutic outcomes when counselors missed opportunities to engage clients in a culturally meaningful dialogue (Davis et al., 2016; Hook et al., 2013; Owen et al., 2014; Owen et al., 2016). In today's Zeitgeist, professionals from all domains that interact with others will likely come into contact with individuals culturally different from themselves (Hook and Watkins, 2015). Thus, humility would be beneficial for those seeking careers that aim to serve or help others. While cultural contexts may pull for professionals to take on an expert role, humility in this context could help professionals accurately assess themselves for limitations or biases and give more power to the client (Gallardo, 2014). Furthermore, humility could help professionals navigate and regulate their emotions and reactions when their beliefs are disagreed with or challenged by clients, thus giving more time to formulate a more humbly perceived response. Ultimately, human beings that stay humble toward another's culture convey the notion that culture is a part of the process of deeply knowing another individual and seeing their cultural identities as integral to the quality of the relationship.

Business Context

A third relationship context that has received some attention in the humility literature is a business or organizational context. Humility might seem counterproductive in the business world today, since many might think one needs to be aggressive or boisterous to succeed (Martin, 2014). Indeed, it might appear that human nature tends to be more competitive and self-focused in the business world rather than staying egoless and other-oriented. However, relationships within and between organizations are likely to thrive, both economically and relationally, when there is a strong foundation of humility (Kriger and Hanson, 1999). Specifically, many researchers have focused on business leaders and theorized that business leaders in particular are key influences in fostering values and virtues in workplace environments because business leaders are in a hierarchical role that serves as a role model for identifying, articulating, and guiding virtuous behaviors (Kriger and Hanson, 1999; Morris, Brotheridge, and Urbanski, 2005; Nielsen, Marrone, and Slay, 2010; Wood and Vilkinas, 2007). Effective leadership in businesses that wish to sustain the longevity of a successful organization are hypothesized to include a blend of humility and strong personal will (Morris et al., 2005). Also, humility has been associated with favorable outcomes among employees in an organization (Wiltshire, Bourdage, and Lee, 2014).

Moreover, expressing humility within an organization has been associated with higher job satisfaction and greater employee engagement. Humility may even help compensate for lower general mental ability among employees (Owens, Johnson, and Mitchell, 2013). In their study of students in business classes, Owen et al. (2013) found team members that were high in perceived humility were positively associated with greater quality of team member contribution on class assignments as well as having a greater individual performance, despite scoring low on self-efficacy, conscientiousness, and cognitive ability tests.

Businesses often have situations in which staying humble could be difficult, such as supervisor-employee interactions, competition for job promotions, or direct competition with other organizations. For example, a successful supervisor or business leader might struggle to remain humble and open to feedback from employees. Also, organizations competing over limited resources might struggle to remain other-oriented and respectful of other companies in the market, thus limiting the potential for cooperation or partnerships. In light of research, humility in a business context would be paramount for buffering against negative relationship consequences from the wear and tear of competition and conflict (e.g., social oil hypothesis), as well as for strengthening relationships within or between organizations (e.g., social bonds hypothesis).

DISCUSSION

Early in the positive psychology movement, psychological research struggled to study humility given the inherent difficulties in defining and accurately measuring humility. To begin to address these challenges, a relational humility model aligned with well-established theory and methods for studying how people perceive traits and virtues in other people. This approach calls for studying humility from a variety of vantage points (i.e., self, target person, others), over time, and in contexts that strain egotism and make humility more difficult to practice. Furthermore, a relational humility model brought to light the importance of the relational context when examining humility given that people often behave differently depending on social cues, relationship factors, and the role they play in various relationships. Moreover, human nature orients itself to make certain relational contexts (e.g., conflicts with others, hierarchical roles) more difficult for individuals to maintain humility and check natural tendencies to be self-oriented versus other-oriented.

Two key hypotheses that help form the backbone of the relational humility model are the social bonds and social oil hypotheses, which further theorize how humility benefits the relational bond and protects or restores the relationship when under stress. A growing body of research has tested these hypotheses and found humility to indeed help develop relationships (e.g., humility is viewed as attractive in potential dating partners), strengthen relationships (e.g., humility is associated with greater relationship satisfaction), and repair relationships (e.g., humility predicts greater likelihood to forgive partner). Although our brief overview of humility research in various contexts (e.g., couples, cultural differences, organizations) was by no means exhaustive, it helped highlight how humility can benefit different relational contexts as well as how humility might be presented and evaluated differently depending on the relational context. Overall, we theorize that humility in relationships of all contexts help form the bedrock for the continual growth and fortification of relational bonds by infusing an accurate view of oneself, a focus on others, and lack of superiority into the very foundation of the relationship.

Limitations and Future Directions

In terms of next steps, research on relational humility has theorized that commitment, more specifically dedication to a partner without constraint, is the mechanism through which perceptions of humility lead to positive relationship qualities, such as forgiveness, closeness, and trust. In other words, humility increases one's dedication to a partner, which in turn leads to positive relationship qualities. While commitment might be a key mechanism contributing to positive relationship quality, we theorize it would need to be the type of commitment that can be a proxy variable to the closeness of the social bond and not commitment used as a constraint holding people in a relationship due to a societal expectation or cultural value. However, most studies thus far have not used strong research designs for evaluating causal inferences implied by the social bonds and social oil hypotheses. To date, we are aware of only one study that employed experimental techniques to demonstrate the causal effect of humility (Van Tongeren et al., 2016). Additional experimental designs must be employed to advance research in this area. Therefore, future research could add to the cross-sectional, correlational research by using more rigorous methodologies (e.g., longitudinal, experimental methods). Also, future studies could examine whether perceptions of humility explain additional variability in relationship commitment above and beyond perceptions of agreeableness, openness, likeability, and other relationship-oriented virtues.

Given that any relational humility models are still fairly new, additional research is needed to explore and test the core tenets. For example, future research could test the social oil hypothesis to see whether humility buffers relationship deterioration from personality qualities such as perfectionism, competitiveness, and having high standards. Also, the literature has not thoroughly tested relational humility models in relationships that are undergoing stressful transitions or may experience drops in relationship quality due to stress. Another limitation is that humility is often difficult to parse from other virtues, so it is possible that humility may not be causally related to positive, prosocial behaviors but instead act as an underlying factor which promotes other virtues more causally proximal. Thus, strong studies using experimental or longitudinal designs are needed to test for theorized mediators.

We see another theoretical area of concern that could be addressed through effective and imaginative methodological approaches. Some contend one might demonstrate too much humility, which could be a liability. That is, there may be drawbacks to acting humbly or being perceived as being too humble. For example, more arrogant individuals may exploit humbler relationship partners. Toward this end, recent research has examined the interactive effects of *both* partners' humility. Advancing what they call the *complementarity of humility hypothesis*, Van Tongeren et al. (2019) argue that the best relational outcomes occur when both relational partners are humble. They present dyadic, other-report longitudinal and physiological data of couples under stress as evidence that only when both partners perceive each other as being high in humility, do relationship outcomes—and individual physiological responses to stress—flourish. Yet when one partner is humble and the other is not, such benefits are not fully realized. Future research should examine the relational contexts in which humility may have limitations or humble individuals may be exploited. Moreover, additional theoretical work could address the distinction between "too much" humility and other distinct psychological states, such as pusillanimity. We see many exciting future avenues of research. Also germane to this, cultural differences in the degree to which humility is valued have yet to be explored. "Too much humility" could be not just that one person might behave so humbly that the other takes advantage, but it could also be a difference in values that creates problems due to crossed expectations. Philosophers and theologians sometimes conceptualize humility differently (see Church and Barrett, 2017; Murphy, 2017; Porter et al., 2017; Roberts and Cleveland, 2017), and such definitional approaches inevitably lead people who adopt them to hold often implicit differences in value. The implications of these philosophical and theological differences are in need of exploration.

Practical Applications

Perceptions of humility are theorized to hold the key to deepening relationships by stabilizing and regulating one's commitment to a person, which allows for the birth of togetherness or "us-ness." On the other hand, the investment into the other is weakened when the target person acts in selfish, arrogant, or disrespectful ways that do not align with humility social norms. From a clinical standpoint, the social oil hypothesis suggests that infusing humility into the training, education, or work of professionals (e.g., psychologists, doctors, and teachers) could allow trainees to embrace humility as a trait, to help protect relationships that may experience ongoing strain. Also, it could be beneficial integrating humility into clinical interventions designed to help individuals going through stressful transitions (e.g., becoming a parent, starting a new job). For instance, humility has been an essential intervention focus for the substance abuse intervention fellowship known as Alcoholics Anonymous, which guides its members toward sobriety in part by portraying and developing a humble mindset.

Another area in which relational humility could be helpful involves successfully navigating people's struggles with balancing the needs of others and their own needs. In this sense, humility could promote greater self-regulation in relationships and reduce the tension in a relationship by caring for the values of each person, allowing individuals to retain their integrity and truthfulness. For example, cultural values may differ between a therapist and client, but humility could allow the therapist to keep their own beliefs intact while still reaching out to explore and respect the client's beliefs. This could also expand to other relational contexts, such as couples, families, and organized groups (e.g., religious, civic, political, business).

Finally, relational humility brings individuals outside of themselves by focusing on others, which could add meaning to their lives by focusing on something greater than themselves. Relational humility could give a person a sense of purpose by enriching the emotional connection and strengthening the social bond to another. Furthermore, one's commitment to the relationship could grow alongside a healthy sense of relational humility and add meaning this way. Togetherness with people closest to us often gives our lives purpose; thus, relational humility could be essential for relationships and the people in them to flourish through the fulfillment of meaning in one's life.

Summary and Conclusion

Humility is an ancient virtue that has recently received some strong scientific interest. After addressing some measurement concerns, research has turned toward advancing and testing theory. A relational humility model conceptualizes humility as arising from an accurate view of self; an other-orientation; and regulation of selfish, egoistic desires. Human nature lends itself to focus more toward the self, for various reasons (e.g., self-promoting, self-protecting), during times where it can be difficult to stay humble (e.g., receiving negative feedback, engaging with someone with different cultural values). Two of its primary research hypotheses—the social bonds hypothesis and the social oil hypothesis—have already begun to receive empirical support. We have suggested that one aspect of commitment—the emotional and social bond—might be the mechanism through which humility affects social outcomes such as strengthening, maintaining, or repairing relationships. Research on the role of humility in a variety of relationships has highlighted many of its benefits in forming, maintaining, and repairing relationships, ranging from close relationships to interactions with dissimilar others. Future work could advance research through more sophisticated methodological designs and theoretical elaboration. In short, research on humility is thriving, yet there is still so much work to be done. Collaborative work centered on advancing research in this domain should prove valuable.

NOTE

1. We would like to thank the generous financial support of the John Templeton Foundation (Grant No. 60622).

REFERENCES

Berry, J. W. 2002. *Cross-cultural Psychology: Research and Applications*. New York: Cambridge University Press.

Bowlby, J. 1977. "The making and breaking of affectional bonds: I. Aetiology and psychopathology in the light of attachment theory." *British Journal of Psychiatry, 130*(3), 201–210.

Çardak, M. 2013. "The relationship between forgiveness and humility: A case study for university students." *Educational Research and Reviews, 8*(8), 425–430.

Chancellor, J., and S. Lyubomirsky. 2013. "Humble beginnings: Current trends, state perspectives, and hallmarks of humility." *Social and Personality Psychology Compass, 7*(11), 819–833.

Church, I. M., and J. L. Barrett. 2017. "Intellectual humility." In *Handbook of Humility: Theory, Research, and Applications*, edited by E. L. Worthington, D. E. Davis, and J. N. Hook, 91–104. New York: Taylor and Francis.

Davis, D. E., K. DeBlaere, J. Brubaker, T. A. Owen, J. N. Jordan, J. N. Hook, and Van D. R. Tongeren. 2016. "Microaggressions and perceptions of cultural humility in counseling." *Journal of Counseling and Development, 94*(4), 483–493.

Davis, D. E., J. N. Hook, E. L. Worthington, D. R. Van Tongeren, A. L. Gartner, D. J. Jennings, and R. A. Emmons. 2011. "Relational humility: Conceptualizing and measuring humility as a personality judgment." *Journal of Personality Assessment*, *93*(3), 225–234.

Davis, D., V. Placeres, E. Choe, C. DeBlaere, D. Zeyala, and J. N. Hook. 2017. "Relational humility." In *Handbook of Humility: Theory, Research, and Applications*, edited by E. L. Worthington, D. E. Davis, and J. N. Hook, 105–118. New York: Taylor and Francis.

Davis, D. E., E. L. Worthington, Jr., and J. N. Hook. 2010. "Relational humility: A review of definitions and measurement strategies." *Journal of Positive Psychology*, *5*, 243–252.

Davis, D. E., E. L. Worthington, J. N. Hook, R. A. Emmons, P. C. Hill, R. A. Bollinger, and D. R. Van Tongeren. 2013. "Humility and the development and repair of social bonds: Two longitudinal studies." *Self and Identity*, *12*(1), 58–77.

Dwiwardani, C., P. C. Hill, R. A. Bollinger, L. F. Marks, J. R. Steele, H. N. Doolin, . . . and D. E. Davis. 2014. "Virtues develop from a secure base: Attachment and resilience as predictors of humility, gratitude, and forgiveness." *Journal of Psychology and Theology*, *42*(1), 83–90.

Dwiwardani, C., A. S. Ord, M. Fennell, D. Eaves, J. S. Ripley, A. Perkins, . . . and R. C. Garthe. 2017. "Spelling HUMBLE with U and ME: The role of perceived humility in intimate partner relationships." *Journal of Positive Psychology*, 1–11.

Farrell, J. E., J. N. Hook, M. Ramos, D. E. Davis, D. R. Van Tongeren, and J. M. Ruiz. 2015. "Humility and relationship outcomes in couples: The mediating role of commitment." *Couple and Family Psychology: Research and Practice*, *4*(1), 14–26.

Fillo, J., J. A. Simpson, W. S. Rholes, and J. L. Kohn. 2015. "Dads doing diapers: Individual and relational outcomes associated with the division of childcare across the transition to parenthood." *Journal of Personality and Social Psychology*, *108*(2), 298–316.

Foronda, C., D. L. Baptiste, M. M. Reinholdt, and K. Ousman. 2016. "Cultural humility: A concept analysis." *Journal of Transcultural Nursing*, *27*(3), 210–217.

Funder, D. C. 1995. "On the accuracy of personality judgment: A realistic approach." *Psychological Review*, *102*, 652–670.

Gallardo, M. E., ed. 2014. *Developing Cultural Humility: Embracing Race, Privilege and Power*. Los Angeles: Sage.

Gergen, K. J. 2009. *Relational Being: Beyond Self and Community*. New York: Oxford University Press.

Hargrave, T. D. 2000. *The Essential Humility of Marriage: Honoring the Third Identity in Couple Therapy*. Phoenix, AR: Zeig Tucker and Theisen.

Holden, C. J., V. Zeigler-Hill, M. N. Pham, and T. K. Shackelford. 2014. "Personality features and mate retention strategies: Honesty–humility and the willingness to manipulate, deceive, and exploit romantic partners." *Personality and Individual Differences*, *57*, 31–36.

Hook, J. N., D. E., Davis, J. Owen, and C. DeBlaere. 2017. *Cultural Humility: A Guide to Engaging Diverse Identities in Therapy.* Washington, DC: American Psychological Association.

Hook, J. N., D. E. Davis, J. Owen, E. L. Worthington Jr., and S. O. Utsey. 2013. "Cultural humility: Measuring openness to culturally diverse clients." *Journal of Counseling Psychology, 60*(3), 353–366.

Hook, J. N., D. E. Davis, D. R. Van Tongeren, P. C. Hill, E. L. Worthington, Jr., J. E. Farrell, and Dieke. 2015. "Intellectual humility and forgiveness of religious leaders." *Journal of Positive Psychology, 10*(6), 499–506.

Hook, J. N., and C. E. Watkins Jr. 2015. "Cultural humility: The cornerstone of positive contact with culturally different individuals and groups?" *American Psychologist, 70*(7), 661–662.

Hopwood, C. J., A. G. Wright, E. B Ansell, and A. L. Pincus. 2013. "The interpersonal core of personality pathology." *Journal of Personality Disorders, 27*(3), 270–295.

House, J. S., K. R. Landis, and D. Umberson. 1988. "Social relationships and health." *Science, 241*(4865), 540–545.

Kelley, H. H., and J. W. Thibaut. 1978. *Interpersonal Relations: A Theory of Interdependence.* New York: Wiley-Interscience.

Krause, N. 2015. "Assessing the relationships among race, religion, humility, and self-forgiveness: A longitudinal investigation." *Advances in Life Course Research, 24*, 66–74.

Krause, N., and R. D. Hayward. 2015. "Humility, compassion, and gratitude to God: Assessing the relationships among key religious virtues." *Psychology of Religion and Spirituality*, 7(3), 192–204.

Kriger, M. P., and B. J. Hanson. 1999. "A value-based paradigm for creating truly healthy organizations." *Journal of Organizational Change Management, 12*(4), 302–317.

Kruse, E., J. Chancellor, and S. Lyubomirsky. 2017. "State humility: Measurement, conceptual validation, and intrapersonal processes." *Self and Identity, 16*(4), 399–438.

Lopez, S. J., and C. R. Snyder, eds. 2009. *Oxford Handbook of Positive Psychology.* New York: Oxford University Press.

Martin, R. 2014, December. "Humility as a desirable personality trait and a construct of effective leadership." Paper presented at the 5th Annual Virtual Conference on Moral Leadership, Virginia Beach, VA, pp. 15–21.

Mittal, R., and P. W. Dorfman. 2012. "Servant leadership across cultures." *Journal of World Business, 47*(4, 555–570.

Moore, C. W. 2014. *The Mediation Process: Practical Strategies for Resolving Conflict.* New York: John Wiley and Sons.

Morris, J. A., C. M. Brotheridge, and J. C. Urbanski. 2005. "Bringing humility to leadership: Antecedents and consequences of leader humility." *Human Relations, 58*(10), 1323–1350.

Mosher, D. K., J. N. Hook, J. E. Farrell, C. E. Watkins, and D. E. Davis. 2017. "Cultural humility." In *Handbook of Humility: Theory, Research, and Applications,* edited by E. L. Worthington, D. E. Davis, and J. N. Hook, 91–104. New York: Taylor and Francis.

Murphy, J. G. 2017. "Humility as a moral virtue." In *Handbook of Humility: Theory, Research, and Applications,* edited by E. L. Worthington, D. E. Davis, and J. N. Hook, 19–32. New York: Taylor and Francis.

Nielsen, R., J. A Marrone, and H. S. Slay. 2010. "A new look at humility: Exploring the humility concept and its role in socialized charismatic leadership." *Journal of Leadership and Organizational Studies, 17*(1), 33–43.

Owens, B. P., M. D. Johnson, and T. R. Mitchell. 2013. "Expressed humility in organizations: Implications for performance, teams, and leadership." *Organization Science, 24*(5), 1517–1538.

Owen, J., I. I. Jordan, A. Terrence, D., Turner, D. E. Davis, J. N. Hook, and M. M Leach. 2014. "Therapists' multicultural orientation: Client perceptions of cultural humility, spiritual/religious commitment, and therapy outcomes." *Journal of Psychology and Theology, 42*(1), 91–98.

Owen, J., K. W. Tao, J. M. Drinane, J. Hook, D. E. Davis, and N. F. Kune. 2016. "Client perceptions of therapists' multicultural orientation: Cultural missed opportunities and cultural humility." *Professional Psychology: Research and Practice, 47*(1), 30–37.

Peters, A. S., Rowat, W. C., and M. K. Johnson. 2011. "Associations between dispositional humility and social relationship quality." *Psychology, 2*(3), 155.

Porter, S. L., A. Rambachan, A. Velez de Cea, D. Rabinowitz, S. Pardue, and S. Jackson. 2017. "Religious perspectives on humility." In *Handbook of Humility: Theory, Research, and Applications,* edited by E. L. Worthington, D. E. Davis, and J. N. Hook, 47–61. New York: Taylor and Francis.

Ripley, J. S., R. C. Garthe, A. Perkins, E. L. Worthington, D. E. Davis, J. N. Hook, . . . and M. Fennell. 2016. "Perceived partner humility predicts subjective stress during transition to parenthood." *Couple and Family Psychology: Research and Practice, 5*(3), 157–167.

Roberts, R. C., and W.S. Cleveland. 2017. "Humility from a philosophical point of view." In *Handbook of Humility: Theory, Research, and Applications,* edited by E. L. Worthington, D. E. Davis, and J. N. Hook, 33–46. New York: Taylor and Francis.

Ryan, R. M., K. W. Brown, and J. D. Creswell. 2007. "How integrative is attachment theory? Unpacking the meaning and significance of felt security." *Psychological Inquiry, 18*(3), 177–182.

Seligman, M. E. P., and M. Csikszentmihalyi. 2000. "Positive psychology: An introduction." *American Psychologist, 55*, 5–14.

Sheppard, K. E., and S. D. Boon. 2012. "Predicting appraisals of romantic revenge: The roles of honesty–humility, agreeableness, and vengefulness." *Personality and Individual Differences*, 52(2), 128–132.

Stanley, S. M., and H. J. Markman. 1992. "Assessing commitment in personal relationships." *Journal of Marriage and the Family*, 595–608.

Tangney, J. P. 2009. "Humility." In *Oxford Handbook of Positive Psychology*, edited by S. J. Lopez and C. R. Snyder, 483–490. New York: Oxford University Press.

Thomas, K. W. 1992. "Conflict and conflict management: Reflections and update." *Journal of Organizational Behavior*, 13(3), 265–274.

Van Tongeren, D. R., D. E. Davis, and J. N. Hook. 2014. "Social benefits of humility: Initiating and maintaining romantic relationships." *Journal of Positive Psychology*, 9, 313–321.

Van Tongeren, D. R., J. N. Hook, M. J. Ramos, M. Edwards, E. L. Worthington, Jr., D. Davis, . . . and R. G. Cowden. 2019. "The complementarity of humility hypothesis: Individual, relational, and physiological effects of mutually humble partners." *Journal of Positive Psychology*, 14(2), 178–187.

Van Tongeren, D. R., J. Stafford, J. N. Hook, J. D. Green, D. E. Davis, and K. A. Johnson. 2016. "Humility attenuates negative attitudes and behaviors toward religious out-group members." *Journal of Positive Psychology*, 11(2), 199–208.

Yalom, I. D. 1995. *The Theory and Practice of Group Psychotherapy*. New York: Basic Books.

Yovetich, N. A., and C.A. Rusbult. 1994. "Accommodative behaviors in close relationships: Exploring transformation of motivation." *Journal of Experimental Social Psychology*, 30, 138–164.

Wallace, J., and W. Louden. 1994. "Collaboration and the growth of teachers' knowledge." *Qualitative Studies in Education*, 7(4), 323–334.

Wiltshire, J., J. S. Bourdage, and K. Lee. 2014. "Honesty-humility and perceptions of organizational politics in predicting workplace outcomes." *Journal of Business and Psychology*, 29(2), 235–251.

Wood, J., and T. Vilkinas. 2007. "Characteristics associated with CEO success: Perceptions of CEOs and their staff." *Journal of Management Development*, 26(3), 213–227.

Worthington, E. L. 1998. "An empathy-humility-commitment model of forgiveness applied within family dyads." *Journal of Family Therapy*, 20(1), 59–76.

Chapter 5

Humility in Four Forms

Intrapersonal, Interpersonal, Community, and Ecological

DARCIA NARVAEZ

INTRODUCTION

The definition of humility that is proposed here is multilayered.[1] The general thesis of this chapter is that a disposition of interpersonal humility develops from the ground up in well-raised human beings within well-supported families and communities where children are supported in meeting their evolved basic needs. Thus, interpersonal humility relies on the behavior of prior generations, making *interpersonal* humility a developmental, intergenerational affair that also fosters an internalized, or *intrapersonal,* humility. But in order to provide appropriate care to the youngest generation, a society or culture needs to be humble toward the basic needs of its members. A third layer of humility occurs at the community level. Modern nations today typically do not fully provide for the evolved basic needs of their youngest members. As a result, they raise individuals whose neurobiological and social grounding presses *against* a disposition of humility and toward self-protective mechanisms that form in response to the stress of unmet needs. Lack of provision for basic needs results, in part, in a lack of humility on the part of a community that in effect moves against the nature of Nature.[2] This contrariness extends to the treatment of the natural world itself, representing another realm of humility I discuss, ecological humility. All four forms of humility—intrapersonal, interpersonal, community, ecological—are interrelated and interactive. See table 5.1 for an outline of the types of humility that I examine in more detail ahead. See figure 5.1 for their interrelations.

INTERPERSONAL HUMILITY

I start with interpersonal humility, which is the typical focus of discussions about humility. As listed in table 5.1, I identify three aspects of interpersonal humility, first, *embodiment*—the functioning of one's neurobiological structures, such as the stress response whose parameters are established in early life. The other two aspects of interpersonal humility mentioned here are *emotion* and *cognition* (the latter could be divided into explicit and implicit cognition, but there is no room here to spell that out, so cognition will be described as one category). Some basic features of *embodiment* and *emotion* are listed in table 5.1, reflecting species-normal human development as a social mammal, but these will be illuminated later, under the section on the development of humility below. The *cognitive* aspects are the usual focus of discussion, and so I start there.

Openness has been identified as a key component of intellectual humility. For example, intellectual humility embraces openness to experience (e.g., Kruse, Chancellor, and Lyubomirsky, 2017). Interpersonal humility, however, must be defined differently. Spezio, Peterson, and Roberts (2019) define relational

Table 5.1 THE LAYERS OF HUMILITY WITH EXAMPLES OF EACH TYPE

	Intrapersonal Humility	*Interpersonal Humility (person to person)*			*Community Humility (intergroup)*	*Ecological Humility (e.g., interspecies)*
		Embodiment	*Emotion*	*Cognition*		
Modesty	Content with self-in-body	Not socially threat reactive	Self-accepting; other-accepting	Open; self-knowledgeable; self-monitoring (e.g., of ego, intellect)	Behaves as a fellow member of a community of communities	Honorable harvest: does not take too much; leaves resources for others
Selflessness	Automatically cooperative with own spirit and self's unique needs	Sociality is pleasurable	Empathic	Minimal ego; communal in thought and habit	Older generation yields to basic needs of younger generation	Limits wants and desires; lives with the biocommunity in mind
Respectfulness	Self-accepting	Relationally attuned to others in multiple nonverbal ways	Emotionally present with others	Hospitable; honors individuality; socially flexible	Honors diversity in development and personality	Honors other-than-human lifeforms

humility as openness to the "I" in the other, "the inclusion of the other as valued together (inseparably) with the self," and they find empirical support for their view in examining interpersonal relations in a L'Arche community.[3] Contrasting intellectual humility's openness with that of relational humility, they point out that intellectual humility can be fairly static and one-way, whereas interpersonal humility is necessarily interactive. One must demonstrate ongoing humility in interactions with the person at hand. This definition is a good starting point for what is posited here. But what is the nature of interpersonal interactions characterized by humility?

Interpersonal humility, in my view, manifests in behavior that is modest, selfless, and respectful. *Modesty* in terms of cognition concerns openness to the other as a dynamic being, accompanied by realistic self-knowledge in terms of capacities and one's place in the world. (This undergoes development throughout childhood and adolescence as one tests and discovers one's capacities and place in the world.) Modesty also includes self-monitoring to keep the ego from inflating or deflating—that is, feeling superior or inferior to the other. Communalism in thought and habit represent the cognitive aspect of *selflessness*, a personal connectedness and egolessness that one brings to a situation, which occurs in supportive growth environments. In contrast, one can become self-conscious (and deflated) in environments where needs are not met and/or emotional expressions are unrecognized or dismissed. However, even in these circumstances the fully humble (adult) person embraces a larger frame than the self and its discomfort, maintaining selflessness, aware that interpersonal connections are deeper, as part of a continuum of being, than they appear. *Respectfulness* is an attitude of hospitality; honoring individuality; and maintaining a readiness to be socially flexible, pliable, and responsive to the other.

The expression of humility shifts by situation according to which relationships are salient and which actions are needed. Humility moves with the relational flow in the moment, co-coordinating action with the well-being of others in mind, maintaining modesty, selflessness, and respectfulness.

The *embodied* bases for humility are also mentioned in table 5.1. The modest individual is not socially threat reactive and selflessly finds social experience pleasurable rather than aversive. The respectful individual is relationally attuned to others in multiple nonverbal ways (coordination of proxemics, kinesics, prosody, and other forms of nonverbal communication[4]). On the *emotional* level, modesty requires a sense of self-trust, rather than distrust, and self-acceptance, a yielding to the deep self, but also to the other, accepting them as they are. Selflessness and respectfulness are apparent in empathy and emotional presence, respectively. Humility is visible in face-to-face encounters when an individual demonstrates appropriate interpersonal and self-coordinated responsiveness to the other in the moment, represented in intersubjective interpersonal verbal and nonverbal communication.

Taking interpersonal humility to be interactive, it won't do for humility to be apparent only once in a while—i.e., in particular situations with specific people, say with one's mother when she is ill. When fully formed, humility is a way of being that individuals carry with them into all situations, infused into all encounters. What I add to the usual discussions of interpersonal humility is a well-constructed neurobiology, the embodiment that underlies the aforementioned capacities. Interpersonal humility is grounded in early experience—support in getting basic needs met without social distress; feeling accepted, loved and respected; having mutually responsive and respectful experiences with multiple different others. The neurobiological substrates of humility development are the next topic.

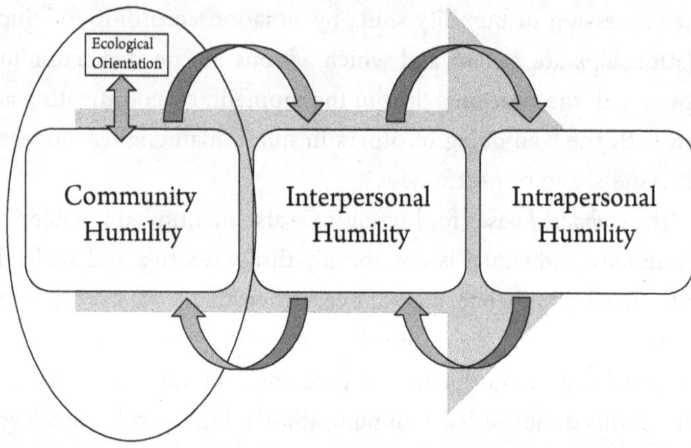

Figure 5.1. Layers of Interactive Influence in Humility Development: Four Types Interrelated Across Generations

DEVELOPMENTAL FOUNDATIONS FOR HUMILITY

Most scholarship focuses on an individual adult's humility. But according to the multilayered definition proposed here, individual interpersonal humility does not develop in social isolation. A child does not come into being alone. She first has a mother, a family, a community, and a system of care. Interestingly, the subsystems and capacities that undergird individual humility are initially shaped in early life by caregivers and communities. Humble communities mold humble members. As a result, humility cannot be considered an individual characteristic alone but must involve multiple generations. Though humility can adhere (or not) to an individual, it can also be attributable (or not) to the community that raises and influences her. We examine this broader framing as we go along.

How does one develop fully blown interpersonal humility? Its groundings are fostered in childhood, especially during babyhood when critical foundations of a human being are established. Humans are born with only 25% of adult brain size at full-term birth. Thus, a great deal of neurobiology is molded after birth, especially in the first months and years of life based on the biochemical "bath" promoted by caregivers (Schore, 2003a, 2003b). Epigenetic and plasticity effects are occurring on multiple levels in multiple sensitive periods, laying the groundwork for capacities later (Knudsen, 2004).

What do babies need to grow well? Every animal evolved a nest to match the maturational schedule of its young. Humans inherited many characteristics of their evolved nest from their social mammalian line (most components are over 30 million years old), but the human neonate increased in immaturity over the course of human evolution to accommodate bipedalism. Human babies need at least another 18 months before resembling a newborn of other animals, save marsupials (Trevathan, 2011). Humanity's evolved nest (or evolved developmental niche) for babies includes a set of experiences provisioned by the community: soothing perinatal experience, extensive breastfeeding and fairly constant affectionate touch, prompt response to needs, multiple adult responsive caregivers, self-directed play with multi-aged mates in the natural world, and positive climate and support (Hewlett and Lamb, 2005). The importance of each of these components has been supported with neurobiological studies (for brief reviews, see Narvaez, Panksepp et al., 2013). When parents yield to the evolved set of needs (e.g., for companionship, affectionate touch, frequent breastfeeding, movement), the child builds a good neurobiology that allows her to be responsive in return. Yielding to the baby means that caregivers maintain the baby's optimal arousal levels, biochemically and psychologically, responding to needs with kindness (in Winnicott's, 1957, term, letting the baby feel "omnipotent"), optimizing normal growth.

The companionship caregiving the human nest provides allows babies to surrender into the arms of the caregiver day after day, night after night.[5] They rehearse a surrender to being-in-place and learn to build and trust intuition and interrelational signaling (Stern, 1985). In these circumstances, emotions and their undergirding neurobiological systems develop well (Schore, 2013). The child learns how to express and interpret emotional signals accurately, learning when to test them or trust them. Trust and humility are interrelated and go hand in hand. Parental trust is transferred to the baby as they humbly meet the child's needs—responding to needs quickly with kindness, promoting calming. When the child communicates their needs and they are met, the child builds confidence that the world will provide, often measured in psychological research as secure attachment, and the young child develops into a cooperative community member (e.g., Bolin, 2010).

Interpersonal humility relies on systems and capacities "all the way down," that is, it is an embodied (neurobiologically-felt) orientation. A well-functioning neurobiology includes self-regulatory systems (e.g., vagus nerve, stress response, neuroendocrine systems like the oxytocinergic system) (Carter and Porges, 2013). These undergird social relations and must function well for virtue enactment generally and for humility specifically. In a neurobiologically well-functioning individual, social skills and microskills are able to develop well (e.g., emerging from good right hemisphere development that is scheduled to take place in early life) (Narvaez, 2014).[6] Concertedly, all these components lead to relational attunement and flexibility in the moment.

Within this developmental nest of support, the child builds layers of self-regulatory capacities, contentment with self-in-body, automatically cooperating with his or her own internal spirit or soul and the self's unique needs, in effect, accepting the self. The individual's implicit social worldview forms into one that is prosocial and trusting because well-functioning subsystems allow one to "lose the ego" appropriately (with compassion and increasing wisdom) in social situations. She develops a modesty of self, feeling like she belongs to and is appreciated by the social group. As she feels respected, she learns to respect others. As her needs are met, she can lose herself in selfless group collaboration. These propensities are capped by deliberate or conscious understandings, narratives, and framings that support relational cooperation and giving over oneself to the other in mutual cooperation.

In this way, the seeds of humility are sown by parents and caregivers.[7] Humility is reliant on neurobiological capacities for emotional resonance with others, which humble parenting supports. As children grow up, they yield in return, allowing themselves to be socialized according to the wishes of parents and community ("committed compliance," Kochanska, 2002). Humble adults raise humble children who are ready to fit into their communities, who go with the flow of communal engagement, leading to an adulthood that supports a community responsive to the needs of its members. Converging evidence across scientific disciplines shows the effects of the nest on capacities (self-regulation, empathy, conscience) for living well and wisely with others (see Narvaez, 2014, 2016, for discussion, and these empirical studies: Narvaez, Gleason et al., 2013; Narvaez, Wang, and Cheng, 2016; Narvaez, Wang, et al., 2013). "Bottom-up" development of humility is a human heritage that emerges from the provision of the evolved nest which is apparent in societies that represent the type of society where humans spent 99% of their genus history, as well as in societies that promote tender care of the young (Narvaez, 2013, 2015). In these societies, great pleasure is taken in babies by the community generally, so that meeting their needs is not onerous but an enjoyable part of social life.

In contrast, nonhumble parenting is exhibited in detached parenting that avoids being too attached or resonant with baby's needs, and instead controls the baby according to adult needs, schedules, and whims. Unhumble treatment of babies starts with medicalized birth practices where babies are forced to be born (instead of signaling when they are ready and starting labor, which varies by about 50 days among babies) and are treated harshly after birth with painful procedures and separation from mother (Klaus and Kennell, 1976/1983; Liu et al., 2007). The ignoring of babies' pain in medicalized birth is mimicked by parents when they proudly ignore baby's cries in order to be "in charge" and "get their lives back," and when they force babies into "independence," for example, by using cry-it-out sleep training to get baby to sleep without them. Most of these practices are based on false beliefs about babies (e.g., you spoil babies if you give them too much attention) that started long ago when parents were isolated from extended family and, lacking community support, began to turn to books for advice. The early advocates were interested in baby control either for reasons of religion (Holt, 1935) or "science" (Watson, 1928) and their behavioristic views still pervade the US parenting landscape (Braden and Narvaez, in press).[8]

As can be inferred from the prior discussion, *cultural humility,* outlined in table 5.1, supports the development of both *intrapersonal* humility (toward the self) and *interpersonal* humility (toward others). But the embodied-self-in-right-relation with multiple layers of functioning includes not only face-to-face relationship(s) in the present moment, which scholarship typically emphasizes, but is intergenerational. That is, humble parents and caregivers pass on humility to their children through their actions toward the child's needs.

The reader no doubt realizes that few children in financially advanced nations today live in developmental systems that foster humility as described earlier. What are the results of a degraded evolved nest? When babies don't receive expected care, the life course gets set on a less-than-optimal trajectory (Cole, Michel, and Teti, 1994). We examine that next.

DEVELOPMENTAL FOUNDATIONS FOR A LACK OF HUMILITY

Too often industrial civilization's practices and capitalism's ideology discourage providing babies with what they crave (need) for optimal development, thereby toxically stressing a developing brain. For example, the US culture promotes unhumble parenting. As one of only three nations with no paid parental leave, parents are pressured to force their babies to be "independent," to leave their children to cry, to consume infant formula, and sleep alone, plus spend many hours separated from parents—all mitigating against species-typical development. When the evolved nest is degraded like this, we can document that fundamental capacities are misdeveloped and trajectories for multiple systems become less than optimal (for reviews, see Narvaez, 2014; Narvaez, Panksepp, Schore and Gleason, 2013), including the development of humility (Narvaez, Thiel, Kurth, and Renfus, 2016).

When communities are not humble toward the needs of the child (due to cultural beliefs or adult self-preoccupation) or are unable to provide the nest due to social circumstances (e.g., war zone), interpersonal humility is not fostered from the bottom up. When parents are set against being humble to their children's needs, they exhibit a hierarchicalism that they imbue into their children (Tomkins, 1965). Children become alienated from their own natures and the natural flow of human existence. By not providing the companionship of the evolved nest, such communities foster people with rigid, brittle, self-protective orientations, "all the way down." That is, their more primitive survival systems are enhanced while the otherwise postnatal growth of humble prosociality is undermined. The survival systems are by their nature not humble because they are about routine self-protection through self-aggrandizement or self-diminishment (guided by the stress response: fight-flight-freeze-faint, and by basic inborn emotions of fear, anger, panic, and seeking; Panksepp, 1998).

Instead of growing prosocial capacities after birth, undercared for individuals are forced into resonating with survival systems ("reptilian" brain; stress response) and resorting to self-protectionist actions such as territoriality, rigid routines, and dominance (sympathetic nervous system) or paralysis (parasympathetic nervous system) (Narvaez, 2008, 2014, 2016). Neurobiology develops in the direction of self-protection with a cacostatic (too much or too little) social orientation (dominance or submission), undermining capacities for humility. Individuals become threat reactive and move routinely into one-up/one-down inegalitarian social relations. Denial of basic need fulfillment forces children into calculated manipulation and deception once they have these capacities. It requires that they take up arms against the resulting anxiety and fear and set themselves against self and others in some fashion. They will necessarily build either a "chip on the shoulder" or self-abnegation (or both)—i.e., a self-protective ego. They become stress reactive, building an ego-dominant self, whose (large, self-protective) ego is easily irritated by things not going their way, manifest in preconscious reactions to perceived threat. Stress hyper- or hypo-reactivity can result in a panicking self that rages, freezes up or shuts down.

Children who are denied the mystery of being alive in the moment, of feeling connected with mother and others, relaxing and sleeping in their arms without survival systems being triggered, do not learn to live well nor with well-constructed emotion systems. They miss the training of the emotion systems through appropriate limbic resonance with caregivers.[9] Limbic resonance is a mammalian need and mammals veer off kilter without it (Lewis, Amini, and Lannon, 2000). Lack of positive reciprocal resonance with mother and others results in a lack of capacity for, then interest in, resonating with others. When caregivers are not responsive and synchronous, the baby learns to prefer the subset of resonance that does work, which can be depressive with a depressed caregiver or erratic with inconsistent care.[10] In any case, toxically stressed youngsters are forced into an isolated one-person psychology, with a sense of loneliness and a restless seeking—for what was not provided when needed for proper development.

Undercare (missing or degraded nest components) in early life undermines human capacities and potential, shaping the individual to be more self-centered, impairing the development of another component of humility, the child's humility toward having needs and accepting vulnerability. When infant needs are disrespected, the child is set on a trajectory of mistrust, need denial, and defensiveness against vulnerability through self-authoritarianism and contempt for needs in others. The child suffers a "primal wound" that will follow him the rest of his life, barring extensive therapy, setting up defensive systems against vulnerability, neediness, and self-awareness (Finman and Gila, 1997). His defensive systems require extensive energy to maintain as they work to suppress emotion and memory, a suppression extended to others through wanting to keep them under control too.

When undercare occurs in early life or trauma is experienced, self-protectionism can become a conditioned reaction that is difficult to mend later. The individual then lacks freedom in the present moment; free will is undermined. The person easily and automatically downshifts to primitive survival systems—shutting down in relationship or moving into the flow of power over others through manipulation and control. Humility is viewed as doormat-ism, as humiliation and submission, a view that comes from underconfidence and lack of trust. Flexible relational attunement falters.

We can take the case of bully and silent victim. Neither is humble. Bullies dominate out of protectionism—they take refuge in feeling powerful because they do not have the capacities to be relationally attuned and egalitarian. Silent victims, or "doormats," are not humble either. They have withdrawn because they don't feel strong enough to demand equal respect. Neither is capable in the moment of honoring their unique selves (see also Morinis, this volume). Domination and submission are cacostatic responses because the flexible attunement of proper development was not supported "all the way down."

To reiterate, for humility to develop in its members from the ground up, rather than intentionally top-down later on, the *community* needs to be humble before the needs of children (and of families so that families can provide the evolved nest). Humans are social mammals whose biology and sociality are co-constructed by their social experience—experiences that are guided by culture and the capacities of elders. In small-band hunter-gatherer societies around the world the co-construction is very similar because child raising is very similar (evolved nest provision), leading to consistent adult dispositions—calm, co-operative, generous—and cultures that support the companionship described (Ingold, 2005). Humility comes easily for a child raised with companionship care of the evolved nest where resonance with the spirit of others is experienced and practiced from the beginning of life. One learns to move *with* others (including other-than-humans), as part of a web of life in which one's self is connected to all other selves—a Commonself, moving *with* instead of *against* them (Ingold, 2005). In short, adults who are humble to the needs of young children initiate societies that are more broadly humble. Intergenerational effects solidify into cultural practices, and culture influences family practices.

Bronfenbrenner's (1979) ecological systems theory identified several social domains of influence on a child's development: *microsystem*: child's realms such as family and school; *mesosystem*: the relations among those systems; *exosystem:* the interrelation of systems beyond the child's experience such as parent workplace and health systems; *macrosystem*: cultural values and laws; and the *chronosystem:* the historical context. In my view, each of these systems can also be assessed for humility, which will support (or not) the development of humility in the child. Do the family and school meet the basic needs of the child? Do they coordinate the provision of needs? Are workplaces and health systems attuned to the parents' needs, which allow them to be better attuned to the child's needs? Do cultural values and laws match up with human needs? In these ways, humility adheres to cultures or communities. This aspect of humility formation aligns with the human capabilities approach (Nussbaum, 2009)[11] where meeting basic needs is required for social justice. In my view, provision of all the components of the evolved nest is a social justice issue for children (Narvaez, Kurth, and Noble, 2018).

ECOLOGICAL HUMILITY

To be thorough about the description of humility, we must address a now obviously key component within a culture—its ecological humility. Can we sort societies into ecologically humble and nonhumble? Robert Redfield (1953, 1956) made a useful sorting of cultural worldviews, boiling them down to two basic incommensurable types (see also Four Arrows, 2016; Four Arrows and Narvaez, 2016). I suggest that in order to distinguish them, we must look not at attitudes but at actions—i.e., worldview in action. I propose that one type of worldview in action is humble and the other not.

The first, more ancient worldview considers the cosmos to be *unified, sacred,* and *moral.* This worldview in action is apparent in earth-centered societies around the world. Redfield (1953) calls it the primitive worldview, but I will call it the indigenous worldview (Four Arrows and Narvaez, 2016). What have these earth-centered societies understood intuitively and applied to their behavior (which science now corroborates; Cajete, 2000; Deloria, 2006; Kimmerer, 2013; Scott, 2017)?

- The earth is full of sentience or living spirit.
- The earth is a self-organizing, complex mystery of dynamic systems that interact on every level (as science now tells

us—from physics and chemistry, to water cycles and atmospheric transformations).
- When a person or society breaks the laws of the earth, suffering ensues.
- Humans are one among many entities living in community.
- Animals and plants must be respected where they are (and science confirms that each ecological system or landscape has a unique balance and needs).

Notice the humility toward nature and natural processes. How these orientations are expressed varies by community, even in the same part of the world, based on the particular nature of the landscape (Descola, 2013). Ecological humility is characteristic of sustainably wise indigenous cultures, including many traditional native American societies (see Cooper, 1998; Deloria, 2006; for reviews, see Narvaez, 2013, 2014).

> To walk the way of the Human . . . the will for the individual person must seek the wisdom to walk a path of harmony with all of life. To walk the Way of the Human is to walk with humility and seek the wisdom to align our will in harmony with the Great Spirit. (WindEagle and RainbowHawk, 2003, 68)

In societies with this orientation, humans are considered one among many siblings in the biocommunity, and they are sometimes most in need of guidance from the older forms of life (plants, animals) (Kimmerer, 2013). Respectful interactions with all relations (animals, plants, rivers, etc.) are fundamental (Descola, 2013). The community exists in a specific landscape, yielding to its needs and facilitating flourishing for all. Food and water sources are shared with other animals. Societies guided by this worldview attend to the basic needs of humans but also to the landscapes in which they move. Earth is viewed as mother, provider of all. Although all living things struggle against the elements (e.g., weather, earthquakes), they live in cooperation with one another (Kropotkin, 2006). Cooperative contracts with predators are maintained, and it is understood that predators eat only when hungry and then tend to take the weaker members (animals might share a watering hole with a predator when it is not hungry). Human hunters prepare themselves to ask respectfully for prey, and a specific animal will give its life to the respectful hunter. In long-time sustainable communities, like the Australian Aborigines and the !Kung of southern Africa who have existed for tens of thousands of years (Balter, 2012; Lawlor, 1991), keeping the biocommunity in balance is essential and guides behavior, requiring deep knowledge of and relationships with the local landscape, knowledge embodied in wise elders who guide the younger.[12] There is a sensitivity to the dangers of ego and intellect (and nonhumility), as wise elders guide the younger away from these pitfalls.[13]

As noted in table 5.1, ecologically humble societies behave modestly in following the "honorable harvest" (Kimmerer, 2013), multiple principles for relating to the natural world that are often implicitly held (e.g., do not take too much of a plant community; leave at least half for others). They maintain a selflessness in limiting wants and desires, living with the biocommunity in mind (Gowdy, 1998). Among the hundreds of uncivilized societies still in existence, as well as the many who still maintain similar worldviews, respect for other-than-humans are built into cultural practices; community rules and traditions inveigh right relationship with the animals and plants that sustain human life (Descola, 2013).

For most of their existence, humans have followed such practices or perished, acting as "fellow-voyagers with other creatures in the odyssey of evolution" (Leopold, 2016, 109). But in the last centuries, humans of dominator cultures have acted differently (Latour, 2013; Sale, 2006; Turner, 1994). This may be due in part to the second worldview in action that began to hold sway. It considers the cosmos to be *fragmented, disenchanted*, and *amoral*. Promulgated by dominator worldviews like Enlightenment philosophy, forms of Enlightenment science,[14] and Enlightenment economics, while maintained by neoliberal forces predominant today (Harvey, 2005), this modern worldview is evident in scientism—the belief that science alone has a claim to truth; in capitalist economics—which detaches from responsible relationships to human, community, and planetary welfare; and in religious traditions that emphasize the earth as a temporary waystation for humans on their way to eternal afterlife (Latour, 2013). Clearly, ecological humility often is hard to discern in these beliefs and accompanying practices.

Europeans colonizing the rest of the world brought with them such views and initially derided the different beliefs about the world they encountered as "superstitious." But it turns out that they are the ones with destructive beliefs, particularly in the United States (Andersen, 2017). A host of false beliefs are destroying life on the planet. What are the false beliefs that exploiters in the Western world have operated under for the last 500 years, still widespread in the United States today and forcefully spread around the world through the primacy and hegemony of capital (Chomsky, 2017; Korten, 2015; Perkins, 2016)? Here is a short list:[15]

- Humans are the pinnacle species.
- Only humans have spirit; the rest of nature is largely inert.
- Nature should be tamed and defeated.
- Humans can separate themselves from natural laws (and live ignorant of them) without risk.

- Western technological and cultural progress are the best/good/right ones/God's will.
- Humans are so smart that their technology will take care of any crises their lifestyles create.

These are not humble beliefs, yet they comprise elements of the narratives that have guided Westernized culture and behavior in recent centuries, leading to colonialization and extermination of people, cultures, and species. "From stories we absorb our goals in life, our morals, and our patterns of behavior" (Merchant, 2003, 3). Accompanying these beliefs has been an elevation of finance over all other areas of life, a belief in the sacredness of money and markets (Korten, 2015), confirmed by a focus on the still common index used to determine societal well-being: gross domestic product (GDP), despite the fact that it rises after natural disasters.[16] When financial concerns come first, basic needs are not necessarily met.

REMEDIES TO FOSTER HUMILITY

The civilized world is full of unnested humans, the walking wounded. We escape into intellectual pursuits or ways we can feel dominant and we are much less social than our ancestors, nearly unable to resonate with other-than-humans. We have difficulty with interpersonal humility if we are stressed or have been raised to be dispositionally distressed (anxious, depressed, stress reactive), which puts us in a more primitive neurobiological substrate that works against humility, undermining higher order perceptions, conceptions, and actions (Narvaez, 2014).

How do we move away from resonance with self-protection, dominance, and conformity? How do we get the chip off the shoulder? How do we learn to stand up with heart? How do we restore our human potential for humility and virtue? First, we need to understand humility as a *developmental* virtue that is grounded initially in early experience. Next, we need to understand that humility adheres not only to people but also social systems (families, neighborhoods, communities, states). Finally, we need to understand that ecological humility is also required for a full-hearted humility. How can we foster humility in the Capitalocene where everything is being commodified and extracted (Moore, 2015)?

Education

To develop interpersonal humility, community members, including future parents, need to be educated about the evolved nest and its effects. Films and videos of humble parenting and its effects need to be part of the cultural landscape. Guided experience with babies during childhood and adolescent provides insight into the benefits of good care. Educational programs like the Roots of Empathy, implemented across Canada, brings a mother and infant into the classroom for nine months (Gordon, 2003).

For children who come from a degraded nest, educators will need to promote calming and healing of dysregulated neurobiological systems to decrease the use of self-protective mechanisms to feel safe and enable better learning and cooperation (Narvaez and Bock, 2014). Educators can provide opportunities to build social trust and social resonance through free play and creative endeavors, which will grow the social self-regulatory skills needed for relational attunement. To develop communal humility, they can expand the child's imagination for multiperspective taking. To develop web-of-life humility, educators can ensure the child's connection to the natural world by helping them develop ecological attachment, landscape consciousness and nature-focused skills and sustainable, wise practices for living. Forest schools are attempting to do these things for younger children but higher education continues to foster Enlightenment's views (Orr, 1991).

Social Policy

To foster interpersonal humility within a society, extended families should be treated by policymakers as the fundamental unit of society (rather than corporations; Michaels, 2011).[17] This would mean providing extensive support (e.g., three years of family leave that includes fathers), not traumatizing babies (e.g., at birth with painful procedures or separation from mother), and through parenting education in schooling and in the community, ensuring that everyone understands child development and evolution's "design" for child raising. Children provided the evolved nest turn into humble adults, as demonstrated by the type of personality among those providing the nest (Ingold, 2005; Narvaez, 2013). In the case of an unnested upbringing, individuals can work on healing themselves (usually with help), though it takes some suffering to overcome one's resistance to being vulnerable and humble.[18]

Culture

Humility does not come about through mere desire or the will to be humble. One needs layers of self-regulation and skills to accomplish it, and these are initially constructed by one's caregivers, community experiences, and only later co-constructed by one's choices of situations and activities. To foster communal humility, meeting basic needs must be central to the goals of a community or society. The human capabilities approach (Nussbaum, 2009) is moving in this direction, but a focus on basic psychosocial needs provided by the evolved nest can provide added guidance (Narvaez, Kurth, and Noble, 2018). When the evolved nest is provided along with lifelong positive social support, we may again see the common emergence of wise and humble elders who ensure that the cycle of basic needs provision continues across generations.

Hopeful Signs

As the neurobiological sciences increasingly demonstrate the lifelong impact of early experience, several initiatives have been taking root around the world such as First Thousand Days, Zero to Three, Child First. The increase in bottom-up efforts to restore "commoning"—the management of earth's riches for collective benefit—represents an effort to promote humility toward nature's ecologies and the benefits of mutual relations for human communities (Bollier and Helfrich, 2015).

CONCLUSION

Humility is essential for the survival of the human species. The current dominant culture of unhumble beliefs and practices is speedily destroying our common wealth. Humility in this chapter has been defined with multiple interacting layers. Humility entails intrapersonal and interpersonal humility—comprised of modesty, selflessness, and respectfulness toward self and others—and shaped by adult humility toward the evolved needs of babies and children. Humble social systems provide for basic humans needs (e.g., the evolved nest for children and social support for all ages), fostering well-being in its effects, and avoiding hubris of ego or intellect. Cultural humility toward the needs of young children is related to a culture's attitude toward natural systems generally.

Ecological humility is the constant awareness that the self is "inseparable from the web of relationships that sustain it" (Macy, 2013, 148). "Wherever we step, whatever we touch and disturb, is a form of interaction with the Earth and therefore should be done with sacred awareness, the awareness of what effect it has on our interdependence" (Brink, 2016, 11).

NOTES

1. The source of these ideas emerged from my reading of long-lasting sustainable societies from humanity's 99%—small-band hunter-gatherer societies (e.g., Bushmen), which greatly contrast with the settled societies that emerged in the last 10,000 years or so (e.g., Narvaez, 2013).
2. "Nature" here refers to how natural systems operate within themselves and with other systems—in concert and with a delicate balance of energy flow and exchange.
3. L'Arche communities are formed by those with and without intellectual disabilities who live together in faith and friendship.
4. Proxemics refers to distance people expect in social relations of various kinds; kinesics entail the body gestures that form part of nonverbal communication; prosody refers to the patterns of sound, such as tenor and tone, in vocal communication (see Hall, 1966).
5. Note that although there are similarities to what is deemed "attachment parenting," the evolved nest is broader and community-based child raising that also meets everyone's basic needs.
6. Though see this source for what to do in adulthood to self-heal when early life did not provide for basic needs.
7. Though there may be ways an individual to self-develop humility top-down later.
8. Can parents be humble to advice but unhumble to their child's needs? Cultures corrupted by arrogance—human superiority to and separation from nature—show unhumbleness toward natural systems generally. The lack of humility is so pervasive in the system that it seeps into parenting as well. If the cultural worldview assumes humans should control nature rather than learn it and respect its ways, this will include babies, who appear, to ignorant adults, to be ungovernable without coercion. Without personal knowledge or knowhow about how to properly meet the needs of a baby, parents turn for advice to the system's

"experts," who may or may not know what they are talking about. Humbling oneself to experts is a way the culture lets parents off the hook for truly knowing and reverencing their child. Thus, parents are driven by ignorance and fear of failure into the hands of unhumble practices. In short, lack of cultural humility, along with ignorance, supports a lack of humility in parenting.

9. Limbic resonance entails social interactional synchrony of sound, movement, and physiological patterns.
10. Resonance refers to the coordination of brain systems (limbic) and body enactment (communicative musicality). Babies coordinate with their caregivers, whether healthy or depressed, leading to established personality patterns. For example, see Bigelow, A. & Rochat, P. (2006). Two-month-old infants' sensitivity to social contingency in mother-infant and stanger-infant interaction. *Infancy*, 9(3), 313-325.
11. Nussbaum identifies 10 central capabilities: life; bodily health; bodily integrity; senses, imaginations, and thought; emotions; practical reason; affiliation; other species; play; control over one's environment in political and material ways.
12. Though some native American teachings lost their guiding power after the European invasion, widespread disease, and the appearance of invincibility of the invaders (Martin, 1978), and the centuries of genocide against native Americans took its toll on the resilience of community traditions (Dunbar-Ortiz, 2014).
13. Lest the reader think that the indigenous worldview is naive and romantic, scientific studies are increasingly supporting it. For example, mutualism and symbiosis govern ecological systems (Bronstein, 2015; Paracer and Ahmadjian, 2000); forests are communities of elders helping youngsters of other species (Wohlleben, 2016); and even the human body relies on a host of microorganisms (whose genes represent 90–99% of genes a person carries).
14. Before the Enlightenment, nature was understood as a benevolent, sometimes wild, mother of all things. With the Enlightenment, seemingly starting with Francis Bacon (who proposed making nature a slave to human interests to regain the dominion over nature that was lost in humanity's Fall in the Garden of Eden), a domination model became increasingly predominant, rationalizing the control and dissection of nature as a resource (Merchant, [1980] 1990).
15. See Merchant, 2003; Worster, 1994; Pinker, 2018.
16. As a gross measure of economic growth, it fails to take into account inequality within the populace. A number of replacement measures have been proposed, but they threaten the status quo and those who hold the reins of power, the oligarchs (see MacLean, 2017).
17. As an example, the Diné (aka, Navajo) do not have a word for any unit smaller than the extended family. Thanks to the editor for pointing this out.

18. Although it is preferable to build one's capacities from the bottom-up as a natural part of development, one can self-heal to at least some degree using top-down methods in adulthood, as Western wisdom traditions assumed was necessary (Bourgeault, 2003; Narvaez, 2014).

REFERENCES

Andersen, K. 2017. *Fantasyland: How America Went Haywire, A 500-Year History*. New York: Penguin/Random House.

Balter, M. 2012. "Ice age tools hint at 40,000 years of Bushman culture." *Science*, 337(6094), 512.

Bigelow, A. & Rochat, P. (2006). Two-month-old infants' sensitivity to social contingency in mother-infant and stanger-infant interaction. *Infancy*, 9(3), 313-325.

Bolin, I. 2010. "Chillihuani's culture of respect and the circle of courage." *Reclaiming Children and Youth Worldwide*, *18*(4), 12–17.

Bollier, D., and S. Helfrich, eds. 2015. *Patterns of Commoning*. Amherst, MA: Commons Strategies Group and Off the Common Books.

Bourgeault, C. 2003. *The Wisdom Way of Knowing: Reclaiming an Ancient Tradition to Awaken The Heart*. San Francisco, CA: Jossey-Bass.

Braden, A., and Narvaez, D. Forthcoming. *Primal Parenting: Lasso the Parent Handlers and Embrace Your Parenting Gifts*. New York: Oxford University Press.

Brink, N. E. 2016. *Trance Journeys of the Hunter-Gatherers: Ecstatic Practices to Reconnect with the Great Mother and Heal the Earth*. Rochester, VT: Bear.

Bronfenbrenner, U. 1979. *The Ecology of Human Development*. Cambridge, MA: Harvard University Press.

Bronstein, J. L., ed. 2015. *Mutualism*. New York: Oxford University Press.

Cajete, G. 2000. *Native Science: Natural Laws of Interdependence*. Santa Fe, NM: Clear Light.

Carter, C. S., and S. W. Porges. 2013. "Neurobiology and the evolution of mammalian social behavior." In *Evolution, Early Experience and Human Development: From Research to Practice and Policy*, edited by D. Narvaez, J. Panksepp, A. N. Schore, and T. Gleason, 132–151. New York: Oxford University Press.

Chomsky, N. 2017. *Requiem for the American Dream: The 10 Principles of Concentration of Wealth and Power*. New York: Seven Stories Press.

Cole, P. M., M. K. Michel, and L. O. Teti. 1994. "The development of emotion regulation and dysregulation: a clinical perspective." *Monographs of the Society for Research in Child Development*, 59(s), 73–100.

Cooper, T. 1998. *A Time Before Deception: Truth in Communication, Culture, and Ethics*. Santa Fe, NM: Clear Light.

Deloria, V. 2006. *The World We Used To Live In*. Golden, CO: Fulcrum.

Descola, P. 2013. *Beyond Nature and Culture.* Translated by J. Lloyd. Chicago: University of Chicago Press.

Di Paolo, E. A., T. Buhrmann, and X. E. Barandiaran. 2017. *Sensorimotor Life: An Enactive Proposal.* Oxford: Oxford University Press.

Dunbar-Ortiz, R. 2014. *An Indigenous People's History of the United States.* Boston: Beacon Press.

Finman, J., and A. Gila. 1997. *The Primal Wound: A Transpersonal View of Trauma, Addiction and Growth.* Albany: State University of New York Press.

Four Arrows. 2016. *Point of Departure.* Charlotte, NC: Information Age.

Four Arrows, and D. Narvaez. 2015. "A more authentic baseline." In *Working for Social Justice Inside and Outside the Classroom: A Community of Teachers, Researchers, and Activists,* edited by N. McCrary and W. Ross, 93–112. Series of Social Justice across Contexts in Education, S. J. Miller and L. D. Burns, eds. New York: Peter Lang.

Gordon, M. 2003. "Roots of empathy: Responsive parenting, caring societies." *Keio Journal of Medicine,* 52(4), 236–243.

Gowdy, J. 1998. *Limited Wants, Unlimited Means: A Reader on Hunter-Gatherer Economics and the Environment.* Washington, DC: Island Press.

Grip, G. 2016. "Prologue: The meaning of life." In *Trance Journeys of the Hunter-Gatherers: Ecstatic Practices to Reconnect with the Great Mother and Heal the Earth,* edited by N. E. Brink, vii–xi. Rochester, VT: Bear.

Hall, E. T. 1966. *The Hidden Dimension.* New York: Random House.

Harvey, D. 2005. *A Brief History of Neoliberalism.* New York: Oxford University Press.

Hewlett, B. S., and M. E. Lamb. 2005. *Hunter-Gatherer Childhoods: Evolutionary, Developmental And Cultural Perspectives.* New Brunswick, NJ: Aldine.

Hogarth, R. M. 2001. *Educating Intuition.* Chicago: University of Chicago Press.

Holt, L. E. 1935. *The Care and Feeding of Children: A Vatechism for the Use of Mothers and Nurses.* 15th ed. New York: Applegate.

Ingold, T. 2005. "On the social relations of the hunter-gatherer band." In *The Cambridge encyclopedia of hunters and gatherers,* edited by R. B. Lee and R. Daly, 399–410. New York: Cambridge University Press.

Kimmerer, R.W. 2013. *Braiding Sweetgrass: Indigenous Wisdom, Scientific Knowledge and the Teachings of Plants.* Minneapolis, MN: Milkweed Editions.

Klaus, M. H., and J. H. Kennell. (1976)1983. *Maternal-Infant Bonding: The Impact of Early Separation or Loss on Family Development.* St. Louis, MO: C. V. Mosby.

Knudsen, E. I. 2004. "Sensitive periods in the development of the brain and behavior." *Journal of Cognitive Neuroscience, 16* (8), 1412–1425.

Kochanska, G. 2002. "Committed compliance, moral self, and internalization: A mediational model." *Developmental Psychology, 38,* 339–351.

Kolbert, E. 2014. *The Sixth Extinction: An Unnatural History.* New York: Henry Holt.

Korten, D. 2015 *Change the Story, Change the Future.* Oakland, CA: Berrett-Koehler.

Kropotkin, P. 2006. *Mutual Aid: A Factor of Evolution.* Charleston, SC: BiblioBazaar.

Latour, B. 2013. *Modes of Existence*. Cambridge, MA: Harvard University Press.

Lawlor, R. 1991. *Voices of the First Day: Awakening in the Aboriginal Dreamtime*. Rochester, VT: Inner Traditions.

Leopold, A. 2016. *A Sand County Almanac*. New York: Oxford University Press.

Lewis, T., F. Amini, and R. Lannon. 2000. *A General Theory of Love*. New York: Vintage.

Liedloff, J. 1977. *The Continuum Concept*. Cambridge, MA: Perseus Books.

Liu, W. F., S. Laudert, B. Perkins, E. MacMillan-York, S. Martin, and S. Graven for the NIC/Q 2005 Physical Environment Exploratory Group. 2007. "The development of potentially better practices to support the neurodevelopment of infants in the NICU." *Journal of Perinatology, 27*, S48–S74.

Kruse, E., J. Chancellor, and S. Lyubomirsky. 2017. "State humility: Measurement, conceptual validation, and intrapersonal processes." *Self and Identity*, 1–40. doi: papers3://publication/doi/10.1080/15298868.2016.1267662.

MacLean, N. 2017. *Democracy in Chains: The Deep History of the Radical Right's Stealth Plan for America*. New York: Viking.

Macy, J. 2013. "The greening of the self." In *Spiritual Ecology: The Cry of the Earth*, edited by L. Vaughan-Lee, 145–158. Point Reyes Station, CA: Golden Sufi Center.

Martin. C. 1978. *Keepers of the Game: Indian-Animal Relationships and the Fur Trade*. Berkeley: University of California Press.

Means, M. L., and J. F. Voss. 1985. "Star Wars: A developmental study of expert and novice knowledge structures." *Journal of Memory and Language, 24*(6), 746–757.

Merchant, C. (1980) 1990. *The Death of Nature: Women, Ecology, and the Scientific Revolution*. New York: HarperOne.

Merchant, C. 2003. *Reinventing Eden: The Fate of Nature in Western Culture*. New York: Routledge.

Michaels, F. S. 2011. *Monoculture: How One Story Is Changing Everything*. Canada: Red Clover Press.

Moore, J. 2015. *Capitalism in the Web of Life: Ecology and the Accumulation of Capital*. London: Versa.

Narvaez, D. 2008. "Triune ethics: The neurobiological roots of our multiple moralities." *New Ideas in Psychology, 26*, 95–119.

Narvaez, D. 2013. "The 99 Percent—Development and socialization within an evolutionary context: Growing up to become 'A good and useful human being.'" In *War, Peace and Human Nature: The Convergence of Evolutionary and Cultural Views*, edited by D. Fry, 643–672. New York: Oxford University Press.

Narvaez, D. 2014. *Neurobiology and the Development of Human Morality: Evolution, Culture and Wisdom*. New York: W.W. Norton.

Narvaez, D. 2015. "The co-construction of virtue: Epigenetics, neurobiology and development." In *Cultivating Virtue*, edited by N. E. Snow, 251–277. New York: Oxford University Press.

Narvaez, D. 2016. *Embodied Morality: Protectionism, Engagement and Imagination*. New York: Palgrave-Macmillan.

Narvaez, D. 2019. "Moral development and moral values: Evolutionary and neurobiological influences." In *Handbook of Personality*, edited by D. McAdams. New York: Guilford.

Narvaez, D., and T. Bock. 2014. "Developing ethical expertise and moral personalities." In *Handbook of Moral and Character Education* (2nd ed.), edited by L. Nucci and D. Narvaez, 140–158. New York, NY: Routledge.

Narvaez, D., T. Gleason, L. Wang, J. Brooks, J. Lefever, A. Cheng, and Centers for the Prevention of Child Neglect. 2013. "The Evolved development niche: Longitudinal effects of caregiving practices on early childhood psychosocial development." *Early Childhood Research Quarterly, 28* (4), 759–773. doi: 10.1016/j.ecresq.2013.07.003.

Narvaez, D., A. Kurth, and R. Noble. 2018. *Basic Needs, Wellbeing and Morality: Fulfilling Human Potential.* New York: Palgrave-MacMillan.

Narvaez, D., J. Panksepp, A. Schore, and T. Gleason, eds. 2013. *Evolution, Early Experience and Human Development: From Research to Practice and Policy.* New York, NY: Oxford University Press.

Narvaez, D., A. Thiel, A. Kurth, and K. Renfus. 2016. "Past moral action and ethical orientation." In *Embodied Morality: Protectionism, Engagement and Imagination,* edited by D. Narvaez, 99–118. New York: Palgrave-Macmillan.

Narvaez, D., L. Wang, and A. Cheng. 2016. "Evolved developmental niche history: Relation to adult psychopathology and morality." *Applied Developmental Science, 20*(4), 294–309. http://dx.doi.org/10.1080/10888691.2015.1128835.

Narvaez, D., L. Wang, T. Gleason, A. Cheng, J. Lefever, and L. Deng. 2013. "The evolved developmental niche and sociomoral outcomes in Chinese three-year-olds." *European Journal of Developmental Psychology, 10,* 2, 106–127.

Nussbaum, M. C. 2009. *Creating Capabilities: The Human Development Approach.* Cambridge, MA: Belknap.

Orr, D. 1991. "What is education for? Six myths about the foundations of modern education, and six new principles to replace them." *In Context: A Quarterly of Humane Sustainable Culture,* Winter, 52. https://www.eeob.iastate.edu/classes/EEOB-590A/marshcourse/V.5/V.5a%20What%20Is%20Education%20For.htm

Panksepp, J. 1998. *Affective Neuroscience: The Foundations of Human and Animal Emotions.* New York: Oxford University Press.

Paracer, S., and V. Ahmadjian. 2000. *Symbiosis.* 2nd ed. New York: Oxford University Press.

Perkins, J. 2016. *The New Confessions of an Economic Hitman.* 2nd ed. San Francisco, CA: Berrett-Koehler.

Pinker, S. 2018. *Enlightenment Now: The Case for Reason, Science, Humanism, and Progress.* New York: Viking.

Plumwood, V. 2002. *Environmental Culture: The Ecological Crisis of Reason.* London: Routledge.

Redfield, R. 1953. *The Primitive World and Its Transformations.* Ithaca, NY: Cornell University Press.

Redfield, R. 1956. *Peasant Society and Culture: An Anthropological Approach to Civilization.* Chicago: University of Chicago Press.

Sale, K. 2006. *After Eden: The Evolution of Human Domination.* Durham, NC: Duke University Press.

Schore, A. N. 2003a. *Affect Dysregulation and Disorders of the Self.* New York: Norton.

Schore, A. N. 2003b. *Affect Regulation and the Repair of the Self.* New York: Norton.

Schore, A. N. 2013. "Bowlby's 'Environment of evolutionary adaptedness': Recent studies on the interpersonal neurobiology of attachment and emotional development." In *Evolution, Early Experience and Human Development: From Research to Practice and Policy,* edited by D. Narvaez, J. Panksepp, A. Schore, and T. Gleason, 31–67. New York: Oxford University Press.

Scott, J. C. 2017. *Against the Grain: A Deep History of the Earliest States.* New Haven, CT: Yale University Press.

Spezio, M., G. Peterson, and R. C. Roberts. 2019. "Humility as openness to others: Interactive humility in the context of l'Arche." *Journal of Moral Education,* 48:1, 27-46, DOI: 10.1080/03057240.2018.1444982

Stern, D. N. 1985. *The Interpersonal World of the Infant.* New York: Basic Books.

Tomkins, S. 1965. Affect and the psychology of knowledge. In *Affect, Cognition, and Personality,* edited by S.S. Tomkins & C.E. Izard. New York: Springer.

Trevathan, W. R. 2011. *Human Birth: An Evolutionary Perspective.* 2nd ed. New York: Aldine de Gruyter.

Turner, F. 1994. *Beyond Geography: The Western Spirit against the Wilderness.* New Brunswick, NJ: Rutgers University Press.

Varela, F. 1999. *Ethical Know-How: Action, Wisdom, and Cognition.* Stanford, CA: Stanford University Press.

Varney, T. R., and P. Weintraub. 2002. *Pre-Parenting: Nurturing Your Child from Conception.* New York: Simon and Schuster.

Watson, J. B. 1928. *Psychological Care of Infant and Child.* New York: W. W. Norton.

WindEagle and RainbowHawk. 2003. *Heart Seeds: A Message from the Ancestors.* Edina, MN: Beaver's Pond Press.

Winnicott, D. W. 1957. *Mother and Child. A Primer of First Relationships.* New York: Basic Books.

Wohlleben, P. 2016. *The Hidden Life of Trees: What They Feel, How They Communicate.* Translated by J. Billinghurst. Vancouver: Greystone Books.

Worster, D. 1994. *Nature's Economy: A History of Ecological Ideas.* 2nd ed.. Cambridge: Cambridge University Press.

Chapter 6

Humility as a Foundational Virtue

JENNIFER COLE WRIGHT

INTRODUCTION

> The truly ethical life is a life in which you encounter yourself as one person among others, all equally real. This means that the legitimate interests of others, insofar as you can anticipate them, will figure on a par with your own legitimate interests in your practical reasoning. . . . For you will find yourself to be only one of the others, the one you happen to know so much about, thanks to being him or her. (Johnston, 2009, 89–90)

The maturely virtuous person—someone who truly embodies the above quote; who is fully attuned and responsive to the needs and interests of others and who experiences them as being as real, legitimate, and as pressing as her own—represents a fairly rare and difficult accomplishment.[1]

As many have noted (and as we all experience) each of us stands, phenomenologically speaking, at the center of the universe. We experience ourselves as the organizing center, not only of a consciousness, but of a consciousness woven together into the form of a life; *our* life.

We experience that life as real and substantial, as something to be lived. Indeed, we experience it as something that *must* be lived—i.e., it comes equipped with a built-in mandate to fulfill certain basic needs and to pursue certain conceptions of the good.

And thus naturally, even though we live in a world filled with needs, it is only a narrow subset (namely, our own), with which we are most intimately familiar and most readily encounter, that press most strongly in upon us and demand our attention. Similarly, though there are many different conceptions of the good, it is naturally our own that strikes us as the most attractive and compelling, the most "true" and worthy of pursuit.[2]

Because of the built-in "centeredness" of our first-person perspective, we experience the gravitational pull of our own needs, desires, interests, beliefs, goals, and values more immediately, continuously, and urgently than we experience those of others'. And though we may choose at times to ignore or resist the pull, it also has the potential to manifest into self-absorption (what Johnston, 2009 calls "self-involvement" or "self-worship"), through which we privilege, prioritize, and favor—in terms of the energy we expend, the thought we give, the resources we dedicate, and the time we allocate—those needs, desires, interests, beliefs, goals, and values, even if we do not intend to do so.[3] This is not simply because they are the ones we happen to know best, but also because they emanate from that center. They, and not others, are *ours*.

As David Foster Wallace stated in a commencement speech:

> Everything in my own immediate experience supports my deep belief that I am the absolute center of the universe; the realest, most vivid and important person in existence. We rarely think about this sort of natural, basic self-centeredness . . . it is our default setting, hard-wired into our boards at birth. (Wallace, 2005)

And this is not a default setting that is easy to change—especially for those of us who live in a culture that, as Wallace (2005) also notes,

> will not discourage you from operating on your default settings, because the so-called real world of men and money and power hums merrily along in a pool of fear and anger and frustration and craving and worship of self.

This is what makes the maturely virtuous person's transcendence of the default setting one of her most central—and striking—accomplishments. She is able to escape the centripetal force of her own natural centeredness, and the biases that arise from it, and is thus able to genuinely *experience* the pull of the others' needs, desires, interests, beliefs, goals, and values as strongly as she does her own, becoming a genuine sister to all of humanity.

Such people have discovered, in Wallace's (2005) words:

> The really important kind of freedom [that] involves attention and awareness and discipline, and being able truly to care about other people and to sacrifice for them over and over in a myriad of petty, unsexy ways every day.

And we see this sort of extended commitment to, and communion with, others clearly demonstrated in the lives of maturely virtuous people. They experience everyone they encounter as having a dignity equal to their own. As Brooks (2015) writes, such exemplars see "the soul of a drug-addled homeless person [as] just as invaluable as the most laudable high achiever" (96). And it is this experience of a deep and abiding connection to, kinship with, and responsibility for others that enables the maturely virtuous to dedicate themselves to helping others—saving lives, addressing injustices, feeding the hungry, tending to the sick, and protecting the weak, vulnerable, and oppressed—often with sacrifice and at great potential risk to themselves (Brooks, 2015; Colby and Damon, 1992; Monroe, 2004, 2012; Oliner, 2003; Oliner and Oliner, 1988).

How does this sort of transformation, this transcendence of our default setting, happen? In this chapter, I will argue that the core catalyst for this transformation, and for the capacity for maturely virtuous engagement more generally, is humility. Further, I will argue that humility—as presented here (and argued elsewhere; see Nadelhoffer and Wright, 2017; Nadelhoffer et al., 2017; Wright et al., 2017; Wright et al., 2018)—should be considered a *foundational* virtue, necessary for the full development and exercise of other virtues and maturely virtuous character.

FIRST, A FEW WORDS ABOUT VIRTUE

It is not the purpose of this chapter to argue for any particular account of virtue—nor is this discussion of the maturely virtuous meant to presume one, except to say that it strongly leans toward some sort of neo-Aristotelian account. Regardless, whatever your preferred account of virtue, it seems relatively uncontroversial to say that the *maturely* virtuous person is someone who is not only typically able to ascertain and do what is called for, ethically speaking, in a given situation, but that she is also typically able to do so appropriately—in the right way, at the right time, and with the right sorts of underlying motivations (see, for example, Annas 2011; Hursthouse, 1999; 2016; Snow, 2010).[4] That is to say, the maturely virtuous person stands in the appropriate relation to the situation to which she is responding and is always "striving for improvement in relation to the right objects, in the right manner, with the right emotions, to the right extent, and so on" (Swanton, 2016, 129).

When asked how it is possible for the maturely virtuous person to accomplish this, many (though certainly not all) virtue ethicists point to practical reasoning, wisdom, or intelligence—a host of interrelated cognitive and affective capacities that allow the maturely virtuous person to accurately identify and evaluate the relevant information and arrive at the appropriate decision about what is required in response to this information (Annas 2011; Hursthouse, 1999; 2016; Russell, 2009; 2013; Snow, 2010). And while it seems clear that such cognitive and affective capacities—developed, honed, and fine-tuned over years of experience—are critical for maturely virtuous engagement, in this chapter I nonetheless want to make the case for the central importance of something arguably more basic.

Being able to do all the things required for maturely virtuous engagement (i.e., identifying and evaluating the relevant information, deciding what to do, and, then in addition, successfully implementing that decision without undue internal interference) requires that the maturely virtuous person be able to cognitively and affectively *experience* and *appreciate* the actual significance—the "weight," as it were—of the many different features of the situation, many of which are not her own and/or are external to her, that contribute to the determination of the appropriate response in a given instance. This requires, at its foundation, the absence—or at least the temporary "quieting"—of interfering and distorting influences.

Central among these interfering and distorting influences are those that arise from the natural centeredness of our phenomenological and psychological constitution. While certainly not the source of *everything* that has the potential to throw a person trying to do the right thing off the mark, many interfering and distorting influences originate from this source, and they are arguably often the most powerful (while often also subtle) influences. Being ever-present, they are also the most likely to continuously distort perception and cloud judgment, interfering with a person's efforts to act appropriately. And they can be particularly pernicious when it comes to the development of mature virtue because they operate (as David Foster Wallace rightly noted) as part of our built-in programming, making them hard to detect and/or dismantle.

As Brooks (2015) observed about the maturely virtuous, through the various experiences they had and hardships they endured,

> they learned to quiet the self. Only by quieting the self could they see the world clearly. Only by quieting the self could they understand other people and accept what they were offering. When they had quieted themselves, they had opened up space for grace to flood in. (13)

Similarly, it is the central thesis presented here is that the interfering and distorting influences that arise from our default setting are most effectively (and perhaps only truly) combated—and ultimately quieted—through the cultivation of humility. This is why we view it as the core catalyst for the transformation undergone by the maturely virtuous discussed above.[5] It is also, as I will argue, why humility should be considered a foundational virtue, necessary for the full development and exercise of all other virtues and mature virtuous character.[6]

NOW, BACK TO HUMILITY

> There is massive consensus across the major religions, that salvation crucially requires overcoming the centripetal force of self-involvement, in order to *orient one's life around reality* and *the real needs of human beings as such*. Given the strength of the centripetal force, it is too easy to invent objects of worship that instead serve as echo chambers for our individual self-worship. (Johnston, 2009, 23–24; emphasis mine)

What this quote suggests is that the centripetal force of our natural centeredness is a source of both *epistemic* and *ethical* distortion—it interferes with our ability to accurately perceive, and fully engage with, both objective reality and the well-being of the other living beings around us.

According to the account of humility, I have developed and defended with others at length elsewhere (Nadelhoffer and Wright, 2017; Nadelhoffer, et al., 2017; Wright, et al., 2017; 2018), humility is an *epistemically* and *ethically aligned state of awareness*. Put another way, humility is a state of awareness in which the distortions mentioned above have been (even if only temporarily) eliminated; a state of awareness free of the epistemic and ethical biases generated by our natural centeredness.[7]

Humility is a state in which we experience *ourselves* in true relation to *all else* (everything and everyone)—allowing us to experience those relations, and their objects, objectively. And while, as a state of awareness, humility is something we can "come into and go out of" (i.e., we can be temporarily or momentarily humble), the *virtue* of humility requires these states of awareness to stabilize into a sort of "standing" or baseline disposition (or trait), such that our cognition, affect, and behavior is continuously informed and influenced by it.[8]

Let us break this down further. By "epistemically aligned," we mean that humility *orients us toward reality*, enabling us to understand and experience ourselves—and all to which we stand in relation—objectively.

> Humility . . . entails an unvarnished and honest assessment of who you are. Without this accurate self-awareness, nothing else in your inner life will come into focus in its true measure. (Morinis, 2007, 46; also this volume)

Among other things, it is the experience of ourselves within the context of our full existence, generating a clear and accurate sense of ourselves as finite, fragile, and imperfect beings, contingent and relationally constituted—part of a vast, complex, and interconnected universe of living beings. As Johnston (2009) mentions, this can be experienced spiritually, as a connection to the divine or some higher force or power, but it can also be experienced more secularly, through an awareness of one's place in, and connection to, the larger natural/cosmic order.

> Humility is having an accurate assessment of your own nature and your own place in the cosmos. Humility is awareness that you are an underdog in the struggle against your own weakness . . . an awareness that your individual talents alone are inadequate to the tasks that have been assigned to you. Humility reminds you that you are not the center of the universe, but you serve a larger order. (Brooks, 2015, 263)

By "ethically aligned," we mean that humility *orients us toward others*, enabling us to truly understand and experience the *"all else"*—e.g., the vast web of interconnected beings whose needs and interests are as morally relevant, as worthy of attention and concern, as our own.

In a discussion on the value of Buddhist meditative practice for virtuous engagement, Flanagan (2015) states of an advanced practitioner that, if questioned about why she has worked so hard to orient her life toward compassion and loving-kindness for all beings, she might reply,

> I saw that my egoism leads to suffering, I saw that I am impermanent, dependently originating, no-self, empty, and part of the flux; this much made me open to feeling my solidarity with all beings who suffer, I began to comprehend myself as less

> bounded; I started to see my fate as a shared fate; and then I felt it—my solidarity, the calling. (187)

In other words, ethical alignment is experienced as the expansion, *not* the contraction, of the force and scope of our own needs and interests. This is because they become interwoven with the needs and interests of others, and as such are no longer experienced as separate, in conflict, and/or in competition, but rather as inextricably and necessarily connected and shared. By experiencing this deep investment in the lives and well-being of others, rather than being merely absorbed with the satisfaction of our own needs and interests, we experience ourselves as grounded by and embedded in, supporting and supported by, the larger living world. Our fates become a shared fate.

> Humility is associated with spiritual perfection. When humility effects depression it is defective; when it is genuine it inspires joy, courage, and inner dignity. (Morinis, 2007, 46)

In other words, the quieting of the interfering and distorting biases generated by our natural centeredness—rather than leading to a sense of alienation or "existential anxiety"—results in a feeling of deep connection and fellow-concern. We experience ourselves not simply *as less* than our centeredness would have us believe but also *as more.*

HUMILITY AS FOUNDATIONAL

Humility is the solid foundation for all virtues.

—Confucius

All virtues and duties depend on humility.

—*Duties of the Heart* (Paquda, 1996).

Humility is the root, mother, nurse, foundation, and bond of all virtues.

—John Chrysostom[9]

Humility "is the base and foundation of all virtues, and without it no other virtue can exist"

—*Don Quixote*, Cervantes ([1630] 2004, 30)

Thus far, I have made two related claims. The first is that humility is necessary for maturely virtuous engagement because the interfering and distorting influences that arise from the natural centeredness of our default setting are most effectively combated—and ultimately quieted—through the cultivation of humility. The second is that humility is necessary for the full development and exercise of other virtues and mature virtuous character. Let us consider each claim in turn.

With respect to the first claim, here is the groundwork that has been laid thus far:

First, I have asserted that maturely virtuous engagement requires typically being able to both ascertain and do what is called for, ethically speaking, in a way that is fully appreciative of the morally relevant features and in sync with the situation (e.g., manner and timing). More specifically, this means that maturely virtuous engagement requires that we are able to perceive, identify, understand, and properly evaluate the significance of the facts with respect to what we ought (or ought not) do.[10] What is more, maturely virtuous engagement requires that we are able to properly weigh the needs, desires, interests, beliefs, goals, and values of all relevant others in determining what we ought (or ought not) do. And finally that, in determining what we ought (or ought not) do, we are able to carry it out without unnecessary internal conflict or "corruption."

I have also argued that accomplishing all of this requires, at its base, a quieting of the interfering and distorting biases that arise from the natural centeredness. In other words, it requires a state of awareness that is *epistemically* and *ethically aligned*—which, according to our account, is humility.

Humility's epistemic alignment orients us toward reality, allowing us to understand and experience ourselves and the world around us as they are.[11] Humility's ethical alignment orients toward others, allowing us to understand and experience ourselves as only one among a host of other morally relevant beings, whose interests are as real, legitimate, and as worthy of attention and concern as our own. Together, they eliminate the many centeredness-generated biases that distort and/or otherwise interfere with our ability to perceive, identify, understand, and properly evaluate the significance of the facts, as well as to properly weigh the needs, desires, interests, beliefs, goals, and values of others, in determining what we ought (or ought not) do. They also silence the internal conflict or "corruption"[12] that would otherwise interfere with us acting on those determinations.

Therefore, humility is necessary for maturely virtuous engagement. Of course, all of this presumes our account of humility, which you may or may not wish to adopt. Thus, we should take a moment to consider our account against the backdrop of other accounts. But first, let us consider our second claim—that humility is necessary for the full development and exercise of other virtues (and mature virtuous character).

While related to our first claim, this is nonetheless a different claim. And it is important at the outset to note that by it we are not just making the claim that humility is an essential virtue to have, along with other virtues (such as courage, honesty, generosity, kindness, patience, and so on), in order to be a maturely virtuous person. The claim is, rather, a stronger one: that humility is necessary for the full (mature) development and exercise of these other virtues.

While a full defense of this claim is beyond the scope of this chapter, we can at least outline what we take to be some points in its favor. To start, it seems reasonable to assume that our natural centeredness, and the many biases that arise from it, would actively work against the manifestation of the other virtues (e.g., courage, honesty, generosity, kindness, patience, and others)—except in those instances where their expression was in line with our own needs, desires, interests, beliefs, goals, and values; where it somehow behooved or otherwise benefited us.

Consider those, for example, who take risks to save others because they enjoy the thrill of the physical challenge and the admiration of their community. This doesn't mean that the sort of heroism we admire in them (even though, when off duty, they may be arrogant, self-inflated, irresponsible, and/or entitled) isn't courage—but it isn't *mature* courage. That is, it is not the expression of a virtue that has become fully attuned to what is called for, ethically speaking, in a wide range of situations. There are many instances outside this particular context (risking one's life to save others) where courage might be required, yet these individuals may be unable to ascertain this and/or act on it, especially when the type of courageous expression required is different from the one to which they have become accustomed. More, insofar as their particular expression of courage as has been enlisted into the psychological service of self-admiration and inflated social egos (the need for which may indicate virtue-relevant damage to private egos), it is likely to be thrown off its mark whenever the biases generated by their self-orientation and absorption are activated.

Or consider honesty. It may be that honesty comes fairly easily, generally speaking. For most of us, it typically only becomes difficult when it puts our needs and interests at risk, or otherwise interferes with them. But, when those situations arise, it becomes challenging to properly adjudicate between our needs and interests and those of the individual(s) with whom we are failing to be truthful. Our needs and interests tend to weigh in much more heavily—even (or perhaps, especially) when it is clear that what we are hiding, or otherwise failing to reveal, reflects poorly upon us and that hiding it is wrong. This makes the silencing of the biases generated by our self-orientation and absorption critical. It allows us to more accurately perform (though it is often more experiential than performative) the "moral calculus" that weighs in favor of our honesty. Among other things, we are able to more clearly appreciate the dignity of the other, whom we harm by not giving her all the facts relevant to her choices and decision-making.

This same kind of story can be told for the other virtues as well—while some partially developed expression of them is possible without humility, in its absence they cannot become mature. Humility is necessary to fully eliminate our self-oriented tendency to view others as inferior, and therefore worthy of scorn and disregard, or unworthy of compassion, kindness, and concern. When considering who should benefit from our time, energy, and resources, humility is necessary to bring the needs of others clearly into view, to generate the grateful joy of being able to generously contribute to their well-being—they who, through luck or circumstance, may have less than we do. Humility quiets the incessant push and pull of our desires, wishes, and fears, facilitating and deepening our capacity for patience, moderation, and modesty. And so on.

It is also worth mentioning here that humility has another critical role to play in the development of mature virtue—namely, *the reduction, and eventual elimination, of vice.* As Roberts and Wood (2007; see also Roberts and Spezio, this volume) note, the defining feature of the humble person is that she lacks the many vices of pride. And as Leary and Banker (this volume) argue, beyond the various accolades and benefits that come from their demonstrated skills and talents, the humble person feels no need to receive special treatment, to be looked on as more worthy or of more value than others—in fact, such behavior would arguably be repugnant to her. Indeed, it is hard to imagine a vice (though one certainly may exist) that does not have as its genesis the tendency toward self-absorption and self-worship that often arises from our default setting.[13]

As such, it makes sense to view humility as residing at the center of the maturely virtuous character. Interestingly, it also suggests (and seems likely given the accounts we have reviewed—see for example, Brooks, 2015; Colby and Damon, 1992; Monroe, 2004; 2012; Oliner, 2003; Oliner and Oliner, 1988) that while moral exemplars differ in many respects from one another, the one virtue they all share—the virtue that stands at the center of the unique moral contributions they have made to their communities and humanity at large—is humility.

BUT, WHY THIS ACCOUNT OF HUMILITY?

We return to the question posed earlier: Why our account of humility? Would other accounts of humility agree with us that it occupies such a privileged position with respect to mature virtue?

First, let us say at the outset that we reject the "self-abnegation" or "lowliness" accounts of humility that can be found in some philosophical and theological approaches (see Nadelhoffer, et al., 2017 for our more extended discussion of this view). This approach aside, over the years humility has received a lot of attention from philosophers and psychologists, who have argued for accounts of humility that encompass a range of interrelated intrapersonal and interpersonal qualities.

Some have defined humility largely in terms of a particular *self-orientation*. For example, Tangney (2000; 2009) identified humility as an accurate assessment of one's talents and achievements, the ability to acknowledge one's mistakes, imperfections, gaps in knowledge, and limitations, along with openness to new ideas, contradictory information, advice, and an appreciation of the value of other people and things. And others have defined humility along similar lines, such as having a moderate or accurate view of oneself (Baumeister and Exline, 2002; Emmons, 1999; Rowatt et al., 2002; Sandage, Wiens, and Dahl, 2001), a willingness to admit mistakes, seek new information, and learn new things (Hwang, 1982; Templeton, 1997), an openness to new or divergent ideas (Gantt, 1967; Harrell and Bond, 2006; Morris, Brotheridge, and Urbanski, 2005; Neuringer, 1991; Templeton, 1995), as well as a relative lack of self-preoccupation, desire to distort information, or otherwise "self-enhance" or make oneself look and feel better (Peterson and Seligman, 2004; Templeton, 1997).

Others have defined humility more in terms of what we might call an *other-orientation,* such as the presence of empathy, gentleness, respect, and an appreciation for the equality, autonomy, and value of others (Halling, Kunz, and Rowe, 1994; Means et al., 1990; Sandage, 1999; Tangney, 2000; 2009), as well as a concern for their welfare (LaBouff et al., 2012). Also, gratitude (Emmons and Kneezel, 2005), a willingness to share credit for accomplishments with others (Exline and Geyer, 2004; Tangney, 2000; 2009; Vera and Rodriguez-Lopez, 2004), as well as a willingness to surrender to God or some transcendent power (Emmons and Kneezel, 2005; Murray, 2001; Powers et al., 2007).

As we have discussed at length elsewhere (Wright, et al., 2017, 2018), one problem with defining humility merely in terms of these (and other) qualities is that it is not clear which of them *constitute* humility and which are simply *related to* it (see Leary and Banker, this volume, for a similar argument). Humble people may indeed possess and express all of the above attributes and qualities, and they may even do so because they are humble, but that does not mean that those attributes and qualities *are* humility. One of the major advantages of our account of humility is that it illuminates its core—i.e., a state of awareness that is free of the epistemically and ethically interfering and distorting biases generated by our natural centeredness—and thus explains the presence of these intrapersonal and interpersonal qualities.

Davis et al. (2012; see also Mosher et al., this volume) take a different approach, proposing that the humility of an individual can only be identified via interpersonal judgments that others in relationship to that individual make about him/her. And, typically, we attribute humility to that individual via the attribution of other capacities or qualities, such as the tendency to express positive other-oriented emotions in one's relationships (e.g. empathy, compassion, sympathy, and love), the ability to regulate self-oriented emotions in socially acceptable ways (e.g. pride or excitement about one's accomplishments), and having an accurate view of self.

While a novel approach that helps address certain worries (see Wright, et al., 2017 for more discussion), it nonetheless collapses back into the other accounts, which define humility in terms of positive personal and interpersonal attributes or qualities possessed by an individual.

Leary and Banker provide yet another account of humility, in this volume. According to them,humility involves the recognition that, however great one's personal accomplishments or positive characteristics may be, one is not fundamentally a more special person because of them and, thus, should not be viewed or treated as special outside the domain of one's accomplishments or characteristics (and sometimes even within it).

While we think this account has a lot to offer—namely, it identifies one of the central outcomes of an epistemically and ethically aligned state of awareness—the concern we have for this account is the same as above. After all, one could ask the humble person *why* she understands that she is not fundamentally more special than anyone else given her accomplishments. And it seems to us that the answer would have to reference something like our account of humility. In other words, we would argue the humble person recognizes her lack of specialness *because* she is in a (temporary or stable) state of epistemically and ethically aligned awareness—it is the state of awareness that generates, or makes possible, this recognition.

Another interesting approach to humility is to view it largely in terms of its "negative character"—i.e., in terms of what it is *not*. As Roberts and Wood (2007) write,

> Humility is opposite a number of vices, including arrogance, vanity, conceit, egotism, grandiosity, pretentiousness, snobbishness, impertinence (presumption), haughtiness, self-righteousness, domination, selfish ambition, and self-complacency. Despite differing from one another in various ways, these vices are all opposites of humility, and therefore definitive of it; we might sum up all of them as "improper pride." (258)

According to this view, humility, rather than being a virtue, is an *absence of vice*. Nonetheless, this account harmonizes with our own in a number of ways. First, our view of humility also involves an absence—namely, the absence of interfering and distorting epistemic and ethical biases generated by our natural centeredness. Second, the biases that we argue humility is free from are precisely the sorts of biases Roberts and Woods (2007) mention in the quote above—all forms of "improper pride." While we would argue that this is not the only form that these biases take, nor the only way that self-orientation and absorption can distort our epistemic and ethical capacities, their idea of improper pride nonetheless captures a good portion of the sorts of distortions we have in mind.

And this leads to exactly the sort of epistemically and ethically relevant clarity we have argued for. For example, they write,

> The humble person is not ignorant of her value or status, but unconcerned about it and therefore inattentive to it. She may appear to be ignorant of her excellence or status, but if she needs to assess herself she can give as accurate an account as the next person; she is just not very interested in such an assessment, thus

> not much inclined to inquire about it, and the evidence for it is not particularly salient for her. (261)

This is not to say that, in their estimation, an absence of vice cannot *become* a virtue. But for humility to be a virtue, Roberts and Wood (2007) argue that we must be able to show how any given expression of it (say, for example, as a lack of concern for status) has an underlying virtuous motive—or, as they write, "We propose that the concern for status is swamped or displaced or put on hold by some overriding virtuous concern" (261), such that the person's humility becomes "coordinated with an intense concern for some apparent good" (263).

Here, we disagree with Roberts and Woods (2007) on two points. First, we would argue that the epistemic and ethical alignment we both appear to agree humility provides is more than a mere absence of vice—it is *itself* an important good. Second, it also seems natural for such an alignment, an absence of bias (or vice), to become coordinated with, and to coordinate, a variety of other goods. For instance, as Roberts and Woods mention, "a disposition to rejoice in the progress of one's students, especially, perhaps, when they advance beyond oneself; and . . . an emotional indifference to the question of the extent of one's own influence on them" (264–265) or a deep, abiding concern for, and joy in, the flourishing of other living beings.

But, perhaps this is not really a disagreement after all. Our argument is that humility is necessary for maturely virtuous engagement and for the full development of other virtues and virtuous character—but that does not mean it is sufficient.[14] This is partly because being in an epistemically and ethically aligned state of awareness does not *by itself* afford you the range of experiences and opportunities to practice that are clearly required for becoming maturely virtuous. But we must also grant that—as Roberts and Woods (2007) point out—it is possible, however unlikely, that a person could experience epistemically and ethically aligned states of awareness and yet somehow be cognitively and/or affectively disconnected from them in such a way as to feel no inclination to act or otherwise respond accordingly. Though we tend to agree with Morinis (2007) that such a state of humility would be a *defective* state of humility, and that genuine humility naturally produces and contributes to a variety of epistemically and ethically virtuous outcomes, a more thorough argument for this would need to be given.

In summary, we view our account of humility as having at least two key advantages over other accounts: first, it clearly illuminates the underlying phenomenological and psychological features of humility such that it (typically) gives rise to the host of intrapersonal and interpersonal, self-oriented, other-oriented, and relational attributes, qualities, and capacities widely discussed by philosophers and psychologists. In other words, it clarifies *why* humble people are more self-aware and accurate in their self-assessment, are mindful of their limitations and fallibility, are open to new information and ideas, are comfortable with both success and failure (and are not inclined to lord the former over, or hide the latter from, others), are modest in their bearing, are compassionate and inclined to care for others, are generous, grateful, and loving. And so on.

Secondly, in so doing, it also clearly illuminates the fundamental importance and value of humility, both as a virtue in its own right and more—as the medium through which virtues develop and mature and vices wither and die; the foundation upon which maturely virtuous character is built.

CULTIVATING HUMILITY

If humility is foundational in the way we have been arguing, then it is important to know how to cultivate it. But how do we do that? The other chapters in the volume have a lot to offer in this topic. For example, Narvaez (this volume) argues powerfully for the importance of early life experiences—experiencing "limbic resonance," and developing a healthy sense of both autonomy and belonging through secure attachment, with caregivers and community members. As her chapter suggests, when raised in a community and culture that fosters the formation of early emotional connected-ness with and deep concern for others, humility will likely also begin to develop early, since the self-oriented biases that emerge as a function of our natural centeredness are being quieted through these social practices and are therefore not given the opportunity to manifest into self-absorption or self-worship.[15]

But, for those of us not raised in this way, both Roberts and Spezio (this volume) and de Vries (this volume) talk about the importance of immersing oneself in what we might call "deep caregiving"—in the former case, through the L'Arche communities with people with disabilities, and, in the latter case, through hospice—where we encounter our own finitude, fragility, and helplessness in the unalterable and unavoidable vulnerability and suffering of others. These circumstances require us to submit to that which is beyond our capacity to change, repair, or solve; or even fully understand. In them, we encounter the edges of our skills and abilities and experience the vast expanse beyond them, what remains unknown, unexplored, unrealized—and yet, nonetheless, a part of us. In response to this, we must give ourselves up to simply loving what is in front of us, without needing to change or "fix" it; to a "selfless respect for reality" (Murdoch, 1970, 93).

Johnston (2009) articulated something similar when he wrote:

> There are large-scale defects in human life that no amount of psychological adjustment or practical success can free us from. These include arbitrary suffering, aging (once it has reached the

> corrosive stage), our profound ignorance of our condition, the isolation of ordinary self-involvement, the vulnerability of everything we cherish to time and chance, and, finally, to untimely death. . . . The redeemed life is a form of life in which we are reconciled to these large-scale defects of ordinary life . . . the idea [that] even in the face of such things there must be a way to go on, keeping faith in the importance of goodness, and an openness to love. (15–16)

Others have spoken of various spiritual practices through which we can cultivate humility. Morinis (this volume, see also Morinis, 2007) discusses the tradition of virtue cultivation in the Jewish faith, called Mussar, which dates back to the 10th century and places the cultivation of humility (*anavah*) at the heart of one's spiritual practice. Here the goal is to learn to *occupy one's rightful space*—"limiting oneself to an appropriate space while leaving room for others" (Morinis, 2007, 49). Of course, it is important to recognize that humility works both ways (as other authors in this volume have pointed out)—it is a sort of "mean" between extremes. So, you must learn, through daily practice, to not only limit yourself to the appropriate space but also to *fully occupy* the appropriate space:

> Arrogance has an insatiable appetite for space. It claims. It occupies. It sprawls. It suffocates others. Every statement in its voice begins with "I." The opposite extreme is self-debasement. Shrinking from occupying any space whatsoever, it retracts meekly inside itself. Its statements would never dare to begin with "I," although, in fact, if we listen carefully, they all do, because, whether we see ourselves as nothing or as everything, we are still preoccupied with the self, and both of these traits are, therefore, forms of narcissism. (Morinis, 2007, 50)

Sometimes, according to Morinis (this volume, see also 2007), learning the boundaries of one's "appropriate space" requires a *humbling* experience—when we are thrown back upon ourselves, shamed for our presumption, or (alternatively) reminded of our responsibility, which we may have shirked, to ourselves and others.[16]

Turning once again to Flanagan's (2015) discussion of Buddhist meditative practices, he argues that meditation facilitates virtue development (and we would argue, the development of humility, in particular) because the dissolution of the self that occurs during advanced meditative practices—where we come to recognize that we are not "substantial" entities, but are instead "relationally constituted," and thus all similarly suffer "the slings and arrows, as well as the pleasures and treasures, of the unfolding" (180)—generates within us a fundamental shift in orientation. We care less about ourselves and more about others. He then argues further:

> What one grasps in the work of meditation, what one experiences, is a calling—something akin to an overpowering desire, which . . . one sees no reason to refuse. One has already both understood and seen that we are all interrelated, that my good is tied up with the good of all other creatures, my ego's guard is down (and it is down for principled reasons), and I am called upon to attend to the suffering of all sentient beings. (187)

At a more secular level, people argue that humility can be cultivated through experiences of awe (Gerber, 2002; Lee, 1994; Stellar et al. , 2018; including this volume)—experiences where we encounter the full impact of our smallness, such as seeing the earth from space, as one tiny blue dot in the vastness of the universe, or standing on the edge of the Grand Canyon, or where we encounter the wondrous beauty of the natural world and of the other beings living in it.

What these many paths to humility seem to have in common is an experience: the (sometimes temporary) revelatory encounter with—and the shifting and quieting of—our natural centeredness. The experience of being knocked off balance, out of a state of self-absorption, so that we can be fully present with the world, others, and ourselves as we are. And with this comes the (again, sometimes fleeting) realization that we are, as individuals, only fragments of a whole, existing in an imperfect world that we did not make or choose, beset by undefeatable difficulties and insurmountable odds. And yet, in precisely these moments, we cannot help but love it, ourselves, and others—the beauty of our imperfection, the grace of our suffering, the indescribable joy of being alive.

NOTES

1. Of course, the frequency of this accomplishment varies across different cultures, with some cultures being much more conducive to the cultivation and development of mature virtue than others. Nonetheless, it seems uncontroversial to say that, relative to the overall population, mature virtue of the sort highlighted in the quote is not a common accomplishment, which is likely why it is revered in most (if not all) cultures.
2. This is not meant to imply that individuals come to these beliefs/values—or even, in some important respects, their needs/interests—on their own, in isolation. They are gained, defined, identified, and shaped by the communities and cultures into which they are born. Nor is it meant to imply that we are naturally "selfish"—it is simply that we naturally experience our own needs, etc., more strongly, immediately, and so forth than we do those of others.
3. It is important to emphasize that while the natural "centeredness" of our experience makes it easier to attend to our own needs/interests than to those of others, this does not necessarily have to manifest into self-absorption and self-worship. In other words, in arguing for our natural centeredness, I am not arguing for a natural "selfishness"—merely for a natural self-oriented bias that we have to work to overcome.
4. Points of clarification: first, while ideally the maturely virtuous person is able to respond appropriately across all ethical contexts, more realistically they are able to exercise their mature virtue in more circumscribed

situations—which may be because certain virtues in their character have been more fully developed than others. Second, while we hold that one's underlying motivational structure is an essential part of maturely virtuous engagement, this is not to say that it has to all or always be consciously accessible. People may respond in the right way to the right features of their environment for the right reasons while not being fully aware they are doing so, especially once—through years of experience—such responding becomes automatic/habitual.

5. Even though I am the sole author of this chapter, I say "we" here (and will do so throughout) when referring to the theory of humility I'm working with here because this is a theory that I developed with others, including Thomas Nadelhoffer, Lisa Ross, Walter Sinnot-Armstrong, and Matthew Echols.
6. We also find ourselves tempted by the stronger claim that humility is sufficient for the full development of (at least some) virtues and virtuous character, at least under normal developmental circumstances. It would certainly seem more than a little odd, given our account, for a person to have cultivated the stable trait of humility and yet not have also developed other mature virtues. The state of humility that we describe seems like precisely the right sort of medium within which other virtues would naturally develop, in the absence of certain constraints and/or barriers. That said, there are several reasons why we do not think we can make this claim—see our discussion about Roberts and Woods's (2007) view below for further discussion.
7. This is similar to what Leary and colleagues call "hypo-egoic" states (a "quieting" of the self), which result in a shift in awareness *away* from oneself and *toward* other things (Leary and Terry, 2012), increased self-regulation (Leary, Adams, and Tate, 2006), a sense of being connected to something larger, and optimal functioning/well-being (Leary and Guadango, 2011).
8. We are not the only ones to make this distinction between state and trait humility. For other discussions see (Kruse, Chancellor, and Lyubomirsky, 2017, including Leary and Banker, this volume).
9. As cited in Tarrants (2011), *Pride and Humility,* retrieved from http://www.cslewisinstitute.org/webfm_send/890.
10. Similarly, mature epistemic virtue requires the person to be able to, perceive, identify, understand, and properly evaluate the significance of the facts with respect to what she ought (or ought not) believe. Though outside the scope of this chapter, we think humility is foundational in this respect as well.
11. This is not to say that we suddenly become omniscient. Rather, it is to say that we are able to encounter the objects of our awareness as they are, without the distortion of the egoic biases that normally interfere with our ability to experience, evaluate, and understand them clearly. The humble person is still saddled with the same physical and cognitive limitations that come with being human (something they are also clearly aware of).

12. At least, those that are centeredness generated. It is conceivable that other forms of conflict and/or corruption could exist.
13. This is not to say that all people who are not humble are vicious, at least not in a robust sense. As we've argued, the default setting of our centeredness takes on the form of natural self-preoccupation, a self-favoring attitude and inclination that, while certainly not exemplary, is not necessarily actively thwarting, nor indifferent to, the needs and well-being of others. It is merely inattentive to them. In this way it is a mild form of vice at most. But this default setting is also vulnerable to further distortion—e.g., narcissism, greed, arrogance, cruelty, megalomania, deception. We might go so far to say that just as humility is a medium conducive to virtue, our default setting is a medium conducive to vice.
14. Though see note 3.
15. Importantly, while the view I have been arguing for holds that "centeredness" is a built-in part of our phenomenological and psychological constitution, this suggests that certain sociocultural practices can function to shift and quiet some of the potentially negative manifestations of this, instilling the capacity for humility—and, thus, for deep felt connection to others—at an early age.
16. Relatedly, in a study with 5th–12th graders, we found a common tendency to reference negative attributes for the humble person, increasingly so the younger they were (highest in 5th–6th graders at 56%, lowest in 11th–12th graders at 10%). In Nadelhoffer et al. (2017), we suggested that this might be because our earliest introductions to humility can be negative—being "put in our place," shamed for being selfish or a braggart, and so forth. And while we did not find much evidence for this in our adult sample (only 2%), we did find that a small percentage (5%) made reference to some form of embarrassment or humiliation being present in their past personal experiences of humility. Collectively, this suggests that one road to becoming humble is *being humbled*.

REFERENCES

Annas. J. 2011. *Intelligent Virtue*. New York: Oxford University Press.

Baumeister, R. F., and J. J. Exline. 2002. "Mystical self-loss: A challenge for psychological theory." *International Journal for the Psychology of Religion, 12*(1), 15–20. doi:10.1207/S15327582IJPR1201_02.

Brooks, D. 2015. *The Road to Character*. New York, NY: Random House Press.

Cervantes. (1613) 2004. *Don Quixote*. New York, NY: Ecco Press.

Colby, A., and W. Damon. 1992. *Some Do Care: Contemporary Lives of Moral Commitment.* New York, NY: Free Press.

Davis, D. E., E. L. Worthington Jr., J. N. Hook, R. A. Emmons, P. C. Hill, and J. L. Burnette. 2012. "Humility and the development and repair of social bonds: Two longitudinal studies." *Self and Identity, 11,* 1–20.

Emmons, R. A. 1999. "Religion in the psychology of personality: An introduction." *Journal of Personality, 67,* 873–888.

Emmons, R. A., and T. T. Kneezel. 2005. "Giving thanks: Spiritual and religious correlates of gratitude." *Journal of Psychology and Christianity, 24*(2), 140–148.

Exline, J. J., and A. L. Geyer. 2004. "Perceptions of humility: A preliminary study." *Self and Identity,* 3(2), 95–114.

Flanagan, O. 2015. "It takes a metaphysics: Raising virtuous Buddhists." In *Cultivating Virtue,* edited by N. Snow, 171–195. Oxford: Oxford University Press.

Gantt, W. H. 1967. "On humility in science." *Conditional Reflex,* 2(3), 179–183.

Gerber, L. 2002. "Standing humbly before nature." *Ethics and the Environment,* 7(1), 39.

Halling, S., G. Kunz, and J. O. Rowe. 1994. "The contributions of dialogal psychology to phenomenological research." *Journal of Humanistic Psychology, 34*(1), 109–131. doi:10.1177/00221678940341007.

Harrell, S. P., and M. A. Bond. 2006. "Listening to Diversity Stories: Principles for Practice in Community Research and Action." *American Journal of Community Psychology,* 37(3–4), 365–376. doi:10.1007/s10464-006-9042-7.

Hursthouse, R. 1999. *On Virtue Ethics.* Oxford: Oxford University Press.

Hursthouse, R. 2016. "Virtue ethics." *Stanford Encyclopedia of Philosophy,* https://plato.stanford.edu/entries/ethics-virtue.

Hwang, C. 1982. "Studies in Chinese personality—A critical review." *Bulletin of Educational Psychology, 15,* 227–242.

Johnston, M. 2009. *Saving God: Religion after Idolatry.* Princeton, NJ: Princeton University Press.

Kruse, E., J. Chancellor, and S. Lyubomirsky. 2017. "State humility: Measurement, conceptual validation, and intrapersonal processes." *Self and Identity, 16*(4), 399–438. doi:10.1080/15298868.2016.1267662.

LaBouff, J. P., W. C. Rowatt, M. K. Johnson, J. Tsang, and G. M. Willerton. 2012. "Humble persons are more helpful than less humble persons: Evidence from three studies." *Journal of Positive Psychology, 7,* 16–29.

Leary, M. R., C. E. Adams, and E. B. Tate. 2006. "Hypo-egoic self-regulation: Exercising self-control by diminishing the influence of the self." *Journal of Personality,* 74(6), 1803–1832.

Leary, M. R., and J. Guadagno. 2011. "The role of hypo-egoic self-processes in optimal functioning and subjective well-being." In *Designing Positive Psychology: Taking Stock and Moving Forward,* edited by K. M. Sheldon, T. B. Kashdan, and M.F. Steger, 135–146. New York: Oxford University Press.

Leary, M. R., and M. L. Terry. 2012. "Hypo-egoic mindsets: Antecedents and implications of quieting the self." In *Handbook of Self and Identity*, edited by M. R. Leary and J. P. Tangney, 2nd ed., 268–288. New York: Guilford Press.

Lee, K. 1994. "Awe and humility: Intrinsic value in nature. Beyond an earthbound environmental ethics." *Royal Institute of Philosophy Supplement*, *36*, 1, 89–101. doi:10.1017/S1358246100006470.

Means, J. R., G. L. Wilson, C. Sturm, J. E. Biron, and P. J. Bach. 1990. "Humility as a psychotherapeutic formulation." *Counselling Psychology Quarterly*, *3*(2), 211–215. doi:10.1080/09515079008254249.

Monroe, K. 2004. *The Hand of Compassion: Portraits of Moral Choice during the Holocaust.* Princeton, NJ: Princeton University Press.

Monroe, K. 2012. *Ethics in an Age of Terror and Genocide: Identity and Moral Choice.* Princeton, NJ: Princeton University Press.

Morinis, A. 2007. *Everyday Holiness: The Jewish Spiritual Path of Mussar.* New York: Trumperter.

Morris, J. A., C. M., Brotheridge, and J. C. Urbanski. 2005. "Bringing humility to leadership: Antecedents and consequences of leader humility." *Human Relations*, *58*(10), 1323–1350. doi:10.1177/0018726705059929.

Murray, A. 2001. *Humility: The Journey Towards Holiness.* Bloomington, MN: Bethany House.

Nadelhoffer, T., and J. C. Wright. 2017. "The twin dimensions of the virtue of humility: Low self-focus and high other-focus." In *Moral Psychology.* Vol. 5: *Virtues and Happiness*, edited by W. Sinnott-Armstrong and C. Miller, 309–371. Cambridge, MA: MIT Press.

Nadelhoffer, T., J. C. Wright, M. Echols, T. Perini, and K. Venezia. 2017. "The varieties of humility worth wanting: An interdisciplinary investigation." *Journal of Moral Philosophy*, *14*, 168–200. doi: 10.1163/17455243-46810056.

Neuringer, A. 1991. "Humble behaviorism." *The Behavior Analyst*, *14*(1), 1–13.

Oliner, S. 2003. *Do unto Others: Extraordinary Acts of Ordinary People.* New York, NY: Basic Books.

Oliner, S., and P. Oliner, 1988. *The Altruistic Personality: Rescuers of Jews in Nazi Europe.* New York, NY: Free Press.

Paquda, Bahya ibn. 1996. *Duties of the Heart.* Translated by D. Haberman. Bilingual edition. Spring Valley, NY: Feldheim.

Peterson, C., and M. P. Seligman. 2004. *Character Strengths and Virtues: A Handbook and Classification.* Washington, DC, and New York: American Psychological Association.

Powers, C., R. K. Naam, W. C. Rowatt, and P. C. Hill. 2007. "Associations between humility, spiritual transcendence, and forgiveness." *Research in the Social Scientific Study of Religion*, 1875–1894.

Roberts, R. C., and W. J. Wood. 2003. "Humility and epistemic goods." In *Intellectual Virtue: Perspectives from Ethics and Epistemology*, edited by M. DePaul and L. Zagzebski, 257–279. Oxford: Clarendon Press.

Rowatt, W. C., A. Ottenbreit, K. J., Nesselroade, and P. A. Cunningham. 2002. "On being holier-than-thou or humbler-than-thee: A social-psychological perspective on religiousness and humility." *Journal for the Scientific Study of Religion, 41*(2), 227–237.

Russell, D. 2009. *Practical Intelligence and the Virtues*, New York: Oxford University Press.

Russell, D., ed. 2013. *The Cambridge Companion to Virtue Ethics*. Cambridge: Cambridge University Press.

Sandage, S. J. 1999. "An ego-humility model of forgiveness: A theory-driven empirical test of group interventions." Dissertation Abstracts International (Jan.), 59, 3712.

Sandage, S. J., T. W. Wiens, and C. M. Dahl. 2001. "Humility and attention: The contemplative psychology of Simone Weil." *Journal of Psychology and Christianity, 20*(4), 360–369.

Snow, N. 2010. *Virtue as Social Intelligence: An Empirically Grounded Theory*. New York: Routledge.

Stellar, J. E., A. Gordon, C. L. Anderson, P. K. Piff, G. D. McNeil, and D. Keltner. 2018. "Awe and Humility." *Journal of Personality and Social Psychology,* 114(2), 258–269. doi:10.1037/pspi0000109.

Swanton, C. 2016. "Developmental virtue ethics." In *Developing the Virtues: Integrating Perspectives,* edited by J. Annas, D. Narvaez, and N. Snow, 116–134. New York: Oxford Press.

Tangney, J. P. 2000. "*Humility*: Theoretical perspectives, empirical findings and directions for future research." *Journal of Social and Clinical Psychology,* 19(*1*), 70–82.

Tangney, J. P. 2009. "Humility." In *Oxford Handbook of Positive Psychology,* edited by S. J. Lopez and C. R. Snyder, 2nd ed., 483–490. New York: Oxford University Press.

Tarrants, J. 2011. "Pride and Humility." *Knowing & Doing,* http://www.cslewisinstitute.org/webfm_send/890

Templeton, J. M. 1995. *The Humble Approach*. New York: Continuum.

Templeton, J. M. 1997. *Worldwide Laws of Life: 200 Eternal Spiritual Principles*. West Conshohocken, PA: Templeton Press.

Vera, D., and A. Rodriguez-Lopez. 2004. "Strategic virtues: Humility as a source of competitive advantage." *Organizational Dynamics,* 33(*4*), 393–408. doi:10.1016/j.orgdyn.2004.09.006.

Wallace, D. F. 2005. Transcription of the 2005 Kenyon College Commencement Address, May 21, 2005. https://web.ics.purdue.edu/~drkelly/DFWKenyonAddress2005.pdf.

Wright, J. C., T. Nadelhoffer, T. Perini, A. Langville, M. Echols, and K. Venezia. 2017. "The psychological significance of humility." *Journal of Positive Psychology, 12*(1), 3–12. doi: 10.1080/17439760.2016.1167940.

Wright, J. C., T. Nadelhoffer, L. Ross, and W. Sinnott-Armstrong. 2018. "Be it ever so humble: Proposing a dual-dimension account and measurement for humility." *Self and Identity, 17*(1), 92–125.

PART II

MORAL HUMILITY IN OUR LIVES

Chapter 7

Humility

The Soil in Which Happiness Grows

PELIN KESEBIR

INTRODUCTION: WHAT WE ARE TALKING ABOUT WHEN WE TALK ABOUT HUMILITY

The word "humility" has it etymological roots in the Latin word *humus*, meaning "earth" or "soil." In this chapter, I argue that humility acts like the soil in which happiness grows. I posit that humility epitomizes a healthy relationship to oneself, to reality, and to others; and it is only on this foundation that enduring happiness can be built. To make my case, I first review the empirical literature linking humility to well-being and then elaborate on the theoretical reasons for this link. Yet before any of this, it is paramount to clarify the meaning of humility—a construct that has proved notoriously difficult to define and measure.

Humility has been dubbed "the gift of perspective" (Hall, 2010). I find it helpful to think of humility as an *ability to see oneself in true perspective and be at peace with it.* Unpacking this broad definition leads us to humility's core features as identified by contemporary psychologists and philosophers. What are those?

Perhaps chief among humility's defining characteristics is a capacity for viewing and a willingness to view oneself accurately (Exline, 2008; Tangney, 2000). In this regard, *seeing oneself in true perspective and being at peace with it* means being able to tolerate an honest look at oneself and non-defensively accepting weaknesses alongside strengths. Humble people thus do not harbor an exaggeratedly high, or exaggeratedly low, sense of self-importance; nor is their self-perception distorted through the lens of their ego's desires and fears. Their relationship to their own self is untroubled, serene, and accepting, rendering unlikely both self-aggrandizing and self-denigrating tendencies. In fact, low levels of self-preoccupation and self-focus (whether that focus is positive or negative) are considered integral to humility, whereas too much attention, energy, and emotional investment devoted to one's self-image points to a lack of it (Tangney, 2000; Wright et al., 2018).

Implied in the definition of humility as an *ability to see oneself in true perspective and being at peace with it* is also the proper positioning of oneself in relation to others. This partly coincides with self-knowledge, in that it is about sensibly discerning where one falls on the various continua on which human beings can be placed. But, at least as crucial to humility as a proper epistemic positioning vis-à-vis others is a proper value positioning. In other words, humble people, even when they rightfully judge themselves as better or worse in some respects relative to others, do not deem themselves as superior or inferior to others on the whole. They do not infer fundamental specialness from their merits, nor fundamental flaw from their faults. Said differently, humble people do not exaggerate the meaning of their differences from others (Leary et al., 2016; Penrose, 2010).

Indeed, humility typically involves a propensity to perceive little difference between oneself and others (Leary, Brown, and Diebels,

2016). This manifests in humble people's pervasively egalitarian views, and their attributing basic worth and dignity to all human beings (Chancellor and Lyubomirsky, 2013). Their interactions with others are thus accepting, kind, and respectful, regardless of with whom they are interacting. Not experiencing themselves as too distinct and separate from others and having an internalized sense that "the entire universe, with one trifling exception, is composed of others" (Holmes, 1927), humble people do not unduly privilege their own views and interests over those of others either. This lower egocentrism and greater attunement to the needs and desires of others has been referred to as the "high other-focus" dimension of humility that complements the "low self-focus" dimension (Wright et al., 2018).

Finally, the *ability to see oneself in true perspective and being at peace with it* also means rightly judging one's place within the larger context of existence and being comfortable with it. Hence, we expect humble people to be more aware and accepting of the fact that against a cosmic scale of time and space, every human being is tiny and insignificant. To be at peace with one's fragility and finitude in a vast and infinite universe is no small psychological feat for an organism wired for self-preservation. What can make it more bearable is a felt connection to something larger than the self—to a reality that extends beyond the exceedingly fragile "me and mine." Indeed, we find that humble people are more sensitive and feel more connected to forces larger than themselves, be this force God, humanity, nature, or the cosmos (Tangney, 2000; Worthington, 2007). On the flip side, a lack of humility is defined by "an undervaluation of that which extends beyond the self, and an overvaluation of self and personal concerns by comparison" (Snow, 1995, 210). The self-transcendent disposition of humble people is also reflected in their perceptions of themselves as part of a web of interdependence (Bauer and Wayment, 2008). Their identities, in that sense, are allo-inclusive: They feel an increased connection to and increased concern for other people and the natural world (Leary, Tipsord, and Tate, 2008).

OF HUMILITY AND HAPPINESS

Having defined humility as a truer, broader, and more accepting perspective of oneself, others, and existence at large, in this section I turn to the relationship between humility and well-being. My first step is to provide a short overview of the existing literature linking humility to physical and mental well-being.*

Even before humility became its own topic of study, significant knowledge had accumulated about psychological constructs resembling a lack of humility and their negative relationship to well-being. Excessive self-focus had already been identified as a hallmark of psychological distress (Ingram, 1990; Leary, 2004), and the costs of narcissism, especially in the interpersonal domain, documented (e.g., Campbell et al., 2005; Campbell, Foster, and Finkel, 2002). More recently, some researchers proposed that *hyper-egoicism* is centrally relevant to a number of psychological disorders that appear dissimilar at first glance (Moore et al., 2016). Hyper-egoicism, standing in stark contrast to humility, refers to a mindset involving a primary focus on and concern with oneself, oftentimes accompanied by a debilitating concern with others' evaluations of oneself. Diverse disorders such as social anxiety disorder, anorexia nervosa, narcissistic personality disorder, or paranoid delusional disorder all bear traces of hyper-egoicism, underlining the well-being costs of high self-focus in its different forms.

* I use the terms happiness and well-being interchangeably in this chapter—to broadly refer to subjectively and objectively desirable states of a person's psychological, physical, and social reality.

Although it is helpful to confirm that a conspicuous absence of humility is associated with various forms of psychological ill-being or distress, this by itself does not constitute evidence that humility promotes well-being. How does the presence of humility, rather than its absence, relate to different components of happiness? In what ways do humble people fare better than those who are not humble? The ability to answer these questions, first and foremost, requires valid and reliable measures of humility. Yet the science of humility is still grappling with measurement issues and no gold standard measure of humility yet exists. Ironically, humbler people will likely tend to underestimate their humility, whereas less humble people will overestimate it, making self-reports of humility even more problematic than self-reports of other personality constructs (Hill and Laney, 2016). It will thus be prudent to bear in mind that the overwhelming majority of the studies reviewed in this chapter rely on these imperfect self-report measures. Although science has learned a lot about humility in the past decades, its measurement remains a humbling endeavor of great importance.

When we review the empirical research, we find scant but promising evidence linking humility to a healthier body and mind. In an early study, Rowatt and colleagues (2006) found that humility correlated positively with mental and physical health in college students (as captured by self-rated mental health, self-rated physical health, number of visits to a counselor, and number of visits to a doctor). A more recent study showed that humbler people report greater happiness and life satisfaction, as well as lower depressed affect and generalized anxiety (Krause et al., 2016). Jankowski and colleagues (2013) too report that humbler people experience fewer depression symptoms.

With regard to the humility-physical health connection, Krause (2010) has documented in a sample of older, religious Americans that those with higher self-reported humility also rated their health more favorably. Of even greater interest, an increase in humility over time was associated with more favorable health ratings over time (Krause, 2012). One way in which humility might positively impact physical health is through reducing stress (also see, Toussaint and Webb, 2017). Relatedly, Krause et al. (2016) demonstrated that humility buffered the effects of stressful life events (e.g., serious illness or injury of a family member, death of a close friend) on four indicators of well-being (happiness, life satisfaction, lower depressed affect, and lower generalized anxiety). The negative impact of these undesirable life events on well-being was reduced for humbler people; furthermore, the benefits of humility were more evident as levels of stress exposure increased.

Recently, Toussaint et al. (2017) reviewed the empirical evidence linking humility to physical and mental health outcomes, and their conclusion too was that the early evidence weighs in favor of the notion that humility is associated with better health and some aspects of well-being. Wright and colleagues (2017) similarly concluded after reviewing the extant literature that humility is a powerfully prosocial virtue with psychological, moral, and social benefits.

WHY WOULD HUMILITY LEAD TO HAPPINESS?

Albeit limited, the scientific literature linking humility to different components of well-being appears encouraging. What are the critical happiness-inducing ingredients of humility? Why do I liken humility to a soil in which enduring happiness grows? My reason for this, as I argue in this section, is that humility represents an optimal way of relating to oneself, which in turn makes it much easier to relate to others and to reality in optimal ways. This sets in place virtuous cycles, ultimately leading to subjectively and objectively more desirable outcomes. In contrast, without the solid foundations of a healthy relationship to oneself, others, and reality, happiness is doomed to stay an artificial and fragile endeavor. To explain why or how, it is imperative to clarify what I mean by happiness, and this is where I turn next.

What We Are Talking about When We Talk about Happiness

Where does enduring happiness lie? Although it is common to conceive of happiness as a state of having satisfied the needs and desires of the ego (e.g., "I'd be happy, if only I could get everything I want, and get rid of everything I don't want"), this seems to be a misunderstanding of the nature of happiness. Even if we set aside for a moment the sheer unreasonableness of asking the universe to give us all that we want, and imagine that we got all we wanted, hedonic adaptation (Frederick and Loewenstein, 1999) would ensure that we would soon get accustomed to our favorable new circumstances and find ourselves with new needs and desires.

Psychological research converges with ancient wisdom and modern self-help in suggesting that happiness is not necessarily the result of having one's desires fulfilled or having good things happening to oneself, but rather a matter of how one sees the world and responds to it. External, situational factors do not seem to have as much of an impact on our happiness as we usually imagine they do. As a case in point, people's circumstances in life, which include demographic and life status variables such as age, gender, marital status, and income, as well as personal history (e.g., having experienced a childhood trauma or won a prestigious award), account for a limited amount of happiness differences among people—about 10% by some estimates (Lyubomirsky, Sheldon, and Schkade, 2005). These and other similar findings emphasize that happiness has less to do with having all one's desires gratified or life constantly going one's way, and more to do with having a healthy state of mind. A healthy state of mind, in turn, comes from having a healthy relationship to oneself, to reality, and to others. These allow for a sturdy, resilient, and durable type of happiness—a fundamental sense of "okayness," an underlying feeling of equanimity and contentment that we can tap into even when things are not going well.

How is happiness, as understood in this way, facilitated by humility? I address this question by examining in detail how humility involves a healthy relationship with oneself, with reality, and with others.

Humility Involves a Healthy Relationship with Oneself

Above, I have defined humility as involving a self that is able to see itself clearly for what it is and is at peace with it. In other words, humble people, while they see themselves for who they are, do not harbor feelings of inferiority; nor do they need to feel superior to others to feel okay. Their lack of self-preoccupation (beyond what is necessary and adaptive) also allows them to connect to others and to the larger world in an open, authentic, unencumbered manner. If we probe deeper into what kind of a self would be capable of these ways of relating, the answer probably is "a deeply secure self." Writings on humility also echo the point that it is the secure who are humble, that "no ego" paradoxically is strong ego. Genuine humility seems to be closely accompanied by a firmly grounded sense of self-worth and calm self-confidence, akin to healthier versions of self-esteem, sometimes referred to as "true self-esteem" (Deci and Ryan, 1995) or "optimal self-esteem" (Kernis, 2003). These stand in opposition to fragile, unstable, or overly contingent forms of self-esteem, which are frequently associated with negative outcomes (Crocker and Park, 2004).

My sense is that nothing is more defining of humility than this kind of well-anchored self-worth—one that does not need continual validation nor is vulnerable to ego-threats. This not only represents an optimal way of relating to oneself but presumably is also the quality from which many of the well-being benefits of humility flow. For one, a secure and enduring sense of self-esteem facilitates the achievement of the sturdier kinds of happiness described earlier. I noted that possibly the most common lay theory of happiness of all—that getting all we want would make us enduringly happy—receives little empirical support and is likely to be ineffective at best and counterproductive at worst. It stands to reason that humility and the accompanying sense of serene self-worth would make people less prone to adopt this happiness strategy: compared to their less humble counterparts who place a heavy emphasis on gratifying their self's needs and wants, humble people should be less likely to have their happiness depend on life going their way all the time. Their more stable and less contingent self-esteem would ensure that their happiness is not kept hostage to the achievements and satisfactions of the ego—that it is not frantically rising and falling, like the stock market, in step with the latest perceived boost or threat to one's self.

With these considerations, Dambrun and Ricard (2011) proposed that self-centered psychological functioning attracts considerable suffering and leads to unstable, fluctuating happiness. A "selfless" psychological functioning, characterized by low levels of self-centeredness and self-importance, on the other hand, is linked to authentic, durable happiness. This theory draws on Buddhist notions of happiness, which regard attachment to the ego as the source of our most disruptive thoughts and a main impediment to lasting peace (Ricard, 2006). Accordingly, to put a premium on the ego leaves us chronically insecure, vulnerable, and threatened, thereby creating an emotional atmosphere antithetical to enduring happiness. Humility, in contrast, allows a less conditional and therefore more lasting kind of happiness—one less tied to the triumphs and tribulations of the ego.

A related way in which humility should enhance well-being is that the healthy sense of self-characterizing humility frees up tremendous amounts of mental and emotional energy that would otherwise go to the exhausting quest of protecting and promoting one's self-image. Excessive self-focus and self-preoccupation, as we saw, have been repeatedly shown to be detrimental to psychological well-being. Not having to live under the tyranny of a needy self, not having to constantly monitor and defend one's self-worth in the eyes of oneself and others should thus confer a substantial degree of inner freedom. This freedom is possibly also what allows humble people to self-transcend, to connect and contribute to entities larger than themselves, which has been uniformly regarded as a recipe for happiness across ages.

The inner freedom born from the secure sense of self characterizing humility presumably also provides the foundation to authenticity—the tendency to act in accord with one's true nature (e.g., one's own values, preferences, needs) as opposed to acting "falsely" to please others or to gain approval (Kernis, 2003). A lack of humility jeopardizes authenticity, in that a heightened preoccupation with others' approval or validation would make people act more in tune with perceived external demands than one's true self, to fabricate a self that is "fitfully designed and distorted to be acceptable to other people" (Harter, 2016, 88). Authenticity, just as the related constructs of intrinsic motivation and self-determination, is robustly linked to psychological well-being (Ryan and Deci, 2000; Wood et al., 2008). This is thus another route by which humility might contribute to happiness and other positive life outcomes.

Humility Involves a Healthy Relationship to Reality

We have discussed how the healthy sense of self underlying humility fosters a mental and emotional outlook that is better suited to enduring happiness. Another essential feature of humility, implied in its definition as "true perspective" and one that should substantially contribute to happiness, is a better alignment with reality. This better alignment, in many ways, is made possible and supported by a healthy relationship to oneself. A secure, calm sense of self can afford an honest look at reality because it operates under the assumption that it can deal with whatever it sees. If the ego's hopes and fears, desires and aversions reign supreme, on the other hand, they tend to corrupt the person's ability to see things clearly and instead result in funhouse mirror-like distortions in the perception of reality.

Greenwald (1980) has famously argued that the ego's cognitive biases are very much like totalitarian information-control strategies: for example, the ego, just like totalitarian regimes, has a penchant for taking responsibility for desired (but not undesired) outcomes or to rewrite history in a way that makes it seem less weak or fallible. We would expect that less humble people would have more "totalitarian ego" tendencies, interpreting situations less based on objective evidence and more based on the implications of the situation for their ego. This detachment from reality, however, should create conflict and psychological distress eventually. Although some have argued that positive illusions foster mental health (Taylor and Brown, 1988), and while there might exist a minimal margin of illusion that leads to positive outcomes (Baumeister, 1989), it is difficult to imagine that serious and chronic aberrations from reality would go unchallenged infinitely. That is because, for us to function effectively in the world, our representation of reality has to overlap with reality. The true perspective characterizing humility should therefore be beneficial to well-being, while its lack should produce undesirable consequences—in the long run, if not always in the short.

In keeping with this idea, Orth and Luciano (2015) showed in a sample of young adults that high narcissism over time led to the occurrence of stressful life events (e.g., serious problems in marriage/relationship, dismissal or serious trouble at work, serious financial problems). This finding is also consistent with research showing that narcissism is negatively associated with life satisfaction in adults (Roberts and Hill, 2012). Although the entitlement/exploitativeness dimension of narcissism was linked to lower life satisfaction across all age groups, some other dimensions (i.e., leadership/authority, grandiose exhibitionism) were associated with higher life satisfaction in adolescents and young adults. This relationship, however, was reversed for adult participants. One way to read this finding is that while positive illusions and a disconnect from reality can confer short-term benefits, in the long run reality catches up with the person.

A sense of entitlement, characterized by pervasive feelings of deservingness, specialness, and exaggerated expectations, is another distinct indicator of low levels of humility. Entitlement exemplifies a less than healthy relationship with reality, in that entitled people expect reality to constantly favor them and to effortlessly bend to their wishes. In addition to the earlier mentioned finding that entitlement is linked to lower life satisfaction, an overview of research by Grubbs and Exline (2016) reveals that entitlement is also a vulnerability factor for psychological distress. According to their model, the unrealistic expectations of entitled people engender a continual vulnerability to external disconfirmation, and when this disconfirmation inevitably occurs, they are more likely to interpret this as an ego-threat and an injustice. Such perceptions not only generate negative psychological states (e.g., dissatisfaction, anger, volatile emotional responses), but also trigger attempts at dealing with these negative emotions by bolstering one's entitled self-concept, leading to a reinforcement of entitled beliefs, thereby initiating the vicious cycle.

We could argue that whereas the disconnect from reality inherent to entitlement sets in motion vicious cycles, humility does the opposite and begets positive dynamics and virtuous cycles. Specifically, we would expect humble people to clash less frequently with reality, given their more accurate mental maps. And even when they do clash, they would likely engage in less defensive and more constructive responses. Their lower ego-involvement, combined with their teachability, would make humble people more prone to accept their mistakes and learn from them, thereby paving the way to more successful outcomes in the future.

Further support for the claim that humble people have a healthier relationship with reality comes from my own work showing that humble people react to reminders of their own mortality in much more constructive and less destructive ways (Kesebir, 2014). Death constitutes the ultimate threat to the self and, as has been posited by terror management theory, can be a source of terrorizing anxiety unless effectively managed (Greenberg, Pyszczynski, and Solomon, 1986). Terror management theory (TMT) argues that this potential for terror is managed by an existential anxiety buffering system, the key ingredients of which are a sense of value, meaning, security, and transcendence. These ingredients are oftentimes provided by self-esteem, faith in one's cultural worldview, and close interpersonal relations. People are thus highly motivated to pursue self-esteem, security, and transcendence within the context of their culture and their close relationships. TMT research has widely documented, however, that these pursuits sometimes take unsavory forms such as self-serving moral disengagement or prejudice and aggression toward those with different cultural worldviews (for an overview, see Kesebir and Pyszczynski, 2012). I was interested in whether humility would thwart these less desirable forms of keeping existential anxiety at bay. Because humility involves a less easily threatened ego that is better aligned with reality and more accepting of its limitations (of which mortality should be one), I reasoned that reminders of the fragility of life and the self should not elicit defensive reactions from humbler people.

In line with my expectations, a series of five studies revealed that higher levels of humility were associated with lower death anxiety and lower defensiveness in the face of death thoughts (Kesebir, 2014). Participants either high in dispositional humility, or experimentally made to feel humility (by being asked to remember a time in their life when they felt humbled), found mortality thoughts less threatening and were less likely to respond to them with prejudicial attitudes toward outgroups or with endorsement of self-serving yet unethical behaviors. Given how unmanaged (or mismanaged) death anxiety is a hallmark of psychological ill-being (Yalom, 1980), the capacity of humility to buffer existential anxiety is very promising. What's more, this finding also emphasizes humility's contribution to a healthy relationship with reality, as reflected in a more accepting and less conflicted relationship with the inexorable fact of our mortality.

Humility Involves a Healthy Relationship to Others

I have argued that humility leads to higher happiness by enabling a better relationship to oneself and a better relationship to reality. What I have not touched upon yet, but is of great consequence, is humility's contribution to better social relationships. Peters and Rowatt (2011) have documented that both self-reported and peer-reported humility is associated with higher perceived quality of one's relationships, even when social desirability and other relevant personality characteristics are statistically controlled. These and many other findings (e.g., Davis et al., 2013; Farrell et al., 2015; Van Tongeren, Davis, and Hook, 2014) leave little doubt that humble people enjoy higher social and relational well-being than their less humble counterparts.

What explains this? How does humility contribute to healthier relationships with others? At the very least, we would expect humbler people to be less likely to alienate others and create interpersonal friction through toxic qualities such as selfishness, entitlement, haughtiness, or contempt. Beyond that, they would probably also possess various qualities essential to the forming and maintenance of healthy personal relationships. For instance, free from exaggerated concerns about what other people signify for their own self-worth or from nervously anticipating their ego's stocks to go up or down with each encounter, humble people should be able to approach others with more openness, ease, and benevolence. Similarly, unencumbered by self-absorption and self-importance, they should feel more connected to others, be more respectful of their perspectives, more sensitive to their needs, and more attentive to their welfare. A large body of research supports these claims by showing humility's associations with helpfulness (LaBouff et al., 2012), generosity (Exline and Hill, 2012), gratitude (Dwiwardani et al., 2014; Kruse et al., 2014), forgiveness (Davis et al., 2011; Dwiwardani et al., 2014; Powers et al., 2007), compassion (Krause and Hayward, 2015), empathy (Davis et al., 2011) and wisdom (Krause, 2016).

The desire to belong is a fundamental human motivation, and good social relationships may be the single most important source of happiness (Baumeister and Leary, 1995; Diener and Seligman, 2002; Reis and Gable, 2003). In contrast, loneliness and poor quality social relationships are strongly associated with low emotional and physical health (Cacioppo and Patrick, 2008; House, Landis, and Umberson, 1988). Given these, it is apparent that humility provides a major pathway toward happiness through its positive effect on social relationships.

Summary

In this section, I offered a theoretical discussion of why we would expect humility to contribute to well-being. To summarize, I have argued that closely intertwined with humility is a secure sense of self and enduring personal worth, which allow the person to afford having a true perspective. The true perspective is embodied as a healthy relationship to oneself, healthy relationship to reality, and healthy relationship to others, which in combination decreases distress and increases well-being. When I have called humility "the soil in which happiness grows," that is what I had in mind: it is impossible to flourish in this world without having harmonious relationships with oneself, with reality, and with others. In this sense, I see humility as foundational to happiness and agree with Nadelhoffer and Wright (2017; see also Wright, this volume) who consider humility a "foundational virtue." According to them, without the proper epistemic and ethical positioning that humility generates, it is impossible to develop other virtues and behave in ways that are fully virtuous. I would add that without that positioning, it is also impossible to achieve enduring happiness.

HOW TO CULTIVATE HUMILITY?

It is beyond the scope of this chapter to provide a detailed discussion of how humility can be cultivated. However, the clear association between humility and happiness makes this an important question, and I would like to briefly touch upon a couple points.

To begin with, the question of how to cultivate humility raises the question of where humility comes from. Despite the paucity of research on this topic, it is safe to assume that a significant portion of variability in humility will be due to genetics, as with any other personality trait. Inherited tendencies to feel more secure (e.g., lower neuroticism), for example, or to be less selfish (e.g., agreeableness), would be expected to relate to humility. In the case of neuroticism and agreeableness, heritability estimates are around .40 (Jang, Livesley, and Vemon, 1996), and for humility, too, we would probably observe comparable numbers. Notwithstanding the genetic component, environmental factors should play a role in the etiology of humility as well. Some incipient empirical and theoretical work has linked humility and related hypo-egoic phenomena to secure attachment (Dwiwardani et al., 2014; Shaver et al., 2016). It stands to reason that an early sense of security conveyed by sensitive and responsive parents would lay the foundation for humility.

Additionally, exposure to exemplars of humility and to practices that lower self-centeredness and promote compassion, as well as the inculcation of values and virtues related to humility (e.g., respect, benevolence, universalism), would be expected to lead children to develop a humbler mindset (Leary, Brown, and Diebels, 2016). This brings us to the importance of culture as a shaping force on humility. Like any virtue, humility needs favorable cultural conditions to thrive, such as the availability and cultural endorsement of humble role models or opportunities to cultivate humility-related values.

Related to the role of cultural factors in shaping self-related processes, we know that narcissism is more prevalent in individualistic cultures than in collectivistic cultures (Foster, Campbell, and Twenge, 2003). Several commentators have noted that the past several decades in the United States witnessed a shift toward radical individualism and the glorification of a self-oriented worldview (e.g., Myers, 2000; Putnam, 2000). Similarly, scholars report a rise in phenomena such as narcissism, psychological entitlement, overcompetitiveness, appearance obsession, and attention seeking (Twenge, 2006; Twenge and Campbell, 2009), denoting an overall decline of humility as a value (also see Brooks, 2015). In our work, we found that this decline is also manifested in cultural products: a survey of a large corpus of American books revealed an average drop of 44.33% in the appearance frequency of the words *humility* and *humbleness* from 1901 to 2000 (Kesebir and Kesebir, 2012). These trends are concerning in light of the well-being benefits accompanying humility.

If we set aside the more distal forces shaping humility, like developmental and cultural factors, and focus on more situational factors, we see emerging empirical evidence on interventions that boost state humility. Ruberton, Kruse, and Lyubomirsky (2017) report three types of interventions that were successful in increasing self-reported and other-observed humility. These interventions involved making participants engage in self-affirmation, practice gratitude, or experience awe. It seems that self-affirmation increased humility by making the ego feel more secure, whereas the gratitude and awe interventions gave participants a better perspective of themselves and promoted feelings of connectedness. Humility interventions, to work, arguably have to make people see things from a broader, truer perspective, while making them feel secure and self-accepting. Future research on this topic will surely be welcomed.

The final point I would like to make concerns the causal directionality of the relationship between humility and happiness. Although this chapter focused exclusively on the effect of humility on happiness, it is virtually certain that happiness would have an effect on humility too. Elsewhere we have argued that virtues and happiness typically operate in a "virtuous cycle" fashion: happiness fosters virtuous behavior, which leads to higher happiness, which in turn facilitates further virtuous behavior (Kesebir and Diener, 2014). It is highly probable that humility is susceptible to similar feedback loops. Positive emotions make it easier to take the focus off of oneself and attend to others, while they also increase the ability to tolerate a more honest look at reality. We would thus expect happiness to increase humility, to the extent happiness makes a person better at seeing reality for what it is and be at peace with it. This bidirectional relationship between happiness and humility could trigger upward spiral processes, leading toward enhanced emotional well-being over time (Fredrickson and Joiner, 2002).

CONCLUSION

The science of humility, albeit young and still struggling with some basic issues, holds a lot of promise for the future. In this chapter, I looked closely at the research and theory linking humility to happiness. Although I discussed a variety of solid theoretical reasons for expecting a close association between humility and happiness, it is prudent to remember that a stronger empirical case for this association still needs to be made. I also cannot deny the possibility that humility, as currently defined by psychologists (and by me in this chapter), might be an overly idealized trait that is hard to encounter in reality. It is not an anomaly, or a degeneracy of character, for a human being to feel insecure in this inherently uncertain, fragile, and dangerous world. Hence, it should not be surprising that the kind of secure ego presumably underlying humility is a rare phenomenon. Even if complete humility might forever elude us, however, in light of what we know about its relationship to happiness, it still seems a worthy goal to patiently strive after.

REFERENCES

Bauer, J. J., and H. A. Wayment. 2008. "The psychology of the quiet ego." In *Transcending Self-Interest: Psychological Explorations of the Quiet Ego*, edited by H. A. Wayment and J. J. Bauer, 7–19. Washington, DC: American Psychological Association.

Baumeister, R. F. 1989. "The optimal margin of illusion." *Journal of Social and Clinical Psychology, 8*, 176–189.

Baumeister, R. F., and M. R. Leary. 1995. "The need to belong: Desire for interpersonal attachments as a fundamental human motivation." *Psychological Bulletin, 117*, 497–529.

Brooks, D. 2015. *The Road to Character*. New York: Random House.

Cacioppo, J. T., and W. Patrick. 2008. *Loneliness: Human Nature and the Need for Social Connection*. New York: W. W. Norton.

Campbell, W. K., C. P. Bush, A. B. Brunell, and J. Shelton. 2005. "Understanding the social costs of narcissism: The case of the tragedy of the commons." *Personality and Social Psychology Bulletin, 31*, 1358–1368.

Campbell, W. K., C. A. Foster, and E. J. Finkel. 2002. "Does self-love lead to love for others?: A story of narcissistic game playing." *Journal of Personality and Social Psychology, 83*, 340–354.

Chancellor, J., and S. Lyubomirsky. 2013. "Humble beginnings: Current trends, state perspectives, and hallmarks of humility." *Social and Personality Psychology Compass, 7*, 819–833.

Crocker, J., and L. E. Park. 2004. "The costly pursuit of self-esteem." *Psychological Bulletin, 130*, 392–414.

Dambrun, M., and M. Ricard. 2011. "Self-centeredness and selflessness: A theory of self-based psychological functioning and its consequences for happiness." *Review of General Psychology, 15*, 138–157.

Davis, D. E., J. N. Hook, E. L. Worthington Jr., D. R. Van Tongeren, A. L., Gartner, D. J., Jennings, and R. A. Emmons. 2011. "Relational humility: Conceptualizing and measuring humility as a personality judgment." *Journal of Personality Assessment, 93*, 225–234.

Davis, D. E., E. L. Worthington, Jr., J. N. Hook, R. A. Emmons, P. C. Hill, R. A., Bollinger, and D. R. Van Tongeren. 2013. "Humility and the development and repair of social bonds: Two longitudinal studies." *Self and Identity, 12*, 58–77.

Deci, E. L., and R. M. Ryan. 1995. "Human agency: The basis for true self-esteem." In *Efficacy, Agency, and Self-Esteem*, edited by M. H. Kernis, 31–50. New York: Plenum.

Diener, E., and M. E. Seligman. 2002. "Very happy people." *Psychological Science, 13*, 81–84.

Dwiwardani, C., P. C. Hill, R. A. Bollinger, L. E. Marks, J. R. Steele, H. N. Doolin, and S. L. Wood. 2014. "Virtues develop from a secure base: Attachment and resilience as predictors of humility, gratitude, and forgiveness." *Journal of Psychology and Theology, 42*, 83–90.

Exline, J. J. 2008. "Taming the wild ego." In *Transcending Self-Interest: Psychological Explorations of the Quiet Ego*, edited by H. A. Wayment and J. J. Bauer, 53–62. Washington, DC: American Psychological Association.

Exline, J. J., and P.C. Hill. 2012. "Humility: A consistent and robust predictor of generosity." *Journal of Positive Psychology, 7*, 208–218.

Farrell, J. E., J. N. Hook, M. Ramos, D. E. Davis, D. R. Van Tongeren, and J. M. Ruiz. 2015. "Humility and relationship outcomes in couples: The mediating role of commitment." *Couple and Family Psychology: Research and Practice, 4*, 14–26.

Foster, J. D., W. K. Campbell, and J. M. Twenge. 2003. "Individual differences in narcissism: Inflated self-views across the lifespan and around the world." *Journal of Research in Personality, 37*, 469–486.

Frederick, S., and G. Loewenstein. 1999. "Hedonic adaptation." In *Well-being: The Foundations of Hedonic Psychology*, edited by D. Kahneman, E. Diener, and N. Schwarz, 302–329. New York: Russell Sage Foundation.

Fredrickson, B. L., and T. Joiner. 2002. "Positive emotions trigger upward spirals toward emotional well-being." *Psychological Science, 13,* 172–175.

Greenberg, J., T. Pyszczynski, and S. Solomon. 1986. "The causes and consequences of a need for self-esteem: A terror management theory." In *Public Self and Private Self,* edited by R. F. Baumeister, 189–212. New York: Springer-Verlag.

Greenwald, A. G. 1980. "The totalitarian ego: Fabrication and revision of personal history." *American Psychologist, 35,* 603–618.

Grubbs, J. B., and J. J. Exline. 2016. "Trait entitlement: A cognitive-personality source of vulnerability to psychological distress." *Psychological Bulletin, 142,* 1204–1226.

Hall, S. S. 2010. *Wisdom: From Philosophy to Neuroscience.* New York: Random House.

Harter, S. 2016. "Developmental and prosocial dimensions of hypo-egoic phenomena." In *Oxford Handbook of Hypo-egoic Phenomena,* edited by K. W. Brown and M. R. Leary, 79–94. New York: Oxford University Press.

Hill, P. C., and E. K. Laney. 2016. "Beyond self-interest: Humility and the quieted self." In *Oxford Handbook of Hypo-egoic Phenomena,* edited by K. W. Brown and M. R. Leary, 243–255. New York: Oxford University Press.

Hill, P. L., and B. W. Roberts. 2012. "Narcissism, well-being, and observer-rated personality across the lifespan." *Social Psychological and Personality Science, 3,* 216–223.

Holmes, J. A. 1927. *Wisdom in Small Doses.* Lincoln, NE: University Publishing.

House, J. S., K. R. Landis, and D. Umberson. 1988. "Social relationships and health." *Science, 241,* 540–545.

Ingram, R. E. 1990. "Self-focused attention in clinical disorders: Review and a conceptual model." *Psychological Bulletin, 107,* 156–176.

Jang, K. L., W. J. Livesley, and P. A. Vemon. 1996. "Heritability of the big five personality dimensions and their facets: a twin study." *Journal of Personality, 64,* 577–592.

Jankowski, P. J., S. J. Sandage, and P. C. Hill. 2013. "Differentiation-based models of forgivingness, mental health and social justice commitment: Mediator effects for differentiation of self and humility." *Journal of Positive Psychology, 8,* 412–424.

Kernis, M. H. 2003. "Toward a conceptualization of optimal self-esteem." *Psychological Inquiry, 14,* 1–26.

Kesebir, P., and E. Diener. 2014. "A virtuous cycle: The relationship between happiness and virtue." In *The Philosophy and Psychology of Character and Happiness,* edited by N. E. Snow and Franco V. Trivigno, 287–306. New York: Routledge.

Kesebir, P., and S. Kesebir. 2012. "The cultural salience of moral character and virtue declined in twentieth century America." *Journal of Positive Psychology, 7,* 471–480.

Kesebir, P., and T. Pyszczynski. 2012. "The role of death in life: Existential aspects of human motivation." In *Oxford Handbook of Human Motivation,* edited by R. Ryan, 43–64. New York: Oxford University Press.

Krause, N. 2010. "Religious involvement, humility, and self-rated health." *Social Indicators Research, 98*, 23–39.

Krause, N. 2012. "Religious involvement, humility, and change in self-rated health over time." *Journal of Psychology and Theology, 40*, 199–210.

Krause, N. 2016. "Assessing the relationships among wisdom, humility, and life satisfaction." *Journal of Adult Development, 23*, 140–149.

Kruse, E., J. Chancellor, P. M. Ruberton, and S. Lyubomirsky. 2014. "An upward spiral between gratitude and humility." *Social Psychological and Personality Science, 5*, 805–814.

Krause, N., and R. D. Hayward. 2015. "Humility, compassion, and gratitude to God: Assessing the relationship among key religious virtues." *Psychology of Religion and Spirituality*, 7, 192–204.

Krause, N., K. I. Pargament, P. C. Hill, and G. Ironson. 2016. "Humility, stressful life events, and psychological well-being: Findings from the landmark spirituality and health survey." *Journal of Positive Psychology, 11*, 499–510.

LaBouff, J. P., W. C. Rowatt, M. K. Johnson, J. Tsang, and G. M. Willerton. 2012. "Humble persons are more helpful than less humble persons: Evidence from three studies." *Journal of Positive Psychology*, 7, 16–29.

Leary, M. R. 2004. *The Curse of the Self: Self-Awareness, Egotism, and the Quality of Human Life*. New York: Oxford University Press.

Leary, M. R., W. K. Brown, and K. J. Diebels. 2016. "Dispositional hypo-egoicism: Insights into the hypo-egoic person." In *Oxford Handbook of Hypo-egoic Phenomena*, edited by K. W. Brown and M. R. Leary, 297–311. New York: Oxford University Press.

Leary, M. R., K. J. Diebels, K. P. Jongman-Sereno, and A. Hawkins. 2016. "Perspectives on hypo-egoic phenomena from social and personality psychology." In *Oxford Handbook of Hypo-egoic Phenomena*, edited by K. W. Brown and M. R. Leary, 47–61. New York: Oxford University Press.

Leary, M. R., J. Tipsord, and E. B. Tate. 2008. "Allo-inclusive identity: Incorporating the natural and social worlds into one's sense of self." In *Transcending Self-Interest: Psychological Explorations of the Quiet Ego*, edited by H. Wayment and J. Bauer, 137–148. Washington, DC: American Psychological Association.

Lyubomirsky, S., K. M Sheldon, and D. Schkade. 2005. "Pursuing happiness: The architecture of sustainable change." *Review of General Psychology, 9*, 111–131.

Moore, K. E., M.A. Christian, E. A. Boren, and J. P. Tangney. 2016. "A clinical psychological perspective on hyper- and hypo-egoicism: Symptoms, treatment, and therapist characteristics." In *Oxford Handbook of Hypo-egoic Phenomena*, edited by K. W. Brown and M. R. Leary, 95–105. New York: Oxford University Press.

Myers, D. G. 2000. *The American Paradox: Spiritual Hunger in an Age of Plenty*. New Haven, CT: Yale University Press.

Nadelhoffer, T., and J. C. Wright. 2017. "The twin dimensions of the virtue of humility: Low self-focus and high other-focus." In *Moral Psychology*, Vol. 5: *Virtue and Character*, edited by W. Sinnott-Armstrong and C. Miller, 309–342. Cambridge, MA: MIT Press.

Orth, U., and E. C. Luciano. 2015. "Self-esteem, narcissism, and stressful life events: Testing for selection and socialization." *Journal of Personality and Social Psychology, 109*, 707–721.

Penrose, B. 2010. "Humility and understanding." *Philosophical Papers, 39*, 427–455.

Peters, A., and W. C. Rowatt. 2011. "Associations between dispositional humility and social relationship quality." *Psychology, 2*, 155–161.

Powers, C., R. K. Nam, W. C. Rowatt, and P. C. Hill. 2007. "Associations between humility, spiritual transcendence, and forgiveness." *Research in the Social Scientific Study of Religion, 18*, 75–94.

Putnam, R. D. 2000. *Bowling Alone: The Collapse and Revival of American Community*. New York: Simon and Schuster.

Pyszczynski, T., and P. Kesebir. 2011. "Anxiety buffer disruption theory: A terror management account of posttraumatic stress disorder." *Anxiety, Stress and Coping: An International Journal, 24*, 3–26.

Reis, H. T., and S. L. Gable. 2003. "Toward a positive psychology of relationships." In *Flourishing: The Positive Person and the Good Life*, edited by C.L. Keyes and J. Haidt, 129–159. Washington, DC: American Psychological Association.

Ricard, M. 2006. *Happiness: A Guide to Developing Life's Most Important Skill*. New York: Little, Brown.

Rowatt, W. C., C. Powers, V. Targhetta, J. Comer, S. Kennedy, and J. Labouff. 2006. "Development and initial validation of an implicit measure of humility relative to arrogance." *Journal of Positive Psychology, 1*, 198–211.

Ruberton, P. M., E. Kruse, and S. Lyubomirsky. 2017. "Boosting state humility via gratitude, self-affirmation, and awe: Theoretical and empirical perspectives." In *Handbook of humility: Theory, Research, and Applications*, edited by E. L. Worthington, Jr., D. Davis, and J. N. Hook, 260–273. New York: Routledge.

Ryan, R. M., and E. L. Deci. 2000. "Self-determination theory and the facilitation of intrinsic motivation, social development, and well-being." *American Psychologist, 55*, 68–78.

Shaver, P. R., M. Mikulincer, B. Sahdra, and J. Gross. 2016. "Attachment security as a foundation for kindness toward self and others." In *Oxford Handbook of Hypo-egoic Phenomena*, edited by K. W. Brown and M. R. Leary, 223–242. New York: Oxford University Press.

Snow, N. E. 1995. "Humility." *Journal of Value Inquiry, 29*, 203–216.

Tangney, J. P. 2000. "Humility: Theoretical perspectives, empirical findings, and directions for future research." *Journal of Social and Clinical Psychology, 19*, 70–82.

Taylor, S. E., and J. Brown. 1988. "Illusion and well-being: A social psychological perspective on mental health." *Psychological Bulletin, 103*, 193–210.

Toussaint, L., and J. R. Webb. 2017. "The humble mind and body: A theoretical model and review of evidence linking humility to health and well-being." In *Handbook of Humility: Theory, Research, and Applications*, edited by E. L. Worthington Jr., D. E. Davis, and J. N. Hook, 178–191. New York: Routledge.

Twenge, J. M. 2006. *Generation Me: Why Today's Young Americans Are More Confident, Assertive, Entitled—And More Miserable Than Ever Before*. New York: Free Press.

Twenge, J. M., and W. K. Campbell. 2009. *The Narcissism Epidemic: Living in the Age of Entitlement*. New York: Free Press.

Van Tongeren, D. R., D. E. Davis, and J. N. Hook. 2014. "Social benefits of humility: Initiating and maintaining romantic relationships." *Journal of Positive Psychology*, *9*, 313–321.

Wood, A. M., P. A. Linley, J. Maltby, M. Baliousis, and S. Joseph. 2008. "The authentic personality: A theoretical and empirical conceptualization, and the development of the Authenticity Scale." *Journal of Counseling Psychology*, *55*, 385–399.

Worthington, E. L. 2007. *Humility: The Quiet Virtue*. West Conshohocken, PA: Templeton Foundation Press.

Wright, J. C., T. Nadelhoffer, T. Perini, A. Langville, M. Echols, and K. Venezia. 2017. "The psychological significance of humility." *Journal of Positive Psychology*, *12*, 3–12.

Wright, J. C., T. Nadelhoffer, L. Ross, and W. Sinnott-Armstrong. 2018. "Be it ever so humble: Proposing a dual-dimension account and measurement for humility." *Self and Identity*, *17*, 92–125.

Yalom, I. 1980. *Existential Psychotherapy*. New York: Basic Books.

Chapter 8

Self-Other Concept in Humble Love

As Exemplified by Long-Term Members of L'Arche

ROBERT C. ROBERTS AND MICHAEL SPEZIO

INTRODUCTION: LIFE IN L'ARCHE COMMUNITIES

In 1964, in the French village of Trosly-Breuil, Jean Vanier began sharing his home and life with two intellectually disabled men, Raphael and Philippe. Prior to that time, he had spent several years in the British navy, and he then studied philosophy and taught at the University of Toronto. He called his home with Raphael and Philippe "l'Arche" (the Ark), and since that modest beginning, more than 150 l'Arche communities have been founded around the world. The residents of these small communities are persons with intellectual disabilities (Core Members) along with "Assistants" who share their life with Core Members, not as caregivers, but as friends who both give and receive care.

In l'Arche communities, Core Members often require help with daily tasks of bodily hygiene. L'Arche teaches new Assistants that when assisting with such tasks, the Assistant should avoid using language that separates Core Members and Assistants and denies mutuality in the shared task. Rather than say, "I am going to give Terry a bath," l'Arche teaches Assistants to say, "I am going to be with Terry for her bath." L'Arche Assistants have reported to us that it sometimes takes several months or years for them to grasp fully the depth of meaning in this seemingly simple change in language, but when they do grasp it, they realize they have changed their view of relationship and mutuality with others.

The members of the l'Arche communities work, play, and celebrate together in ordinary houses located in ordinary neighborhoods. They cook, clean, listen to music, watch TV, go to coffee shops and football games; they live together. Vanier strongly emphasizes the primary place of joy in their common life—enjoyment of the activities and celebrations they share, but above all enjoyment of one another's persons and of the affirming affection they have for each other. Affirmation of a person's belonging to the community as a unique individual says to each member in l'Arche, "You matter to me and to our community," and recognizes each member's equality in having power to define the community by saying this to others. Both Core Members and Assistants receive and carry out this sacred task in mutual humility.

This chapter explores and attempts to explain this transformation of character. Central to our account will be the concept of *humble love* or *loving humility*. We take these expressions to designate an intersection of two mutually supporting virtues: humility and the special kind of love known as *agapē*—love which, in a sense that we will explain, is indiscriminate or universal.

THE ALLIANCE OF LOVE AND HUMILITY

Historically, these virtues seem to have been conceived together. Neither is conceptually salient in several ancient philosophical traditions (Platonic, Aristotelian, Stoic) that have influenced the West, but they appear together in the New Testament, with strong anticipations in the Hebrew Bible. Humility of a kind seems characteristic of Socrates, but without being named and explicitly discussed, as many other virtues are in Plato's dialogues. Socrates's "humility" is presented not as a virtue that everyone should exhibit, but as particular to his special calling to be a gadfly to Athens (*Apology* 30e) and a midwife of ideas serving those with whom he conversed (*Theaetetus* 150b–e).

By contrast with classical philosophical texts, humility is salient in the New Testament, where it is associated with love. Central loci for the virtue are Philippians 2.1–11 and John 13.1–5, 12–17.

> So if there is any encouragement in Christ, any incentive of love [*agapē*], any participation in the Spirit, any affection and sympathy, complete my joy by being of the same mind, having the same love, being in full accord and of one mind. Do nothing from selfishness or conceit, but in humility [*tapeinophrosunē*] count others better than yourselves. Let each of you look not to his own interests, but also to the interests of others. (Phil. 2.1–4)

Paul goes on to speak of how Christ divested himself of the privileges of Godhead and took on human form and, indeed, the form of a servant of humankind, even dying the death of a criminal for the sake of humankind. Paul urges the Philippian congregation to divest themselves, in like manner, of selfishness and conceit, and to practice serving one another. In a narrative illustrative of this point, John the Evangelist reports:

> Before the feast of the Passover, when Jesus knew that his hour had come to depart out of the world to the Father, having loved [*agapēsas*] his own who were in the world, he loved them to the end. And during supper, when the devil had already put it into the heart of Judas Iscariot, Simon's son, to betray him, Jesus, knowing that the Father had given all things into his hands, and that he had come from God and was going to God, rose from supper, laid aside his garments, and girded himself with a towel. Then he poured water into a basin, and began to wash the disciples' feet, and to wipe them with the towel with which he was girded. (John 13.1–5)

As in the Philippians passage, Jesus is a model for disciples to follow: he tells them, "I have given you an example, that you should also do as I have done to you" (v. 15). Jesus's illustration of humble love is set on the night before his death on a cross (Phil. 2.8) to which Paul refers as the ultimate act of humble love. Let us now try to say what each of the virtues in this compound virtue contributes, and how each contribution relates to the other.

THE CONTRIBUTIONS OF HUMILITY AND LOVE

We noted that the Greek word for love (*charity* in an older translation) in the quoted New Testament passages is *agapē*. *Agapē* is "neighbor"-love, and *neighbor* (Greek *plēsion*, "near one") is a symmetrical concept (if A is a near one to B, then B is a near one to A). This internal symmetry of the concept suggests the equality of A and B. The l'Arche communities, by their structure and their teaching, foster the construal of all members of the community (and all persons outside the community) as of equal value.

The internal symmetry of *agapē* explains why Jesus can answer the lawyer's question, Who is my neighbor? (that is, Which *others* are my neighbors?) with a parable about the Samaritan who was a good neighbor to the wounded one abandoned by the side of the road. That is, the Samaritan was the good neighbor because of being moved by the other's suffering and acting out the notion of a self that connects it intimately with the other (Luke 10.25–37). The symmetry of the concept of neighbor suggests that the cognitive structure of *agapē* unites a concerned conception of the other with a concerned conception of oneself. This symmetry of *agapē* is evident in two main dimensions of the virtue, which we will call *cherishing the other* and *willing the other's good.*

You cherish the other by affirming that the other is precious, valuable, or dear. Cherishing someone leads you, if there is sufficient time and proximity, to practices in which you experience joy in her presence, are glad to see her, enjoy doing activities *with her,* even when you are personally indifferent to those activities in her absence. While cherishing those who belong with us can lead to negative consequences such as in-group bias, the notion of cherishing in l'Arche, being completely independent of the qualifications of the Normal (success in competitions, superiority of skills and power, and so forth) intentionally applies to all, both inside and outside of l'Arche. That is, the unique loveliness of each individual is repeatedly affirmed, as is the diversity of their gifts and their belonging to the community. These affirmations, which flow from the symmetry of *agapē,* enhance the cherishing of others and deepen one's own sense of belonging as well.

When immersed in a foreign culture, if we overhear someone speaking our dialect, we tend to have warm feelings toward her even if we have never met and will never meet. We feel "kinship" with her.[1] It is a matter of how we "see" the other. A person whose practiced, integrative use of the concept of neighbor is as wide as that of

Jesus will construe herself as a "near one" to others and, in a mutually reinforcing manner, similarly construe as a "near one" every person she meets, regardless of that person's "qualifications" or material similarities or dissimilarities.

The other element of neighbor-love, willing the other's good, is closely connected with cherishing the other. When we cherish other things than people—art treasures, mementos, objects of our own creation, for example—we do care for them in the sense of wanting them to remain intact and in good condition. But, not being persons, they don't profit *for themselves* from our care. If they have been improved or maintained, that is nothing *to them*, and our act of caring for them may be entirely for our own sake. When we care for another person, by contrast, we wish to benefit her life for *her own* sake. And this *for the other's sake* is characteristic of *agapē*. When the Samaritan noticed the wounded man by the roadside, his cherishing vision of the wounded one was the felt desire to help him. The text says, "seeing him, he was moved in his gut [*esplanchnisthē*: this is the typical New Testament word for compassion], and he went to him." He wanted his life saved and his wounds healed *for him*. As Alasdair MacIntyre has noted, this should not be confused with self-ignoring altruism.[2] The Samaritan's cherishing the wounded one and willing his good is not a general, apersonal orientation, nor does it emerge from outside the symmetrical character of neighbor-love. In cherishing the wounded man and willing his restoration, the Samaritan is, in a way, acting on his own behalf, as kin to the wounded one. Think of a mother who cares for her sick child. Is she acting for his sake or for her own? Neither answer, in abstraction from the other, is right; she acts *as his mother* for his sake. Her sake is his sake and his is hers. As Fr. Gregory Boyle would say, there is "no daylight separating them."[3] That's how "near" the Samaritan is to the man in the ditch, in the Samaritan's agapic construal of the other in relation to himself. This will be true of all the forms of *agapē*—not just compassion, but also generosity, gratitude, and forgiveness.[4] When we cherish another, we cherish him or her as a person, and thus as one whose life as a person—which can go well or badly for *him or her*—matters to us, who are kindred persons. This is one way that cherishing is connected with willing the other's good.

Another way is that when we act on the other's behalf in fostering the other's life, we consolidate our understanding of ourselves as cherishing the other, and we elide the typical barriers that language and thought place between self and other. People who foster others speak of "investing themselves" in the other, and so they build a sense of being bonded with the other. We can well imagine that, as the Samaritan washes and binds the wounds, the tenderness of his hands, as expressing his will for the other's healing and safety, both enacts and supports his cherishing. If the other then responds by cherishing *us* and perhaps by fostering *our* life in some way (say, by affirming that we, too, matter and belong), the other becomes all the more precious to us and our bond deepens. Let this suffice as our account of the contribution of love to the alliance of humble love. What does humility contribute?

Taking our cue from the quoted Philippians passage, we propose to think of humility in its opposition to what we might call the vices of pride. Paul sets humility in opposition to selfishness (*eritheia,* which might also be translated "rivalry" or "strife"; the idea seems to be that of a struggle for ascendancy over other people) and conceit (*kenodoxia,* which might also be translated as "vainglory" or "vanity"; here the idea seems to be that of "empty" management of others' impressions of oneself—that is, just for the sake of being admired, adulated, or envied by the others). We propose to read *eritheia* and *kenodoxia* as stand-ins for the whole family of vices that orient us by a false conception of personal importance. Humility, then, involves the absence or mitigation of any of a family of vices marked by an inappropriate concern for one's (our) own importance or the importance of belonging to one's group, or (in other words) a concern for one's importance under a range of false descriptions.

We distinguish five groups by their kinds of false descriptions: the vices of *distorted agency* (selfish ambition, domination, and hyper-autonomy); *empty self-display* (vanity and pretentiousness); *corrupt entitlement* (arrogance, presumption); *invidious comparison* (snobbery, self-righteousness, invidious pride, and envy); and *tribal superiority* (racism, ethnicism, sexism, homophobia, etc.). Central to each of these vices is a concern for personal importance. They differ from one another in how that importance is conceived, either as *having been* achieved or as *to be* achieved. We all want to be important as persons, but we can differ in how we conceive that importance, and also in whether we think of ourselves as having or lacking it. In the following schema, we sketch the thought (the concerned construal of self in relation to the other) that defines each of the vices.

1. The prides of distorted agency (selfish ambition, domination, and hyper-autonomy).

   Selfish ambition: I can make myself important as a person by achieving accomplishments that will arouse people's admiration, applause, and envy because these accomplishments are greater than those of others.

   Domination: I make myself important as a person by controlling others' actions and emotions, so that they become extensions of my agency.

   Hyper-autonomy: I am more important as a person, the fewer people I depend on for what I am and do.

2. The prides of empty self-display (vanity and pretentiousness).

   Vanity: I am important as a person to the extent that people admire, applaud, and envy me.

Pretentiousness: I make myself important as a person by displaying myself so that people admire, applaud, and envy me.

3. The pride of corrupt entitlement (arrogance, presumption).

   Arrogance (presumption): My importance as a person is increased by my having special privileges and entitlements.

4. The prides of invidious comparison (snobbery, self-righteousness, invidious pride, and envy).

   Snobbery: I gain importance as a person by belonging to elite (superior) classes or groups.

   Self-righteousness: I have importance as a person to the extent that I am morally better than someone.

   Invidious pride and *envy*: I am important as a person in inverse proportion to other people's lesser importance as persons. Or, I am unimportant as a person in inverse proportion to other people's greater importance as persons.

5. The prides of tribal superiority (*racism, ethnicism, sexism, homophobia*, etc.).

   We (members of my "tribe"—race, ethnicity, sex, etc.) have greater value as persons and so are worthy of more respect and concern than persons who don't belong to our "tribe."

These sketches bring out clearly both the social nature of these vices—the fact that they are about the self *in relation to* another or others—and their *anti*social nature—that their sociality is of an alienating or distancing kind. Selfish ambition would turn others into "losers" and admirers. Domination would reduce others to auxiliaries or even chattel. Hyper-autonomy tends to be stingy with credit owed to others. Contrariwise, humble love seeks the full individual development of the other and rejoices in the excellence of the other's agency. Vanity and pretentiousness conceive others nonmutually as potential or actual admirers or enviers. Contrariwise, humble love compassionately sees the other as having needs, including the need for recognition and respect, and is moved to build up the other by communicating affection, respect, and appreciation. Arrogance or presumption is disrespectfully competitive in seeking *greater* privileges and entitlements than others, and encroaches on others' rights, in claiming false entitlements. Contrariwise, humble love doesn't insist on its own entitlements except where these serve some purpose deeper than the satisfaction of its own ego, and in general claims entitlements where and because they serve the good of the community. Snobbery, self-righteousness, and invidious pride, in conceiving oneself as having special importance, conceive the other invidiously as lacking such importance; and envy, in its frustrated quest for similarly comparative importance, is offensive in the same way. Humble love, by contrast, appreciates the importance of the other independently of the criteria that make for invidious comparisons. The vices of tribal superiority are social in positing a circumscribed "we"-self and are alienating in pitting that "superior" we-self against outsiders who are conceived as less important because they don't belong to the favored group. Humble love, by contrast, works with an *encompassing* "we," a we that invites personal inclusion of everyone, affirming that all belong, regardless of race, religion, gender, sexual orientation, education, economic class, and all the rest.

A person with perfectly virtuous humility would be completely without any of these vices. Very likely no mere human being is perfect in this way, so we count, as being virtuously humble, people who are unusually *low* in their concern to have such misconceived importance and minimally disposed to conceive the social world in the ways that the concern involves. The vices of pride are all psychological schemas that disable us for human relationships marked by cherishing one another and wishing one another well without discrimination of abilities, class, power, comeliness, moral uprightness, or tribe. Humility thus favors the development of *agapē*, and so *agapē* is evidence of effective, enactive humility.

Jean Vanier's conception of human beings as fulfilled by humble love implies a conception of human nature bent toward the giving and receiving of tender personal attention in the context of a community of persons formed to give and to receive in this way. But as we have seen in our exposition of the vices of pride, and as we will see more clearly in the following section, human beings are prone to undermine their own happiness and fulfillment by a kind of egoism that undermines mutual affection and endangers or destroys community. Vanier is a Catholic, and his realism about these two contrary tendencies in human nature reflects his context and formation in that tradition. As Blaise Pascal notes, "The true religion must teach greatness *and* misery."[5] Though human nature as we experience it is paradoxical, the balance of the two tendencies is not ultimately equal, according to Vanier and his Church. Human nature as humble and loving is primary, and human nature as egoistic and conflictual is secondary.

L'ARCHE COMMUNITIES AS MATRICES OF HUMBLE LOVE

People who join a l'Arche community—both Core Members and Assistants—are often in retreat from typical Western secular society. Vanier writes,

> I know young couples who, tired of life and of the stress experienced in business, join l'Arche. They seek communities like ours where they can live a more humane life, with an approach to liberation from the tyranny of the Normal. They find there a life shared with persons of disability. They learn from them what is essential to life: receiving and giving, and this implies

> disciplining themselves to welcome the other who is at the same time so different and so near to themselves.[6]

The Normal is an ethos, a way of being concerned about and understanding one's life and how it is going. It is a system of concepts for construing self in relation to others against the background of these concerns and the associated understanding.[7] It is a mindset that pervades secular culture and seeps into the minds of its participants without explicit announcement. It is often presented by educational, political, and economic institutions and scholars as "common sense," as "rationality." The stealthy nature of this ethos is a feature of its tyranny; its schemas often go so unnoticed that those seeing, choosing, and acting under their influence aren't aware of their tyranny. It is, after all, the Normal. But that is not to deny that people immersed in the Normal may become disillusioned with it—more or less vaguely aware that it isn't "working" for them as a way to live. The Normal is a dehumanizing ethos, but it never succeeds in completely rooting out people's humanity. Even those who are most profoundly under its spell remain potentially accessible and susceptible to a genuine human gaze or out-reaching gesture. The young people to whom Vanier refers in the above quotation are a case in point. People's humanity, bruised and bruising as it may be by the assaults of the Normal, coexists with and resists it. Vanier is not saying that l'Arche communities are completely free of the Normal's influence nor that healthy humanity is completely absent from secular society. But in l'Arche communities, members cultivate together a heightened awareness of the perversity of the Normal to human nature, and simultaneously dedicate themselves to one another to actualize an alternative mode of life, one of mutuality. This dedication and the community it seeks to realize are never fully realized, never even close to perfection. Thus, Vanier and those in l'Arche repeatedly emphasize the messiness and difficulty of life together, and the dynamic interplay of forgiveness and celebration necessary to live it. Forgiveness recognizes the harms resulting from actions and systems still in the grip of the Normal within l'Arche. Celebration recognizes the authentic and full humanity of each human being and the emergence of this humanity as each member, with the sure support of the community's welcome and assurance of belonging, shows increasing glimpses of full mutuality. It is critical to keep this dynamic at the core of l'Arche at the very fore of this paper's account of the self-other-concept in l'Arche, and of its relation to humble love.

A person in the grip of the Normal is driven by "the desire for power, the need to appear as the best, to be recognized and appreciated" (51). He wants to possess or wield power over the other (105), to achieve, excel, prevail in competitions with others, insisting on achievement and excellence at any price (107). He wants to become "an achiever admired in other people's eyes" (76). He has "a judgmental attitude—'I'm right and you're wrong,' 'I belong to the élite, and you are poor' "—that makes it difficult to work with other people (203). It sometimes shows up in "mutual flatteries and amorous rivalries" (225). It causes people "to live in a lie, to be shut up in a culture of self-glorification by human society" (225). It is a culture of "achievement, excellence, and proper appearance" (228), of "commerce and rivalry" (225) that tends to crush the weaker members of our society. From these descriptions we can see that the tyranny of the Normal is constituted largely of the concerns and thoughts that belong to the vices of pride, and that humility will be a significant target of nurture in resisting the tyranny.

Notice that many of these features are not bad in themselves and may even be socially necessary. They are not inconsistent with humble love. Achievement, competence, success, excellence, and differential power can all be benign and not expressive of any vice. Without some of them, a distinctively human way of life would be impossible. Vanier points out that l'Arche itself, in matters of its administration, "understands itself as bringing together community life, spirituality, and a desire to be competent, successful, and professional" (233). He repeatedly says that all people need to develop their potential.[8] The criticism of competence and success is really criticism of *attitudes toward* these—in particular, the attitudes marked by the tyranny of the Normal. These goods become vices of the Normal by being turned into measures of the fundamental worth of persons. Typical concerned construals of self-other under this dictatorship include the following:

> *I am worthless if my grades don't put me in the top 25%.*
> *Well, at least I'm more successful than [so-and-so].*
> *I'm so afraid they'll find out about my past and refuse to be seen with me.*
> *If I admit how much help I got, I'll lose face.*

By Vanier's reckoning, all the understandings definitive of the vices of pride are *false*: the real value of persons is *not* conditioned on success, self-sufficiency, superiority, power over others, and the like. That is part of the explanation of their status as vices. But it is not the whole explanation. The vices warp our interpersonal relationships, undermine our eudaimonia, and darken our intellects. This is true not only for people with disabilities but also for everyone who is ruled by the tyranny of the Normal, including those marked by the Normal as "winners." Unlike the young couples so disillusioned with Western secularism that they retreat into communities like l'Arche, many people fail to realize, or realize only by vague discomfort about their lives, that something is wrong. But among those less able to satisfy the demands of the Normal, the felt need to establish their worth by achievement and superior performance translates into outright self-deprecation, psychic pain, and discouragement leading to lethargy, apathy, and depression. It "ravages the lives of people with disabilities, the aged, and many poor people" (24).

Vanier often makes the point about the universal human need for love and affirmation by referring to our infancy.

> Because the baby is loved, he isn't afraid; he doesn't need to hide himself, but is exposed, completely naked in all his vulnerability, and is happy. The mother's love, her tenderness, her sweet words, show the baby who he is: he's precious, he has value, he is somebody. (76)

The mother has the same need as the child, and the child's happy response to her expressed admiration speaks to this need:

> At the same time, his trust touches the mother's heart, and she learns from him who she is. (76)

Namely, that she too is precious and beautiful, and someone who matters.

In this developmentally early mutuality between mother and child, the tyranny of the Normal may have little influence. Her love for him may count as humble love, inasmuch as none of the concepts that shape the vices of pride infect her construals of him and herself. And the same can be said of the child's love for the mother. But as the child gets older, the noxious influence of that tyranny tends to creep in more and more, both inside and outside the family to which the child belongs.

> Then, little by little, the child grows, and he enters the world of the Normal. He needs to succeed, to get good grades, become an achiever admired in other people's eyes, and so conform to his parents' "wishes." Thus he risks losing his consciousness of being a person, formed in communion and freedom. Will he, one day, rediscover the gaze that earlier told him, "I love you as you are,

> not because of your successes; I love your abilities and your body just as they are"? (76–77)

The need for love—for belonging to someone and receiving the joy of her joy in one's existence—persists, but the spirit of the Normal has now transformed it. It is now no longer grounded in mutuality, vulnerability, and belonging, but in a quest for superior status and approval that is conditioned on performance or some other attribute such as beauty, talent, or position. The approval is no longer conceived as that of mutually belonging persons in loving communion, but now as applause, adulation, or even envy. The fact that envy can satisfy this concern underlines how far the transformation of one's need to be loved has deviated; for envy, while it is a kind of approval, is closer to enmity than it is to love.

All the attributes that the Normal makes into conditions for the importance of persons may be beneficial when they are not made into such conditions. Nevertheless, for people who have been immersed in the Normal and thoroughly indoctrinated in its values and ways, it is spiritually necessary that they be stripped, somehow, of those conditions if they are to gain what Vanier calls "life." A confrontation with death can sometimes have this effect, as can a dramatic and unavoidably perceptible moral failing, or a confrontation with the decline of old age, or some other "humbling" experience. This stripping of the conditions of worth, however, requires a context of mutual belonging and mattering; *mere* stripping will lead only to despair and shame.

THE BIRTH OF HUMBLE LOVE

Recall what Vanier said about those who, having become disillusioned with Normal life, come into a l'Arche community:

> They find there a life shared with persons of disability. They learn from them what is essential to life: receiving and giving, and this implies disciplining themselves to welcome the other who is at the same time so different and so near to themselves. (109)

These two sentences identify three essential features of the community's power to give "life" free of the constraints of the Normal: sharing life with persons of disability, receiving and giving, and disciplining themselves. Let's consider each of these dimensions of the l'Arche experience.

Sharing Life with Persons with Disabilities

Persons with intellectual disabilities have difficulty managing daily needs, including aspects of hygiene, nutrition, shelter, and earning a living income. So, they are often mischaracterized as having "no use." They have reduced powers to achieve impressive feats, to exercise power, to prevail in competitions, and to garner the admiration of others, and so they are generally excluded from elite circles and from participating in cultures of self-glorification. Their exclusion is often complete. This is why they suffer so intensely from living under the demands of the Normal. They are not easily given to the pleasures of the vices of pride but are exquisitely susceptible to their humiliations. The susceptibility indicates a need—the universal human need for communion with others that is falsified by the vices of pride and, more broadly, by the tyranny of the Normal. When an Assistant-to-be enters the l'Arche fellowship, he or she undertakes to live in a relationship of equality of value with persons who have all the need and capacity for love that any human being has but who do not typically exhibit the need in the competitive, exclusionary, and perverse ways of the Normal. So, as that new Assistant participates in the community, she learns—from the community's example and her own inclusion—to let go of the devices and desires of the vices of pride, forming a spirit of humble love.

Receiving and Giving

Participation in the community involves many things—comforting one another in times of distress, celebrating birthdays and other events together, eating together, cooking, washing dishes, doing household chores, talking about life, solving problems, playing games, etc. But in all such activities, the ethos of l'Arche encourages the construal of the activities as *receiving* and *giving*, that is, receiving *from the others* and giving *to them*, all in the context of fellowship. Vanier sometimes criticizes what he calls "generosity," and he means, among other things, a kind of giving to the poor that withholds the personal presence of the giver. The rich person "doesn't have time" to spend with the recipients of his bounty (nor feels comfortable being with them) but writes a check and is done with it. The kind of giving that characterizes l'Arche is giving *and receiving* in the close encounter of friendship; it is a giving of oneself more than anything else, and thus involves being present with the other and acknowledging the giver's neediness of attention and blessing from the other.

We can also bring out this special character of l'Arche by contrasting it with what is known as "caregiving." In the institutions from which some of the Core Members have come to l'Arche, caregivers "care" for the clients or patients and these receive the "care." In another sense, the caregivers may or may not care about the wards as persons, but in such institutions the relationship is construed as asymmetrical. The caregiver "gives" to the ward but receives nothing from him or her (instead, she receives a salary from the institution). In l'Arche, by contrast, there are no caregivers, only members. Everybody is both a receiver and a giver. A significant defect of caregiving institutions is that those "cared for" come to feel useless, passive, having nothing to give. Their fundamental human need for agency—to make a contribution to others—goes unsatisfied. So, caregiving comes to be dehumanizing. Vanier emphasizes that in a real community, everybody gives and everybody receives. He applies the biblical notion of "gift."[9] In a community, every member has a gift—something special to contribute to the life of the community—and each member receives benefits from the others.

Another contrast will bring out the relevance of l'Arche's "receiving and giving" for humble love. Aristotle expresses what seems to be a natural human intuition about receiving and giving when he tells us that the "great-souled man" (the *megalopsychos*) "is the sort of man to confer benefits, but he is ashamed of receiving them; for the one is the mark of a superior, the other of an inferior."[10] Vanier points out repeatedly that the Core Members of l'Arche—people with intellectual disabilities—are often the ones more experienced in what it means to be human and often act as transformative teachers of that humanity for the Assistants. One of the lessons they teach Assistants is that the so-called normal Assistants are themselves disabled. The great-souled person's concern to be superior to the beneficiary strikes many of us as unloving (ungenerous) as well as unhumble. An ability to receive graciously—to concede to the other, as appropriate, the pleasure of giving, and to acknowledge one's need of the other's gifts—is characteristic of a generosity in friendship that Vanier finds lacking in Aristotle's concept of this virtue.[11] Furthermore, hyperautonomy, the insistence on not being indebted to others, is one of the vices of pride. The mutual receiving and giving across the l'Arche membership—a dynamic which Assistants often say benefits them by way of moral insight and transformation far more than it benefits the Core Members—is both an expression and a support of humble love.

Self-Discipline

The third feature of the l'Arche experience is the self-discipline in humble love that members need to implement to live as community life leads, guides, and supports them. People who enter the l'Arche community have often been deeply accustomed to the norms of the Normal; it has firmly formed their dispositions of alien-making concerned perception of self and other. However dissatisfied they may have become with the tyranny of the Normal, they are still to some degree enraptured by and in servitude to it. Even when they have the presence of mind to withhold reflective endorsement from their perceptions of self-other like envy, invidious pride, vanity, and self-righteousness, they may still *see* self and other as related in those ways. So it is part of the ethos of l'Arche to *expect* that life in community will present frustrations and irritations, that these will be ongoing, that they are opportunities for growth, and that spiritual growth will very likely be a slow process. Far from being a panacea, life in the l'Arche community presents its own special problems, and among these is the discovery of painful flaws in oneself that may have been less evident under the cover of Normal life. Vanier says,

> As Martin Luther King used to say, to avoid despising others, so different from ourselves, it is indispensable that we accept ourselves, with our weaknesses and disabilities. Only then can we enter humbly and with great respect in an authentic relation of person to person, a true mutuality. It's the work of a whole life, a long and beautiful road that takes us up towards the universal and the infinite, but also down to the places of misery and filth such as we find in others and in ourselves, for God frequents the places where distress, sickness, and mud are the reigning order of things. (83)

Though the road is not easy, it is beautiful. Commenting in 2009 about the fact that l'Arche had lasted for 45 years and had grown from one to 135 communities, Vanier says,

> If people come to live at *L'Arche* and stay a month, a year, or forty years, it's because they're happy and experience pleasure. No Assistant stays here from duty, because he "ought to." None stays for the purpose of doing a "good deed." (23)

SELF-OTHER CONSTRUALS OF HUMBLE LOVE

Let's look at a couple of anecdotes to illustrate the concerned understanding of self and other (the conceptual schema) characteristic of humble compassion, respect, and friendship to see what the dynamic relation might be between these virtues and the vices of pride. The first is about a simple encounter between Vanier and a young woman visiting the abbey in which he is taking a retreat:

> A young woman who has just arrived at the abbey happens to meet me in a hallway and we exchange names, nothing more. Three days later she sees me in the dining hall and asks whether we can meet. We seat ourselves and she tells me the story of her depression. She tells me, "It was as though I had a big snake in me." A period in the psychiatric hospital, disappointment with her psychiatrist, a family conflict, a twin sister who died before birth; her whole story and her way of telling it touch me. Then she asks me who I am. "No, I'm not Belgian, but Canadian, born in Switzerland, and I studied in England." We open ourselves to one another. On parting, she says "Thank you, Mr. Vanier."—"Jean, everybody calls me Jean," I respond. She calls me by my first name, and I pronounce hers. This encounter, marked by respectful mutual trust,[12] caused a light to sparkle in me. I departed with a lighter heart, a smile on my lips, a heart full of gratitude to life. She revealed to me that I was a person, and I revealed to her

> that she was a person. This fortuitous encounter revealed life to us, and opened us to something beyond [*à un au-delà*]. (223–224)

She initiates the conversation because of some intuitive sense, born, perhaps, of their brief encounter in the hall, that Vanier can be trusted with her story: he will not use her or put her down. She wants to be heard, not as an opportunity for vain self-display, but because she wants the human communion of someone who will listen with sympathetic interest. He listens to the story of her life with genuine interest in *her*, in who she is and what she has been through, and this interest is not instrumental. He does not construe her emotions and her behavior as having some reference to himself and his importance; *she* is what is important to him in this conversation. But that self-transcendence doesn't exclude him from his construal: in seeing her as his neighbor he sees himself as her neighbor, as a fellow human being whose business, in this moment, is to be *with* her. He thinks of himself (though probably non-focally—his focus is on her) as her companion in this brief moment, as someone to accompany her through her story and reflections. This according of interest to her is gift-like, giving of himself, and in giving, he receives: "her whole story and her way of telling it touch me." She takes a like interest in his story, and a kind of mutuality supervenes: "We open ourselves to one another." Further intimacy is confirmed by his inviting her to call him by his first name, and her doing so, then his uttering hers, all sustaining the mutual interest that has marked the encounter. In their mutual generous and grateful attention, they both feel joy in being alive as human persons. And somehow, their encounter has given them both a sense of belonging to something greater and more basic than the finite world in which they live.

Our second anecdote from Vanier illustrates what is essential about l'Arche because it is about a personal encounter with a person with a disability. Vanier writes,

> Pierre, an Assistant who lives at l'Arche, told us of a magical moment, a moment of grace and transformation, that he experienced with Françoise. She's seventy-six, blind, bed-ridden, afflicted with a severe disability, unable to speak. After the meal one day she put her hand on his and smiled at him. Pierre's being became a smile. He felt—he saw—life appear suddenly from the fragile body of Françoise. At that moment, he lowered the guard-barriers of his own fear (fear of not being at a height). He no longer sought power, nor acclaim; he experienced an encounter that revealed a new meaning of life to him. (53)

The touch and smile of Françoise somehow penetrated the wall of Pierre's concerns about his superiority, his power, and his reputation—all concerns engendered by the tyrannical ethos of the Normal in which he had been so long immersed—and said to him, as it were, "I love you." And lowering the barrier guarding his self-understanding, he responded by beholding the personal loveliness of her soul. A constant theme of Vanier's thought is that people with disabilities are in a unique position to teach others about the meaning of life. They do so by teaching (by showing) the irrelevance, in questions of personal worth, of the criteria that the ethos of the Normal imposes: a person's worth as conditioned by his or her achievements, power over others, talents, competencies, education, righteousness, good looks, membership in élites, and the like.

But persons with disabilities can dissolve these features of someone's moral outlook only if they, who so notably lack such conspicuous glories, have communities of belonging and inclusion to call home, and thus have the opportunity to show themselves to be full human beings. They must be able, by their palpable humanity, to call those beguiled by competition, power, prestige, and applause to something higher and more humane. This they do, in l'Arche, by being constant companions over time, and by being persistently viewed and treated as full members just as they are. This moment of "revelation" appears to be a consequence of a perhaps rather long preparation of both Pierre and Françoise. Pierre has received instruction in the philosophy of l'Arche—the sort of teaching that we find in Vanier's writings—and has been faithfully caring for Françoise in an effort to live out this philosophy. Pierre's faithfulness and his cheerfulness in meeting her needs have made an impression on Françoise's injured consciousness; they have made inroads on her defenses. In the revelatory moment that Pierre reported, these inroads yielded her appreciative construal—a full-fledged perception—of his goodness to her, and she who had heretofore been so apparently unresponsive reached out, touched him, and smiled. Her smile and touch gave substance to the teachings, against the background of Pierre's months or years of faithful care, and yielded his appreciative construal—a full-fledged perception—of her affirmation of his own belonging and beauty. In this moment of communion, each turned away from the world of the Normal and perceived the other with the eyes of humble love.[13]

NOTES

1. Kinship as a characterization of belonging to one another is salient in the thought and work of Fr. Gregory Boyle. See his *Tattoos on the Heart* (2010).
2. MacIntyre, 1999, 160.
3. Boyle, 2010, 205.
4. These virtues of love are differentiated by applying to different situations and so implying different kinds of actions. Compassion applies where another is suffering or lacking in some way; generosity applies where we can share good things—time, energy, possessions, the benefit of a doubt—with another; gratitude applies where another has done us a favor; forgiveness applies where

another has wronged us. But all of these virtues, insofar as they are agapic, involve the same symmetrical pattern of self-other construal.

5. *Pensées* 494, http://www.gutenberg.org/files/18269/18269-h/18269-h.htm, italics added.
6. Between June 7, 2009 and August 22, 2010 Vanier exchanged letters with Julia Kristeva concerning societal approaches to problems associated with disability. Their exchange was published as *Leur regard perce nos ombres* [*Their gaze pierces our shadows*] 2011, 109. Page numbers in parentheses hereafter refer to this book. The translation is by Roberts.
7. For discussion of the notion of a concern-based construal, see Roberts, 2013, chapters 3–5.
8. See, for example, Vanier, 1998, 153.
9. See Vanier, 2001a, 50–55, where Vanier discusses I Corinthians 12 and Dietrich Bonhoeffer's *Life Together*.
10. Aristotle, 1980, book 4, chapter 3.
11. Vanier, 2001b, 184–185.
12. Note the distrust created by the vices of pride and the tyranny of the Normal. Trust is a communal virtue begotten of humility, the absence of the vices of pride. Note also the role of "name-calling" in the expression and nurture of trust. It seems that "life" and "the *au delà*" have the same referent. We are reminded of the passage in the Gospel of John where Jesus refers to himself as "the life." This helps make sense of Vanier's saying that he felt grateful *to* life. Ordinarily, one is grateful *for* life *to* someone who has saved one's life, or the divine.
13. This chapter was produced with the support of a grant from the Templeton Religion Trust by way of the Self, Motivation, and Virtue project of the Institute for the Study of Human Flourishing at the University of Oklahoma. The views expressed here are the authors' only, and not necessarily those of the Templeton Religion Trust.

REFERENCES

Aristotle. 1980. *Nicomachean Ethics*. Translated by W. D. Ross, edited by J. Ackrill and J. Urmson. Oxford: Oxford University Press.

Bonhoeffer, D. 1954. *Life Together*. New York: Harper and Row.

Boyle, Gregory. 2010. *Tattoos on the Heart: The Power of Boundless Compassion* New York: Free Press

Boyle, G. 2017. *Barking to the Choir: The Power of Radical Kinship*. New York: Simon and Schuster.

MacIntyre, A. 1999. *Dependent Rational Animals.* Chicago: Open Court.

Roberts, R. 2013. *Emotions in the Moral Life.* Cambridge: Cambridge University Press.

Vanier, J. 1998. *Becoming Human.* Mahwah: Paulist Press.

Vanier, J. 2001a. *Community and Growth.* Rev. ed. Mahwah: Paulist Press.

Vanier, J. 2001b. *Happiness, Aristotle for the New Century.* Translated by Katherine Spink. New York: Arcade.

Vanier, J., and J. Kristeva. 2011. *Leur regard perce nos ombres* [*Their gaze pierces our shadows*] Paris: Librairie Arthème Fayard.

Chapter 9

Humility and Helplessness in the Realization of Limitations within Hospice

KAY DE VRIES

INTRODUCTION

Humility has variously been associated with religiosity (Exline and Geyer, 2004), forgiveness (Sandage and Wiens, 2001; Davis et al., 2010), attention (Weil, [1951] 1973; Sandage et al., 2001; de Vries, 2004), generosity (Exline and Hill, 2012), good psychological adjustment (Tangney, 2000; Kupfer, 2003), cultural awareness (Foronda et al., 2016), and good leadership (Rego et al., 2017; Morris et al., 2005). Wuthnow (1991) and Brehony (1999) examined the lives of ordinary individuals who help and care for others in extraordinary ways, and they equate humility with compassion, generosity, courage, loyalty, mercy, forgiveness, love, honesty, faith, tolerance, altruism, and empathy. Humility may also be viewed as something of an art form, an independent order of reality where humility, so understood, requires acceptance of a mystery beyond argument, perhaps "beyond human" (Cooper, 2002, 360). Cooper proposes that humility as a traditional virtue is in accordance with and to mystery, and this requires an orientation more attitudinal than intellectual.

There has, until recently, been little empirical work carried out that has directly addressed this construct within the field of psychology. Using empirical data, Tangney (2000) lists some key features when conceptualizing humility that include an accurate sense of one's abilities and achievements; the ability to acknowledge one's mistakes, imperfections, gaps in knowledge, and limitations (often with reference to a higher power); openness to new ideas, contradictory information, and advice; and an ability to keep one's abilities and accomplishments in perspective. The range of recent definitions are generally inclusive of these key features, and Exline and Geyer (2004) summarize their conceptualization, suggesting humility involves a non-defensive willingness to see the self accurately, including strengths and limitations.

A concept of humility, as a psychotherapeutic formulation, proposed by Means et al. (1990) characterizes it in four ways: a willingness to admit one's real inadequacies; a recognition that one cannot control all interpersonal interactions; a general attitude of patience and gentleness with others; and a platform from which empathy is fostered. In the context of this chapter I will use a theoretical characterization developed by Kunz et al. (1987) drawn from a study of individuals' experiences of humility or of being humbled using dialogal phenomenological methodology.[1] The researchers concluded that the phenomenon of humility cannot be identified or grasped in its entirety; however, this depiction offers a useful foundation in the context of interpreting the experiences of staff in hospice services to which this paper refers. I will therefore utilize the following characterization throughout:

> It eludes literal interpretation. It is the mysterious ground from which words and actions speak to another. By definition, it is

> hidden from the humble person. It evokes admiration from others but cannot be managed by the humble person. Through the humbling event, humility emerges as a momentary self-acceptance from the ground of personal limitation. This is preceded by an experience of surprise, awe, and wonder. The humbled is disengaged from the trap of striving for an achievable perfection by beginning to accept his/her own imperfection. A person finds a new perspective for an understanding of his/her place in the world. Humility is manifest in compassion for others through the desire and felt-sense of responsibility to care for those in need. It is a nurturing respect for life in all its aberrant manifestation, as well as its beauty. Humility is an act of hospitality, which embraces the wounds of life's alienation and invites us into a larger, human community. (Kunz et al., 1987, 18, 19)

In this chapter I draw on the works of a number of philosophers, predominantly those of Emanuel Levinas, George Kunz, Iris Murdoch, and Simone Weil.

HOSPICE AS A LIMINAL SPACE

The formulation by Kunz et al. (1987) has congruency with the origin of the word "hospice" in proposing humility as "an act of hospitality." The term "hospice," a derivative of the Latin *hospes,* meaning "host or guest," and *hospitium,* meaning "hospitality," can be traced back to medieval times when Christian orders and monasteries welcomed travelers, thereby providing a place of shelter and rest. Because great numbers of the pilgrims were in ill health, many spent their last days there. The culture of hospice fundamentally retains historical Christian foundations and a religious presence, within which are implications of humility at a level not found in other healthcare settings. This culture suggests a model of liminality and sacredness for hospice; hospice provides a liminal space metaphorically structured to manage the process of dying (Braude, 2012; Stanworth, 2004; Lawton, 1998a, 1998b, 2000; Froggatt, 1995, 1997). These authors draw on the work of van Gennep (1960) and Turner (1969) in conceptualizing hospice as a liminal space within which death may be seen as a rite of passage. According to Van Gennep (1960) "rites of passage," or "transitions," are manifest by three phases. Separation from "what was" (detachment of the individual or group from an earlier fixed point in the social structure); margin (or threshold), where the individual passes through a cultural realm that has few or none of the attributes of the past or coming state; and aggregation, the "next," where the passage is accomplished. During this passage their behavior is normally passive or humble; they must obey their instructors implicitly and accept arbitrary penance, such as what clothes to wear, if any, and physical mutilation, without complaint (Turner, 1966). The attributes of liminality are frequently likened to death, transition, being in the womb, invisibility, traveling, the wilderness, lodging, sacred institution, and reference to the mystical (Turner, 1966). These are also posited as being features of hospice ideology. Some of the hospice value-based principles that contain these attributes of liminality are dying as a journey; crossing thresholds; a waiting room for the dying; hospice as family; hospice nurses as "ritual specialists" who control the passage of dying in various ways (Froggatt, 1995, 1997); and hospice as a symbolically protected environment (de Vries, 2006; Froggatt, 1995, 1997).

Lawton (1998a, 1998b, 2000) presents a less idealized view of liminality and hospice space, likening hospice to an abattoir where "dirty dying" occurs through sequestration of the unbounded/disintegrating body and that during the dying process the person experiences invisible suffering. This supports the premise that it is likely the so-called sacredness of hospice has become somewhat diluted and overshadowed by the medicalization of hospice care (Karsoho et al., 2016; Floriani and Schramm, 2012; McNamara and Rosenwax, 2007; Clark, 2002; James and Field, 1992; Field, 1994; Walter, 1994; Bradshaw 1996). The view that the original spiritual values have diminished and the values have become those of the medical "expert" where skills and techniques offer efficacy in treatment and suppression of conflict where death is no longer a truth to be confronted, but a process to be managed (Bradshaw, 1996), is not universally true of contemporary hospice. Medicalization of hospice has been challenged and "secularization of hospice" was the pragmatic approach taken to reconcile questions and tensions about its faith and religious orientation and relationship to medicine, and its status as a community (Clark, 1998, 2001). Clark (2001) suggests that secularization resolved the tensions between hospice as a sacred place and as a medical facility and has resulted in a model applicable in both contexts.

In a study examining the stories of 25 hospice patients and a period of participant observation, Stanworth (2004) revealed constructed metaphors that expressed patients' sources of meaning and sense of self in a non-religious language of spirit. Stanworth (2004) showed that this "spiritual" "story making" exists within contemporary hospice care and may be accessed through the attention of the silent listener. This supports Froggatt's (1995) position that a sacredness re-emerged (or had not been lost) that embraces the medical interventions where the nurses, as ritual specialists, hold the "special knowledge" of pain and symptom control. Regardless of medical interventions, hospice remains the one organization that provides an environment in which death, one of the greatest mysteries of life, is a regular and repeated occurrence. Throughout history people have repeatedly reported being humbled by death; consequently, it can be assumed that humility is present at some moments, however transient, within this environment.

Hospice is also an environment in which people suffer, often at an extreme level. On some occasions, sedation is administered not only to reduce patient suffering but also to reduce the caregivers' suffering or distress and anxiety, and those of others within the immediate environment. Particularly when cognitive impairment is present, caregivers can be "driven" to sedate or medicate patients in order to relieve the caregivers' suffering, an action that is, according to Sundararajan (1995), fundamentally a form of violation. This violation relates to the right of the Other to be inaccessible and unresponsive to treatment and the inherent difficulty we have in accepting that cure is not an option (Sundararajan, 1995). This struggle to face suffering without hope of cure is found "not in the rightness of our values or of our ethos but in a demanding alertness that intensifies our sense of suffering in the absence of its resolution or removal" (Scott, 1990, 119). The struggle to face suffering without hope of cure requires a challenging vigilance that deepens the sense of suffering in the absence of its resolution or removal.

It is the suffering and weakness of the Other that creates the ethical command that calls for the Other to be served in their need (Levinas, 1961, 1985; Kunz, 1998).[2] Levinas (1961) maintains that subjectivity is formed in and through our helplessness to attend to the Other; it is primordially ethical, not theoretical. For Levinas, ethics begins only when the Other is recognized as prior to the I, that is, our responsibility for the Other is not driven by our partiality but gives meaningful direction and orientation to our being in the world. Furthermore, once the ethical responsibility to the Other has been realized, then the ethical responsibility automatically extends to all others (Levinas, 1961, 1972, 1985, 1998; Kunz, 1998).

Kunz (1998) refers to this as the power of weakness or the power of others to inspire the caregiver (self) to an authentic freedom in the service of others: "While the others' weakness remains weak, this weakness is the source of their power" (Kunz, 1998, 157). Ramsay

(2000, 147), as a young physician, found in her response to carrying out an observation study in a hospice: "there was something much older and more powerful in the face of which modern medicine and my professional training was impotent." In other words, the "space of ethics" and the power of the vulnerability of the extremely sick and dying "solicit assistance in helpless silence" (Wyschogrod, 1992, 66). We are rendered silent by the Other's suffering; however, the struggle to respond means we care (Levinas, 1961). "The silent world is a world that comes to us from the Other . . . silence is not a simple absence of speech . . . it is the inverse of language: the interlocutor has given a sign, but has declined every interpretation; this is the silence that terrifies" (Levinas, 1961, 91). Terrifying, I suggest, fits with the definition of humility as an experience of "awe and wonder" (Kunz et al., 1987) that is beyond emotion. The powerlessness and helplessness personifies a sense of humility for the person witnessing suffering that is beyond adequate description for that person (Kunz et al., 1989) rendering them silent. As suggested earlier, they may then be predisposed to sedate the person who—in their eyes—is experiencing extreme suffering.

SELF-KNOWLEDGE OF HUMILITY AND AWARENESS OF LIMITATIONS

With most other virtues, such as courage, patience or kindness, there is little problem with self-knowledge or being aware of the virtue, but with humility this virtue is threatened by proper knowledge, especially knowledge of humility itself (Kupfer, 2003).[3] The neurological symptoms of variant CJD develop and progress extremely quickly, from deterioration of cognitive processes, memory, and concentration to the person becoming severely disorientated. They become unable to perform complex sequential tasks, have tremor and rigidity, slurred speech, swallowing difficulties, visual disturbances with possible cortical blindness, and seizures in the final stages.

> **Family Member (crying while speaking):** Watching somebody actually um, starve to death is the most horrendous, horrendous thing to watch. Someone who had been so vibrant, somebody so young. That last, that last week when everything had been taken away from her. When she couldn't hear, couldn't move, couldn't eat, when she couldn't drink, she couldn't laugh, smile, talk, listen, eyes half closed . . . and just praying she would go soon. (de Vries, 2006, 221)

The weakness of the suffering person is paradoxically powerful (Kunz, 1998). Suffering is at the heart of the paradox of the power of weakness, and the hospice teams "suffered" in the presence of the "powerful weakness" of the person with variant CJD. The dying person is not responsible for their weakness—and even more powerfully—variant CJD patients were young and were "innocent victims" of biotechnological tampering;[4] they were the "undeserving" sufferers (Kunz, 1998). Hospice staff could only guess and hope that they had managed to relieve the suffering of the patients with this disease. They were rendered helpless by the horrific nature of the symptoms and by the inability of these patients to communicate, due to the dementia component of the disease.

When, during the study mentioned above, I took the pilot findings back to the first focus group to check my interpretation, they could identify with and confirm theoretical categories of "Novelty," "Controlling" and "Becoming knowledgeable," but not that of "Humility" (de Vries, 2006). Their responses to this were "we were just doing our job," "it was the team effort," and "it was continuity of care." My interpretation of this response was that they were again demonstrating humility, as had been evident from initial interviews, in that they were understating the high standard of care provided. This provides some endorsement of the problem of self-knowledge of humility and how, when it does occur, it cannot be managed by the humble person (Kunz et al., 1987; Kupfer, 2003). That is, the humble person is rendered embarrassed and awkward and does not know how to comfortably respond to a compliment, in this case related to their care practices, consequently they downplayed their achievements.

However, lack of awareness or self-consciousness of humility does not necessarily entail ignorance of the self (Skillen, 1995). There was a "sense of self-satisfaction" about the level and standard of care that staff had provided, and this suggests pride in their work that is compatible with humility. The helplessness of the young dying person with dementia symptoms gave meaning to the caregivers' caring. The caregivers felt an inner need to care for the patient in keeping with Levinas (1972), in that the suffering and mortality of others are the responsibility and moral ethics of the self and that the "humanity of the human" is found in the acknowledgment that the other person comes first. The fact that the caregivers fulfilled their own needs by caring for the patient did not necessarily equate with self-centeredness. The importance of self-knowing and self-care have been identified as prerequisites to the ability to provide holistic, compassionate care for others (Mayeroff, 1971; Wuthnow, 1991; Brehony, 1999).

One healthcare assistant excused herself by saying, "that sounds terribly pompous" when talking about how proud she was that the patient's skin was still intact, "and part of that was due to me." Similarly, faced with recognition of their generosity, humble people acknowledge this superior status albeit with embarrassment (Skillen, 1995). The healthcare assistant felt that she had overstepped the mark just by being proud of her work, however, as Comte-Sponville (2003, 141) remarks; "Humility . . . doubts everything, particularly itself." This should not be understood as a "habit of self-effacement" but as a "selfless respect for reality" (Murdoch, 1970, 93), which requires the abandonment of excessive pride or self-confidence (Cooper, 2002) and is the mean between self-denigration and arrogance (Kupfer, 2003). Kunz (1998, 171) extends this continuum suggesting, "too much substitution of the self into service of the Other would seem slavish . . . too much sacrifice of the self's own needs would seem masochistic."

Humility "evokes admiration from others" (Kunz et al., 1987), and family members of the patients with variant CJD repeatedly expressed how wonderful the hospice was. They wanted to be interviewed so they could tell me about their experiences of "excellent" care. As one family member referred to the hospice: "it was like getting to Shangri La when we got here." The hospice as a metaphorical Shangri La (Hilton, 1933) was repeated on several occasions by this family member; describing the hospice as Shangri La echoes the ideology of the idealized model of liminality (Braude, 2012; Stanworth, 2004; Froggatt, 1995, 1997), fitting within attributes of liminality applied to sacred places such as monasteries (Turner, 1969). It is particularly interesting that this family member chose to use this term in relation to hospice, which is a place connected to death and dying, when Shangri La was a mythical place of extreme longevity and possible everlasting life. "Shangri La" provided a symbolic metaphor for the hospice, reflecting the origins of hospice and the ideology of liminality. Implicit within the symbol of Shangri La is that a space is created in which people are "living" in peace and harmony and where there is potential for everlasting life, symbolically speaking. The original philosophy of hospice as a sanctuary, a place of hospitality where dying was "cloaked" is a primary task of hospice. Families experienced the hospice as the epitome of what the organization stands for in the eyes of the public, a place of hospitality and a safe retreat, a sanctuary, being like "home" or "family" (de Vries, 2006; Froggatt, 1995, 1997).

In accordance with the Latin root of the word humility, *humus*, people who are humble have their feet planted firmly on the earth and go about their lives in a steady, level-headed way; they are earthbound and unpretentious, which keeps them from being excessively proud of their achievements (Kupfer, 2003). The staff showed an unpretentious earthbound orientation that kept them, as humble people, from being carried away with their achievements. Study participants did not claim humility. I claim it for them.

The rewards achieved by the staff link to the internal rewards of altruism (Campbell, 1984; Mayeroff, 1971; Wuthnow, 1991). Murdoch (1970, 67), takes a position in keeping with the idea of ordinariness and goodness, suggesting good is analogous to prayer but not prayer of "any quasi-religious meditative technique, but something which belongs to the moral life of the ordinary person." This supports the principle that the lives of "good," but often ordinary, people have always inspired other people (Murdoch, 1970; Wuthnow, 1990; Skillen, 1995, Brehony, 1999). In referring to people who work "selflessly" in the service of others, Kunz (1998, 4) suggests that these people "find goodness outside themselves in their clients, goodness needing help; and they respond with selfless service." He suggests that these people have replaced their egos with Others, referring to this as radical altruism. Radical altruism is a radical alternative to egoistic theories of ethics (Kunz, 1998). Egoistic theories center on the assumption that the ego is instrumental in self-initiating its good intentions and actions. However,

> [t]he radical alternative to egoistic theories of ethics points out that the neediness and worthiness of others, calls us to responsibility prior to our reason, beyond our individual desire for

> happiness, before forming any contract with others, generates the ethical command. (Kunz, 1998, 20)

There is, however, a need for large doses of self-interest in much of the practice of altruism (Mayeroff, 1971; Wuthnow, 1991), and the reward for caring is internal and comes in relation to pride in a job well done and a high degree of self-love (Skillen, 1995). The first principle of Levinas's (1961) ethical philosophy is the dignity of the Other. Levinas also forcefully states that the self can have nothing to offer the Other and cannot fulfill their responsibility to the Other if they have not nurtured themselves, as expressed by Kunz (1998, 175): "The self must set aside time, energy, and interest in order to develop itself to have something to offer to others." Levinas placed limits on the possibilities of altruism for this very reason. For example, ordinary people working in rescue services that require risk when attending to the needs of others, often without stopping to consider the consequences, or the risk to themselves, were also very well able to care for themselves (Wuthnow, 1991; Brehony, 1999). If people did not take care of themselves, they would quickly find they were unable to care for others (Wuthnow, 1991). The biblical injunction, "love your neighbor as yourself," is a practice that is a crucial element in the process of providing care (Campbell, 1984). Furthermore,

> Pride in a job well done is not pretentious, it does not distance; rather it goes with an honest awareness of what I have done and the extent of my dependence on the co-operation of others and on various conditions. There is nothing incompatible between pride, in this sense, and humility, (Mayeroff, 1971, 25)

In undertaking care of the variant CJD patients the hospice staff neither overdramatized their weaknesses nor flaunted their strengths;

they took pride in their care practices while at the same time acknowledging their limitations.

Humility requires not just an awareness of but also a willingness to honestly and appropriately acknowledge or "own" one's limitations, and the humility of knowing one's limitations is an important element of competence in healthcare practice. The hospice teams had "done the best they could," reached their limits of expertise, and were prepared to admit to this. Humility, then, is not a lack of awareness but "is the *extreme* awareness of the limits of all virtue and of one's own limits as well" (Comte-Sponville, 2003, 140;my emphasis). The weakness of the Other calls to the responsibility of the caregiver, yet the caregiver does not have the power to reduce the suffering and is humbled by this limitation where "the Other is infinitely nearby commanding help, and infinitely distant, always exceeding our total understanding and our power to control" (Kunz, 1998, 17). Consequently, the staff had disengaged from the trap of striving for an achievable perfection by beginning to accept their limitations (Kunz et al., 1987). "The needs of others are infinite, and so is my responsibility to them . . . but my capacity to meet the needs of others is finite, no matter how I suffer" (Kunz, 2002).

This "power of weakness" proposes that the experience of meeting the weakness of the Other, in this case the dying person with this new, horrific disease, moved caregivers in a way that is congruent with a concept of humility. Encountering the case of the person with variant CJD engendered "awe and surprise" (Kunz et al., 1987) and horror. The "horrific" nature of the disease was portrayed in many ways, and the following terms and phrases were found repeatedly in the data: "worst thing I've ever seen," "worst possible nightmare," "just a nightmare," "horrendous," "the most horrific disease I've ever seen," "I've never seen anything like it," and "the shock of actually seeing her."

The abject body is both fascinating and repulsively horrifying, and it is humbling to realize the precariousness of our own position and how any one of us may be one diagnosis away from the same experiences as the Other for whom we are caring (Waskul and van der Riet, 2002). Witnessing a young person displaying severe and debilitating neurological symptoms and behaviors, which are associated with dementia, was profoundly horrifying and disturbing for participants. Yet they were also profoundly respectful of and toward these patients, adhering to the definition: "humility is nurturing respect for life in all its aberrant manifestations" (Kunz et al., 1987).

COLLECTIVE HUMILITY

Humility appears to be less a personality attribute that qualifies the individual person and more of a relational quality between people, or as the context of the relation where humility "invites us into a larger, human community" (Kunz et al., 1987). Disinterested effort in work for others requires *collective humility*, in which people labor for each other in a community and for the common good (Kunz, 1998, 187), and where humility nurtures deep collegiality within teams (Wadell, 2017). I propose that the teams manifested a collective humility of this type, but that it is a paradoxical feature of hospice care and transient or "momentary" (Kunz et al., 1987); it is not present at all times. I call this paradoxical as the environment is conducive of humbling experiences through moments, events, and engagements experienced by the teams in being with, and caring for, the dying, providing care that is palliative rather than curative; while, at the same time, hospice has a medicalized and controlling function in attending to the symptoms of dying people.

Hospices are not "faith" communities, however, people of faith are drawn to them; and while people of faith are not necessarily humble, the practice of caring for the dying and bereaved within hospice engenders a collective humility that has associations with spirituality and religiosity that are not necessarily or obviously overt. The understanding of spirituality within hospice has evolved. The original religious definition of spirituality as a relationship with God or a divine other, which provided a faith tradition that served a principal function of providing an ethical underpinning and a set of core beliefs, has been replaced by a definition of spirituality as the personal and psychological search for meaning (Bradshaw, 1996). Hospice now embraces a secular humanistic approach as discussed earlier. However, the collective humility demonstrated by the team facing this new disease, does not fit easily into a religious or secular framework. An ethical framework underpinned it, where the staff were not only responsible to the Other (dying patient), they were also responsible to others within their team who shared the responsibility toward the Other:

> I must reflect not only on my responsibility, but also on the responsibility of others to other Others. I must engage in conversation and action with others to design, organize, and implement how each person's responsibility fits into the complex of responsibilities, and how we all fit together not simply to provide for the common good as the whole, but for the common good to serve the good of each individual. (Kunz, 1998, 182)

Each person is responsible for all yet cannot do it all (Kunz, 1998). Staff had no information that could assist them in providing the type of hospice care that they were familiar with and aspired to provide. They had little or no knowledge about many aspects of the symptoms and clinical progress of variant CJD; added to this were concerns that changes in the condition of the patient(s) may have been due to some fault, "whether it was something that we had or hadn't done," in their management of care, continually reminding them of their limitations. Participants were completely open about their limitations and made no pretense about having a specialized knowledge about the disease to family members. As characterized by the definition I have used to ground this discussion (Kunz et al., 1987), they experienced "momentary self-acceptance from the ground of personal limitation."

What also occurred was a powerful sense of learning from each other within the teams, including learning from family members, reflecting Murdoch (1997, 373): "Not to pretend to know what one does not know—is preparation for the honesty and humility of the scholar [practitioner] who does not even feel tempted to suppress the fact which damns his theory." Lack of knowledge about this new disease, searching for knowledge, to enable the best care for the people with variant CJD, was open, honest, and freely expressed by staff; and extensive and concerted efforts were made to find ways to manage the care of these people with excellence. This ability of the participants to admit to limitations, to not having answers, but to have demonstrated every effort to become knowledgeable about the new disease and means of managing it engendered family members' total trust of the hospice team.

The root of the word "trust" is clearly linked to truth, and trust means more than hoping to receive reciprocal support from another, but that it is mutual and requires authentic cooperation (Kunz 1998). Participants expressed that serving the families (and the patients) was a privilege of the order that they had never experienced. Within this trusting relationship the caregivers' spiritual needs were also met (Kunz, 1998), much in the manner articulated by Jean Vanier (1995, 2013) on the relationships that develop between those people with severe learning difficulties and their caregivers in the L'Arche communities (discussed in Roberts and Spezio, this volume).

The above discourse affirms the suggestion that humility is an indispensable virtue to learn or nurture for practicing with excellence, and it is impossible for healthcare practitioners to achieve excellence without nurturing the virtue of humility, both as individuals and within teams (Wadell, 2017). There was recognition that team cohesion was part of the culture of hospice care, and the desire and felt-sense of responsibility to care for those in need. I have equated the care provided by this team as a collective humility and the "radical altruism" described by Kunz (1998) discussed earlier.

The empirical evidence thus presented would suggest that humility arises from experiences in unexpected ways and that, perhaps, as a means of connecting moral theories or settling moral questions within the practicalities of life, we should—as proposed by Wyschogrod (1992)—return to such ethical studies as the reading of the narratives of saintly lives. Or, at the very least, we should revisit ethical and moral notions of caring for the dying that have been at best marginalized or at worst omitted from discourse on healthcare. In doing so, perhaps we can draw on hospice founding principles of a community that embraces religiosity, spirituality, and secular humanism and reject the prevailing ideas of rationalism and positivistic science.

CONCLUSION

Humility implies a space beyond emotion that may be momentary and transient. It is a space that is silent because there is no adequate way of expressing what is experienced, where there are no more questions that can be asked and therefore no answers to what is experienced; a place that may be even "beyond human" (Cooper 2002). Murdoch (1970) attempts to show that goodness equates with humility. That is, the sovereignty of good is congruent with humility; "the humble man . . . although he is not by definition the good man, perhaps he is the kind of man who is most likely of all to become good" (Murdoch

1997, 385), and also with love, in that good is the magnetic center toward which love naturally moves. "When true good is loved, even impurely or by accident, the quality of the love is automatically refined, and when the soul is turned towards [the] Good the highest part of the soul is enlivened" (Murdoch, 1970, 100). Murdoch asserts that goodness, over freedom and right action, should be the goal but that "right action, [and] freedom in the sense of humility, are the natural product of attention to the Good" (1970, 69). Murdoch (1970) admits to borrowing from Simone Weil and her concept of "attention" to express the idea of a just and loving gaze as a characteristic and proper mark of the active moral agent underlying things that are familiar to us in ordinary life. Weil ([1951] 1973) saw "good" as more esoteric however, proposing that good "is mysterious, and consists in non-action and in activity that does not act," similar to Levinas who asserted good as "beyond being," as irrevocably and irreversibly the obligation to responsibility that precedes freedom and non-freedom. "The passivity, unconvertible into present, is not a simple *effect* of a Good which would be reconstructed as cause of this effect; the Good *is* in this passivity, the Good that strictly speaking doesn't have to *be* and *is* not" (Levinas 1972, 54). For Weil, "activity that does not act" is commanded through attention. Here though she acknowledges the enormous difficulty in achieving true attention. "Those who are unhappy [dying] have no need for anything in this world but people capable of giving them attention. The capacity to give one's attention is a very rare and difficult thing; it is almost a miracle; it *is* a miracle" (Weil 1977, 9). For Levinas, "being-for-the-other" is based on a relationship where the essence of the self is to seek the good revealed in others, not only related to a relationship where the other is suffering. Levinas is adamant that within the interaction, as he sees it, there is no expectation of reciprocity.

Being in the presence of the overwhelming weakness of the Other took hospice professionals caring for dying people into a space and experience of complete powerlessness and helplessness that was, however, transient. I believe that the experiences described in this chapter reflect the historical and founding basis of the religiosity and spiritual focus of the hospice movement. It also, perhaps, reflects the "type" of person who is drawn to work in that setting. The ability to be present with the dying contributes to experiencing humility and fits a new paradigm of healing, focusing on care instead of cure and defining excellence in terms of humility and sensibility as opposed to power and mastery, concepts that aptly fit an exemplary form of hospice care.

NOTES

1. The historical and philosophical origins of dialogal phenomenology are based on the works of thinkers who saw the role of dialogue as central to the process of understanding and the search for truth. There is an explicit recognition that steps or procedures cannot be followed mechanically and that the dialogal and collaborative approach is more process than procedurally oriented (see Halling and Leifer, 1991; Halling et al., 1994).
2. Levinas refers to the Other in this manner in reference to the irreducible alterity (philosophical and anthropological term meaning "otherness") of the other—over the irruption of the Other that permits access to the absolute. He takes the same approach when referring to good. Murdoch (discussed later in the chapter) also refers to good in this manner, although it is unclear whether she attributes good with the absolute at the level at which Levinas does.
3. CJD belongs to a group of diseases known as transmissible spongiform encephalopathies (or prion disease) that are known to occur in both humans and animals. It is widely accepted that variant CJD is the result of contamination from bovine spongiform encephalopathy (BSE), a prion disease of cattle, and was classified a "new" disease. The BSE (mad cow disease) epidemic that occurred in in the UK in the mid-1980s originated from animals consuming feed that was contaminated with scrapie, a sheep prion disease.
4. The believed mode of transmission of variant CJD speaks of a pollution of a kind that attacks the young through the innocent act of, for example, eating a hamburger. The mode of infection for variant CJD and the age of those infected fits with the premise that some individuals do not necessarily experience stigma, such as "innocent victims of HIV," i.e., hemophiliacs and babies who

have acquired HIV through blood produces or maternal transmission (Sontag, 1988). The biotechnology that caused the BSE crisis is an example of the manufactured risk identified in discussions about political, technological, cultural, and economic globalization.

REFERENCES

Brehony, K. A. 1999. *Ordinary Grace: An Examination of the Roots of Compassion, Altruism, and Empathy, and the Ordinary Individuals Who Help Others in Extraordinary Ways*. New York: Riverhead Books.

Braude, H. 2012. "Normativity unbound: Liminality in palliative care ethics." *Theoretical Medicine and Bioethics*, 33, 107–122. doi 10.1007/s11017-011-9200-2.

Bradshaw, A. 1996. "The spiritual dimension of hospice: The secularisation of an ideal." *Social Science & Medicine*, 43, 409–419.

Campbell, A. V. 1984. *Moderated Love: A Theory of Professional Care*. London: Society for Promoting Christian Knowledge.

Clark, D. 1998. "Originating a movement: Cicely Saunders and the development of St Christopher's Hospice, 1957–1967." *Mortality*, 3(1), 43–63. doi:10.1080/713685885.

Clark, D. 2001. "Religion, medicine, and community in the early origins of St. Christopher's Hospice." *Journal of Palliative Medicine*, 4(3), 353–360.

Clark, D. 2002. "Between hope and acceptance: The medicalisation of dying." *British Medical Journal*, 324, 905–907.

Comte-Sponville, A. 2003. *A Short Treatise on the Great Virtues: The Use of Philosophy in Everyday Life*. London: Vintage.

Cooper, D. E. 2002. *The Measure of Things: Humanism, Humility, and Mystery*. Oxford: Clarendon Press.

Davis, D. E., J. A. Hook, E. L. Worthington, D. R. Van Tongeren, A. L. Gartner, and D. J. Jennings. 2010. "Relational spirituality and forgiveness: Development of the Spiritual Humility Scale SHS." *Journal of Psychology and Theology*, 38(2), 91–100.

de Vries, K. 2004. "Humility in nursing practice." *Nursing Ethics*, 11(6), 577–586.

de Vries, K. 2006. "Caring for the person with variant Creutzfeldt-Jakob disease within the hospice service." PhD diss., University of Surrey, London.

Exline, J. J., and A. L. Geyer. 2004. "Perceptions of humility: A preliminary study." *Self and Identity*, 3(2), 95–114. doi.org/10.1080/13576500342000077.

Exline, J. J., and P. C. Hill. 2012. "Humility: A consistent and robust predictor of generosity." *Journal of Positive Psychology*, 7(3), 208–218. doi.org/10.1080/17439760.2012.671348.

Field, D. 1994. "Palliative medicine and the medicalization of death." *European Journal of Cancer Care, 3*, 58–62.

Floriani, C. A., and F. R. Schramm. 2012. "Routinization and medicalization of palliative care: Losses, gains and challenges." *Palliative & Supportive Care, 10*(4), 295–303. doi.org/10.1017/S1478951511001039.

Foronda, C., D. L. Baptiste, M. M. Reinholdt, and K. Ousman. 2016. "Cultural humility: A Concept analysis." *Journal of Transcultural Nursing, 27*(3), 210–217. doi: 10.1177/1043659615592677.

Froggatt, K 1995. "Keeping the balance: Hospice work, death and emotions." PhD diss., South Bank University, London.

Froggatt K. 1997. "Rites of passage and the hospice culture." *Mortality, 2*(2), 123–136.

Halling, S., and M. Leifer. 1991. "The theory and practice of dialogal research." *Journal of Phenomenological Psychology, 22*(1), 1–15.

Halling, S., G. Kunz, and J. O. Rowe. 1994. "The contributions of dialogal psychology to phenomenological research." *Journal of Humanistic Psychology, 34*(1), 109–131. doi:10.1177/00221678940341007.

Hilton, J. 1933. *Lost Horizon*. London: Macmillan.

James, N., and D. Field. 1992. "The routinization of hospice: Charisma and bureaucratization." *Social Science and Medicine, 34*(12), 1363–1375.

Karsoho, H., J. R. Fishman, D. K. Wright, and M. E. Macdonald. 2016. "Suffering and medicalization at the end of life: The case of physician assisted dying." *Social Science & Medicine, 170*, 188–196.

Kunz, G. 1998. *The Paradox of Power and Weakness*: Albany: State University of New York Press.

Kunz, G. 2002. "Simplicity, humility, patience." In *Levinas, Ethics and the Practice of Psychology*, edited by E. E. Gantt and R. N. Williams, 118–142. Pittsburgh, PA: Duquesne University Press.

Kunz, G., D. Cligaman, R. Kortsep, B. Kugler, and M. Park. 1987. "A dialogal phenomenological study of humility." Paper presented at the Sixth International Human Science Research Conference. University of Ottawa, Canada, May 28.

Kupfer, J. 2003. "The moral perspective of humility." *Pacific Philosophical Quarterly, 84*, 249–269.

Lawton, J. 1998a. The Disintegration of Self: A Study of Patients in a Day Care Service and a Hospice in England. PhD Thesis. Cambridge: University of Cambridge.

Lawton, J. 1998b. "Contemporary hospice care: the sequestration of the unbounded body and 'dirty dying.'" *Sociology of Health and Illness, 20*(2), 121–143.

Lawton, J. 2000. *The Dying Process: Patients' Experience of Palliative Care*. London: Routledge.

Levinas, E. 1961. *Totality and Infinity*. Translated by Alphonso Lingis. Pittsburgh, PA: Duquesne University Press.

Levinas, E. 1972. *Humanism of the Other*. Translated by Nidra Poller. Urbana and Chicago: University of Illinois Press.

Levinas, E. 1985. *Ethics and Infinity*. Translated by Richard A. Cohen. Pittsburgh, PA: Duquesne University Press.

Levinas, E. 1998. *Otherwise than Being: Or Beyond Essence*. Translated by Alphonso Lingis. Pittsburgh, PA: Duquesne University Press.

Mayeroff, M. 1971. *On Caring.* Translated by Alphonso Lingis. London: Harper and Row.

McNamara, B., and L. Rosenwax, 2007. "The mismanagement of dying." *Health Sociology Review, 16*(5), 373–383.

Means, J. R., G. L. Wilson, C. Sturm, J. E. Biron, and P. J. Bach. 1990. "Theory and practice: humility as a psychotherapeutic formulation." *Counseling Psychology Quarterly, 3*, 211–215.

Morris, J. A., C. M. Brotheridge, and J. C. Urbanski. 2005. "Bringing humility to leadership: Antecedents and consequences of leader humility." *Human Relations, 58*(10), 1323–1350. doi.org/10.1177/0018726705059929.

Murdoch, I. 1970. *The Sovereignty of Good*. London: Routledge.

Murdoch, I. 1997. *Existentialists and Mystics: Writings on Philosophy and Literature*. London: Chatto and Windus.

Ramsay, N. 2000. "Sitting close to death: A palliative care unit." In *Observing Organisations: Anxiety, Defence and Culture in Health Care,* edited by R. D. Hinshelwood and W. Skogstad, 142–151. London: Routledge.

Rego, A., B. Owens, S. Leal, A. I. Melo, M. P. Cunha, L. Gonçalves, and P. Ribeiro. 2017. "How leader humility helps teams to be humbler, psychologically stronger, and more effective: A moderated mediation model." *Leadership Quarterly, 28*(5), 639–658.

Sandage, S. J., and Wiens, T. W. 2001. "Contextualizing models of humility and forgiveness: A reply to Gassin." *Journal of Psychology and Theology, 29*(3), 201–211.

Sandage, S. J., T. W. Wiens, and C. M. Dahl. 2001. "Humility and attention: The contemplative psychology of Simone Weil." *Journal of Psychology and Christianity, 20*(4), 360–369.

Scott, C. E. 1990. *The Question of Ethics: Nietzsche, Foucault, Heidegger*. Bloomington: Indiana University.

Skillen, A. 1995. "Can a good man know himself?" *Philosophical Investigations, 18*(2), 151–155.

Sontag, S. 1988. *Aids and Its Metaphors.* London: Penguin Books.

Stanworth, R. 2004. *Recognising Spiritual Needs in People Who Are Dying.* Oxford: Oxford University Press.

Sundararajan, L. 1995. "Patient as the Other." *Humanistic Psychologist, 23*, 53–70.

Tangney, J. P. 2000. "Humility: Theoretical perspectives, empirical findings and directions for future research." *Journal of Social and Clinical Psychology, 19*(1), 70–82.

Turner, V. 1966. *The Ritual Process: Structure and Anti-Structure*. New York: Cornell University Press.

Turner, V. 1969. *The Ritual Process: Structure and Anti-Structure*. London: Penguin Books, Random House.

Vanier, J. 1995. *An Ark for the Poor: The Story of L'Arche*. Toronto: Novalis.

Vanier, J. 2013. *The Heart of L'Arche: A Spirituality for Everyday Life*. London: SPCK.

van Gennep, A. 1960. *The Rites of Passage*. Translated by Monika B. Vizedome and Gabrielle L. Caffee. London: Routledge and Kegan Paul.

Wadell, P. J. 2017. "Humility: An indispensable virtue to learn for practicing with excellence." *Health Progress*, 52–56. www.chausa.org.

Walter, T. 1994. *The Revival of Death*. London: Routledge.

Waskul, D. D., and P. van der Riet. 2002. "The abject embodiment of cancer patients: Dignity, selfhood, and the grotesque body." *Symbolic Interactionism*, 25(4), 487–513.

Weil, S. (1951) 1973. *Waiting on God*. Translated by E. Craufurd. New York: Harper and Row.

Weil, S. 1977. *The Simone Weil Reader*. Edited by G. A. Panichas. New York: Moyer Bell.

Wuthnow, R. 1991. *Acts of Compassion: Caring for Others and Helping Ourselves*. Princeton, NJ: Princeton University Press.

Wyschogrod, E. 1992. "Who is Emmanuel Levinas?" *Sh'ma: A Journal of Jewish Responsibility*, 22(429), 65–67.

Chapter 10

Humility in Competitive Contexts

MICHAEL W. AUSTIN*

INTRODUCTION

Among philosophers, humility has its share of skeptics. Aristotle, for example, does not include it in his catalogue of virtues. David Hume pejoratively describes humility as a "monkish" virtue (Hume, 1983, 73–74). And contemporary philosopher Tara Smith argues that pride, rather than humility, is a virtue (Smith, 2005, 90–116). Others, however, have defended different conceptions of humility as a virtue, in both religious and secular forms (Austin, 2018; Boyd, 2014; Byerly, 2014; Garcia, 2006; Richards, 1992). I will not defend the more general claim that humility is a virtue. Rather, I will argue that it is an apt trait for competitive contexts. This is important because one might think that humility is a virtue in some realms of life but not others, and it is likely that competitive contexts are included in the latter realms for the skeptic. In what follows, I will first describe a particular conception of the virtue of humility. I will then

* I would like to express my appreciation to Jennifer Cole Wright, Nancy Snow, and the participants at the conference, "Humility: Its Nature and Function," October 2016 (sponsored by the Institute for the Study of Human Flourishing at the University of Oklahoma), for the helpful questions, insights, and suggestions which helped to improve this chapter.

discuss some possible problems that arise when we consider how this trait might function in competitive contexts by examining how humility is an apt trait for the competitive realms of sport, business, and academia.

DEFINING HUMILITY

Contemporary philosopher Tara Smith thinks of humility as something akin to self-denigration, as an irrational view in which an individual takes herself to have very little value. On this view, the humble person does not desire much, has little ambition, and projects a belittling self-image to other people. She makes do with as little as she can and has a low estimate of her self-worth (Smith, 2005, 97–98). However, humility can and should be understood in other ways. I believe we should think of humility as lying on an Aristotelian mean between the deficient trait of self-denigration and the excessive trait of egoistic pride.

On the intuitive conception of humility that I favor, this virtue includes both *proper self-assessment* and a *self-lowering other-centeredness* (Austin, 2012). The term "proper" here refers to both the *accuracy* of one's self-assessment and *the level of concern* with such assessment that the humble person possesses. The humble person tends not to inflate his own importance, abilities, or character. Nor does he expend excessive time or effort thinking about them.

The second aspect of this intuitive definition—a self-lowering other-centeredness—captures the dispositions that the humble person possesses concerning others. The humble individual will have a prima facie tendency to place the interests of others before her own. This involves particular kinds of preferential judgments, desires, and actions concerning others and one's relationship to them. The humble person will be disposed to place the interests of others ahead of her own, as is appropriate given the circumstances. This does not require self-abasement or an irrational disregard for her interests in the context of interpersonal relationships. The humble person need not *always* place the interests of others ahead of her own, but she is disposed to do so as is appropriate, given the circumstances and dictates of prudence. This disposition is not a moral maxim that all must follow in all circumstances, but rather a disposition that the ideally humble person possesses and is able to rightly express as the virtue of prudence dictates in the relevant circumstances for such expression.

Other-centeredness does not solely refer to other persons. It refers also to nonhuman animals, the natural world, and other entities that have value. It also can refer to moral ideals such as justice and compassion. The idea is that the humble person is turned outward, away from herself toward other creatures and values that merit her attention and focus. Related to this, Joseph Kupfer's account of humility includes the claims that it (i) "orients individuals to objectively worthwhile things in the world," and (ii) "involves appreciating and promoting the value of things apart from their significance for our own interests and needs" (Kupfer, 2003, 253). Similarly, Dietrich von Hildebrand argues that humility fundamentally includes a response to value. He says that for the humble person "[t]he inward nobility of good, its intrinsic beauty, touches his heart and delights him. In his devotion to the good, he participates in the harmony of values; his soul is bright and serene, free from the corrosive poison that eats at the heart of the proud" (Hildebrand, 1997, 18). A humble person, then, appreciates objectively valuable elements of reality, such as the beauty of the natural world, artistic and scientific achievements, moral values (e.g. justice), moral virtues (e.g. compassion), or God. Other objectively valuable things mentioned by Kupfer include family, community, and work. These goods transcend our own narrow self-interests. The humble person not only appreciates such goods, but she is also motivated to serve or advance them through her actions.

In order to clarify what a more fine-grained definition of humility might include, consider the conceptualizations of this trait that are present in some recent work in psychology. One contemporary psychological model of personality structure—the HEXACO model—includes the claim that there are six major dimensions of personality, one of which is Honesty-Humility (Ashton and Lee, 2007). The inclusion of the category of Honesty-Humility as one of the major dimensions of personality structure is justified by several empirical findings concerning the link between these two traits (Ashton and Lee, 2007, 161). For my purposes, I will focus on the conception of humility employed by the model (Lee and Ashton, 2012). People who score high on the Honesty-Humility factor of personality avoid exploiting, manipulating, or deceiving others. They do not possess a sense of entitlement relative to taking advantage of others, nor do they want comparatively more than other people.

Several other conceptual components of humility can be found in psychological explorations of this trait (Exline and Hill, 2012). Contrary to what many hold, humility does not include nor does it imply low self-esteem or a lack of assertiveness. In a summary of some of the psychological literature on humility, Julie Exline and Peter Hill state that it includes "an orientation toward others . . . a non-defensive willingness to see the self accurately, including strengths and limitations . . . the ability to acknowledge mistakes, imperfections, gaps in knowledge . . . openness to new ideas . . . keeping one's abilities and accomplishments in perspective; low self-focus or an ability to 'forget' the self; and an appreciation of the value of all things" (Exline and Hill, 2012, 208). We can formulate an analysis of humility grounded in the intuitive definition offered above as well as the understandings of humility that are operational in contemporary psychology. As is evident from the above, humility can be seen as having both self-regarding and other-regarding elements. That is, some aspects of this trait are focused on the self, while other aspects are concerned with our relationships to other people as well as other things of value in the world.

I now propose the following as central elements of a definition of the virtue of humility. While I do not argue for this conception of humility here, this is at least one plausible way of understanding what constitutes this virtue. This is sufficient for my present aim, namely, to argue that on a particular plausible understanding of the virtue, humility is an apt trait for competitive contexts. Consider the following claims about the nature of humility:

(H1) Humility includes proper self-focus and accurate self-assessment.
(H2) Humility disposes its possessor, prima facie, to put the interests of others ahead of her own.
(H3) Humility involves an accurate recognition of and a proper response to objective value in the world.

Given this understanding of the virtue of humility, is it an apt trait for human beings as we interact in competitive contexts?

WHAT DOES IT MEAN FOR HUMILITY TO BE "AN APT TRAIT FOR COMPETITIVE CONTEXTS"?

For a trait to be *apt* for competitive contexts, it must function such that it helps enable one to pursue and perhaps obtain the ends of such contexts. It is important to note that the aims of competitive contexts tend to be pluralistic. For example, in sport the aims might include winning, demonstrating moral and athletic excellence, a display of beauty, or cultivating character. In philosophy (and ideally the academy more generally), one's aims might include the acquisition of knowledge, the cultivation of intellectual and moral virtue, obtaining a grant to fund one's research, or exemplifying forms of human excellence. It seems to me that humility is apt for achieving such ends. I will explore some ways in which this is the case in what follows.

There is a feature of humility that is especially relevant for competitive contexts and supports the claim that it is an apt trait for them. One implication of (H1) is that the humble person will have a proper lack of concern about how others view her. There are times when concern for what others think is proper and even virtuous. For example, one may rightly be concerned about a misunderstanding of one's intentions or motives, when they are good but misperceived as wrong or selfish. However, the humble person will tend not to be concerned—or to have a very low concern—about how others regard her and especially her status (Roberts and Wood, 2003, 261–263). With this in mind, we can see that potential barriers to engaging in certain forms of risk-taking are removed. Pride, by contrast, can erect barriers to taking risks that one might otherwise take. The arrogant and self-centered person may suffer from a form of insecurity that prevents him from risking failure in the eyes of others, whereas the humble person will be less prone to such insecurity. Humility, then, can motivate and strengthen both proper ambition and risk-taking. Consider the fact that many people fail to embark upon an ambitious path in some aspect of life because they fear failure. Often, part of this fear is grounded in a concern with what others will think of them if they fail. For example, someone might strongly want to play soccer in college, but fear that she does not have what it takes to succeed. One reason that such a person might not embark on this path is that she fears what others will think of her if she fails to reach this goal. Humility, however, frees her from this concern, because she truly does not care that others might consider her a failure of some sort if she is unsuccessful. Humility can be conducive to risk-taking and proper ambition because it removes a prominent barrier to both, namely, being overly concerned about what other people think. Humility can play another important role in such situations. Recall (H1), which includes the claim that humility involves accurate self-assessment. Given this, humility includes an important form of self-knowledge in such circumstances related to our own abilities. Humility can undermine unreasonable fears of failure if one has a justified belief or even knowledge that one has the relevant capacities conducive to success. If the foregoing is correct, then humility becomes a very useful virtue for competitive contexts. It might be argued, however, that humility is not apt for such contexts. In the next section, I consider and reject this claim.

HUMILITY AND COMPETITIVENESS: A CONFLICT?

Jan Boxill observes that competition is "[o]ne of the most controversial features of our society. It is condemned by Marxists, championed by capitalists, deemed a necessary evil in education, and is necessary to and dramatized in sport" (Boxill, 2014, 343). Some believe that competition produces excellence, while others claim that it produces unnecessary tension at best and significant harm at worst. Alfie Kohn, a prominent critic of competition, argues that it is harmful and does not promote excellence, contra the claims of its defenders (Kohn, 1987). Kohn offers several criticisms of the claim that competition is a good. For instance, he argues that competition is harmful to our self-esteem because it encourages us to define our value as persons by what we have accomplished, or failed to accomplish, particularly with respect to our victories and defeats in competitive contexts (e.g. the classroom, the office, the playing field). Kohn also claims that competition teaches us to see others as obstacles to our own success, which creates interpersonal hostility. If competition is a necessary evil, and if it is harmful and fails to yield excellence, then it seems there are good reasons for skepticism concerning the claim that humility is a trait that is well suited for competition. I will discuss this in more detail below. First, consider a deeper and closely related problem, namely that there is a *conflict* between humility and competition. More specifically, one might think that the trait of humility conflicts with the trait of competitiveness. If this is so, then the humble person should either avoid competition or set humility aside when she enters competitive situations.

Historically, it appears that humility did not appear in some catalogues of virtues at least in part because it was not thought to be apt for competitive contexts, such as war, sport, politics, drama, or philosophical argumentation (MacIntyre, 1984, 131–145). Alasdair MacIntyre claims not only that humility does not appear in any Greek list of the virtues but also that it could not do so (MacIntyre, 1984, 136). This is so because the *agon,* or contest, plays a central role in classical Greek society. Virtues such as courage were prized in that context. MacIntyre observes that the character of the *agon* changes over time. First, the contest of war is suspended in order to create time and space for the contest of the Olympic Games. This periodic suspension of war between Greek city-states yields a way of contrasting a Greek from a barbarian. Greeks are members of a city-state entitled to attend the Olympic Games, whereas barbarians have no such right. The *agon* also changes its form within city-states. Here, the contest arises in the debates that occur in political assemblies and courts of law (politics), the plotlines of comedies (drama), and philosophical argumentation in the form of dialogue (philosophy). For MacIntyre, it is crucial to understand that "the city-state and the *agon* provide the shared contexts in which the virtues are to be exercised" (MacIntyre, 1984, 138). These contexts inform how people conceive of the virtues as well as what traits end up on the relevant catalogue of virtues. However, one can agree with these points—that context informs one's conception of virtue and which traits count as virtues—without following the ancient Greeks in their rejection of humility as a virtue suitable for competitive contexts. In order to see why humility might not be apt for competitive contexts, it will be helpful to achieve some clarity with respect to the nature of the trait of competitiveness.

In a brief discussion of competitiveness, Robert Adams argues that even if it is a generally beneficial trait, it does not follow that competitiveness is a virtue (Adams, 2006, 55–56). Adams argues that competitiveness, as it is normally understood, is not a moral excellence for human beings. It does not help make one a morally good individual. On his conception of competitiveness (which is similar to the Greek view elucidated by MacIntyre), it can include hostility to the interests of others and a desire to do better than they. Adams claims that the desire to do *well* is virtuous, but the desire to do *better than others* is not. For him, competitiveness includes the desire that others "do less well," and this is "hardly a mark of a virtue" (Adams, 2006, 56). A similar understanding of competitiveness is present in the work of Kohn, who makes a distinction between structural competition and intentional competition (Kohn, 1986, 3–5). Structural competition is exemplified in a situation where there are one or more winners and one or more losers. The success of some requires the failure of others. Intentional competition has to do with the attitudes of individuals. A person may desire to do better than others, that is, be intentionally competitive, whether or not a structural competition exists. An athlete may have the desire to defeat her opponent in a 100-meter race (structural and intentional competition). Another individual may try to prove he is the most intelligent person at the faculty meeting (intentional but not structural competition). Both of these aspects of competition are relevant as we consider the virtue of humility within competitive contexts. A context might be competitive because of the structure or the intentions of the relevant persons, or both. In any of these cases, the trait of competitiveness may play a role.

Competitiveness, then, on the common understanding Adams discusses and Kohn criticizes, can be conceived of as follows:

(C1) Competitiveness includes the desire to do better than others.
(C2) Competitiveness includes particular forms of hostility to the interests of others, in certain contexts.

If this is correct, then there is not only a conflict but also a contradiction between the trait of competitiveness and the virtue of humility. First, there is a tension between (H1) and (C1). The humble person, according to (H1), will have a proper level of self-focus that will often mean a low level of self-focus and even a tendency to forget herself. It is perhaps unclear how this can be true of a person who also has the desire to do better than others, as (C1) claims will be true of the competitive person. (C1) involves a degree of focus on the self in comparison to others that at least initially seems in conflict with (H1). Second, and more problematically, (H2) and (C2) appear to contradict one another. On (H2), the humble person will tend to put the interests of others ahead of her own, while on (C2) the competitive person will be hostile toward the interests of others. Concern for and hostility toward the interests of others are contradictory dispositions. If this is so, then surely humility is not an apt trait for competitive contexts.

RESOLVING THE CONFLICT: HUMILITY IN THE CONTEXT OF SPORT

There are numerous ways in which one might address this conflict. One could simply accept that humility is incompatible with competitiveness and therefore accept that it is not apt for competitive contexts. Alternatively, one could redefine humility in such a way that no conflict between it and competitiveness arises, perhaps by conceiving of it as a purely self-regarding virtue having to do with self-knowledge. A third possibility, the one that I pursue here, is to conceive of competitiveness and the nature of competition in such a way that the conflict with humility is resolved. This is promising in part because the foregoing definition of competitiveness that gives rise to the conflict is flawed. It also clarifies some of the ways in which humility is an apt trait for competition in general and competitive sport in particular.

In order to resolve the conflict between humility and competitiveness, I will offer a different understanding of the trait of competitiveness than the one Adams employs. While I agree with Adams that this is the way many normally think of this trait, the competitive person need not be hostile to the interests of others. Nor need he have the narrow desire to do *better than* others in order to compete *well*. For example, he might focus on pursuing excellence over and above (or rather than) merely doing better than his opponent.

Before considering these issues in the context of sport, it seems to me that the tension between (H1) and (C1) could potentially be resolved in a straightforward way. Perhaps what is proper, as (H1) prescribes, in certain competitive contexts is to have the requisite level of focus on one's own performance that enables one to attempt to compete well. That is, one might desire to do better than others in a competitive context without having an improper type or amount of self-focus. For now, I merely raise this as a possible way to resolve the tension between (H1) and (C1). In what follows, I focus on reconceiving competition and competitiveness in order to harmonize humility and competitiveness, as well as show how humility is apt for competitive contexts.

In order to see another way in which competitiveness can be conceived, consider the context of sport. Many coaches, athletes, and fans think of competition as a battle and operate with a conception of competitiveness much like that Adams describes. But according to David Shields, those who think of competition in this way are not thinking about true competition but rather *decompetition* (Shields and Bredemeier, 2011). Decompetition is a devolvement of true competition, and as such is its opposite. Its basic guiding metaphor is warfare, and so opponents are enemies. In decompetition, the motive is something extrinsic to the game: fame, wealth, or egoistic feelings of superiority. The goal is victory via dominating one's opponent, and the emotions that come with the conquest of that opponent. The point is to win by whatever process will deliver a victory. However, there are other ways of thinking about the nature of competition, or what Shields calls true competition. Shields points out that the root meaning of competition from its Latin origin is "to strive with"—not "against." Competitors strive with each other to achieve excellence. The basic metaphor of true competition is that of partnership. Each competitor needs the other in order to pursue and hopefully achieve excellence. True competition, then, is a form of cooperation. True competitors are motivated by their love for the game and their desire to achieve excellence according to its rules and standards. The goal is developing and displaying excellence, and to experience the joy, hope, and excitement that accompany strenuous play. True competitors still value winning and seek victory, but what has greater value is the process itself. They value winning, and they see sport as serious play. The play element is not lost on them. Winning matters, but it is not everything. When athletes in a competition approach it in this manner, they have the potential to exemplify (H2). Rather than cheating to win, for example, they embrace the process so that they and their opponents can pursue excellence together. For instance, an elite athlete could exemplify (H2) by refusing to seek an advantage via performance-enhancing drugs, motivated in part by her concern for fair competition. She is willing to sacrifice a better chance at victory and the external goods it might bring to her in part because to seek such an unfair advantage is selfish. She exemplifies (H2) when she sacrifices her interests in acquiring such goods in order to provide a fair competition to her opponent. Shields's views about the nature of true competition are reflected in some recent work in the philosophy of sport that will help us see how humility is consistent with competitiveness and apt for competitive contexts.

For example, consider one recent attempt to resolve the conflict between competitiveness and humility from philosopher of sport Eric Gilbertson, who distinguishes virtuous and vicious forms of the trait of competitiveness (Gilbertson, 2016). Gilbertson observes that on some understandings, competitiveness simply amounts to the desire to win or be better than others at some activity or pursuit. He rejects this analysis, and he observes that it is at least possible that a competitive person may be such by virtue of enjoying competition, or perhaps "in terms of her desire for meaningful competition among worthy competitors (who perform at or near their best)" (Gilbertson, 2016, 412). The virtuous competitor, for Gilbertson, respects the game and those she competes against. She displays the appropriate level of modesty with respect to her own talents and abilities and is willing to face adversity and lose (but does so with humility). The vicious competitor, however, has such a strong desire to win that it "overwhelms other attitudes, such as the desire to win fairly or legitimately, and the belief that loss or failure does not necessarily mean that one has failed to do one's best" (Gilbertson, 2016, 416–417).

Given this, Gilbertson would reject both (C1) and (C2) as elements of what it means to be competitive. If this is correct, then this is one way to harmonize humility with competitiveness. On this solution, the tension between humility and competitiveness, particularly between (H1) and (C1), is resolved by rejecting (C1) as a proper analysis of competitiveness. I prefer a different approach that includes the claim that (C1) is true but rejects the idea that it must be vicious—thereby rejecting (C2)—by conceiving of sport in a particular manner. In order to see how this might work, consider that at one point in his paper, Gilbertson states that the virtuous competitor "is not primarily concerned with defeating her opponents, but rather with challenging, and being challenged by, them, in the interest of developing her competitor's capabilities as well as her own" (Gilbertson, 2016, 419). This view of the virtuous competitor fits very well with Robert Simon's influential conception of sport, in which he takes it to be a cooperative activity. He argues that competition in sport is best thought of as *a mutual quest for excellence through challenge* (Simon, 2003). On this view, sport is a cooperative venture marked by the pursuit of excellence rather than a combative quest for dominance. For Simon, athletes ought to compete in a cooperative manner. If they do, part of their motivation for seeking victory is not only to bring out the best in themselves but also in their opponent. This approach presupposes respect for persons, which includes respecting their interests. Each athlete needs her opponent to pursue excellence, because this supports her in her own pursuit of excellence. In so doing, they provide a challenge to each other in a way that fosters both of their interests in cultivating athletic excellence in their sport. In these ways, athletic competition is cooperative, and one can be a competitive athlete in ways that are consistent with (H2) and (H3).

A different way of harmonizing humility with competitiveness has to do with the actual implications of (C1) and (C2) in the context of sport. It is not clear that they pose a problem for the claim that humility is an apt virtue for sport. Consider (C1). It is not clear to me that seeking to do better than someone else is necessarily morally suspect, as Adams maintains. For example, if two elite cyclists are competing against one another in the Tour de France, and each believes that he is truly the best, then one function of the competition is to provide evidence for or against that belief. It seems at least consistent with moral goodness as well as the virtue of humility to seek to demonstrate one's greater level of excellence via athletic competition by trying to do better than one's opponent if the end is not mere victory. If other ends are also in play, including realizing one's own excellence, cooperatively fostering the excellence of one's opponent, and ideally revealing the truth about who is in fact the better cyclist, then this is not only consistent with humility but also potentially indicative of it. Part of the function of athletic competition is to ascertain what is true with respect to the abilities and performances of the athletes. This may exemplify humility, in particular (H3), as the competitors and others gain such knowledge. In addition, having this knowledge is in the interests of both competitors, in a manner that is consistent with (H2). Of course, the loser will not enjoy losing, and in fact may find it very unpleasant, but he nevertheless may enjoy the competition itself. And this lack of enjoyment does not entail that losing is not in his interests, if the loss is an accurate reflection of the relative abilities of the competitors and their performances on the day (and perhaps even when it is not).

I reject the assumption that seeking to defeat and in fact defeating one's opponent is not in their interests. Losing is sometimes in one's interests. As noted above, it can give one a more accurate self-assessment, and, in this way, it can support the cultivation of humility, that is (H1). Moreover, losing can yield the opportunity for cultivating other virtues like persistence, courage, modesty, patience, and certain forms of practical wisdom. A loss can foster moral growth and athletic excellence as it motivates one to improve, to become more excellent. Given the potential results of both moral growth and a continued or even more determined pursuit of athletic excellence as responses to losing, seeking to defeat an opponent can be consistent with (H2). There are goods to be had via one's response to losing.

One objection to the above is that talk of the pursuit of excellence in sport (or the public good in business or justice in politics) is that these more lofty ideals are mere window dressing. The actual aim is to defeat everyone else using the tools that will secure this goal, such as money, manipulative rhetoric, cunning strategy, power, cheating, and intimidation. As Robert Roberts puts it, "the underlying philosophy tends to get covered up by subordinating the 'winning' to some more noble goal such as 'excellence,' the good of the company or the public good, or democracy and justice. But the real guiding goal in the bloody business is to be on top" (Roberts, 1993, 159). I think this is unfortunately and quite often an accurate diagnosis. In sport, for example, many use the rhetoric of excellence while their actions reveal (C1) and (C2), sometimes by morally objectionable means. The proper response to this problem is not to abandon the higher ideals, as some would claim (not Roberts, however). The proper response is to adopt the higher ideals and put victory in its proper place. The virtue of humility can help us do just that. Sport is a human creation. Its values, structures, and aims are up to us. Sport can exemplify great beauty, goodness, and other forms of human excellence. Humility, in particular (H3), can help us appreciate such values and orient ourselves toward them in a proper manner (Boyd, 2014). This is another reason that it is an apt trait for sport.

Humility can also keep our desire for the pursuit of our own excellence in check. One implication of (H1) is that we are not self-sufficient; many of the goods we achieve and the excellences we possess cannot be realized by us on our own. We are dependent on others, and humility helps us see this, acknowledge it, and act accordingly. It places us in a community with others, and the interdependence it affirms can also act as a check on becoming self-absorbed in our pursuit of excellence. Robert Adams offers helpful observations with respect to humility as it contrasts with such self-absorption:

> I think there is a form of humility that is also a form of love of excellence, a form of humility that focuses on the excellence there is or can be much more than on the excellence of one's own part in it. If one is humble in this way, one will want to participate in excellence that transcends one's own or extends beyond one's own. In this context one will relax one's interest in the thought that one's own excellence might stand out in some way amidst the general excellence. Such humility may demand of me that I focus more on the excellence of what *we* are doing than on the excellence of *my* part in it. If I think that I have participated in a particularly excellent collective performance, for example, I may spoil or cheapen my enjoyment of that excellence if I let my mind go very far in trying to distinguish my own excellence in the matter from that of others. (Adams, 2006, 169)

Humility helps us and others work together in the pursuit of excellence. In this way, humility is an important social virtue that can help communities with a common goal, such as a team, flourish.

A similar type of argument can be employed in any human endeavor in which objective values are present or relevant, including competitive endeavors. Humility disposes its possessor to not only be aware of the values in play but also to integrate them properly into her character and actions. In the next section, I consider the aptness of humility in the realm of business.

RESOLVING THE CONFLICT: HUMILITY IN THE CONTEXT OF BUSINESS

In their research concerning competitiveness as it relates to business, Mudrack, Bloodgood, and Turnley consider some of the ethical implications in business for two varieties of competitiveness

(Mudrack, Bloodgood, and Turnley, 2012). They observe that competition is thought by many to be inevitable in the realm of business. For individuals in that realm, the trait of competitiveness is "viewed by many as desirable and normatively correct at the individual level" (Mudrack, Bloodgood, and Turnley, 2012, 347). Given the working definition of competition that Mudrack et al. use—"social comparisons involving an unequal distribution of rewards or scarce resources deriving from the relative performance of the participants in an activity" (Mudrack, Bloodgood, and Turnley, 2012, 347)—and the battle for survival and profit present in business, such attitudes might be expected.

However, humility need not conflict with competitiveness in the context of business. To see how, consider that Mudrack et al.'s analysis of competitiveness in the context of business follows a similar strategy utilized by philosophers of sport, namely, conceiving of competition and competitiveness in ways that are not vicious. So conceived, there is no conflict between competitiveness in business and the virtue of humility. The form of competitiveness that does conflict with (H1)–(H3) is *hypercompetitiveness*, which consists of "an indiscriminate need to compete and win, and perhaps more significantly to avoid losing and make others lose whatever the cost" (Mudrack, Bloodgood, and Turnley, 2012, 348). This is related to the notion of decompetition discussed previously in the context of sport. We can think of hypercompetitiveness as a trait that correlates with the state of affairs captured by the notion of decompetition. In particular, hypercompetitiveness is a trait suitable for such states of affairs but not for true competition. Moreover, those who possess this form of competitiveness are often arrogant, in contrast with (H1). They have a general lack of concern for other people and are not inclined to put the interests of others over their own. Such an inclination is in direct conflict with (H2). In some cases, the desires that hypercompetitive people have for money, attention, or power over others override any possible concerns about how these ends are achieved. For example, such people are willing to engage in insider trading, and they do not see this as unethical. This is arguably inconsistent with (H3), as it fails to properly value and response to objective values such as justice, fairness, and integrity.

By contrast, *personal development competitiveness* does not include the belief that winning is the most significant aspect of competition (and related dispositions). Rather, persons with this trait

> focus on self-discovery, self-improvement, and task enjoyment and mastery when competing. Such persons spend little time comparing themselves with others, and tend to respect opponents. In this view, other people are viewed as helpers and partners who furnish opportunities for growth and self-discovery rather than as rivals. (Mudrack, Bloodgood, and Turnley, 2012, 349)

In addition, Mudrack et al. observe that people who possess personal development competitiveness are unlikely to act in unethical ways, because doing so is counterproductive to the aims of competition as they conceive of it and because it is unfair and therefore disrespectful to opponents as persons. It is clear that there is no conflict between personal development competitiveness and the virtue of humility. There is no conflict with (H1)—humility includes proper self-focus and accurate self-assessment—because the individual who possesses this form of competitiveness spends little time focusing on herself and, in a balanced manner, seeks the self-knowledge described in (H1) through the competitive process. There is no conflict with (H2), which is the claim that humility disposes its possessor, prima facie, to put the interests of others ahead of her own, because in order to respect another person, in some contexts, requires this disposition to be actualized via the acts an agent performs. This is true in part because when I see my opponent not as a rival, but rather as a person and even a partner, this will tend to foster psychological attitudes related to (H2)—for example, unselfishness, empathy, and concern for the welfare of others—and motivate me to exemplify (H2) in action. Seeing an opponent as a rival is likely to have the opposite effect, as this perspective is more conducive to hypercompetitiveness and apt for the paradigm of decompetition. Finally, personal development competitiveness is also consistent with (H3) and reveals that (H3) is apt for competitive contexts in business, as the person who has personal development competitiveness accurately recognizes and properly responds to objective value in these contexts insofar as she respects others and refuses to treat them in an unethical manner for the sake of winning in business.

Finally, consider another way in which it is arguably the case that humility is apt for the competitive context of business. In his discussion of a five-year study focused on what moves a company from being good to becoming great, Jim Collins concludes that humility plays a central role (Collins, 2001). In this study, 11 of the 1,435 companies that made the *Fortune* 500 between 1965 and 1995 qualified as being "good to great." To be characterized in this manner, a company had to follow a pattern. First, it had to generate cumulative stock returns at or below those of the general market for 15 years. Next, it had to undergo the occurrence of a transition point. Following this point, the company had to generate returns of at least triple the market rate over the next 15 years. Any company that was part of an industry that followed this pattern was removed from the study. This was done in order to rule out industry-wide success as a factor in a particular company's move from good to great. What is relevant for my claim that humility is an apt trait for such competitive contexts is that humility was identified as an important characteristic of the CEO's of each of these 11 companies that were identified as a "good to great" company. The combination in a leader of the traits of humility and "intense professional will" (Collins, 2001, 68) was found to be a catalyst for the statistically rare transformation of a company from good to great. Moreover, there was a lack of humility and a determined professional will in the leaders of comparison companies that did not make the transition from good to great. Given this, the presence and centrality of humility in those who lead companies through such transformations is an important piece of evidence in support of the claim that humility can help foster business success and is apt for the competitive context of business. In the final section, I consider humility's aptness for academia and in particular my own discipline of philosophy.

HUMILITY IN ACADEMIA

I had read and believed that philosophy is the love of wisdom; then I attended a professional philosophy conference. After becoming more familiar with the way that philosophy was often practiced, I learned that for many philosophy is actually about constructing a theory in some realm of philosophical inquiry and holding onto that theory until your dying breath, no matter what sort of logical and argumentative gymnastics this requires. Protection of one's professed theory, and one's reputation, often trumps truth and wisdom in such cases.

Less cynically, perhaps, it is not always clear what the aims of philosophic inquiry are. Ideally, I would argue the aims should include both knowledge and wisdom, among other things, rather than reputation, honor, status, or power over other people. Humility does conflict with and is not apt for the pursuit of reputation, honor, status, or power as ultimate ends. However, the humble philosopher—take this as a thought experiment rather than seeking to bring a concrete example to mind—will not necessarily fail to be humble if she receives any of these as a result of her work. However, she will not make them the ends of her work *qua* philosopher. Moreover, she will be willing to lose or forgo reputation, honor, status, or power. As (H1) instructs, she will seek to be aware of the force of these temptations for her. For example, she may reach a very unpopular conclusion and engage in public descriptions and defenses of her position, because she values knowledge and wisdom and is convinced of the truth of her unpopular view. Because she is humble, she values truth and the good that it might do others, as (H2) prescribes. Therefore, she will not seek to protect her reputation at the cost of knowledge and wisdom. She is also willing to defend her view on the basis of the strength of the relevant evidence, and she is open to whatever counterevidence or arguments might necessitate she revise or change her view. Humility is apt for the competitive context of academia in general and philosophy in particular, because it can orient us to the objective goods in our area of inquiry in this way. In addition, if (H3) is exemplified in this context, then we should at least be willing to be shown that we are wrong or mistaken, as this can move us closer to the objectively valuable goals of wisdom and knowledge.

CONCLUSION

Humility is an apt virtue for competitive contexts. It is clear that humility is inconsistent with some understandings of competitiveness. But when competition and the trait of competitiveness are conceived of as having morally valuable ends, rather than mere victory or dominance at all costs, humility is not only consistent with competitive contexts but is an apt trait for them. The humble person, all else being equal, is more likely to succeed as she pursues excellence in sport, business, or academia.

REFERENCES

Adams, Robert. 2006. *A Theory of Virtue*. New York: Oxford University Press.

Ashton, Michael and Kibeom Lee. 2012. *The H Factor of Personality*. Ontario: Wilfrid Laurier Press.

Ashton, Michael and Kibeom Lee. 2007. "Empirical, theoretical, and practical advantages of the HEXACO model of personality structure." *Personality and Social Psychology Review, 11*, 150–166.

Austin, Michael W. 2018. *Humility and Human Flourishing: A Study in Analytic Moral Theology*. New York: Oxford University Press.

Austin, Michael W. 2014. "Is humility a virtue in the context of sport?" *Journal of Applied Philosophy, 31*, 203–214.

Austin, Michael W. 2012. "Defending humility: A philosophical sketch with replies to Tara Smith and David Hume." *Philosophia Christi, 14*, 461–470.

Boxill, Jan. 2014. "Competition." In *The Bloomsbury Companion to the Philosophy of Sport*, edited by Cesar R. Torres, 343–344. London: Bloomsbury.

Boyd, Craig A. 2014. "Pride and humility." In *Virtues and their Vices*, edited by Kevin Timpe and Craig A. Boyd, 245–256. Oxford: Oxford University Press.

Byerly, T. Ryan. 2014. "The Values and Varieties of Humility." *Philosophia, 42*, 889–910.

Collins, Jim. 2001. "Level 5 leadership: The triumph of humility and fierce resolve." *Harvard Business Review, 79*, 66–76.

Exline, Julie J., and Peter C. Hill. 2012. "Humility: A consistent and robust predictor of generosity." *Journal of Positive Psychology, 7*, 208–218.

Garcia, J. L. A. 2006. "Being unimpressed with ourselves: Reconceiving humility." *Philosophia, 34*, 417–435.

Gilbertson, Eric. 2016. "Vicious competitiveness and the desire to win." *Journal of the Philosophy of Sport* 43, 409–423.

Hildebrand, Dietrich von. 1997. *Humility: Wellspring of Virtue*. Manchester, NH: Sophia Institute Press.

Holowchak, M. Andrew, and Heather L. Reid. 2011. *Aretism: An Ancient Sports Philosophy for the Modern Sports World*. Lanham, MD: Lexington Books.

Hume, David. 1983. *An Enquiry into the Principles of Morals*. Indianapolis: Hackett.

Kohn, Alfie. 1986. *No Contest: The Case Against Competition*. Boston: Houghton Mifflin.

Kohn, Alfie. 1987. "The case against competition." Blog. http://www.alfiekohn.org/article/case-competition/.

Kupfer, Joseph. 2003. "The moral perspective of humility." *Pacific Philosophical Quarterly, 84*, 249–269.

MacIntyre, Alasdair. 1984, *After Virtue*. 2d ed. Notre Dame: University of Notre Dame Press.

Mudrack, Peter E., James M. Bloodgood, and William H. Turnley. 2012. "Some ethical implications of individual competitiveness." *Journal of Business Ethics, 108*, 347–359.

Richards, Norvin. 1992. *Humility*. Philadelphia, PA: Temple University Press.

Roberts, Robert C., and W. Jay Wood. 2003. "Humility and epistemic goods." In *Intellectual Virtue: Perspectives from Ethics and Epistemology*, edited by M. DePaul and L. Zagzebski, 261–263. New York: Oxford University Press.

Roberts, Robert C. 1993. *Taking the Word to Heart: Self and Other in an Age of Therapies*. Grand Rapids, MI: Eerdmans.

Shields, David, and Brenda Bredemeier. 2011. "Contest, competition, and metaphor." *Journal of the Philosophy of Sport 38*, 27–38.

Simon, Robert L. 2003. "Good competition and drug-enhanced performance." In *Sports Ethics*, edited by J. Boxill, 175–181. Malden, MA: Blackwell.

Smith, Tara. 2005. "The practice of pride." In *Personal Virtues*, edited by Clifford Williams. New York: Palgrave Macmillan.

Chapter 11

Humility and Decision-Making in Companies

ANTONIO ARGANDOÑA

INTRODUCTION

A few decades ago, the pioneering work of Anscombe (1958), Foot (1978), MacIntyre (1984), and other philosophers opened the way for a new approach to virtue theory that, a few years later, emerged in business ethics through the writings of Solomon (1992) and others. Since then, the literature on virtues in management has grown extensively.

Humility (and its complementary virtues such as modesty, patience, docility, or magnanimity, or its opposing vices such as pride, arrogance, haughtiness, boasting, and narcissism) has been the subject of a large number of theoretical and empirical studies, from both the psychological (Davis et al., 2011; Exline and Geyer, 2004; Peterson and Seligman, 2004; Rowatt et al., 2006) and ethical viewpoints (Argandoña, 2015a; Frostenson, 2016; Molyneaux, 2003; Roberts and Wood, 2003), with many applications in management and leadership (Chatterjee and Hambrick, 2007; Collins, 2001; Hayward et al., 2006; Hiller and Hambrick, 2005; Li and Tang, 2010; Morris et al., 2005; Nielsen et al.,

2010; Ou et al., 2017; Owens and Heckman 2012; Owens et al., 2013; Owens et al., 2015; Picone et al., 2014; Sousa and Dierendonck, 2017; Tang et al., 2015; Vera and Rodriguez-Lopez, 2004).

So there already exists a considerable body of critical knowledge about the importance of humility in teamwork, management, and leadership. However, the reader of this copious literature is justified in feeling dissatisfied: apart from their scholarly interest, what do these articles contribute to our understanding of the manager's task and training? What normative reasons can be given to people who wish to possess this virtue?

In this chapter,[1] I try to explain the role of virtues in general and humility in particular, as exercised by managers, developing what seems to be the main argument for someone who is responsible for running a business: managers must be ethical if they want to be excellent managers.[2] If they are not ethical, they might be financially successful and acknowledged for their successes but, as MacIntyre (1984) pointed out, success is not a synonym for excellence (Beabout, 2013). What goes wrong in the haughty or arrogant manager? And does a humble manager really manage "differently"—and better?

This chapter begins with an explanation of what managing is and the role played by virtues in managerial work. It then presents humility and what makes the humble manager "different," and puts forward some ideas about how this virtue can be acquired and closes with conclusions.[3]

MANAGING

An organization (e.g., a firm, a sports club, an NGO, a political party, but also a family or a group of friends who are planning an outing) is a community of people who cooperate to achieve a purpose in which they are all interested, albeit perhaps for different reasons. Furthermore, in a business organization, the results achieved must meet certain economic efficiency requirements and assure the organization's continued existence over time. In all cases, management of the business organization (or firm) is put in the hands of a person or a team of people.

The managerial task consists of designing and developing a profitable business project and running it in the specific context of the market. So that this can be done, those who own the resources that the firm needs must be willing to contribute them to the project as owners, managers, employees, suppliers, or distributors; for example, in the case of employees, they are sought, selected, trained, motivated, and rewarded by the firm's management so that their contribution will be sufficient and appropriate, both now and in the future.

Managing people, therefore, consists of proposing a project, motivating those who take part in it, and coordinating their work so that the firm's goals are attained. And not just in the present, because people learn (knowledge, abilities, attitudes, and virtues) and change their motivations, contributions, and relationships. Thus, managing a firm is also optimizing each individual's contribution, not just to obtain financial results but also to develop the human and professional qualities of the people on which the firm's distinctive capabilities and competitive advantages depend.

Activating and aligning with people's motivations are the keys to gaining their voluntary participation in the project. There are three types of motivation (Pérez López, 1991): extrinsic, what the agent hopes to receive from the organization, which may be financial (salary, career opportunities) or non-financial rewards (recognition); intrinsic, for what the agent does in the organization (job satisfaction and learning operative knowledge and skills); and transcendent,[4] or prosocial, when the agent acts to achieve a positive or negative result in other people (rendering service to customers or society, assist a colleague, or improve environmental quality within the firm).

Human action puts into motion a series of knowledge learning and skill, and virtue or vice development, processes. These processes happen in any case, even if the people concerned are not aware of them or do not wish them: they improve (or worsen) their knowledge and practices, they "learn" to take an interest in other people's welfare (or ignore it), and they "teach" others with their actions and attitudes. For example, when employees lie to customers, they are developing, to a greater or lesser extent, the vice of lying and are causing real or potential harm to their customers. And if their superiors instruct them to lie or tolerate it, they are also being untruthful and unfair to customers and employees.

This learning is important because it impacts the task of gaining employees' voluntary participation in the firm's project, which, as we have said, is an important part of the managerial task. In view of the three types of motivation, managers must achieve three types of results: first, generate financial return to satisfy the extrinsic motivations of their employees (basically, their remuneration) and those of their suppliers, lenders, and owners; second, create an atmosphere within the firm and its environment where employees feel sufficiently satisfied with the work they perform and its results, including the acquisition of knowledge and skills (and corresponding advancement), this is the content of their intrinsic motivation; and, last but not least, devote attention to transcendent, or prosocial, motivations, so that the firm can become a genuine community of people who are treated with respect, who help each other, who learn to take an interest in other people's needs (Melé 2012): in short, who can improve their virtues or, at least, prevent them from deteriorating.

In acting in this manner, managers are also satisfying their own personal motivations: extrinsic (remuneration, recognition, career opportunities), intrinsic (satisfaction, operational learning), and prosocial (service), as well as developing their virtues (or vices) as individuals and as professionals: they are being, or learning to be, excellent professionals, which is a manifestation of a virtuous life.

And, by these means, the human community we have called a "firm" can become an organization that is not only efficient and profitable but also ethical—although never to a complete degree, due to the inherent limitations of any human initiative.[5] This is not something that only needs to be done once: it is a task that must be performed daily, sometimes with steps forward and sometimes with setbacks. Decisions do not happen on their own but are part of continued or repeated projects, which give rise to repeated interactions between managers and employees, and they have lasting consequences for the agents' characters. And this is precisely why ethics is important in organizations.

Managers' moral responsibilities go beyond their individual decisions because they also encompass the firm's mission, organization, structure, and culture. "Managers who want to create and maintain ethics in their organizations need to know how structures, systems, people, and culture can be deployed to accommodate ethical behavior and make unethical behavior disadvantageous" (Hartman, 1998, 553).

However, it may happen that, faced with these demands, managers may take fright and wish to scale down the scope of their responsibilities because the problems they face are highly complex; they often lack the necessary information; they are exposed to intense market pressures and must make decisions under an obligation to ensure results with authority and professionalism, knowing that any mistakes may have serious consequences; they do not have time to engage in unhurried ethical reflection; and the environment in which they must operate is not sensitive to these issues. And, above all, managers may have difficulties in evaluating the consequences of their decisions on other people and on themselves (Argandoña, 2015b). It would seem that Abbà (1992) was thinking of these challenges when he said:

> It is relatively easy to make a decision of principle; the problems arise when such a complex and fragile subject as is the human subject seeks a path for execution in the midst of complicated, varied situations. Problems arise for reason, which must seek, anticipate, remember, invent, take into account so many relevant circumstances and, before that, differentiate them, judge and draw up a precise directive; problems for will, which must express new desires and interests, surmounting obstacles, preexisting inclinations, indifference; problems for emotional appetites, which have so much weight here; docility to allow oneself to be spurred forward or held back, to modify one's own goals, to bow to the demands of higher opinions. (127–128)

To resolve these perplexities, business ethics often resort to deontological or utilitarian criteria. The former are useful as guides for action but are not sufficient when it comes to making decisions in a specific situation, in which, for example, different principles may be invoked that lead to opposing decisions. And utilitarian criteria are also useful, but they do not take into account how the action is performed and who performs it, that is, how it contributes to shaping the decision-maker's character and ethical quality. Therefore, Abbà (1992) proposes: "This is the place, where fundamental decisions readily collapse, where virtue must reside" (128). Consequently, we must reflect on the role of virtues in the managerial task.

VIRTUES

Roughly, a virtue is "a deep-seated trait of character that provides (normative) reasons for action together with appropriate motivations for choosing, feeling, desiring, and reacting well across a range of situations" (Alzola, 2012, 380). It is an acquired, firm, stable quality that helps perform actions focused on excellence, not mechanically but with freedom and effort.

Basically, virtues perform four functions in people's lives and, especially, in the lives of people who run human organizations, in accordance with the four components or elements explained by Aristotle (1999): intellectual, emotional, motivational, and behavioral (see Alzola, 2015; Hartman, 2015).

First, a virtuous person "perceives a situation rightly—that is, notices and takes appropriate account of the salient features of a situation" (Hartman, 2008, 322) because she has developed the abilities that enable her to understand and adequately weigh the situation's ethical content, not on an abstract level through application of general principles, but in the present environment and for the specific people affected by it. This is the intellectual dimension of virtue.

Second, virtues are "dispositions not only to act in particular ways but also to feel in particular ways" (MacIntyre, 1984, 149): this is the emotional function. Virtuous managers are sensitive to the events and people that cross their path. The intellectual and emotional perceptions of situations and people activate the motivational dimension: virtuous managers are moved by appropriate motives, not by fear of reprisals or unpleasant consequences, or for convenience.[6]

And lastly, virtuous people carry out the chosen actions, because they have the necessary strength of will to overcome short-term pressures and the temptations that may turn them from this path: this is the behavioral dimension (Alzola, 2012; Argandoña, 2011a; Polo, 1996). Virtues "will sustain us in the relevant quest for the good, by enabling us to overcome the harms, dangers, temptations and distractions which we encounter, and which will furnish us with increasing self-knowledge and increasing knowledge of the good" (MacIntyre, 1984, 219).

In business ethics, managers' decisions are usually studied as isolated actions. However, managers are not performers of isolated actions but of a conduct, of a set of more or less ordered and interrelated actions that arise from their deepest and most enduring intentions, processes, and emotions (Abbà, 1992). All this forms part of moral character, which is "an individual's characteristic patterns of thought, emotion and behavior associated with moral/ethical and immoral/unethical behavior" (Cohen et al., 2014, 6).

Managers' daily work demands and makes possible the development of intellectual and moral habits (virtues) that help them in their decisions—although this does not mean that all of them achieve this development. Virtues are not automatic mechanisms or routines in the decision-making process; they do not dictate the specific actions that must be performed but enhance the agent's ability to choose and act (Abbà, 1992, 172).

To summarize, virtuous managers have the possibility of becoming excellent managers because they are developing the habits that enable them to make better decisions, both now and in the future, avoiding negative evaluative learning (vices) and, insofar as possible, facilitating positive learning (virtues), both in themselves and the people who depend on them.[7] On this foundation, it is possible to develop an understanding of the different ways in which each of the virtues and, in our case, humility acts.

HUMILITY

Humility is a strength of character associated with the virtue of temperance, which moderates the natural instinct to put oneself in front, to show superiority, stature or pre-eminence (Pieper, 1965). In the past, it has sometimes been identified with a lack of self-esteem, and it was not considered a desirable trait for people in positions of government or leadership or those invested with authority. However, once it started to be understood properly, it became a full member of the list of virtues required for organization management.[8] Humility can be conceived as a means between two extremes (Aristotle, 1999), by excess (degradation, pusillanimity, shyness, submission) and by default (pride, vanity, conceit, arrogance, haughtiness).

When we say that a person is humble, we are highlighting four features of their behavior, corresponding to the four dimensions of virtue that we have explained earlier: intellectual, emotional, motivational, and behavioral;[9] in turn, these dimensions can be viewed from an intrapersonal or interpersonal viewpoint (Argandoña, 2015a; Davis et al., 2011).

Intellectual Dimension

Humble people possess realistic and objective self-knowledge (Aquinas, 2006, II-II 161, 6; 162, 3 ad 2). This knowledge arises from two sources: their own experience and self-reflection, with all its biases and limitations, and what other people know about them and convey to them.

Self-knowledge encompasses the agents' abilities and understandings, personality and character, cognitive and operational strengths and weaknesses, their imperfections, material and spiritual assets and liabilities, and the consequences of all this: their accomplishments, errors, and successes. That is why Teresa of Avila said that "humility is to walk in truth" (1921, VI, 10.7).[10]

Objective self-knowledge is the means for realistic self-assessment and self-esteem (Brennan, 2007): the humble subjects do not despise themselves and neither do they find any reason to unduly glorify themselves, which eliminates barriers in dealings with other people. For managers, self-knowledge is essential if they are to make good decisions, shoulder their responsibilities, be more transparent, make less mistakes, be accountable, not hide or justify their mistakes, not have hidden agendas, etc.

The knowledge that humble people have of themselves cannot be separated from their knowledge of external reality, including other people, because that reality points to possibilities and limits in their actions and it enables them to define their "position in the world," which also forms part of their self-knowledge.

Motivational Dimension

Knowledge serves to motivate, and, in turn, motivation promotes knowledge. Humility is not an abstract disposition but is deployed in the concrete circumstances of each situation; figuratively speaking, we can imagine that agents possess a "database" that contains their knowledge and experience and from which they draw, in each case, what they consider relevant for understanding themselves and their environment, and this generates motivations to act. Here we identify five aspects of this motivational dimension:

First, attitudes or dispositions toward self-knowledge.[11] These include (1) the development, with effort and perseverance, of the necessary capabilities and skills to accomplish self-knowledge, and the willingness to continue doing it in the future or, at least, to not prevent it; (2) the attitude (operative habit) to recognize one's defects and errors, one's accomplishments and abilities, to learn, to ask for forgiveness, to correct the former and nurture the latter—including recognition of the possibility of acting improperly; (3) the disposition to judge and appraise oneself realistically and, insofar as possible, objectively, and the self-respect that comes from this; (4) the disposition to always act in accordance with one's self-knowledge, that is, to be sincere and not try to hide one's weaknesses or exaggerate one's strengths; (5) the stable disposition to not be satisfied with what one sees in oneself and to try to improve;[12] and (6) the possibility of being a model for others and the responsibility of leading by example.

Second, attitudes toward the knowledge of external reality. In order to make good decisions, the agents need the right dispositions to have objective and impartial knowledge about their environment. This forms part of the virtue of humility,[13] allowing recognition, for example, of the limitations imposed by the environment on the agent's ability to influence it.

Third, openness to others. This is the agents' disposition to receive information about themselves, allowing themselves to be known and corrected (teachability). This openness manifests in qualities such as not feeling threatened by the knowledge that others have about one, not admit feelings of inferiority or superiority, not comparing oneself with others, being willing to learn from everyone, not depending on superiors', peers', or inferiors' approval, not concealing or justifying mistakes, not hiding successes or accomplishments but not exaggerating them either, not holding grudges, always being willing to forgive, asking for counsel, and so on. All these attitudes are very important in the management of organizations.

Fourth, attitudes toward others. Humility combines with a battery of social virtues that receive input from self-knowledge and the attitudes and dispositions mentioned earlier. People who know and respect themselves are able to recognize the capacities, strengths, merits and achievement of others, without exaggerating or belittling them; judge them with honesty, without looking for failures or hidden intentions in their actions; show respect to others; exercise benevolence and justice; help them, share projects with them, give them opportunities, are patient, show empathy and approachability and many other character traits.[14]

Agents who value humility as a virtue will also try to foster it in others, to empower them, to encourage them to act, to be accountable, to take into account other people's specific abilities and to give them appropriate responsibilities, to propose shared goals, and many other traits (Sousa and Dierendonck, 2017). One outcome of all this may be an atmosphere of trust and cooperation within the organization: breaking barriers, respecting, listening, and inviting everyone to take part, supporting initiatives and participation, putting the firm's interest before personal interests, and so on.[15] Another outcome may be the avoidance of negative learning (everyone is able to accept their responsibilities, they know themselves, they are willing to ask for forgiveness, and take into account others), and a further step could be to support people's development—including their ethical development. This in turn fosters unity in the firm, first around the mission or purpose but also as a human group with some form of friendship (Argandoña, 2011b).

Low self-focus is a summary of the previous attitudes: not being full of oneself, keeping one's skills and achievements in perspective, not concentrating on oneself, giving value to other people's merits, capabilities, results, etc.

Emotional Dimension

Emotions may act as motivators for humility, triggering or enhancing attitudes and dispositions related with this virtue, in a positive (giving prominence to other people) or negative sense (reacting with envy to other people's success). Emotions can also inhibit these attitudes. Self-command or self-control helps prevent feelings and emotions from interfering with correct decisions.

Behavioral Dimension

Virtue is not confined to knowing what needs to be done or to the wish to do it, but it also moves the will to put into practice what has been decided.[16] The disposition to practice humility facilitates the exercise of other virtues, or is even a necessary condition for them (as several other contributors to this volume suggest), to the extent that it is often difficult to identify it as a distinct virtue. To quote the author of *Don Quixote*, humility "is the base and foundation of all virtues, and without it no other virtue can exist" (Cervantes, 2004, 30). Lack of humility is an impediment to exercising these virtues (generosity, willingness to listen and forgive, courtesy, respect, patience, and many others) and, therefore, to performing acts that would objectively be good governance. But the arrogant or vain manager would not understand this.

Other people are likely to first identify the actions related with these virtues connected with humility, and only later, through reflection and observation, will they understand how humility supports these virtues. In any case, behavior toward others will be mediated by these other virtues.[17] Humility gives its best fruit when it is combined with them, producing an excellent moral character (Hartman, 1998). Among these virtues, there are two that deserve particular attention. One is prudence or practical wisdom, *auriga virtutum*, or the driver of all virtues (Aquinas, 2006, I-II, 2, 1). It is prudence that enables us to judge, in each specific case, whether a humble action is an act of virtue: for example, whether it is advisable to place trust in team members who may be trying to manipulate a decision for their sole personal benefit. The other virtue is magnanimity, the twin virtue of humility, which engages the will with that which tends toward the sublime (Aquinas, 2006, II-II, 129, 1). Magnanimous people know that they are called to do extraordinary things and they make themselves worthy of them, acting with humility, sincerity, and honesty, without any conceit or flattery (Pieper, 1965). Llano (2004) points out that humility is the virtue that guides decisions in the study and diagnosis phase and magnanimity in the decision phase.

HOW TO DEVELOP HUMILITY?

Humility is a virtue that everyone needs, particularly those whose job is to manage people. But it is not an easy virtue to learn. In the previous section, we presented many specific actions that show how a humble person behaves. Here, we will complete these recommendations with a few general ideas.

Operative habits or virtues, humility too, are acquired by the voluntary, free, and deliberate repetition of acts, with effort and perseverance and appropriate motivations (Abbà, 1992; Argandoña, 2011a; Aristotle, 1999; Aquinas, 2006; Pérez López, 1991). Some authors consider that humility is not a virtue because it supposes acting against reason (Spinoza), it goes against the intimate feelings of people (Hume), or it is characteristic of a slave morality (Nietzsche). At most, they accept utilitarian arguments, in that humility offers a certain tranquility of conscience to people and contributes to social stability. However, considered from the point of view of human action in organizations, as we have presented before, humility is a necessary virtue, especially for people who hold positions of authority and government. There does not have to be anything negative in the recognition of what each person owes to external factors (genetic, education, help received from others), in the objective assessment of the environment and of the people, or in the orientation toward social purposes or valuable ideals. Because, in addition, humility tends to go hand in hand with magnanimity and greatness of soul, so that it cannot be said to be something unnatural.

Humility cannot be an end in itself because that could easily lead to conceit concealed behind feigned humility—showing external signs of humility to be recognized as humble is a manifestation of pride. The motivations to acquire humility must be honest; the agent must pursue ends such as becoming a better person or a better manager, setting a good example, or creating an atmosphere of trust within the organization; not extrinsic ends, such as economic profit or social standing (Abbà, 1992). Logically, in the early stages of moral progress, people will have difficulty in acting against their spontaneous motivations, which will lead them to compare themselves with others, exaggerate their merits or mask their failings; with time, practicing the virtue will consolidate these motivations.

Managers who seek to improve the quality of their humility should understand the reasons that make this virtue desirable, for them, for the firm, and for others. Being familiar with the arguments developed, for example, in this article is not a requisite, but they should have at least an intuitive knowledge that, normally, will come from their personal background and, above all, from the example given by other people (Haidt, 2001; Rhonheimer 2011). In any case, nobody learns to be humble by reading manuals or attending ethics classes: becoming humble requires a conscious decision, even though initially one may not understand sufficiently the underlying reasons for behaving like this; usually, the example given by others will be sufficient.[18]

As said, a key component of humility is self-knowledge, which requires self-examination and reflection: for example, asking oneself frequently why one does something and what are the motives for one's actions, distinguishing between what gives pleasure and what is salutary. If actions contrary to the virtue are discovered in the process of this examination, they must be acknowledged, without transferring blame to others, without justifying oneself, instead apologize and start again.

In this personal reflection process, one may be helped by certain negative indicators, for example, envy at other people's successes or abilities; thoughts of superiority (or inferiority) with respect to other people; the need to be accepted by superiors, peers, or subordinates; the tendency to talk about oneself and make oneself the center of attention in relationships; or lack of impartiality in one's judgments (for example, the tendency to only accept information that is to one's favor). Other indicators of a possible lack of humility, particularly in organizations, are fear of ridicule, which discourages participation in a sincere, open dialog; fear of failure, which paralyzes decision-making; hiding errors or not giving account of the decisions made and their results; avoiding passing bad news upward or "forging ahead" without facing problems which, therefore, shows no genuine commitment to solving them.

Self-knowledge draws mainly from other people's vision of the manager and his attitude toward these manifestations, including the willingness to ask honest, demanding advisers for advice, ask for and accept help, and show appreciation for opinions, even when they are critical.[19]

An important aspect of managers' humility is how they view others, particularly their colleagues and subordinates: acknowledge people's dignity, respect them and give them the importance they deserve; know them and, therefore, listen to them, ask for their opinion, be open to their ideas and try to understand their thoughts and, most importantly, their emotions. Managers must acknowledge their employees' abilities because they all have something to contribute. When assessing them, it is important to first point out their positive aspects before talking about the negative aspects; the assessment performed must be used not only to judge subordinates' performance but also to realize their learning abilities and their possibilities for improvement.

The outcome of the managers' attitude may be a greater level of employees participation: give them responsibilities matched to each employee's circumstances and abilities, let them know that they have their manager's confidence, and let them learn to exercise their responsibilities; pay attention not only to their short-term performance but also to their learning and their long-term human and professional development; be patient, be demanding but also be ready to help; pull them upward, encouraging them to take on responsibilities: managers must conjugate "we" before "I."

Humble managers and employees mean humble firms. This cannot be achieved via public relations and communication but through rules, culture, and incentive systems that lead to shared missions; a culture of dialogue within the firm and with its external stakeholders; the minimum of red tape; balanced power structures that do not generate privileges within the organization; fair compensation criteria; career opportunities, etc.

CONCLUSIONS

Firms are, above all, communities of people who cooperate to achieve a purpose that is in everyone's interest, albeit for different reasons. Managers' task is to get everyone to participate voluntarily in this common project, which not only needs knowledge and technical expertise but, above all, also virtues that allow the moral development of the managers and the rest of that community.

Virtues enable a fuller understanding of the firm's situation, because they take into account the consequences of managers' decisions for themselves, for other people, and for the organization. This broader understanding leads to a special sensitivity, a greater motivation to act, and the necessary strength to overcome resistance. This is the transformative role of virtues in management.

Humility plays a key role in the management task. The vices contrary to humility (arrogance, hubris, vanity, conceit, boastfulness, and vainglory, among others) start as deficiencies in knowledge about oneself, one's projects, one's environment, and one's position in it. Thus, humble managers have developed, to a greater or lesser extent, the operative habit of knowing themselves, their capabilities, virtues, and accomplishments, their weaknesses and shortcomings, and of allowing themselves to be known by others and learn from them. The consequence of this operative habit is realistic and humble knowledge, which makes this virtue operative in managerial work. This attitude toward self-knowledge is confirmed with the will's decision to act in accordance with it, showing itself openly as it is, without trying to exaggerate its positive aspects or conceal the negative ones.

The disposition to know oneself is manifested in interpersonal relationships, which are not selfish because, if they nurture the habit of knowing, assessing, and respecting themselves, they will also be in a position to know other people, their capabilities and accomplishments, their successes and failures, and they will be able to appraise them, respect them, and help them. The humble person's behavior toward other people is developed through a range of prosocial virtues: love, affinity, modesty, courtesy, respect, gratitude, acknowledgement, trust, patience, etc.; these virtues may be present, to a greater or lesser degree, in arrogant or haughty people, but when combined with humility they enhance the abilities of a good leader.

Managers are motivated to be humble when they try to do what is good for others (customers, suppliers, employees, owners) and for themselves, that is, to act with transcendent or prosocial motivation (Pérez López, 1991).[20] If people systematically act moved by the desire to serve customers, help colleagues, and develop the firms' human community, they will probably "learn" new ways and motives to fulfill other people's needs, especially if it is projected onto the firm's mission, structure, and culture. One consequence of this is that humility can never be assumed as won or lost but must be built each day.

The humility exercised by managers will probably spread to other stakeholders, but it may be a slow process, or it may not happen at all, because it depends on those people's individual freedom. However, humble managers will improve according to the quality of their motivations: that is why we said that the deepest reason why managers should be virtuous is that they wish to be excellent managers. On the other hand, humility can never be an invitation to inaction, passivity, or conformism. Humble managers will often have to be heroic to live this virtue themselves (mediated by prudence) and to give it life for others, without compromising the goals of the firm.

Virtues do not guarantee the financial success of a company, which depends on many conditions, some of them external to the firm (demand, credit, costs, technology, competition), others internal (structure, organization, culture, technology), within the manager herself (technical and financial knowledge, abilities, attitudes, and values) and within other people in the organization (knowledge and abilities, willingness to cooperate, commitment, trust, loyalty). However, if managers have not developed a moral character, there are many reasons to believe that the firm will not progress as a human community, even if it achieves spectacular financial results in the short term.

NOTES

1. This chapter is part of the activities of the CaixaBank Chair of Corporate Social Responsibility, IESE Business School, University of Navarra.
2. There are other "instrumental" reasons, based on the economic outcomes of virtue-based management (Frostenson, 2016).
3. The article's narrative thread is taken from Pérez López (1991, 1993), as developed in Argandoña (2008a, 2008b, 2015b).
4. It is called transcendent because it transcends the agent.
5. This does not guarantee maximum profit or maximum share value, because that also depends on external factors such as the market, credit, or competition.
6. Alzola (2008, 354) highlights this dimension when he reminds us that "human beings are morally weak, especially when confronted with a resolute authority, a unanimous group which sees the world in a very different way than they do, or an intense situation that elicits 'counterdispositional' behaviors. Our weakness is not just cognitive—i.e., situational pressures make us lose our moral compass—but also motivational. We avoid exposing ourselves to disruptive social situations by telling others what we think."

7. But virtues are not enough: excellent people seek the goods of their actions, which constitute the ends of their behavior; they respect ethical norms and implement virtues (Polo, 1996).
8. It is not a "role-specific" virtue but rather a "comprehensive" virtue that is necessary for all people and at all times (Audi, 2012, 278).
9. Many authors give a list of the ingredients of humility; for example, accurate self-assessment of abilities and achievements, self-awareness of mistakes and limitations, openness to new ideas, information and advice from others, capacity to keep successes and accomplishments in perspective, low self-focus, and appreciation for others (Tangney, 2005); self-awareness, developmental orientation or teachability, appreciation of others' strengths and contributions, and low self-focus (Owens, 2009); willingness to view oneself accurately, displayed appreciation for others, and openness to feed-back (Owens et al., 2013), to which Ou et al., (2014) add low self-focus, self-transcendent pursuit, and transcendent self-concept.
10. This differentiates true humility from the abasement or negation of one's own abilities: humble people know what they have, although they do not attribute to themselves the merit of having them. However, in postmodern societies where the concept of truth is blurred, humility becomes mere outward appearance; for that reason, its external manifestations, like abasement or self-humiliation, are interpreted, mistakenly, as manifestations of true humility.
11. In this article, words are used such as "attitudes" or "dispositions" to designate the nature of the operative habits or virtues, without seeking to give them the technical meaning they have in psychology, such as, for example, "behavioral dispositions to act in conformity with certain rules of action" (Alzola 2015, 295).
12. This may be viewed as an act of arrogance; whether it is, will depend on the agent's intention.
13. Here it belongs to what some authors call the transcendent dimension of humility (Furey, 1986): to feel connected or part of a reality that is greater than oneself, such as God, the universe, beauty, science or moral perfection.
14. The humble person seeks to develop authentic personal relationships with other people that have an epistemic (i.e., they contribute to psychological development, self-understanding, self-conception, and the ability to examine oneself with a critical eye), emotional (i.e., they offer the opportunity to express one's feelings and engage in interactive relationships) and moral value (i.e., they develop character traits that are only possible in authentic relationships, such as gratitude and love) (Sakalaki and Fousiani, 2012).
15. In the relationships that are formed in an organization, the two parties, manager and employee, are active agents and both must actively practice virtues, albeit, obviously, with different characteristics. Cf. Pérez López (1993), Argandoña (2015b). Humility is a necessary virtue for both sides of a

command-obedience relationship: the persons who command must be receptive to the initiative of the persons who obey, and they will not be fit to command if they are not able to obey, and the persons who obey must always obey with initiative, which implies a certain exercise of command.

16. People who are really humble try to correct their mistakes but do not pretend to be recognized as perfect, which could be a lack of humility.
17. This means that humility has an indirect role in shaping leadership.
18. This intellectual exercise may be useful for avoiding misunderstandings about what humility is, such as highlighting excessively the negative aspects of one's character or playing down the positive aspects, showing hesitancy in decision-making, setting unambitious goals or trying to keep everyone happy when giving instructions. This also implies a correct purpose of the firm: if it is to maximize profit, this is unlikely to give rise to the need for management humility, except as an instrumental virtue.
19. Managers must make decisions that are not to everyone's liking, and it will not always be opportune to ask for advice from people who, for example, do not know all the data or cannot see the big picture or do not have the ability to interpret the decision's objectives, but they should always be open to feedback.
20. Normally, there are several motivations behind each action; the key is to identify the dominant one, that is, that which will prevail in the event of conflict.

REFERENCES

Abbà, G. 1992. *Felicidad, vida buena y virtud*. Barcelona: Ediciones Internacionales Universitarias.

Alzola, M. 2008. "Character and environment: The status of virtues in organizations." *Journal of Business Ethics*, 78(3), 343–357.

Alzola, M. 2012. "The possibility of virtue." *Business Ethics Quarterly*, 22(2), 377–404.

Alzola, M. 2015. "Virtuous persons and virtuous actions in business ethics and organizational research." *Business Ethics Quarterly*, 25(3), 287–318.

Anscombe, G. E. M. 1958. "Modern moral philosophy." *Philosophy*, 33, 1–19.

Aquinas, T. 2006. *Summa Theologiae*. Cambridge: Cambridge University Press.

Argandoña, A. 2008a. "Integrating ethics into action theory and organizational theory." *Journal of Business Ethics*, 78(3), 435–446.

Argandoña, A. 2008b. "Anthropological and ethical foundations of organization theory." In *Rethinking Business Management: Examining the Foundations of Business Education*, edited by S. Gregg and J. R. Stoner Jr. 38–49. Princeton: Witherspoon Institute.

Argandoña, A. 2011a. "Las virtudes en una teoría de la acción humana." In *La persona al centro del Magistero sociale della Chiesa,* edited by P. Requena and M. Schlag, 49–71. Roma: Edusc.

Argandoña, A. 2011b. "Beyond contracts: Love in firms." *Journal of Business Ethics,* 99(1), 77–85.

Argandoña, A. 2015a. "Humility in management." *Journal of Business Ethics,* *132*(1), 63–71.

Argandoña, A. 2015b. "Consistencia y ética en la toma de decisiones." Working Paper WP-1128, Barcelona: IESE Business School.

Aristotle. 1999. *Nicomachean Ethics.* Translated by T. Irwin. Indianapolis: Hackett.

Audi, R. 2012. "Virtue ethics as a resource in business." *Business Ethics Quarterly,* 22(2), 273–291.

Beabout, G. R. 2013. *The Character of the Manager: From Office Executive to Wise Steward.* New York: Palgrave Macmillan.

Brennan, J. 2007. "Modesty without illusion." *Philosophy and Phenomenological Research,* 75(1), 111–128.

Cervantes, M. de. 2004. *The Dialog of the Dogs.* London: Hesperus Press. (Original in Spanish, 1613.)

Chatterjee, A., and D. C. Hambrick. 2007. "It's all about me: Narcissistic chief executive officers and their effects on company strategy and performance." *Administrative Science Quarterly.* 52(3), 351–386.

Cohen, T. R., A. T. Panter, N. Turan, L. Morse, and Y. Kim. 2014. "Moral character in the workplace." *Journal of Personality and Social Psychology, 107*(5), 943–963.

Collins, J. 2001. "Level 5 leadership: the triumph of humility and fierce resolve." *Harvard Business Review,* 79(1), 67–76.

Davis, D. E., J. N. Hook, E. L. Worthington, D. R. Van Tongeren, A. L. Gartner, D. J. Jennings, and R. A. Emmons. 2011. "Relational humility: Conceptualizing and measuring humility as personality judgment." *Journal of Personality Assessment,* 93(3), 225–234.

Exline, J. J., and A. L. Geyer. 2004. "Perceptions of humility: a preliminary study." *Self and Identity,* 3(2), 95–114.

Foot, P. 1978. *Virtues and Vices and Other Essays in Moral Philosophy.* Berkeley: University of California Press.

Frostenson, M. 2016. "Humility in business: A contextual approach." *Journal of Business Ethics, 138*(1), 91–102.

Furey, R. J. 1986. *So I'm Not Perfect: A Psychology of Humility.* New York: Alba House.

Haidt, J. 2001. "The emotional dog and its rational tail: A social intuitionist approach to moral judgment." *Psychological Review, 108*(4), 814–834.

Hartman, E. M. 1998. "The role of character in business ethics." *Business Ethics Quarterly,* 8(3), 547–559.

Hartman, E. M. 2008. "Socratic questions and Aristotelic answers: A virtue-based approach to business ethics." *Journal of Business Ethics, 78*(3), 313–328.

Hartman, E. M. 2015. *Virtue in Business: Conversations with Aristotle.* Cambridge: Cambridge University Press.

Hayward, M. L., D. A. Shepherd, and D. Griffin. 2006. "A hubris theory of entrepreneurship." *Management Science, 52*(2), 160–172.

Hiller, N. J., and D. C. Hambrick. 2005. "Conceptualizing executive hubris: The role of (hyper-)core self-evaluations in strategic decision-making." *Strategic Management Journal, 26*(4), 297–319.

Li, J., and Y. Tang, 2010. "CEO hubris and firm risk taking in China: The moderating role of managerial discretion." *Academy of Management Journal, 53*(1), 45–68.

Llano, C. 2004. *Humildad y liderazgo. ¿Necesita el empresario ser humilde.* Mexico: Herberto Ruz.

MacIntyre, A. 1984. *After Virtue: A Study in Moral Theory*. 2nd ed. Notre Dame: Notre Dame University Press.

Melé, D. 2012. "The firm as a community of persons. A pillar of humanistic business *ethos." Journal of Business Ethics, 106*(1), 89–101.

Molyneaux, D. 2003. "'Blessed are the meek, for they shall inherit the earth': An aspiration applicable to business?" *Journal of Business Ethics, 48*(4), 347–363.

Morris, J. A., C-M. Brotheridge, and J. C. Urbanski. 2005. "Bringing humility to leadership: antecedents and consequences of leader humility." *Human Relations, 58*(10), 1323–1350.

Nielsen, R., J. A. Marrone, and H. S. Slay, 2010. "A new look at humility: Exploring the humility concept and its role in socialized charismatic leadership." *Journal of Leadership and Organizational Studies, 17*(1), 33–43.

Ou, A. Y., A. S. Tsui, A. J. Knicki, D. A. Waldman, Z. Xiao, and L. J. Song. 2014. "Humble chief executive officers' connections to top management team integration and middle managers responses." *Administrative Science Quarterly, 59*(1), 34–72.

Ou, A. Y., D. A. Waldman, and S. J. Peterson. 2017. "Do humble CEOs matter? An examination of CEO humility and firm outcomes." *Journal of Management, 44*(3), 1147–1173.

Owens, B. P. 2009. "Humility in organizations: Establishing construct, nomological, and predictive validity." *Academy of Management Best Papers Proceedings.* Briarcliff Manor: Academy of Management.

Owens, B. P., and D. R. Hekman. 2012. "Modeling how to grow: An inductive examination of humble leader behaviors, contingencies, and outcomes." *Academy of Management Journal, 55*(4), 787–818.

Owens, B. P., M. D. Johnson, and T. R. Mitchell. 2013. "Expressed humility in organizations: Implications for performance, teams, and leadership." *Organization Science, 24*(5), 1517–1538.

Owens, B. P., A. S. Wallace, and D. A. Waldman. 2015. "Leader narcissism and follower outcomes: The counterbalancing effect of leader humility." *Journal of Applied Psychology, 100*(4), 1203–1213.

Pérez López, J. A. 1991. *Teoría de la acción humana en las organizaciones. La acción personal*, Madrid: Rialp.

Pérez López, J. A. 1993. *Fundamentos de la dirección de empresas*. Madrid: Rialp.

Peterson C., and M. Seligman, eds. 2004. *Character Strengths and Virtues: A Handbook and Classification*. New York: Oxford University Press.

Picone, P. M., G. B. Dagnino, and A. Minè. 2014. "The origin of failure: A multidisciplinary appraisal of the hubris hypothesis and proposed research agenda." *The Academy of Management Perspectives, 28*(4), 447–468.

Pieper, J. 1965. *The Four Cardinal Virtues: Prudence, Justice, Fortitude, Temperance*. New York: Harcourt, Brace and World.

Polo, L. 1996. *Ética. Hacia una versión moderna de los temas clásicos*, Madrid: Unión Editorial.

Roberts, R. C., and W. J. Wood. 2003. "Humility and epistemic goods." *Intellectual Virtue, 1*(9), 257–298.

Rhonheimer, M. 2011. *The Perspective of Morality. Philosophical Foundations of Thomistic Virtue Ethics*. Washington: Catholic University of America Press.

Rowatt, W. C., C. Powers, V. Targhetta, J. Comer, S. Kennedy, and J. Labouff. 2006. "Development and initial validation of an implicit measure of humility relative to arrogance." *Journal of Positive Psychology, 1*(4), 198–211.

Sakalaki, M., and K. Fousiani. 2012. "Social embeddedness and economic opportunism: A game situation." *Psychological Reports, 110*(3), 955–962.

Solomon, R. C. 1992. *Ethics and Excellence: Cooperation and Integrity in Business*. New York: Oxford University Press.

Sousa, M., and D. van Dierendonck. 2017. "Servant leadership and the effect of the interaction between humility, action, and hierarchical power on follower engagement." *Journal of Business Ethics, 141*(1), 13–25.

Tang, Y., J. Li, and H. Yang. 2015. "What I see, what I do: How executive hubris affects firm innovation." *Journal of Management, 41*(6), 1698–1723.

Tangney, J. P. 2005. "Humility." In *Handbook of Positive Psychology*, edited by C. R. Snyder and S. J. Lopez, 411–419. New York: Oxford University Press.

Teresa of Avila, 1921. *The Interior Castle* or the *Mansions*. 3rd ed. London: Thomas Baker. (Original in Spanish 1588.)

Vera, D., and A. Rodriguez-Lopez. 2004. "Strategic virtue: Humility as a source of competitive advantage." *Organizational Dynamics, 33*(4), 393–408.

Chapter 12

Frederick Douglass and the Power of Humility

DAVID J. BOBB

INTRODUCTION: HUMILIATION AND THE EARLY LIFE OF FREDERICK DOUGLASS

The word humility is derived from the Latin word *humus,* which refers to the earth or ground. For the first eight years of Frederick Douglass's life, he knew no bed except the dirt floor beneath him. Born a slave on the eastern shore of Maryland, and owned by one of that state's wealthiest men, Colonel Edward Lloyd, Douglass had a hard childhood marked by the daily humiliations of human bondage. In fact, humiliations were the only constant in his life, for his childhood, as Douglass recalled, was "without an intelligible beginning."[1]

Officially named Frederick Augustus Washington Bailey by his mother, who died when her son was only eight years old, young Freddie did not know the identity of his father, thought to be the white man who was chief slave overseer for Douglass's owner. Enslaved for the first two decades of his life, Frederick wrote in his first autobiography, *Narrative of the Life of Frederick Douglass, an American Slave,* that no matter the season, at the plantation he lacked a bed and had nothing to wear except a single long shirt. He and his fellow child slaves (he was not allowed to live with his mother, whom he saw rarely during his childhood) ate from the ground, with the mush that was their only food served from a trough, so that they ate "like so many pigs" (Douglass, [1845] 1994, 33). Killing a runaway slave in Douglass's time in Maryland was not a crime, and although young Freddie did not suffer routine whippings, he witnessed physical brutality against others daily (Douglass, [1845] 1994, 31). As Douglass summarized his plight in his third autobiography, *Life and Times of Frederick Douglass*, "The contrast between the condition of the slaves and that of their masters was marvelously sharp and striking. There was pride, pomp, and luxury on the one hand, servility, dejection, and misery on the other" (Douglass, [1881] 1994, 505).

One incident of humiliation in particular etched itself into young Freddie's memory. With more than 500 slaves, including Douglass, under his ownership, Colonel Edward Lloyd took special interest in the maintenance of his stable of horses, cared for by a slave called "old Barney." Douglass relates a moment that he called "one of the most heart-saddening and humiliating scenes I ever witnessed":

> These two men [old Barney and Col. Lloyd] were both advanced in years; there were the silver locks of the master, and the bald and toil-worn brow of the slave—superior and inferior here, powerful and weak here, but *equals* before God. "Uncover your head," said the imperious master; he was obeyed. "Take off your jacket, you old rascal!" and off came Barney's jacket. "Down on your knees!" Down knelt the old man, his shoulders bare, his bald head glistening in the sunshine, and his aged knees on the cold, damp ground. In this humble and debasing attitude, that master, to whom he devoted the best years and the best strength

> of his life, came forward and laid on thirty lashes with his horsewhip. The old man made no resistance, but bore it patiently, answering each blow with only a shrug of his shoulders and a groan. I do not think that the physical suffering from this infliction was severe for the whip was a light riding-whip; but the spectacle of an aged man—a husband and a father—humbly kneeling before his fellow-man, shocked me at the time; and since I have grown older, few of the features of slavery have impressed me with a deeper sense of its injustice and barbarity than did this exciting scene. I owe it to the truth, however, to say that this was the first and last time I ever saw a slave compelled to kneel to receive a whipping. (Douglass, [1881] 1994, 510)

This incident revealed to Douglass that the core of chattel slavery's subjugation of women and men was an effort to annihilate their humanity (Bobb, 2013, 159). Slavery denied the equality of all human beings before God and sought the humiliation of those deemed "inferior" because humiliation was among the most effective tools used in dehumanization.

As Douglass was moved from the rough St. Michael's plantation to his slave master's home in the city of Baltimore, Douglass began to reflect more on the meaning of humiliation and liberation. Teaching himself to read, as his mother before him had managed to do, Douglass came to see in reading an escape from enslavement. Douglass's slave master in Baltimore reprimanded his wife when he learned that she was helping Douglass read the Bible because "knowledge unfits a child to be slave" (Douglass, [1881] 1994, 527). Overhearing this exchange, Douglass wished nothing more than to be unfit. Yet he wondered often—as the same people who read him the Bible invoked its teachings to compel him to enslavement—if he would ever have any other destiny than that of a slave. It seemed to young Frederick that he might never be free.

HEALTHY PRIDE AND THE DEVELOPMENT OF HUMILITY

Humility is a hard-won virtue. It is not natural to human beings but must be intentionally honed. Requiring a keen self-knowledge, humility is a mean between self-aggrandizement and self-debasement. Its opposite is arrogance, not healthy pride. Humility requires introspection of the kind that Douglass displayed from an early age. It demands a reckoning with one's faults and a realization of one's opportunities. It does not insist on personal debasement. While healthy pride inspires self-confidence, humility counsels against overconfidence. Healthy pride instills a sense of agency and claims the rightful dignity of each human being. Humility guards against an unchecked ego. It upholds the claims of agency and dignity, and it warns against claims of unwarranted superiority. In its moral dimension, humility enables action consistent with the virtue. In its intellectual dimension, humility helps human beings realize their fallibility.

In Douglass's self-portrayal of his 20 years as a slave, the words "humility" or "humble" are used only pejoratively and mainly to refer to the mentality to which slaves were beholden that said Christianity sanctioned enslavement. This idea of false humility, or slavish self-debasement, was foisted on him. What Douglass replaced it with over time was healthy pride and genuine humility.

At the age of 13, Douglass scraped together enough money to purchase a copy of *The Columbian Orator,* in which he encountered some of the great speeches in world history, including those delivered by Socrates, the Roman statesman Cato the Younger, and George Washington. A dialogue between a fictional slave and a master impressed Douglass the most, even though it included the unlikely scenario of the slave gaining manumission because the master could not defend the injustice of the slave's condition. Reason rather than force and will prevailed in this account. According to Douglass, this unexpected outcome for the slave moved Douglass to consider whether his own plight might be similarly remedied. Douglass wondered if "the mighty power and heart-searching directness of truth penetrating the heart of a slaveholder and compelling him to yield up his earthly interests to the claims of eternal justice" could be realized in his own life (Douglass, [1881] 1994, 533).

A revelation from *The Columbian Orator* was to guide the rest of Douglass's life. "I had now penetrated," he concluded, "to the secret of all slavery and of all oppression, and had ascertained their true foundation to be in the pride, the power, and the avarice of man." For Douglass, arrogance marked the antithesis of "the principles of liberty." Arrogance, or unhealthy pride, combined with power and avarice were the "foundation" of the slave empire and "of all oppression" (Douglass, [1881] 1994, 533). Healthy pride is the opposite of arrogance, for with the discovery of healthy pride comes the negation of enslavement's power.

Douglass felt liberated, even vindicated, by this revelation because up to this point in his life he had been subjected to relentless propaganda from religiously minded masters that slavery was institutionalized and sanctioned by God—for the benefit of both slave and master. It was part of a divine plan for Douglass's life that he be a slave. The self-abnegation that resulted from this ideological lie was insidious, for it kept enslaved women and men like Frederick Douglass convinced that they had no inherent self-worth. The arrogance, or unhealthy pride, of the slave interest denied the slave any sense of self or healthy pride. The process by which this was accomplished was in the steady stream of humiliations suffered by enslaved people, all of which amounted to a denial of any healthy pride.

This "positive good" school of thinking about slavery, popular in the early and mid-19th century in the United States not just in the South but also throughout various intellectual and elite circles in the North and South, bedeviled Douglass in his early life precisely because of its rank hypocrisy. As he discovered the power of reason, he could see that those who cloaked their views in pseudo-religion and pseudo-science (it was supposed by many in the positive good school that both the Bible and science dictated that whites were the master race) were relying on arguments devoid of any intellectual integrity. "There is not a man beneath the canopy of heaven that does not know that slavery is wrong for *him*," Douglass later would write (Douglass, [1852] 1999, 196). His revelation even as a 13-year-old young man told him that overweening pride, combined with power and greed, was the real foundation of the slaveholding ideology. There was no rational foundation to the argument that had been presented to him, despite the slave masters' insistence that their position was consistent with the laws of nature and justice. Instead of being rooted in natural law, slavery's real foundation was an unhealthy, overweening pride. Whereas the slave interest couched their defense of slavery in reason, it was in fact only a rationalization.

The revelation of overweening pride's central place in human affairs that came from his reading of *The Columbian Orator* later prompted Douglass's understanding of its central place in the cause of the American Civil War and of the entirety of human oppression. It motivated him to become an enemy of institutionalized pride. Still, despite the progress in Douglass's intellectual understanding of slavery that came with the revelation of pride's central place in human affairs, 13-year-old Douglass was a long way from being free. Douglass was caught in a downward spiral in which his intellectual acuity only exacerbated the misery of his condition. The more he reflected on human liberty, the more he knew of what he was deprived. "This everlasting thinking distressed and tormented me; and yet there was no getting rid of this subject of my thoughts. Liberty, as an inestimable birthright of every man, converted every object into an asserter of this right. I heard it in every sound, and saw it in every object. It was ever present to torment me with a sense of my wretchedness"

(Douglass, [1881] 1994, 534). Freedom was in the air, yet Douglass was unable to breathe.

Abraham Lincoln said that America was God's "almost chosen people." In the same speech in which Lincoln used this expression, he also pronounced himself "a humble instrument in the hands of the Almighty" (Lincoln, [1861] 1953, 236). Lincoln used each phrase only once in the entire corpus of his more than 2 million recorded words. Yet these references, combined with the strong civil religious content of Lincoln's political philosophy, reveal an appeal to a higher mission for America, one that is ordained from on high—or at least consistent with a divine purpose. In an early speech, given before Lincoln had turned 30 years old, he beseeched "every lover of liberty" at the Young Men's Lyceum of Springfield, Illinois, to follow the nation's laws. "As the patriots of seventy-six did to the support of the Declaration of Independence, so to the support of the Constitution and Laws, let every American pledge his life, his property, and his sacred honor." This "political religion," as Lincoln called it, demanded of Americans that they "sacrifice unceasingly" upon its "altars" (Lincoln, [1838] 1953, 112).

Whereas Lincoln had throughout his life a fondness for America that led him to propound a "political religion" in its devotion, Frederick Douglass maintained a much more fraught relationship with the nation of his birth. As a 13-year-old, Douglass emerged from his intellectual awakening about pride's central place only to see with greater clarity the evils of slavery. Rejecting the deceit that told him nature or God ordained him to be a slave, Douglass came to see slavery in its true colors. Liberty was his lodestar, but he did not yet know how to secure his freedom.

Having identified unhealthy pride as the problem at the heart of slavery, Douglass had yet to develop the healthy pride that would allow him to escape his enslavement. Douglass relates how he gained this healthy pride in his autobiographical account of being sent to the slave-breaker Edward Covey, known in Maryland as among the most savage of those whose job it was to break the wills of slaves. At the age of 16, Douglass was sent away from Baltimore to be broken. "There was neither joy in my heart nor elasticity in my frame as I started for the tyrant's home," Douglass later wrote (Douglass, [1881] 1994, 563). His desire to read was diminished, as Douglass needed all his energy to work. Covey was "[c]old, distant, morose, with a face wearing all the marks of captious pride and malicious sternness, he repelled all advances" (Douglass, [1881] 1994, 566). So intense was the forced labor, and so unrelenting the beatings, that Douglass "was sometimes tempted to take [his] life and that of Covey, but was prevented by a combination of hope and fear" (Douglass, [1881] 1994, 572).

Douglass's intellectual awakening had stirred in him a moral uprising. Having been "humbled, degraded, broken down, enslaved, and brutalized" (Douglass, [1881] 1994, 575), Douglass stated, "I would have exchanged my manhood for the brutehood of an ox" (Douglass, [1881] 1994, 583). But refusing to give up, Douglass steeled his soul so that his body could resist the tyrant. As he would later say, in his most famous speech, "Self-Made Men," "The soul is the main thing" (Douglass, 1874, 21). Even though every beating felt more than Douglass could bear, he mustered the energy one day to fight back against Covey. Recognizing in his soul that he did not fear death, he thereby gained the ability to resist the physical predation of Covey. In this act of resistance, which left Covey attempting to order other slaves to help him against Douglass—to no avail—Douglass encountered what he called a "turning point." For Douglass, "This spirit made me a freeman in *fact,* although I still remained a slave in *form*" (Douglass, [1881] 1994, 591, italics in original).

Although it took Douglass many months before he was able to liberate himself "in form" by escaping to the North, the decisive moral act on which his freedom turned was his discovery that he need not fear death. The decisive moral understanding was that the message he had heard all his life—that he was a slave because God and the order of the universe said he should be—was false. What Douglass had been told throughout his life, that "God required them to submit to slavery and to wear their chains with meekness and humility," was a lie (Douglass, [1881] 1994, 534).

For Douglass, "humility" in this sense was something pressed upon him. It was not authentic humility but forced humiliation. In fact, his entire life as a slave was enforced humiliation—abject and awful. This humiliation characterized his first 20 years of life. Even after his escape from slavery, humiliations followed him throughout his life, from churches that distributed the elements of Holy Communion in segregated lines, to the everyday condescension that marked his conversation with too many white people. Abolitionists, Douglass said, were often the worst because of how they talked down to black people.

Yet, once Frederick Douglass achieved his intellectual awakening, and then his moral epiphany, he was able to see himself for who he really was. Before, in his unenlightened state, subjected to the physical attacks of Edward Covey, Douglass frequently wished that he was an animal, or a "brute." Once enlightened about the prospect of freedom, and awakened to his inherent dignity, Douglass gained a sense of self that was healthy pride.

Whereas unhealthy pride, or arrogance, sanctions the idea of chattel slavery, healthy pride entails the proper understanding of the dignity of the human person. Each human being, Douglass came to believe, is equal in possession of natural, or human, rights. The universal application of healthy pride is equal rights for all people. "*Right* is of no sex—Truth is of no color—God is the Father of us *all*, and we are brethren" was the masthead of *The North Star*, the newspaper Douglass started in 1847. Within this revelation was the path to true humility. And if humility is in part knowing one's own limitations (curbing one's arrogance) and infusing one's ambitions with respect for the inherent dignity of others, then healthy pride is overcoming the limits unduly imposed by others in order to stand as an equal to all.

HUMILITY AS A MORAL VIRTUE

By Douglass's own account, the humiliations and struggles heaped upon him in his period of enslavement were enough to make him contemplate suicide. Yet upon facing death, Douglass gained a moral clarity that made him strong. This moral epiphany also helped him overcome any bitterness that at later points in his life might have overwhelmed him. In two remarkable letters Douglass wrote to his former slave owner, Thomas Auld, who was outspoken about his Christianity, and his brother, Hugh, with whom Douglass lived while in Baltimore, he forgives the men for holding him as a slave. His healthy pride opened the way to genuine humility.

In 1848, when Douglass was only 30, and 10 years out of captivity, he wrote an open letter to Thomas Auld in *The North Star.* On the occasion of the 10th anniversary of Douglass's "emancipation," he wrote about the injustice against himself but was particularly indignant at the thought of three of his four sisters still languishing under Auld's control, their current state unknown to Douglass because of their inability to read or write: "You have kept them in utter ignorance, and have therefore robbed them of the sweet enjoyments of writing or receiving letters from absent friends and relatives. Your wickedness and cruelty committed in this respect on your fellow-creatures, are greater than all the stripes you have laid upon my back, or theirs. It is an outrage upon the soul—a war upon the immortal spirit, and one for which you must give account at the bar of our common Father and Creator" (Douglass, 1848, 116). Pledging to make Auld's name known as a way of unmasking the hypocrisy of slave owners who use Christianity to cover their sins, Douglass nonetheless closed by saying that he "entertain[s] no malice towards you personally. There is no roof under which you would be more safe than mine, and there is nothing in my house which you might need for your comfort, which I would not readily grant. Indeed, I should esteem it a privilege, to set you an example as to how mankind ought to treat each other" (Douglass, 1848, 116–117).

To Hugh Auld, Thomas's brother, and the man who said that if Douglass continued to learn to read from his wife that he would be unfit for slavery, Douglass wrote a letter in 1857, on the 20th anniversary of his running away. In a much shorter letter, sent privately, Douglass requests some information that Hugh Auld alone would know and writes, in passing, "I love you, but hate Slavery." Desirous of knowing a particular date related to his captivity, Douglass closes his appeal for the information, "We are all hastening where all distinctions are ended, kindness to the humblest will not be unrewarded" (Douglass, 1857).

For Douglass, humility helped him forgive those who enslaved him. It allowed him to resist the bitterness that could have consumed him. Healthy pride helped him gain confidence in his dignity as a human being. In this combination alone came the possibility that he could contend with the humiliations that were part of his life—past, present, and future.

Healthy pride does not ensure against any humiliation. Rather, healthy pride ensures that humiliation need not be overwhelming. The healthy pride that Douglass discovered gradually as a young man included a growing sense of self-importance. Humility helps rein in self-importance so that it does not grow too large. When one's life is full of humiliations, as was Douglass's, it is easy to lapse into self-abnegation. That is what Douglass's tormentors wanted, after all: that his sense of self-worth would shrink to the place where he would not assert his humanity. The "soul-crushing and death-dealing character of slavery," against which Douglass fought, came from arrogance that supposed that some human beings were born to be slaves (Douglass, [1855] 1994, 184). Against this ideology Douglass had to recover his dignity.

Even as Douglass gained notoriety for his rhetorical skills, and grew to become one of America's best known orators, there were constant reminders of the indignities of being a free black. One incident related by Booker T. Washington encapsulates all of this. On one train trip Douglass took in Pennsylvania, despite having paid the same train fare as white passengers, he was relegated to the baggage car. Some well-meaning white passengers apologized for the incident, with one saying, "I am sorry, Mr. Douglass, that you have been degraded in this manner." To this Douglass retorted, "They cannot degrade Frederick Douglass. The soul that is within me no man can degrade. I am not the one that is being degraded on account of this treatment, but those who are inflicting it upon me" (Washington, 1906, 100).

If overweening pride—the kind that overwhelms an individual soul and makes it amenable to evil—is the "foundation" of slavery and oppression, healthy pride ensures that dignity may be upheld. Dignity is not earned by anyone; it is something that all human beings possess by virtue of being human. But a person whose condition is one of perpetual degradation does not *feel* dignified. It is difficult for them to even claim their dignity with healthy pride. When such a claim is made, liberation of the sort Douglass related on that Pennsylvania train is the result. One knows one's self-worth, and nothing can take that away. To deny another's worth is to denigrate your soul, not theirs.

HUMILITY AS AN INTELLECTUAL VIRTUE

Humility and healthy pride go together. And if healthy pride is not an opposite of humility, neither is healthy ambition. Often erroneously displayed as passive or inert, the humble individual is not a wallflower. For the enlightened Frederick Douglass, after his escape from slavery, his ambition was strong, and he was keen on determining how he would channel his ambition.

Frederick Douglass was mainly a man of action. Yet also as a man of the written and spoken word, Douglass labored throughout his adult life to be guided wherever the evidence in a particular debate led him. An intellectually humble person is willing to accept correction, admit mistakes, and change course. An ideologue, on the other hand, refuses to be guided by evidence and hews to a way of thinking despite evidence to the contrary. Intellectual humility is premised on the importance of falsifiability.

As an ex-slave, Douglass quickly became a much sought-after speaker. Ignited by the abolitionist writings published in William Lloyd Garrison's newspaper, *The Liberator*, Douglass became active in the abolitionist cause almost immediately and met Garrison in 1841, three years into his life as a freeman. Douglass was on the same dais as Garrison in that first meeting, and both speakers were equally impressed by the other. To Garrison, having heard Douglass a second time, the uneducated slave was so eloquent he "would have done honor to Patrick Henry" (Stauffer, 2008, 82). Douglass's career as a speaker took off, and soon he was traveling the country speaking on behalf of abolition.

The movement to abolish slavery in America had many factions, but its dominant strain, led by Garrison, critiqued the US Constitution as a blood-soaked covenant. The Declaration of Independence was clear in its affirmation of liberty and equality for all, but its call was not heeded. For Garrisonians, politics was a trap that would force compromise where none was possible. Moral purity demanded ideological rigidity and viewed any violent resistance to slavery as unjustified. Captured wholly by their view of Christian virtue, Garrisonians were a powerful force in antebellum America.

Douglass entered the Garrisonian wing of the abolitionist cause, its majority faction, on fire for the cause as a whole. As he experienced more of the day-to-day vicissitudes of trying to be opposed to slavery without being involved in politics, Douglass, along with many other former slaves who were part of the 500,000-person community of American freemen, struggled to see how the abolitionist movement could be effective without a political arm. For instance, Douglass's newspaper, *The North Star*, did not condemn those who voted, even though Garrison's *Liberator* was staunchly opposed to voting of any kind.

On another important issue Douglass started to break from his mentor Garrison. Whereas the Garrisonians held to a strictly anti-constitutional line, Douglass, influenced by the abolitionist Gerrit Smith, began to reconsider his stance. For all of his abolitionist career, Douglass had followed Garrison in loathing the Constitution, considering it an elaborate cover for the ongoing protection of the institution that had taken his first 20 years of life. That such a document could be the governing instrument of America meant to Douglass, following Garrison, that both the compact and the country were irremediably corrupt. The corruption went so deep to leave Douglass deeply alienated from the homeland. "I have no love for America, as such; I have no patriotism," Douglass wrote in 1847. "I have no country. What country have I? . . . I have not, I cannot have, any love for this country, as such, or for its Constitution. I desire to see its overthrow as speedily as possible, and its Constitution shivered in a thousand fragments" (Douglass, [1847] 1999, 77–78).

As the slaveholding interest amassed more power in the late 1840s, and the positive good school defending slavery grew more powerful, Douglass started to rethink his views on non-violence and on the Constitution. Having reluctantly come to the conclusion that violent resistance was going to be necessary to end slavery, Douglass also changed his mind on the status of the Constitution. On May 23, 1851, Douglass published "Change of Opinion Announced" in his newspaper, in which he announced that the Constitution was an anti-slavery document (not a pro-slavery document). The implications of his reversal were profound: Douglass now affirmed that political activity must accompany moral persuasion.

Douglass displayed a considerable amount of intellectual humility in breaking with his mentor. Intellectual, or epistemic, humility is the counterpart to moral humility. Just as Douglass was able to forgive those who owned him when he was an enslaved person, Douglass also was willing to admit when he wrong and reverse course on long-entrenched matters of ideology. Instead of digging into positions long held, Douglass was willing to subject his views, and those of his close comrades in the movement, to criticism. He was not afraid of reversing himself or offending others when it became clear to him that his previous views were mistaken. In rejecting Garrisonianism, Douglass declared an openness to the political process he had previously eschewed. He avoided the self-righteous moral preening that followed Garrison throughout his career. By admitting where he had been wrong, Douglass was able to draw upon the fixed principles of the Declaration (equality and liberty for all) *and* the flexible (amendable) quality of the Constitution. The Constitution's protection of slavery, Douglass maintained, resembled the scaffolding of a "magnificent structure," which was removable upon the building's completion (Douglass, [1863] 1999, 536).

Douglass's intellectual humility allowed him to change his historical, political, and legal views. In his willingness to reimagine the arguments against slavery, and the means by which justice could be achieved, Douglass recognized that the critical factor was not the American past, but a just future. He invokes the spirit of '76 not to instill a fidelity to the rule of law, as did the young Lincoln, but to abolish unjust laws, such as the laws that allowed slavery.

Whereas for Garrisonians America's constitutional past was something to be avoided, for Douglass, America's past could be overcome. The flawed Constitution could be repaired, since only its façade, not its foundation, had to be replaced. Whereas Douglass as a Garrisonian had to see the United States' government as illegitimate, in his new stance Douglass could see the US government as legitimate but flawed.

Douglass also shifted his stance about politics, moving from a thoroughgoing anti-political stance to one in which political action was embraced. This meant Douglass jettisoned the political passivity of Garrisonianism and replaced it with radical political rhetoric (working within political parties that could articulate radical abolitionism) and prudential political action. He began supporting Republican Party candidates who had a chance of winning.

Finally, by adapting his philosophy of constitutional interpretation, which previously was inflexibly fixed on what might be called the original intention of the Constitution's framers, Douglass allowed a more capacious view that took into account a combination of original meaning and dynamic interpretation. In short, Douglass moved from being an anti-political activist who was alienated from America, and opposed to its pro-slavery Constitution, to a political abolitionist ill at ease with contemporary America but inspired by its anti-slavery, pro-liberty Constitution. Unchanged in all of this movement was Douglass's abiding passion for the principles of the Declaration of Independence.

Douglass's change of opinion cost him his friendship with his mentor William Lloyd Garrison, who not only broke thoroughly with Douglass on grounds of the philosophical disagreements, but he also implied that Douglass had shifted his views only to garner financial support from a wealthy abolitionist who was contributing to the success of Douglass's newspaper. Douglass was saddened by the breach but continued throughout the rest of his life to credit Garrison as a hero and mentor.

HOPE FOR UNIVERSAL EQUALITY

In his life as an ex-slave, Douglass fought for justice for all people and hoped for the kind of universal equality articulated in the American Declaration. He aimed to fulfill what the founders had started by making real the rhetoric of "All men are created equal." He wished to do so not only for Americans of African descent but also for women. "All rights for all" was the motto of *The North Star,* and the guiding purpose of Douglass's work.

For Douglass, humility helped guard against hopelessness. At the beginning and end of Douglass's 1852 speech on the meaning of the Fourth of July, which was his most famous speech, he invokes hope. Hope for Douglass began with the Declaration of Independence. July 4th is Declaration day, and for Douglass, as he told those gathered in Rochester, "The 4th of July is the first great fact in your nation's history—the very ringbolt in the chain of your yet undeveloped destiny" (Douglass, [1852] 1999, 191). The "saving principles" of the Declaration must be followed without fail. As great as the principles are, they are no help if not followed. America had gone astray, Douglass charged, and departed from those principles. July 4th to the slave is a hypocrisy. "To him, your celebration is a sham; your boasted liberty, an unholy license; your national greatness, swelling vanity; your sounds of rejoicing are empty and heartless; your denunciation of tyrants, brass fronted impudence; your shouts of liberty and equality, hollow mockery" (Douglass, [1852] 1999, 196). Compounding the hypocrisy is the complicity of Christianity, which by staying silent on the creation and maintenance of slavery, and perpetuating the evil institution of slavery "favors the rich against the poor" and "exalts the proud above the humble" (Douglass, [1852] 1999, 201).

Douglass's speech is a jeremiad against pride run amok and a warning to those who would extol America inordinately. "Americans! Your republican politics, not less than your republican religion, are flagrantly inconsistent. You boast of your love of liberty, your superior civilization, and your pure Christianity, while the whole political power of the nation (as embodied in the two great political parties) is solemnly pledged to support and perpetuate the enslavement of three millions of your countrymen." As Douglass continues, you Americans "pride yourselves on your Democratic institutions, while you yourselves consent to be mere *tools* and *body-guards* of the tyrants of Virginia and Carolina." All are in thrall to "a system begun in avarice, supported in pride, and perpetuated in cruelty" (Douglass, [1852] 1999, 202). This system, built on pride, begets further pride, a sign of a nation out of control and worthy of destruction. Still, Douglass concluded "I, therefore, leave off where I began, with hope." His practical hope is that the global connectedness of all nations will break down the pernicious pull of tradition. "No nation can now shut itself up from the surrounding world and trot round in the same old path of its fathers without interference" (Douglass, [1852] 1999, 205).

Almost a decade after the July 4th speech, and just a month into the Civil War, Douglass published an article in his newspaper, *Douglass' Monthly*, in May 1861, in which he argued that the hubris of slavery had brought on the "nemesis" of civil war. "At last our proud Republic is overtaken," he begins. Having ignored the warnings against the inhumanity of slavery, America went about "strengthening the arm of his guilty master, till now, in the pride of his giant power, that master is emboldened to lift rebellious arms against the very majesty of the law, and defy the power of the Government itself" (Douglass, [1861] 1999, 450). Ending slavery is the only way to win the war caused by slavery.

Douglass's hope for America's future was that it could overcome its nemesis. The victory for equality in the Civil War, followed immediately by necessary constitutional changes, was not nearly enough. As Reconstruction faltered, Douglass's disappointment with the American people grew more intense. Slavery's abolition was a profound victory, but it had to be followed by greater action to ensure the attainment of equal civil rights, and the integration of black Americans into society.

SELF-MADE MEN

For Douglass, a combination of healthy pride and humility informed his idea of the "self-made man," which was one of the most important themes of his post–Civil War oratory. Crafted as a constructive response to his disappointment with Reconstruction's failings, the approximately 50 speeches he gave on the self-made man included self-help advice for Americans of African descent, and admonition to all Americans about what could be done in light of larger political failings. The argument he makes in "Self-Made Men" help connect his biography to the social and political story of America, for in this speech Douglass reveals how his mature political philosophy includes a counterpoise between humility and greatness.

Although Douglass came to love America, it was a love complicated by the long complicity of Americans in the perpetuation of slavery as an institution and as a legacy. The several years Douglass spent in England and Scotland made him see the United States through a different lens. His admiration of France, too, affected the way he saw America. Douglass had a cosmopolitan outlook, but he eventually became proud of being an American. It was a hard journey, and his pride in America grew only as the institution of slavery withered away. By 1870, he could say, "We are a great nation—not we colored people particularly, but all of us. We are all together now. We are fellow-citizens of a common country. What a country—fortunate in its institutions, in its Fifteenth amendment, in its future" (Douglass, [1870] 1991, 272).

American greatness, for Douglass, was elusive, for America in his depiction was always on its way to a better place. As he said in "Self-Made Men," it is often noted by foreign observers that there is "no repose in America" (Douglass, 1874, 35). "Self-Made Men" is a reflection on greatness, and what makes a person great. Rejecting the idea that men are born great, he celebrates a work ethic that can bring progress. "When we find a man who has ascended heights beyond ourselves; who has a broader range of vision than we and a sky with more stars in it than we have in ours, we may know that he has worked harder, better and more wisely than we" (Douglass, 1874, 12–13). For Douglass, greatness must be earned.

The self-made man, for Douglass, must have the right combination of humility and healthy pride. Examples of self-made men include Abraham Lincoln ("the king of American self-made men") (Douglass, 1874, 27); the African American scientist Benjamin Banneker, who went from slave to architect of the nation's capital; and Toussaint L'Overture, the leader of the 1791 Haitian revolution who came up from slavery (Douglass, 1874, 29). For Douglass, America has been especially hospitable to the rise of the self-made man, in large measure because work is rewarded in the United States. The "free spirit" of the American people, who exercise sovereignty, buoys "both labor and laborer. The strife between capital and labor is here, comparatively equal. The one is not the haughty and powerful master and the other the weak and abject slave as is the case in some parts of Europe" (Douglass, 1874, 31). With the notable exception of slavery, this prevailing condition is among the most important reasons why America is such fertile soil for self-made men.

The main reason that self-made men are numerous in America is the meritocratic society. "In Europe, greatness is often thrust upon men. They are made legislators by birth" (Douglass, 1874, 32). This is not true in America, where George Washington, Jr., or Andrew Jackson, Jr., Douglass notes, are no more likely to be president than "the sons of Smith or Jones" (Douglass, 1874, 33–34). Because Americans are not bound by antecedents, the future is open. "We have as a people no past and very little present, but a boundless and glorious future," Douglass said. "With us, it is not so much what has been, or what is now, but what is to be in the good time coming" (Douglass, 1874, 34). For Douglass, the opportunity to succeed or fail is vital. Of every American it can be rightly said, "If he cannot be President he can, at least, be prosperous. In this respect, America is not only the exception to the general rule, but the social wonder of the world." Europe "inspires little of individual hope or courage," Douglass said (Douglass, 1874, 34).

The challenge with the self-made men, Douglass concludes his address, is that "self-made men," especially those of the educated sort, "are not generally over modest or self-forgetful men" (Douglass, 1874, 37). They are prone to "egotism" (Douglass, 1874, 37–38). As he noted about Andrew Jackson, "A man indebted for himself to himself, may naturally think well of himself" (Douglass, 1874, 38). What is important is having the wherewithal to correct this tendency. "That a man has been able to make his own way in the world, is a humble fact as well as an honorable one. It is, however, possible to state a very humble fact in a very haughty manner, and self-made men are, as a class, much addicted to this habit" (Douglass, 1874, 38). This tendency alienates self-made men from the rest of society, but it need not. Addictions can be broken, and self-made men can buck the trend.

NATIONAL IMPLICATIONS

Douglass could lecture authoritatively on self-made men because he was one. As a slave, he gained personal insight into the arrogant core of oppression. Later in life, this made him acutely aware of the problem of political and social oppression. Douglass's discovery of his own dignity—what came to be his healthy pride—made possible his rise in American society. As a self-made man, he was aware of unhealthy pride, which manifests itself as egotism. As a political leader, Douglass was aware of the national implications of unhealthy pride.

In 1876, exactly 11 years after Lincoln's assassination, Frederick Douglass was the keynote speaker at the dedication of the Freedman's Memorial, in Lincoln Park, Washington, DC. Douglass paid honor "to an American great man" (Douglass, [1876] 1999, 617) and in addressing his "fellow citizens," insisted that "we disclaim everything like arrogance and assumption" (Douglass, [1876] 1999, 618). The statue of Lincoln that was being dedicated, called *Emancipation,* depicts a shackled slave, wearing nothing but a loincloth, kneeling at the feet of the Great Emancipator. In Douglass's prepared remarks, he does not comment on the statue, but mainly notes that although great, "In his interests, in his associations, in his habits of thought, and in his prejudices, [Lincoln] was a white man." Following this, Douglass told the white members of the 25,000-strong crowd, including President Ulysses Grant, and speaking of his fellow African Americans, "You are the children of Abraham Lincoln. We are at best only his stepchildren" (Douglass, [1876] 1999, 618). According to Howard University professor and historian John Cromwell, Douglass departed from his prepared text to comment on the statue, criticizing it because it "showed the Negro on his knees when a more manly attitude would have been indicative of freedom" (Araujo, 2014, 157). Old Barney was on his knees, Douglass might have recalled, but old Barney's children need not be.

In Douglass's view, any celebration of America would have to be qualified with recollection of old Barney, or the slow, faltering way in which slavery came to be condemned over the course of the 18th and 19th centuries. It would be tempered by the depiction of the black man in the statue *Emancipation.* Throughout his career, whenever Americans around him praised America, Douglass was quick to agree about its many outstanding qualities, but equally quick to remind his interlocutors of its many failings. The self-made nation, like the self-made man, should be careful not to think too highly of itself. Hubris in a nation is as bad as hubris in a human being. Humility is a quality to be prized in people and nations alike, for in its practice is the possibility of equality and justice for all.

NOTE

1. Douglass, *My Bondage and My Freedom,* in Douglass, 1994, 157. Douglass wrote three autobiographies, the first of which was *Narrative of the Life of Frederick Douglass,* published in 1845, seven years after he escaped from slavery. The second, *My Bondage and My Freedom,* was published in 1855, while the first edition of the third autobiography, *Life and Times of Frederick Douglass,* came out in 1881. As Douglass advanced in age beyond his captivity, and the threat of his recapture was ended, he was able to be more frank about his ordeal.

REFERENCES

Araujo, Ana Lucia. 2014. *Shadows of the Slave Past: Memory, Heritage, and Slavery.* New York: Routledge.

Douglass, Frederick. (April 22, 1870) 1991. "At Last, At Last, the Black Man Has a Future: An Address Delivered in Albany, New York." Series One, Vol. 4 of *The Frederick Douglass Papers,* edited by John R. Blassingame and John R. McKivigan, 265–272. New Haven, CT: Yale University Press.

Bobb, David J. 2013. *Humility: An Unlikely Biography of America's Greatest Virtue.* New York: Nelson Books.

Douglass, Frederick. (July 6, 1863) 1999. "Address for the Promotion of Colored Enlistments." In *Frederick Douglass: Selected Speeches and Writings*, edited by Philip S. Foner, 533–538. Chicago: Lawrence Hill Books.

Douglass, Frederick. 1857. Letter to Hugh Auld, October 4. https://www.gilderlehrman.org/content/i-love-you-hate-slavery-frederick-douglass-his-former-owner-hugh-auld-1857.

Douglass, Frederick. 1848. Letter to Thomas Auld, September 3. In *Frederick Douglass: Selected Speeches and Writings*, edited by Philip S. Foner, 111–117. Chicago: Lawrence Hill Books.

Douglass, Frederick. (1881) 1994. "Life and Times of Frederick Douglass." In *Autobiographies*, edited by Henry Louis Gates, Jr. New York: Library of America.

Douglass, Frederick. (July 5, 1852) 1999. "The Meaning of July Fourth for the Negro." In *Frederick Douglass: Selected Speeches and Writings*, edited by Philip S. Foner, 188–206. Chicago: Lawrence Hill Books.

Douglass, Frederick. (1855) 1994. "My Bondage and My Freedom." In *Autobiographies*, edited by Henry Louis Gates, Jr. New York: Library of America.

Douglass, Frederick. (1845) 1994. "Narrative of the Life of Frederick Douglass." In *Autobiographies*, edited by Henry Louis Gates, Jr. New York: Library of America.

Douglass, Frederick. (May 1861) 1999. "Nemesis." In *Frederick Douglass: Selected Speeches and Writings*, edited by Philip S. Foner, 450–451. Chicago: Lawrence Hill Books.

Douglass, Frederick. (April 14, 1876) 1999. "Oration in Memory of Abraham Lincoln." In *Frederick Douglass: Selected Speeches and Writings*, edited by Philip S. Foner, 615–624. Chicago: Lawrence Hill Books.

Douglass, Frederick. (May 11, 1847) 1999. "The Right to Criticize American Institutions." In *Frederick Douglass: Selected Speeches and Writings*, edited by Philip S. Foner, 75–83. Chicago: Lawrence Hill Books.

Douglass, Frederick. 1874. "Self-Made Men." Address before the students of the Indian Industrial School, Carlisle, Pennsylvania. https://www.loc.gov/item/mfd.29006/.

Lincoln, Abraham. (January 27, 1838) 1953. "Address Before the Young Men's Lyceum of Springfield, Illinois." Vol. I of *The Collected Works of Abraham Lincoln*, edited by Roy P. Basler, 108–115. New Brunswick, NJ: Rutgers University Press.

Lincoln, Abraham. (February 21, 1861) 1953. "Address to the New Jersey Senate at Trenton, New Jersey." Vol. IV of *The Collected Works of Abraham Lincoln*, edited by Roy P. Basler, 236–237. New Brunswick, NJ: Rutgers University Press.

Stauffer, John. 2008. *Giants: The Parallel Lives of Frederick Douglass and Abraham Lincoln*. New York: Twelve.

Washington, Booker T. 1906. *Up from Slavery*. New York: Doubleday.

PART III

INTELLECTUAL HUMILITY

Chapter 13

Self-Trust and Epistemic Humility

C. THI NGUYEN

INTRODUCTION

We are fallible beings. Our calculations, judgments, and decisions rest on methods and abilities that are not, and cannot be, perfectly secured against mistake. Though we must trust our mental abilities in order to think and act, that trust must be impeachable. Yet we often ignore our cognitive fallibility in certain domains, such as the moral, the aesthetic, and the religious. We seem to think, in these domains, the fact that others disagree with us should not reduce our confidence in our own beliefs. This is in stark contrast to how we conduct our cognitive lives in other domains, like the perceptual and the scientific, where we usually take certain forms of disagreement as clear reasons to decrease our confidence and certain forms of agreement to increase our confidence.

There seems to be something special about the domains of the moral, aesthetic, and perhaps even the religious, something that demands that we make up our own minds about what we believe and what we will do. We ought not bow down to authority; we ought not simply obey moral gurus and art critics and spiritual leaders the way we follow the prescriptions of our doctors and mechanics. So, as this line of thinking goes, we ought not simply believe because we are told in these special domains, even if the tellers are experts. We ought to strive for, say, moral judgments that proceed only from our own understanding, that gel with our genuine and sincere moral intuitions. Though conversations with others might prompt me to consider new arguments or reasons, in the end I ought to make up my own mind for myself.

The moral discussion here leans on what, to many, is a clear intuition about our obligations to think through moral matters for ourselves. There is, it seems, nothing wrong with unquestioningly following my doctor's orders. But there seems to be something wrong with unquestionably obeying a moral authority; that strikes many as a form of problematic servility. What might explain that intuition? According to Robert Paul Wolff, it's because there is a special requirement for moral judgment—a requirement that we be morally autonomous.

> Since the responsible man arrives at moral decisions which he expresses himself in the form of imperatives, we may say that he gives laws to himself, or is self-legislating. In short, he is autonomous. As Kant argued, moral autonomy is a combination of freedom and responsibility; it is a submission to laws that one has made for oneself. The autonomous man, insofar as he is autonomous, is not subject to the will of another. He may do what another tells him, but not *because* he has been told to do it. (Wolff, 1970, 13–14)

Others have attempted to explain the intuition without the direct invocation of Kantian autonomy. Robert Hopkins has explained the intuition in terms of a special requirement for moral understanding—that we must grasp the specifically moral grounds for our moral beliefs. When we acquire moral beliefs through on testimony, we may have social grounds, but not moral grounds, for our moral beliefs (Hopkins, 2007). Similarly, Philip Nickel argues that moral decisions are so dependent on subtle details of the exact state of affairs that an actor must have moral understanding in order to accurately respond to changing conditions (Nickel, 2001; for a more detailed survey and critical discussion of these issues in moral testimony, see McGrath, 2011; Driver, 2006; Nguyen, 2010). Similarly, most aesthetic theorists believe that our aesthetic judgments ought to arise from our own direct experiences (Wollheim, 1980, 233; Whiting, 2015; Hopkins, 2011). Malcolm Budd, for example, argues that aesthetic judgments express one's actual appreciation of the aesthetic qualities in an object. To claim that a dancer is graceful is to express one's appreciation of the particular way in which that dancer achieves gracefulness, rather than just attributing some abstract property to them. But testimony, in and of itself, doesn't give us an appreciation of those aesthetic qualities (Budd, 2003; for critical discussion of these claims about aesthetic testimony, see Meskin, 2007; Laetz, 2008; Robson, 2015; Nguyen, 2017). Thus, it is thought, we should be intellectually self-sufficient in these special domains. It is the demand for intellectual self-sufficiency that seems to license us to ignore both expert testimony and disagreement. If we demand absolute intellectual self-sufficiency in these special domains, then we ought not trust others, and we ought to ignore their testimony, be it supportive or condemnatory of our own beliefs.

In my view, permitting ourselves this exaggerated form of epistemic independence is a mistake, even in such peculiar realms. We ought, instead, to be *epistemically humble*—that is, we ought to recognize our own cognitive fallibility, in these peculiar realms, and let others' disagreement affect our confidence. The demand for complete self-sufficiency is an exaggeration of a more plausible consideration: namely, that there is something wrong with abject subservience—with giving up on all attempts at reasoning and understanding and submitting our will to another. While there is something wrong with total intellectual subservience, responding with epistemic humility in the face of disagreement is not actually a form of intellectual subservience. It is, instead, a distinct and active intellectual process, part of our epistemically responsible procedure for checking the functioning of our own cognitive abilities. Employing this procedure does not count as subservience; it is, in fact, the very reverse. Unthinking subservience is a form of disengagement from the deliberative process. The drive to seek evidence of corroboration and discorroboration, the drive to use others to check ourselves, comes from the very same values that lead us to abhor subservience: values of understanding, epistemic self-perfection, and responsibility for our beliefs. Using social sources of information to corroborate and discorroborate our cognitive abilities is actually a form of increased rational engagement and part of a mature cognitive life. And acquiring epistemic humility in the face of disagreement is the active and engaged response to genuine evidence of our own potential unreliability.

TRUST AND SOCIALLY EMBEDDED KNOWLEDGE

Let's start by acknowledging that the requirement for radical intellectual self-sufficiency is something of a peculiar bird.[1] In many realms, such as the empirical and the scientific, the volume of knowledge and skill required for any reasonable cognitive life far surpasses the capacities of a lone human mind. We may master one or two areas of specialist knowledge, but no single person can adequately understand modern medicine, nutrition, automotive repair, computer software architecture, and meteorology. Thus, we must often trust the testimony and judgment of others (Hardwig, 1985, 1991; Goldberg, 2010; Millgram, 2015). This trust is not necessarily blind; we may choose whom to trust for good reasons, but at some point, we must adopt beliefs without understanding the direct evidential grounds for those beliefs for ourselves. In doing science and going to the doctor, we must trust.

But things seem very different in certain non-empirical domains. Though we don't hold every person responsible for understanding their medical beliefs, we do seem to require every person to be responsible for arriving at their own moral beliefs independently, through their own reasoning and understanding.[2] Thus, one might think that the demand for such radical autonomy, wherever it might be found, shields us against any impact from disagreement. The existence of moral and aesthetic disagreement shouldn't impact our degree of self-confidence because in those domains we are supposed to trust only ourselves.

Much has been written recently about disagreement in general, and how we ought to rationally revise our beliefs when we encounter disagreement. The debate is usually framed as one between the positions of "steadfastness"—that one ought to ignore the existence of disagreement—and "conciliationism"—that one ought to adjust one's degree of belief in response to the existence of disagreement.[3] The focus of these debates has often been on empirical judgments and other sorts of ordinary judgments to which no radical demand for self-sufficiency seems to apply. I will presume that conciliationism is the correct position for disagreement over empirical judgments, and otherwise leave that discussion to the side. I am interested, instead, in examining the seemingly asymmetric impact of disagreement between empirical domains and domains like the moral, aesthetic, and religious.

Let's focus on disagreements over *unsecured judgments*. An unsecured judgment is any judgment where the judger's degree of confidence exceeds their justificatory resources. The category includes what are often called brute intuitions—substantive judgments based on phenomenal seemings. For example, I might make an unsecured judgment that torture is wrong simply because it strikes me as obviously wrong. But the category also includes loose applications. That is, even if I had a well-secured moral principle—perhaps I accept a Kantian argument to the conclusion, "Do not use others as means"—a hasty application of that principle to a particular situation might not be well-secured.[4] I will assume that most or all of our moral, religious, and aesthetic judgments are unsecured, while our empirical and scientific judgments are, for the most part, secured. Those cognitive domains where judgments are largely unsecured, I call *unsecured domains*.

Interestingly, these apparently unsecured domains are also the ones in which we seem to face the most pervasive disagreement. There are three possible responses to that pervasive disagreement. First, we might be moved to become *epistemic nihilists* about the domain. Since our judgments are already unsecured, the existence of disagreement could move us to abandon any and all hope of obtaining knowledge or reasonable belief in that domain. Second, we might become *epistemic dogmatists* and think that we should simply hold firm to our self-trust and ignore disagreement. The thought here might be something like this: given that we are permitted to hold beliefs here without sufficient justification, our beliefs are somehow beyond the grip of the usual sorts of justificatory practices. Thus our beliefs are immune to the usual effects of disagreement. The final position, in between the two extremes, is *epistemic humility,* which holds that, though one may still retain some degree of belief in the face of pervasive disagreement, that disagreement ought to lead to some loss of self-confidence.

WHY NOT EPISTEMIC NIHILISM?

Why not abandon any claim to knowledge in the relevant domain when faced with pervasive disagreement? In metaethics, pervasive disagreement is often used as a consideration in favor of moral nihilism.[5] This maneuver is made plausible by the lack of a satisfying account of why we should trust our moral judgment. But recent developments in epistemology promise to fill this gap, for all forms of unsecured judgment.

The most plausible approach to epistemology presently available, to my mind, is entitlement theory, also known as the theory of epistemic warrant.[6] Entitlement theory shows when and how it is reasonable to accept unsecured judgments. By applying the developments of entitlement theory to thinking about unsecured judgments, we can carve a reasonable middle path between nihilism and dismissal. Entitlement theory arises in opposition to the Cartesian approach to knowledge. To paint with a broad brush, the Cartesian approach demands that we secure our foundations—that we provide a proof or account for any and all of our beliefs. But this demand seems impossible to satisfy. If we begin by distrusting all our beliefs and faculties until given a reason to trust them, then we shall never trust them, for any possible supporting reasons could only arise from some already trusted belief or faculty.[7] Consider the following principle:

Prior Justification Demand: in order to reasonably trust a given mental ability, we must have a prior account giving us a reason to think that ability is reliable.

It is something like this principle that is behind both the Cartesian approach to knowledge and justification, and the ensuing skepticisms that seem to plague all attempts to provide a complete Cartesian justification of any piece of knowledge. This is easy to see in the perceptual realm. We have some perceptual experience: it seems to us that we see an apple. Suppose the Prior Justification Demand is correct. Then, in order to trust our senses and believe that there is, in fact, an apple before us, we would need a justification for believing that our visual system was functioning well. But any account of the proper functioning of our perceptual faculties will have to make some references to some scientific theory—to optics, chemistry, to neurobiology. Trusting those scientific theories would itself depend on using data gathered with the senses. A vicious circle threatens. If we demand a prior account showing us that our perceptual system works before we are willing to accept it, we'll never get one, because the very sciences that might vet our perceptual systems themselves depend on a basic trust in our perceptual systems.

This circularity is even more apparent when we turn to our basic cognitive abilities. If we demand a convincing argument for trusting our cognitive abilities before we are permitted to trust them, then we'll never get anywhere at all, because the very act of finding and evaluating arguments depends on the substantive exercise of our cognitive abilities. Tyler Burge, in "Content Preservation," gives an argument for the necessity of default self-trust toward our cognitive abilities (Burge, 1993). When we reason, says Burge, we usually must trust our short-term memory. When an agent rehearses the steps of an argument, they mentally focus on a single step, and then store the results of that step in short-term memory in order to move on to the next step. If they don't trust their short-term memory, they might substitute some other cognitive resource, like writing steps down. But then they've simply shifted their dependencies from one fallible cognitive ability to another fallible one—in this case, from memory to reading and writing. We must rely on some storage facility in order to perform any complex reasoning. But we also cannot demand of ourselves that we provide some piece of reasoning to support the reliability of those storage abilities before we trust them, since all reasoning depends on those storage abilities.

Once we see that any act of reasoning depends on trusting some mental abilities, we can see that the problem lies with the Prior Justification Demand itself. If we cannot trust any of our mental abilities unless we have an argument justifying our trust, then we will never be able to trust ourselves. It thus follows from the Prior Justification Demand that we cannot reasonably trust any of our beliefs. Human knowledge seems impossible, and radical skepticism looms. The proper response, suggests entitlement theory, is not to give up on the possibility of knowledge, but to reject the Prior Justification Demand. As Crispin Wright argues, anything like the Prior Justification Demand leads to radical skepticism about all knowledge, and so must be rejected (2004, 164–175). Thus, the only place we can begin cognitive life is to tentatively trust, without argument, our cognitive abilities. We cannot begin with the Cartesian demand for proof for all our starting points. We must, instead, flip the burden of proof. Instead of distrusting our cognitive abilities until given a reason to trust them, we should begin by trusting our cognitive abilities until we discover reasons why we should not.[8] The right methodology by which to conduct our epistemic lives is not one of default epistemic miserliness, but one of default epistemic generosity. Trust widely, and whittle down from there. That epistemically generous approach is the only way into having any sort of cognitive life at all.

This trust is, however, only tentative; it is vulnerable to future defeat. Unlike the intuitionism of an earlier era, entitlement theory doesn't purport to offer us unshakeable foundations for knowledge. Entitlement theory instead claims that approaching our cognitive abilities with initial trust is the only viable approach. This doesn't mean that we can trust ourselves absolutely; it only means that tentatively accepting our cognitive abilities is permissible as a default stance. We're entitled to assume that our cognitive abilities work, but this is only an opening assumption, and open to revision from future evidence.

If we accept entitlement theory, we have a basis for self-trust with regard to unsecured judgments, like moral, aesthetic, and religious ones. Let's take a brief tour. Burge suggests the Acceptance Principle as a basic principle of reasoning:

> A person is entitled to accept as true something that is presented as true and that is intelligible to him, unless there are stronger reasons not to do so. (Burge, 1993, 467)

And Jim Pryor offers the following basic principle:

> We have immediate prima facie justification for believing those propositions that our experiences basically represent to us—whichever propositions those turn out to be. (Pryor, 2000, 539).

Lawrence Sklar suggests Methodological Conservatism:

> The very fact that that a proposition is believed can serve as a warrant for some attitude to be rationally maintained in regard to believing it. (Sklar, 1975, 375)

In all these cases, the proffered criterion for entitlement is surely broad enough to catch the sorts of unsecured judgments we've been talking about. It covers moral intuitions: it strikes me that it's wrong to manipulate people's actions through hypnosis. It covers aesthetic judgments: I look at Van Gogh's *Irises* and find it to be disturbingly beautiful. It covers religious experiences: I am full of a sense that God is watching me with love and approval. In all those cases, I (a) have something presented to me as true and intelligible, (b) have a proposition basically represented to me in experience.[9] And if I form a belief, based on those experiences, I am permitted to (c) maintain those beliefs simply because I have them.

Thus, any entitlement theory formulated along the lines of Pryor's, Sklar's, or Burge's easily justifies our tentative opening trust in our moral intuitions, aesthetic judgments, and religious experiences. Beyond these examples, we can reasonably expect other entitlement theories to be similarly expansive. Entitlement theories are constructed to capture the way in which everyday knowledge works. They begin with a commitment to the reasonableness of everyday knowledge. Thus, entitlement theories are likely to have quite minimal conditions for granting entitlements, because entitlement theories must grant entitlements to non-reflective agents—the holders of most everyday knowledge. Entitlement theory ought not demand extensive knowledge of the nature, structure, and inner workings of one's cognitive abilities as prerequisites for being entitled to trust those abilities. This would leave most people out at cognitive sea. It is likely, then, that other plausible entitlement theories will also offer a basis for self-trust over unsecured judgments.

WHY NOT BE AN EPISTEMIC DOGMATIST?

Entitlement theory grants us self-trust, but does it also force us to trust others? We have disposed of an easy route to epistemic nihilism through entitlement theory. But perhaps entitlement theory permits the other extreme, licensing dogmatism of a particularly epistemically individualist variety. What matters here is the scope of entitled trust. If one's epistemic entitlements cover only one's own beliefs, intuitions, etc., then dogmatism might easily follow. After all, I am entitled to believe my own unsecured beliefs but have no reason to accept your unsecured beliefs. A philosophically self-aware dogmatist might reason in the following way: "I am entitled to believe that eating meat is OK, because it seems to me intuitively true. You believe that eating meat is wrong. Nothing forces me to believe you; after all, I am entitled to believe what seems to me true, and you don't seem to me to be right at all. In fact, I have a very good reason to think you wrong—namely, that I have a reasonable belief that eating meat is OK, and you disagree with me. Thus, our disagreement is, in fact, a reason to dismiss you as irrational." In other words, the opening position of tentative self-trust does not, by itself, guarantee epistemic humility. Entitlement theory seems to leave the door open to the following position: I trust only myself. I treat my opening beliefs as tentative but only treat them as subject to revision from pressure from my other beliefs. To see this, simply imagine the epistemic position of Mr. Arrogant. Mr. Arrogant takes himself as justified in tentatively trusting his intuitions. He has the following intuition: everybody else is incredibly stupid and untrustworthy. His starting positions are tentative because they might be defeated by his other beliefs, but he seems to have sealed himself from any revision based on the testimony of others. Mr. Arrogant seems to be licensed, by entitlement theory and his intuitions, to hold a kind of epistemic solipsism.

This seems like a terribly unfair way to apply one's entitlements. I argue, instead, that any entitlement to self-trust will generalize, in the right conditions, to trusting others. Thus, the right default stance is that disagreements matter, and that we should lose confidence in our beliefs in the face of them.[10] Mr. Arrogant is reasoning badly. He is failing to see how self-trust forces interpersonal trust, which in turn brings epistemic humility.

The details here depend on which entitlement theory you pick. Burge's account, for example, extends epistemic entitlements to any "comprehensible cognitive resource." The testimony of others is as comprehensible to me as my own internal cognitive resources are, and so the basis I have for self-trust automatically extends to trusting others. Thus, a Burgean account indicates that we should take a posture of epistemic humility, rather than epistemic dogmatism, in response to disagreement. But this isn't as easy with other accounts. For example, Sklar's account grants an entitlement to continue believing any belief one holds. One might perfectly well start by holding the belief that one is right and everybody else wrong. Similarly, Pryor's account grants an entitlement to any basic representational experience—and though my own intuitions count as representational experiences to me, the testimony of others does not. Both Sklar's and Burge's accounts seem to support Mr. Arrogant's approach.

But even in those more narrowly scoped entitlement theories, we can show that, given our entitlement to our self-trust, we ought to trust others. This is because the mechanisms that underlie the reliability of my own unsecured judgments are, to the best of my knowledge, shared by other human beings. Thus; the entitlement I have to tentatively trust my own cognitive abilities extends to tentatively trusting the cognitive abilities of others. If I am to trust my own vision, I ought to substantively trust the vision of other people, for their visual equipment is, to the best of my knowledge, similar to mine. Similarly, if I am to trust my own moral judgments, then I ought to extend a similar order of trust to the moral judgments of those who have cognitive equipment similar to mine. My goal here is to show that this generalization argument, which is uncontroversial for empirical matters, must also extend to unsecured domains. Any entitlement theory that licenses thinking of myself as prima facie truth-tracking requires that I also think of others sufficiently like me as prima facie truth-tracking.

Suppose it strikes me *p*, and so, as I am entitled, I believe that *p*. Suppose that *p* is some judgment about the world outside my brain—that there is an apple here, that torture is wrong, that God loves me. Since the content of that judgment is an objective claim,

I must take myself to have some ability to reliably track objective, mind-independent facts. In trusting myself, I am imputing to myself some reliable ability for tracking the truth—for reliably getting onto states of affairs outside of me. That reliability is the explanation for the purported correctness of my judgments. Entitlement theory implies that I am reasonable in imputing to myself such a reliable ability, even lacking an account of why the ability is reliable. Now we turn our gaze to other people. Ought we to trust them? Yes, for trusting others follows from trusting ourselves. With entitled but unsecured judgment, we trust that our cognitive abilities are reliable, but we can give no account of why or how. We don't know what our abilities are like, how they function, the basis for their reliability; we don't even know, in many cases, which cognitive abilities we're using. But we do know that certain other people—our peers—are cognitively very similar to us, on the whole. They seem to have mostly the same abilities; we seem to be able to understand each other and reason very similarly in most situations; we seem to have the same physical apparatus, and we seem to come from similar sources—similar genetic material, a similar evolutionary background.[11] Given that we have no particular account of where in our mental makeup our moral truth-tracking ability resides, and many reasons to think that the mental makeup of others is largely like our own, we have many reasons in favor of taking others to be our moral peers and few reasons against.

Any entitlement that licenses me in thinking of myself as rational thus requires that I think of others as rational, provided I have reason to think that they are sufficiently like me. What counts as "sufficiently like me"? It's very hard to say because of the impoverished nature of our epistemic self-knowledge. In the situation of entitlement, I don't have enough information to draw the line precisely. But for my peers, there are many empirical reasons to think that they're similar to me, and no prima facie categorical reason to think they're not. There are, of course, sometimes contingent reasons to think that certain people aren't as truth-tracking as I am—they're biased, they're angry, they haven't thought things through as long as I have, they don't have the background or education I have in a particular area. But the proper initial presumption, given that they're people rather like me, is that they're also rational like me, and thus approximately as morally reliable.

To summarize:

The Generalization Argument

1. Suppose that I am entitled to believe some unsecured judgment that *p*. That means that I am entitled to accept that *p*, until shown otherwise.
2. If that belief is about some external state of affairs, then I must take myself to have some reliable faculty, ability, or other resource for accurately getting to that state of affairs.
3. Empirical evidence indicates that other people have similar faculties, abilities, and cognitive resources to mine—they have similar biology, etc.
4. For entitled but unsecured belief, I don't have a complete account of which cognitive faculties I'm using.
5. Since I know certain people to be in general cognitively similar to me, then I have reason to think they are in general as reliable as I am.
6. If I take my own faculties to be sufficiently reliable to give me reasons to believe, then I must think that the faculties of cognitively similar people also give me reasons to believe.

C: Thus, for those people for whom I have some empirical evidence of cognitive similarity, their testimony that *not-p* gives me some reason to believe *not-p*.

In short, since I take my own faculties to provide me with substantive reasons to believe and since, for some other agents, I have every reason to believe that their faculties are like mine and little reason to suspect they are unlike, then I ought to believe that their faculties are also well functioning, and thus should take them as providing substantive reasons to believe.[12] The generalization argument manifests the spirit of epistemic humility, and gives it a rational basis. It highlights the fact that others have similar backgrounds and belief processes, and argues that, at least from an entitlement start, the rational implications of those similarities is doubt in the face of disagreement.

Of course, this argument is only one about the proper presumptions and starting points. The presumption of parity with other biologically similar beings can be broken, for example, by evidence that one side has more relevant training or education in the domain. But the point here is that the right opening presumption lies on the side of presuming epistemic parity with others, and that the burden of proof lies with demonstrating disparity.

The argument I've given clearly applies to empirical abilities, but why should we take it to apply to moral, aesthetic, or religious judgment? I think that, in fact, the argument applies more strongly to unsecured judgments than to secured ones. The crux of the argument from generalization is that given that I don't know very much about the source of my reliability, general features of cognitive similarity weigh more. The argument applies most clearly to unsecured judgments precisely because they are the most mysterious of our purportedly objective faculties. We don't have to rely on general features for assessing vision because vision is so well understood, and we have a well-developed and trustworthy method for assessing the reliability of visual systems. It is when we lack such an account that we must default to general cognitive similarity, and our account of moral cognition is, at the moment, terribly impoverished.

Our moral intuitions, aesthetic judgments, and religious experiences may strike us as obviously true, clear as day. But none of us has any basis to claim an especially privileged relationship to the moral, aesthetic, or religious domain. We are each merely one cognitive agent among many, all looking at the same set of facts.

If it's true that we can find such disagreements over most of our moral judgments, then we will have arrived at a qualified form of moral skepticism—not the radical skepticism of the nihilists, but a constrained skepticism, one which leads to reasonable doubt and moderate suspicion. Notice that this constrained skepticism is not born of some abstract possibility of failure; it is born of substantive empirical evidence that we might, in fact, have malfunctioned somewhere in our own process of judgment. This is not merely some abstract thought experiment, where we merely raise the possibility that we are, say, just brains in vats being fed illusory data. When we discover disagreement in the world, this gives us a positive reason to increase our degree of belief in our possible failure. Since this skepticism is contingent on acquiring certain types of empirical evidence, the amount and degree of suspicion engendered by disagreement will vary from one person to another. A very cosmopolitan person may run across a larger number of disagreements than somebody who has never left their small hometown. This has some very striking consequences. For example, somebody who has had the opportunity to encounter many other people ought, rationally, be more epistemically humble; if they are not epistemically humble, they are being irrational. Somebody deprived of that opportunity might reasonably be less humble, for they haven't had a chance to encounter the relevant evidence.[13]

DISAGREEMENT AND THE AUTONOMY REQUIREMENT

Of course, one might think that the genuine barrier to using the testimony of others wasn't epistemic but something else. Perhaps we have every epistemic reason to trust the testimony of others, but some non-epistemic requirement for intellectual autonomy prevents us from using that testimony.[14] Interestingly, versions of this requirement crop up both in the discussion of moral testimony and the discussion of aesthetic testimony. Robert Paul Wolff argues, in a distinctly Kantian mood, that our moral beliefs are subject to a special requirement for autonomy. Let's call this the requirement for *moral understanding*—that we ought to understand the basis for our own moral beliefs. Note that there is no parallel requirement for empirical understanding. I have plenty of beliefs about which repairs my car needs, which medicines I need to take, and what foods are healthy, for which I do not understand the basis. My beliefs here are based on the testimony of my mechanic, my doctor, and nutritional watchdog institutions. Again, the requirement for understanding seems to show up in the other realms we've considered. For example, we seem to demand something like aesthetic understanding for our aesthetic judgments. This, it seems, is why we demand that people only judge those artworks which they have encountered for themselves, based on aesthetic experiences they have had for themselves.

Let's suppose that there is an Understanding Requirement for certain domains which demands that one's judgments proceed from one's own understanding.[15] Furthermore, let's suppose, as Wolff and Hopkins have suggested, that any such requirement isn't based in epistemic considerations. Rather, they are based in considerations of autonomy, which override epistemic considerations in certain domains. That is, Wolff allows that the fact that a moral authority believes some moral principle gives me good evidence to believe that principle, but it is considerations of my own moral autonomy that forbid me from acquiring a belief in that principle merely through testimony. Thus, considerations of autonomy would override my generalization argument, which only yields epistemic reasons to trust others. It may be that the generalization argument tells me that, in fact, disagreement gives me evidence that I might be wrong, but it is not evidence that I should actually use. Using this evidence, which came to me from testimony, might lead me to accurate beliefs, but it would also involve doing something worse: morally wronging myself by destroying my moral independence.

I will assume, for the purposes of argument, that there is an Understanding Requirement for moral, aesthetic and, in some religious traditions, religious judgment as well, and assume that its considerations of autonomy can trump evidence.[16] But such a requirement cannot be unlimited. As we've seen, we cannot hold the Understanding Requirement for all empirical knowledge. We must trust others to give us information about observations, scientific conclusions, and engineering assessments. For example, we must trust others to assess the reliability of functional systems for us. I get on a plane because I trust, via an institutionalized system of informational disbursal, the testimony of aeronautical engineers and mechanics, and the related testimony of the scientists who have developed the physical theories on which those engineers and mechanics rely. I trust their judgments that types of systems on my plane work, and I trust the judgments of the engineers who have given my plane its most recent safety checks. I implicitly trust those judgments because I rely on them in my decision to get on the plane. In believing that my plane is safe, I am, in fact, trusting others' judgments with my life, without any understanding of the basis for those judgments.

So, we have granted the Understanding Requirement in the moral, aesthetic, and religious domains. This means that we cannot acquire new moral belief, aesthetic belief, or religious belief via testimony (but see note 13), because we would not understand the basis for that belief ourselves. But crucially, such a direct importation of belief through testimony is not the only way to use that testimony. There are, in fact, two pathways for using a piece of such testimony. Let's call them the direct path and the indirect path.

Suppose that there is somebody that I have reason to trust testifies that *p*, where *p* is a moral belief. The *direct path* would be to acquire a belief that *p*, based on their testimony that *p*. Notice that the direct path opens one sort of doorway to epistemic humility. Suppose I trust you, morally speaking. If I held some moral belief, based on my intuitions, and you testified to the contrary, based on your intuitions, then I would have some reason to decrease my confidence in my own moral belief. But the direct path is forbidden by the Understanding Requirement. If I am modifying my moral beliefs based merely on your testimony that *p*, then I am giving a belief epistemic weight in my own system of moral beliefs, without accepting your argument for *p*.

But there is also an *indirect path* for using that testimony. Suppose that I believe *p*, and you testify the opposite. I have now discovered the empirical fact that we disagree. And given that I have reason to trust myself and reason to trust you, then the fact that we disagree gives me reason to think that somewhere, in at least one of our cognitive processes, somebody must have made a mistake. And until I have located that mistake, the fact that we disagree gives me reason to doubt the reliability of both my cognitive process and yours. I have positive, empirical evidence that I might have been mistaken (and that you might, too), and this is a reason to reduce my self-confidence in both of us. This is an empirical pathway to epistemic humility.

Notice that while the direct pathway violates an Understanding Requirement for moral beliefs, the indirect pathway does not. This is because I do not acquire a *moral belief* through testimony; I acquire an *empirical belief* based on the fact that we disagree. The indirect pathway relies on acquiring, through testimony, only empirical beliefs about the reliability of cognitive systems. Notice that the end result is the same; in both cases, I might give up my original belief. It is the pathway, and the nature of what I acquire through testimony, that varies. Imagine I believe, firmly, that premarital sex is wrong. You testify that you think that premarital sex is absolutely fine. If I take the direct pathway, I acquire from you some moral reasons to believe that premarital sex is fine, which *cancels out* some of my belief in the wrongness of premarital sex. If I take the indirect pathway, I acquire from you some reasons to doubt my reliability, which *undermines* my confidence in my own reasoning. To put it another way, in the direct pathway, I have acquired some of the credential force of your moral belief without being able to give the grounds for that belief. I am not moved by your argument that premarital sex is fine, but I let your belief sway me. In the indirect pathway, I acquire an empirical belief (i.e., that there is disagreement) based on grounds that I possess—observational evidence. Furthermore, I can explain why disagreement affects my belief: the disagreement gives me reason to think something has gone wrong.

This is not a cheap trick. The indirect pathway emerges from the fact that we must substantively trust our cognitive systems in order to acquire things like moral and aesthetic beliefs. The confidence we have in our beliefs emerges from complex systems of other networked beliefs. My belief that I am sitting on a chair right now emerges both from my experience of the sensory perceptions of a chair, but also my trust in the reliability of the associated systems of perception. Similarly, any confidence I have in my moral, aesthetic, or religious beliefs must come from some combination of those experiences, and my entitled trust in the reliability of their underlying cognitive systems and abilities. Thus, disagreement in the moral, aesthetic, and religious realms can generate self-doubt without violating the Understanding Requirement, because there is a pathway by which we can get to self-doubt from disagreement over moral, aesthetic, or religious issues, without our actually acquiring any new moral, aesthetic, or religious beliefs through testimony. Similarly, agreement can improve our self-confidence by offering corroborative evidence of the well-functioning of our systems. But the indirect pathway allows changes to our degree of self-confidence, based only on acquiring empirical evidence about the likely reliability of our cognitive systems that underlie our ability to get to moral, aesthetic, and religious matters.

But the Understanding Requirement is not entirely toothless here. For those domains where it applies, it does forbid one from acquiring any new beliefs through testimony. Instead, it only permits one to modify the degree of certainty in beliefs one already has. For example, suppose I went to the museum and found Van Gogh's *Irises* beautiful but found that Picasso's *Nude Descending a Staircase* left me entirely cold. I then encounter a very trustworthy, aesthetically sensitive friend and relay my experiences. My friend agrees with me that *Irises* is beautiful but suggests that Picasso's painting is also beautiful and urges me to look again to see what I have missed. The Understanding Requirement says that I cannot acquire directly the belief that Picasso's painting is beautiful via testimony.[17] I can, however, acquire the belief that I might be mistaken because a trustworthy person disagreed with me. Similarly, I cannot simply add my friend's assessment of the beauty of *Irises* to mine and increase my degree of belief in the beauty of *Irises* directly, but I can treat our agreement as a kind of corroboration of my own judgment and increase my confidence in the conclusion I arrived at through my own experiences and understanding.

What I am saying is not so mysterious. Consider an everyday case where we seek understanding. Suppose that I am studying with my friends for a calculus test. My goal, in doing the problems with my friends, is to get an understanding of calculus. It would be useless, in the study session, to simply copy my friends' answers, for that would promote no understanding. But we do employ a procedure of corroboration and discorroboration. We all work at the same problem together, and then check to see if we got the same answer or not. The point is that disagreement gives us evidence that somebody has made a mistake, and agreement gives us evidence that we all properly understand what's going on. It doesn't decrease my understanding to use disagreement and agreement in this way. In fact, using social evidence as part of a self-checking procedure promises to increase my understanding by putting the evidence of my failure in my hands, and spotlighting my own misunderstandings. The same is true in moral, aesthetic, and religious cases. Of course, using social evidence in this way doesn't provide a guarantee for success—it is simply one moderately reliable method for self-check among many.

In fact, if the goal here is to increase intellectual autonomy, I have done so by using my trust in others via the indirect pathway. I am in further contact with the reasons for self-trust or self-doubt. They are socially sourced reasons, but they are social reasons I understand. I have, in fact, collected the evidence of disagreement and agreement myself, and understand the reasons why disagreement or agreement should lead me to adjust my degree of self-confidence. When we acquire epistemic humility from the existence of disagreement, via the indirect pathway, we are not making ourselves subservient to another and abandoning our intellectual responsibilities. We are, instead, embracing our intellectual responsibilities more fully and actively by seeking out the social forms of evidence by which we may begin to transform our self-trust from merely entitled into something more thoroughly investigated.

For many theorists, the whole reason to accept the Understanding Requirement in the first place is the value of autonomy. When we take things on testimony, without thinking through them for ourselves, we give up having our own understanding of the grounds for our belief. But the use of disagreement along the indirect pathway doesn't involve reducing our understanding. In the indirect pathway, we have contact with the evidence—that others disagree—and understand the grounds for why disagreement matters. In that case, the reasons that drive us to autonomy tell us to seek out possible disagreements. In fact, we make ourselves more autonomous when we have investigated the world for possible disagreement, and when we take that disagreement into consideration. We are more actively participating in our assessment of all the relevant considerations—in this case, most especially in the assessment of our own cognitive reliability. Thus the value of autonomy can give us reason, not only to refuse to accept certain kinds of testimony, but to also actively seek out those who disagree with us. We have reason to become more intellectually cosmopolitan, to seek out those with different backgrounds and different approaches, who might disagree with us. Epistemic humility is thus an active pursuit, one powered, at least in part, by considerations of autonomy.

EPISTEMIC HUMILITY AND ITS CONSEQUENCES

So what are the consequences of disagreement, and of epistemic humility, if we are not allowed to acquire new beliefs through testimony? Let me briefly sketch two. First, some actions may require, for their justification, very high degrees of confidence in the relevant beliefs. It's plausible to think, for example, that choices about how I conduct my life in wholly private ways demand very low degrees of confidence. I take a walk the long way on an autumn day because it strikes me that it might be nicer, even though there's a substantial chance I'm wrong; that whisper-thin justification is enough. But when I choose to intervene in the lives of others, especially against their will, we demand much higher degrees of confidence. In that case, the existence of disagreement can be a basis for eroding my self-trust and confidence in my cognitive abilities enough to prevent me from acting in such a way toward others. Epistemic humility, then, can lead to my refraining from intervening in the lives of others, precisely because such interventions call for a higher standard of certainty.

Second, without epistemic humility, the considerations of the Understanding Requirement threaten to make one's own moral, aesthetic, and religious beliefs entirely unassailable. Cognitive life, in these domains, where we take ourselves as reasonably entitled to self-trust, but where we leave out the possibility of social discorroboration, is one that permits excess self-confidence. One's own understanding of morality, aesthetic life, and the religious universe can continue onward, unimpeded, self-reinforcing its way to greater degrees of self-confidence. Socially sourced epistemically humility puts the brakes on our entitled beliefs. It introduces to us the possibility that we might be wrong, even in those cases where we do not even understand why we trust ourselves to be right.

NOTES

1. A lengthier version of this argument can be found in (Nguyen, 2011, 35–82). However, my earlier argument was focused exclusively on moral judgment; the argument here has been generalized to cover a larger variety of judgments.
2. How this requirement is hashed out varies considerably. One option is that we think that, in these domains, understanding is required for knowledge. In that case, knowledge could not be gained through testimony. Another option is to think that there is some requirement external to the demands of knowledge—say a moral requirement—such that moral knowledge without moral understanding could in fact be gained through testimony, but that it would be wrong, on non-epistemic grounds, to use that testimony. It might, for instance, be a violation of some requirement for autonomy. I have attempted to be neutral on this debate; for further discussion see Hopkins, 2007.

3. The literature here is vast, but Christensen (2013) contains clear statements of the key positions. See also Christensen, 2007; Elga, 2007; Kelly, 2005, 2008, 2010; Feldman, 2006; Lackey, 2010.
4. A similar approach to mine has been offered by Michael Huemer as a form of intuitionism about ethical judgment (Huemer, 2001, 2005). I take my view here to be in a very similar spirit to his, though differing in many small details. Most importantly, my analysis is aimed at a slightly larger phenomenon. His view directly addresses raw moral intuitions about particular cases but not loose applications.
5. Sarah McGrath provides a good recent overview of these arguments (McGrath 2008).
6. For a superb overview of entitlement theory, including a discussion of its historical roots, see Wright, 2004.
7. The clearest exposition of this thought occurs in Wright 2004, 168–175.
8. The reasoning here is not simply practical. The Cartesian approach to knowledge depends on holding the principle P, that every belief, to be reasonably held, be deducible from another reasonable belief. If P is true, then it self-applies, and this shows that it is not reasonable to hold P. Therefore, we ought to hold P false, and drop the universal demands for grounds.
9. For a significant elaboration on this argument, please see Nguyen, 2011, 35–54. My earlier arguments, however, are restricted to moral judgments; the present paper generalizes those arguments.
10. I consider other sorts of dismissal arguments in Nguyen, 2011, 88–130.
11. This argument should also work for a monotheist creationist, who, I take it, takes all humans to have been created by the same God.
12. I originally offered the generalization argument in Nguyen, 2011. Linda Zagzebski (2012) offers an argument in a very similar spirit. However, mine is built against the background of entitlement approaches to epistemology, while hers is built to suit a virtue theoretic approach to epistemology.
13. The issue of the relationship between upbringing, opportunity, and epistemic responsibility is a complex one, which I plan to explore at greater length in future work.
14. I am influenced here by Robert Hopkins's discussion of the unusability thesis in aesthetic testimony (Hopkins, 2011).
15. I am leaving here what "understanding" consists in as fairly flexible, to be compatible with a wide variety of accounts. In particular, I leave unspecified whether emotions and other affective states could or could not count as understanding.
16. Some religious traditions treat religious knowledge as something essentially passed through testimony—those traditions do not hold to an Understanding Requirement and are left out of this analysis. The analysis applies to those religious traditions that require some sort of personal religious experience or

personal judgment and response to religious texts. Greco (2017) summarizes the philosophical tradition of applying the Understanding Requirement to religious judgment (and offers some criticisms).

17. I here present here the Understanding Requirement in the way it is normally presented in the literature on aesthetic testimony. In Nguyen, 2017, I argue that the Understanding Requirement, as stated, doesn't fully capture the complexity of aesthetic judgment. There are, I claim, two kinds of aesthetic judgment—a cognitive one, concerning the value of the work, and an affective one, concerning my felt responses. I claim that our intuitions Understanding Requirement actually apply most strongly to affectively involved judgments that make reference to our responses, but not less affectively involved judgments of value. If one accepted my view, then the Understanding Requirement would cover claims like, "It's so beautiful!" but not claims like, "That painting is of great artistic value and ought to be preserved." Which is exactly why we do, in fact, permit ourselves to rely exclusively on aesthetic testimony in deciding what to put in museums but not in our own homes. My claim here is that even for the most affectively entangled responses, like, "It's beautiful!," the disagreement of another can give me reason to think my initial response might have missed something and motivate me to look again.

REFERENCES

Budd, M. 2003. "The acquaintance principle." *British Journal of Aesthetics, 43*(4), 386–392.

Burge, T. 1993. "Content preservation." *Philosophical Review, 102*(4): 457–488.

Christensen, D. 2007. "Epistemology of disagreement: The good news." *Philosophical Review, 109*, 457–488.

Christensen, D., and Jennifer Lackey, eds. 2013. *The Epistemology of Disagreement: New Essays*. Oxford: Oxford University Press.

Driver, J. 2006. "Autonomy and the asymmetry problem for moral expertise." *Philosophical Studies: An International Journal for Philosophy in the Analytic Tradition, 128*(3), 619–644.

Elga, A. 2007. "Reflection and disagreement." *Nous, 41*(3), 478–502.

Feldman, R. 2006. "Epistemological puzzles about disagreement." In *Epistemology Futures*, edited by Stephen Hetherington, 216–326. Oxford: Oxford University Press.

Goldberg, S. 2010. *Relying on Others: An Essay in Epistemology*. New York: Oxford University Press.

Greco, J. 2017. "Testimony and the transmission of religious knowledge." *Epistemology and the Philosophy of Science, 53*(3), 109–147.

Hardwig, J. 1985. "Epistemic dependence." *Journal of Philosophy, 82*(7), 335–349.

Hardwig, J. 1991. "The role of trust in knowledge." *Journal of Philosophy, 88*(12), 693–708.

Hopkins, R. 2007. "What is wrong with moral testimony?" *Philosophy and Phenomenological Research, 74*(3), 611–634.

Hopkins, R. 2011. How to be a pessimist about aesthetic testimony. *Journal of Philosophy, 108*(3), 138–157.

Huemer, M. 2001. *Skepticism and the Veil of Perception*. Lanham, MD: Rowman and Littlefield.

Huemer, M. 2005. *Ethical Intuitionism*. New York: Palgrave Macmillan.

Kelly, T. 2005. "The epistemic significance of disagreement." *Oxford Studies in Epistemology, 1*, 167–196.

Kelly, T. 2008. "Disagreement, dogmatism, and belief polarization." *Journal of Philosophy, 105*(10), 611–633.

Kelly, T. 2010. "Peer disagreement and higher-order evidence." In *Disagreement*, edited by Richard Feldman and Ted A. Warfield, 183–217. New York: Oxford University Press.

Lackey, J. 2010. "A justificationist view of disagreement's significance." In *Social Epistemology*, edited by Adrian Haddock, Alan Millar, and Duncan Pritchard, 145–154. Oxford: Oxford University Press.

Laetz, B. 2008. "A modest defense of aesthetic testimony." *Journal of Aesthetics and Art Criticism, 66*(4), 355–363. http://www.jstor.org/stable/40206364.

McGrath, S. 2008. "Moral disagreement and moral expertise." *Oxford Studies in Metaethics, 3*, 87–108.

McGrath, S. 2011. "Skepticism about moral expertise as a puzzle for moral realism." *Journal of Philosophy, 108*(3), 111–137.

Meskin, A. 2007. "Solving the puzzle of aesthetic testimony." In *Knowing Art*, edited by Matthew Kieran and Dominic McIver Lopes. Dordrecht: Springer.

Millgram, E. 2015. *The Great Endarkenment: Philosophy for an Age of Hyperspecialization*. Oxford: Oxford University Press.

Nguyen, C. T. 2010. "Autonomy, understanding, and moral disagreement." *Philosophical Topics, 38*(2), 111–129.

Nguyen, C. T. 2011. "An ethics of uncertainty." PhD diss., University of California, Los Angeles.

Nguyen, C. Thi. 2017. "The uses of aesthetic testimony." *British Journal of Aesthetics, 57*(1), 19–36.

Nickel, P. 2001. "Moral testimony and its authority." *Ethical Theory and Moral Practice, 4* (3), 253–266.

Pryor, J. 2000. "The skeptic and the dogmatist." *Nous, 34*, 517–549.

Robson, J. 2015. "Norms of belief and norms of assertion in aesthetics." *Philosopher's Imprint, 15*(6), 1–19.

Sklar, L. 1975. "Methodological Conservatism." *Philosophical Review, 84*(3), 374–400.

Whiting, D. 2015. "The glass is half empty: A new argument for pessimism about aesthetic testimony." *British Journal of Aesthetics, 55*(1), 91–107.

Wolff, R. P. 1970. *In Defense of Anarchism*. New York: Harper and Row.

Wollheim, R. 1980. *Art and Its Objects.* 2nd ed. New York: Cambridge University Press.

Wright, C. 2004. "Warrant for nothing (and foundations for free)?" *Aristotelian Society Supplementary,* 78(1), 167–212.

Zagzebski, L. 2012. *Epistemic Authority*. New York: Oxford University Press.

Chapter 14

Understanding Humility as Intellectual Virtue and Measuring It as Psychological Trait

MEGAN C. HAGGARD

INTRODUCTION

As a whole, philosophers, theologians, and psychologists have found it easier to define humility by what it is not. On one end of the spectrum, humility is the opposite of arrogance and narcissism, but not simply a lack of them, though it may be devoid of the vice of pride (Davis, Worthington, and Hook, 2010; Roberts and Wood, 2003; Tangney, 2009; Worthington, 2008). On the other end, humility is not self-deprecation, low self-esteem, or even modesty (Davis et al., 2010; Roberts and Wood, 2003). Further complicating matters, there is a distinct lack of consensus about how to measure humility. Davis and colleagues (2010) argue that a single self-report measure is not sensitive enough to accurately separate self-enhancers and narcissists from those with legitimately high levels of humility.

What remains most needed in the study of humility is the benefit of a well-crafted theoretical basis that incorporates these proposed facets. Relying on what humility is not for a definition has left the field of study confused and underpowered, shuffling between the folk understanding of lacking self-focus, which is all too often paired with modesty (Seligman and Peterson, 2004) and an epistemological concept of low status-seeking behaviors (Roberts and Wood, 2003; 2007). As intellectual humility begins to gain traction as an important and distinct type of humility, building measures with reference to theory will not only help organize current and future work but also allow for more deliberate and careful understandings of trait processes.

Moving beyond previous conceptions of intellectual humility as the opposite of narcissism or intellectual arrogance, I advocate for a spectrum understanding of intellectual humility as opposed to the more common binary definition (Haggard et al., 2018). The spectrum understanding posits that true intellectual humility lies at the mean between an excess of intellectual humility (intellectual servility) and the deficiency of intellectual humility (intellectual arrogance). Finally, connections between intellectual humility and the cognitive, motivational, affective, and behavioral outcomes from recent studies from positive psychology are explored. In sum, this chapter will provide a comprehensive analysis of the virtue of intellectual humility as a personality trait in psychology, which varies in its expression along a continuum, as well as future avenues for application, conceptualization, and experimentation.

HUMILITY AS AN INTELLECTUAL VIRTUE

Previous Accounts

Attempting to distinguish domains within a single virtue, such as humility, is in direct contrast to previous work in positive psychology that seeks to create meaningful groups of virtues. In addition, theorists have disagreed about the primary components that make up humility. As a member of a group of virtues, Worthington (2008) places humility with forgiveness and compassion, but Seligman and Peterson (2004) consider it a temperance-based virtue. In reference to its composition, Bollinger and Hill (2012) contend that there is a component of self-awareness needed in humility, whereas Chancellor and Lyubomirsky (2013) claim openness to new information is a key aspect. Tangney (2000; 2009) offered one of the first full empirical descriptions of humility, including the following components: accurate assessment of one's abilities/achievements, acknowledgement of one's imperfections/limitations, openness to new ideas, keeping one's abilities/achievements in perspective, relatively low self-focus, and appreciation of the value of all things. This all-encompassing definition demonstrates the inherent issues in attempting to place the virtue of humility in a single category. Unlike other virtues like gratitude, which is primarily focused on the actions of others or the surrounding environment, or self-control, which is based on reining in various internal states, humility requires both knowing oneself intimately while maintaining an open orientation toward the outside world (Bollinger and Hill, 2012).

As with the study of most personality traits, this struggle between the need to understand what humility is and is not, as well as what it does and does not do, has delayed construction of an adequate scale to measure it (Barenbaum and Winter, 2008). The psychological examination of virtues in particular has wavered between embracing the wholly factor-analytic model of determining traits, such as Peterson and Seligman's work on values in action (2004), or extracting information about traits through theory-guided or folk psychology approaches. Though humility is included as a core personality trait by some theorists (see the HEXACO personality inventory, Ashton and Lee, 2008), it is also grouped with facets that may not be purely humility, such as greed avoidance or honesty.

Issues concerning composition and delineation of intellectual humility have impacted research as well. Recent considerations of intellectual humility as an independent virtue arise mostly from Roberts and Wood (2003; 2007), who describe it as a primarily epistemic good. Low concern for intellectual status, an intrinsic desire for knowledge and truth, low intellectual domination, and a lack of unwarranted intellectual claims highlight their definition of intellectual humility. In essence, any concern that would potentially lead to intellectual vanity or arrogance is not present or not of great importance to an intellectually humble individual. These traits, in turn, help foster the spread of epistemic goods and other virtues not just in the individual but also in those around the individual. For instance, intellectual humility does not only help an individual to pursue truth and knowledge effectively but also influences the colleagues and subordinates of this individual, creating an environment in which intellectual exploration flourishes. It is an epistemic factor that is integral in the "acquisition, maintenance, transmission, and application of knowledge" (Roberts and Wood, 2007, 272).

However, Roberts and Wood (2003; 2007) note that this primarily negative definition can potentially fail to distinguish between those who are truly intellectually humble and those who are somehow limited in their abilities (i.e., frontal lobe damage), who may lack concern only because their brain is unable to produce such thoughts. There are two signs that may help make this distinction: first, that virtuous intellectual humility will often appear with other virtues, whether moral or intellectual. Second, a complete lack of any concern is not the ultimate goal of virtuous intellectual humility. Instead there must be some level of appropriate concern about one's level of knowledge for what warrants it (e.g., one's career). A core aspect of Roberts and Wood's (2007) conception of intellectual humility is an appropriate level of concern with appropriate topics for virtuous reasons. For instance, a professor should be at least slightly concerned with achieving tenure if they wish to continue to cultivate and learn from students. Indeed, this level of concern may lead to continued cultivation of intellectual humility and other virtues.

From an evolutionary perspective, Gregg and Mahadevan (2014) offer a combined understanding of both intellectual arrogance and intellectual humility as the involvement of the ego or lack thereof with one's beliefs, respectively. For intellectual arrogance, this also corresponds to the "inclination to regard a belief as truth because it is one's own" (2014, 8). This is demonstrated using the spontaneous preferences for one's own theories effect (SPOT effect), which shows that individuals are more likely to remain confident in a theory concerning obviously fabricated information about fictional alien species in the face of disconfirming evidence when it is attributed to them, but not when attributed to another person or to no one at all (Gregg, Mahadevan, and Sedikides, 2016). They provide evidence of an "own theory" bias rooted in intellectual arrogance, similar to other cognitive biases such as the Dunning-Kruger effect or better-than-average effect[1] (Kruger and Dunning, 1999; Sedikides et al., 2014): yet, there were no direct tests of the connection between intellectual humility and the tendency to seek the truth, even at the expense of original beliefs.

Gregg and Mahadevan also theorize that intellectual humility is not the polar opposite or lack of intellectual arrogance: for instance, intellectual humility is not the tendency to consider a belief false simply because it is one's own (opposite), nor is it the presence of critical thinking in reference to one's beliefs. It involves "due deference to an epistemic principle that one subjectively regards as having legitimate authority" (2014, 11). This crucially alters the conception of intellectual humility beyond attention and concern, adding that, in the face of appropriate evidence, an intellectually humble individual must abandon one's original beliefs if proven wrong.

The connection to our evolutionary roots lies in the transmission of belief from generation to generation, where both intellectual arrogance and humility played large roles. While intellectual arrogance thrived in situations of intellectual dominance (e.g., the Spanish Inquisition), intellectual humility was more prominent in the intellectual traditions of the Academy (e.g., Socratic method). Young individuals with erroneous beliefs who deferred to better trained and better informed teachers after having their reasoning carefully critiqued kept the practice of intellectual humility in education thriving.

Despite differing and, at times, competing definitions, both Roberts and Wood (2007) and Gregg and colleagues (2014) agree that virtuous intellectual humility relies on an appropriate amount of concern at times, whether with one's intellectual status or with the fallibility of one's own theories. While on the surface it may appear that these accounts adhere to a binary understanding of intellectual humility, there are important aspects of each that rely on a more spectrum or "golden mean" interpretation.

Intellectual Humility as a "Golden Mean"

In order to synthesize and clarify work on intellectual humility, Whitcomb and colleagues (2015) addressed the state of the psychological trait and philosophical concept. The primary conclusion of their investigation focuses the definition of intellectual humility on the owning of one's intellectual limitations and proper attentiveness to them. Intellectual limitations can include, but are not limited to, cognitive deficits, cognitive mistakes, gaps in knowledge, and knowledge-related character flaws. One must own his or her intellectual limitations at the appropriate time and place—not own all of them all the time, thus contributing to low self-esteem and, eventually, servility—but also, one must not ignore all of them all of the time, as an arrogant, conceited person does. As in the Aristotelian tradition, intellectual humility requires the "golden mean" of appropriate, or proper, attentiveness, which lies between the extremes of two vices, an excess and a deficiency.

Whitcomb and colleagues (2015) incorporate this into their understanding of intellectual humility by placing both proper intellectual humility and proper intellectual pride precisely between the vices of intellectual arrogance and intellectual servility (see also Morinis, this volume). While intellectual humility requires an appropriate acknowledgment of intellectual limitations, since too little recognition results in intellectual arrogance and too much in intellectual servility, intellectual pride requires an appropriate acknowledgment of intellectual strengths. When one focuses too much on these strengths, then intellectual pride may become intellectual arrogance. Conversely, too little recognition of one's strengths is intellectual servility. It is important that an intellectual humility measure be crafted with this spectrum understanding in mind (see figure 14.1). Instead of intellectual humility as the opposite or lack of intellectual arrogance, it now occupies the space between intellectual arrogance

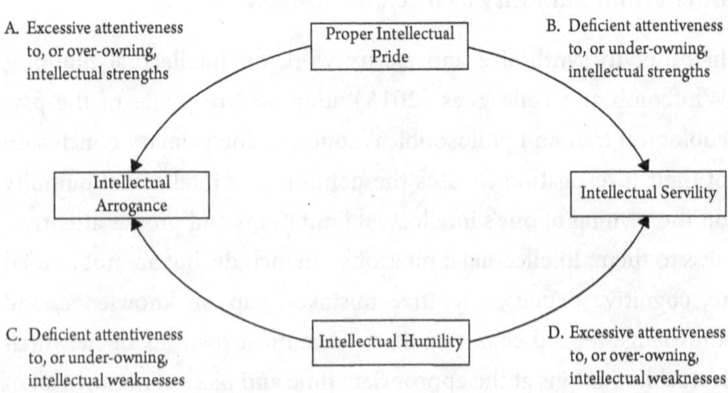

Figure 14.1. Diagram of the Relationship between Proper Intellectual Pride, Humility, Arrogance, and Servility.

Source: Adapted from Whitcomb et al., 2015, 351

and intellectual servility. One manifestation of intellectual servility would be an individual so consumed by their real or perceived limitations that they lack any willingness to seek out new information, ask questions, or alter their knowledge in any way (Whitcomb et al., 2015).

Whitcomb and colleagues also argue that possessing intellectual humility for the aim of some other end, such as a promotion, greater monetary gain, or better reviews from peers or subordinates, does not equal the attainment of the virtue of intellectual humility, which draws on Roberts and Wood's (2007) argument that intellectual humility does not include concern about things external to the pursuit of knowledge and truth. Their final definition refers to this distinction, as intellectual humility is an "intellectual virtue just when one is appropriately attentive to, and owns, one's intellectual limitations because one is appropriately motivated to pursue epistemic goods" (Whitcomb et al., 2015, 10). An individual may think of him- or herself as intellectually humble, or get others to think so, for the purpose of seeking accolades and rewards, but will not attain the virtue. While a virtuously intellectually humble individual may obtain promotions or awards in his or her pursuit of knowledge, it cannot be her primary motivation. Therefore, it is necessary to measure some aspect of appropriate motivation along with appropriate limitations owning. As opposed to only some aspects of intellectual humility lying on a spectrum, as with Roberts and Wood (2007) and Gregg and colleagues (2014), the limitations-owning conception of intellectual humility places all aspects of intellectual humility on a spectrum—appropriate recognition of one's intellectual limitations, appropriate discomfort with the presence of those limitations, and appropriate levels of motivation to pursue knowledge, truth, and overcome these limitations.

As suggested in the previous sentence, owning one's intellectual limitations should be accompanied by a host of related cognitive, behavioral, affective, and motivational outcomes, including owning one's mistakes caused by one's intellectual limitations, engaging more knowledgeable others when unsure of a particular topic or piece, and feeling the need to correct one's intellectual mistakes when pointed out while not begrudging the critics. Making connections like this between social outcomes and personality traits has long been underexplored in personality research, yet it would be incredibly useful for crafting a rich understanding of a trait (Back and Vazire, 2015).

Measurement of Intellectual Humility as Trait

In order to separate the measurement of intellectual humility from the issues of humility assessment more generally, Samuelson and colleagues (2014) empirically explored the virtue folk-knowledge surrounding intellectual humility. They asked over 300 individuals to list 10 descriptors of a wise, an intellectually humble, or an intellectually arrogant person. They discovered 39% similarity between the descriptions provided for a wise person and an intellectually humble person, but near zero resemblance between the descriptions of the intellectually arrogant person and the wise or intellectually humble persons. Next, participants evaluated the prototypicality of each descriptor for the three groups, including some based on Roberts and Wood's (2003) conception of intellectual humility, such as "seeks the truth" and "accurate self-assessment." Again, the descriptors of intellectually humble and wise persons shared considerable overlap, but still had significantly more unique prototypical traits than similar traits.

Overall, Samuelson et al. (2014) found that all descriptors for each of the three categories fit into either knowledge-based or social dimensions. In addition, people's lay theories of intellectually humble individuals included the characteristics of being humble, loving learning, being intelligent, and respectful of others, whereas wise individuals were rated as having experience, being rational, and being reflective. By contrast, intellectually arrogant individuals were seen as opinionated, educated know-it-alls. Samuelson et al. (2014) posit that their results show the clear distinction between intellectual humility and other related virtues, such as wisdom, further demonstrating the need for a trait measure of intellectual humility alone.

Positive and personality psychologists used this impetus to construct an intellectual humility measure in three different ways– updating or altering other measures of humility (Hook et al., 2015; McElroy et al., 2014), creating their own measure (Hill, Laney, and Edwards, 2014; Hoyle et al., 2016; Leary et al., 2017), and collaborating with outside thinkers, particularly philosophers, before developing a measure (Haggard et al., 2018; Krumrei-Mancuso and Rouse, 2016). Each pathway has provided useful evidence for the study of intellectual humility and has brought needed attention to the many facets of this understudied virtue.

Drawing on work by Davis and Worthington (2010), Hook and colleagues (2015) have primarily focused on defining intellectual humility as a unique division of the larger understanding of humility. Hook and colleagues' (2015) first attempt to create an intellectual humility measure resulted in simply changing the prompt of their cultural humility scale (2013) from "Regarding the core aspect(s) of my cultural background, my counselor . . . " to "Regarding different types of religious beliefs and values, the clergy/minister . . . ". While this is an easy distinction for measuring the perceived humility of another, it lacks needed specificity for a self-report measure of intellectual humility, especially one that could be utilized in the general population.

In order to remedy this conflict, McElroy and colleagues (2014) began with the original cultural humility scale, but they expanded the two-factor structure into intellectual openness and intellectual arrogance. They argue that intellectual humility is primarily being aware of limits and regulating arrogance with regard to intellectual matters. Essentially, intellectual humility should be examined in instances where ideas or knowledge are negotiated or observed. However, this scale, like the cultural humility scale, has been used mostly for other-reports of intellectual humility, not self-reports. For instance, the original factor structure was determined and validated by asking participants to rate not themselves, but a parent. Further studies asked individuals to rate a person who was most or least intellectually humble, modest, or driven (McElroy et al., 2014) or a religious leader (Hook et al., 2015). While an other-report measure is certainly of use, it may need to be reframed as a self-report measure and relies heavily on the binary interpretation of intellectual humility as the opposite pole of intellectual arrogance.

Several other researchers (i.e., Hill et al., 2014; Hoyle et al., 2016; Leary et al., 2015) opted to create their own self-report scales of intellectual humility, primarily influenced by Roberts and Wood (2003) and Gregg and Mahedevan (2014). Hill and colleagues (2014) identified three factors present in their 17-item intellectual humility scale: perspective taking, low concern for intellectual status, and low intellectual defensiveness. The low concern for intellectual status and low defensiveness are very similar to Roberts and Wood's (2007) conception of intellectual humility as lacking intellectual vanity and arrogance. The perspective-taking factor might be better characterized as deference to knowledgeable others or openness to criticism, as it includes items such as "I am willing to accept feedback from others, even if it is negative" and "It is important that the way I think considers others' perspectives as well as my own." Though open-mindedness toward new opinions and criticism is an important aspect of intellectual humility, in large amounts it may be more indicative of intellectual servility. More research using this scale is needed to further explore its usefulness; as of now, a confirmed factor structure remains undetermined.

Instead of developing a single self-report measure of intellectual humility, Hoyle, Leary, Deffler, and colleagues (2016; 2017) posit that a general intellectual humility scale and a specific intellectual humility scale are necessary to fully understand the construct. Beginning with an earlier definition of intellectual humility put forth by philosophers and positive psychologists, they conceptualized it as "recognizing that a particular personal belief may be fallible, accompanied by an appropriate attentiveness to limitations in the evidentiary basis of that belief and to one's own limitations in obtaining and evaluating relevant information" (Leary et al., 2017, 3). While this embraces the importance of limitations owning, it does not fully reflect the truth-seeking, epistemological motivations of intellectual humility, which are connected to and help cultivate the virtue.

The general intellectual humility scale is comprised of only six items, all of which reference altering one's beliefs in the face of new evidence or because they could be wrong. The scale demonstrated positive relationships with openness, agreeableness, need for cognition, and other intellectual virtues, and showed negative relationships with dogmatism, intolerance of ambiguity, and self-righteousness. Surprisingly, it was not shown to be related to narcissism or social vigilantism, both of which represent an important dimension of negative convergent validity.[2]

Using the specific intellectual humility scale, developed by Hoyle and colleagues (2016), requires that researchers or participants include a relevant intellectual domain or topic of interest. A sample item includes "I recognize that my views about ________ are based on limited evidence," where a researcher would fill in the domain of interest (Hoyle et al., 2016). In validating the scale, the authors used diverse domains, including politics and manners, as well as topics differing in personal importance, such as abortion and intelligent life on other planets. While they did not find a clear connection between issue specificity and general intellectual humility, they did discover that individuals who held extreme views (regardless of content) were less likely to be intellectually humble. Still, the limitation of needing to pick a topic that is both of interest and well-documented enough to be used diminishes its applicability to the overall understanding of intellectual humility as a virtue.

Finally, following the extensive philosophical investigation by Whitcomb and colleagues (2015), Krumrei-Mancuso and Rouse developed a scale to include their conclusions, identifying intellectual humility as "a non-threatening awareness of one's intellectual fallibility" (2016, 5). The resulting scale, the comprehensive intellectual humility scale, includes four factors—independence of intellect and ego, openness to revisiting one's viewpoint, respect for others' viewpoints, and lack of intellectual overconfidence. The scale predicted open-mindedness over and above demographic variables such as age and education, as well as other measures of humility, intellectual humility (McElroy et al., 2014), intellectual arrogance (McElroy et al., 2014), individualism, and understanding. There was limited information concerning its predictive ability of related but negative constructs, including narcissism and psychological entitlement, and about its relation to specific behaviors, cognitions, or feelings associated with intellectual humility. However, as its name suggests, it offers the most comprehensive understanding of intellectual humility, especially as it is experienced by the self and how it interacts with others' beliefs.

While these previous measures offer important evidence and information as to the structure and content of intellectual humility, they also demonstrate some limitations that can be addressed within the limitations-owning perspective. For instance, while the comprehensive intellectual humility scale (Krumrei-Mancuso, and Rouse, 2016) and general intellectual humility scale (Leary et al., 2017) both adeptly capture the connection between intellectual humility and a willingness to alter one's views when new evidence is found, they lack the inclusion of a motivational factor and a recognition that focusing too much on one's limitations could lead to negative outcomes. Instead, the limitations-owning perspective shifts importance away from a binary-only conception of intellectual humility to a spectrum, where there is both the potential for too little acknowledgment of limitations (intellectual arrogance) and too much awareness of them (intellectual servility). It is also the only perspective that includes the recognition that a motivation to pursue knowledge is a crucial component of intellectual humility.

Limitations Owning as Intellectual Humility

The limitations-owning intellectual humility scale includes three main facets to capture true, virtuous intellectual humility—owning one's intellectual limitations, appropriate discomfort with intellectual limitations, and a love of learning (Haggard et al., 2018). The owning intellectual limitations factor, which requires an awareness of one's limitations as well as their impact, and appropriate discomfort factor, which involves not being overwhelmingly threatened by the presence of limitations, bring the understanding of intellectual humility into a spectrum understanding as opposed to a binary one, where it is the "golden mean" of owning limitations and discomfort with them that leads to virtuous intellectual humility. The love of learning factor touches on the needed motivational component behind intellectual humility, which is a desire to seek the truth, not concerns about other goals or outcomes.

It is crucial to attempt to understand both what intellectual humility is and is not, and the limitations-owning perspective provides a clear solution: owning intellectual limitations without being subservient to them while being motivated to pursue knowledge (Whitcomb et al., 2015). This interpersonal and intrapersonal orientation requires that an individual be self-aware without being self-obsessed, be respectful of others' beliefs and opinions without the need to control them, and seek out new information without overestimating or underestimating one's intellectual standing. The metacognitive self-awareness inherent in intellectual humility requires self-regulatory and attentional resources; it is difficult to engage in intellectual humility when one's cognitive resources are overwhelmed with more pressing issues and one's attention is diverted. The dual processing model (Evans and Stanovich, 2013; Kahneman, 2011) details that humans rely on both intuitive (fast, automatic, and effortless) and reflective (slow, effortful, and deliberate) cognitive processing. Individuals are more inclined to utilize intuitive processing when cognitive resources, such as attention and self-control, are low, and engage reflective processing when one can devote adequate resources to contemplate the issue at hand. Both processes are parts of human nature, yet are used in different circumstances and, at times, contrary ways (see Kahneman, 2011, for review). Similarly, intellectual humility may not be the first instinct of some, particularly those under cognitive duress, with impaired cognitive abilities, or with overlearned or conditioned associations; however, when resources are available and accessed by the individual, intellectual humility can be second nature.

The limitations-owning perspective of intellectual humility has shown positive connections with related open and flexible personality and cognitive traits, especially openness to experience, agreeableness, cognitive reflection, authentic pride, and assertiveness (see Haggard et al., 2018, for a full review). It is negatively associated with restrictive thinking styles and self-important traits like closed-mindedness, dogmatism, overclaiming knowledge, and hubristic pride. Therefore, intellectual humility is positively connected to behaviors and traits that engage slower, more effortful reflective processing and negatively correlated with quicker and more automatic intuitive processing. In addition, the positive correlation between the limitations-owning scale and authentic pride, which is related to self-control and a sense of purpose in life, and the negative correlation with hubristic pride, which is connected to extrinsic motivation for fame and impulsivity, are also important to understanding the relationship between intellectual humility and pride (Carver and Johnson, 2010). Reflecting early work by Roberts and Wood (2007), intellectual humility and vicious pride operate in opposition to each other, whereas virtuous pride and intellectual humility rise and fall together.

Lastly, the investigation into the social cognitions and limitations-owning perspective establish preliminary evidence of how intellectual humility is manifest in outward worldviews and behavior. Specifically, individuals higher in limitations-owning intellectual humility were more likely to engage in cognitive reflection, more likely to detect fictional foil items, and less likely to engage in displays of intellectual dominance. These connections give a fuller picture of what it means to be a truly intellectually humble individual, including more deliberative and flexible thinking. These findings signal that intellectual humility research should expand beyond the simple connections of different trait measures and toward a theoretical understanding built on behavioral data and outcomes.

IMPACT OF INTELLECTUAL HUMILITY

Recent research into the structure and nature of intellectual humility demonstrates that it is not simply a nice, tepid virtue to set upon a shelf. It can encourage individuals to reflect more carefully on their gut reactions and biases; it is related to more genuine assessment of one's abilities and triumphs; and it is predictive of exploring new experiences and having an open-minded orientation to difficult questions (Bollinger and Hill, 2012; Haggard et al., 2018;

Krumrei-Mancuso, 2017). These are important to shaping an individual who can examine several viewpoints without bias or threat, make clear-headed decisions by weighing evidence appropriately, and is able to see beyond themselves in critical situations (Whitcomb et al., 2015). In order to combat the increasingly ethnocentric, reactive dialogue many politicians and leaders engage in, intellectual humility stands as a powerful though quiet alternative that often yields far better results (Davis et al., 2016; Peterson and Seligman, 2004). As predicted by Roberts and Wood (2007), new research suggests that individuals with higher levels of intellectual humility also engage in other virtues and prosocial values such as gratitude, empathy, tolerance, and open-mindedness (Krumrei-Mancuso, 2017).

An ongoing investigation by Catalyst, a nonprofit specializing in inclusion of women in business, in six countries has found that business leaders who practice humility by admitting mistakes, learning from criticism, and seeking the help of others, increase workers' feelings of belongingness and inclusion (Prime and Salib, 2014). Simply put, intellectually humble leaders inspire good work and promote good working relationships. Social contagion of a leader's intellectually humble behavior contributes to improved collective strategic orientation, strategic focus, and, often, business successes (Owens and Hekman, 2016). Intellectual humility not only builds better leaders but also inspires better work and more satisfied workers. Businesses such as Google also seek out intellectual humility as an important characteristic for their employees at all levels (Friedman, 2014). Similarly, doctors and other medical professionals are beginning to realize the potential impact of intellectual humility in medical education. Gruppen (2014) calls for renewed importance of the intellectual humility embedded within the Hippocratic Oath in medical education, which states "I will not be ashamed to say 'I know not,' . . . when the skills of another are needed for a patient's recovery" (quoted on p. 54).

With the profile of intellectual humility increasing in research, civic, business and medical spheres, it is imperative that its measurement be theoretically based, psychometrically strong, easy to use, and related to specific motivational, cognitive, and emotional outcomes. The limitations-owning scale meets these criteria, as does the comprehensive intellectual humility scale (Krumrei-Mancuso and Rouse, 2016). It also is related to concrete social-cognitive outcomes that can engender intellectual humility in the self and others by example, which benefits not only virtue epistemology and positive psychology, but can also have wide-ranging impacts in business, politics, and in the creation of a more civil society.

NOTES

1. The Dunning-Kruger effect demonstrates that individuals tend to hold extremely favorable views of themselves, even in domains of knowledge or ability where they score below or far below the average. For instance, someone who ranks in the 12th percentile believes they rank in the 62nd percentile (Kruger and Dunning, 1999). The better-than-average effect also shows overly positive self-enhancement in character traits such as kindness and law-abidingness in populations noted to lack these traits, such as prisoners.
2. Negative convergent validity demonstrates a negative relationship between the trait and an expected opposite trait. In this case, we would expect both narcissism and social vigilantism, a need for others to believe the same as you do, to have a negative correlation with the trait of intellectual humility. Not finding this relationship may signify that the measure is not strong enough to capture this facet of the trait.

REFERENCES

Aristotle. 1999. *Nicomachean Ethics*. Translated by M. Ostwald. Upper Saddle River, NJ: Pearson.

Ashton, M. C., and K. Lee. 2008. "The HEXACO model of personality structure and the importance of the H factor." *Social and Personality Psychology Compass*, 2(5), 1952–1962. https://doi.org/10.1111/j.1751-9004.2008.00134.x.

Back, M. D., and S. Vazire. 2015. "The social consequences of personality: Six suggestions for future research." *European Journal of Personality*, 29(2), 296–307. http://doi.org/10.1002/per.1998.

Barenbaum, N. B., and D. G. Winter. 2008. "History of modern personality theory and research." In *Handbook of Personality: Theory and Research*, edited by O. P. John, R. W. Robins, and L. A. Pervin. New York, NY: Guillford Press.

Bollinger, R. A., and P. C. Hill. 2012. "Humility." In *Religion, Spirituality, and Positive Psychology: Understanding the Psychological Fruits of Faith*, edited by T. G. Plante, 31–47. Santa Barbara, CA: Praeger/ABC-CLIO.

Carver, C. S., and S. L. Johnson. 2010. "Authentic and hubristic pride: differential relations to aspects of goal regulation, affect, and self-control." *Journal of Research in Personality*, 44(6), 698–703. https://doi.org/10.1016/j.jrp.2010.09.004.

Chancellor, J., and S. Lyubomirsky. 2013. "Humble beginnings: Current trends, state perspectives, and hallmarks of humility." *Social and Personality Psychology Compass*, 7(11), 819–833. http://doi.org/10.1111/spc3.12069.

Davis, D. E., K. Rice, S. McElroy, C. E. DeBlaere, C. Choe, D. R. V. Tongeren, and J. N. Hook. 2016. "Distinguishing intellectual humility and general humility." *Journal of Positive Psychology*, *11*(3), 215–224. http://doi.org/10.1080/17439760.2015.1048818

Davis, D. E., E. L. Worthington, and J. N. Hook. 2010. "Humility: Review of measurement strategies and conceptualization as personality judgment." *Journal of Positive Psychology*, 5(4), 243–252. http://doi.org/10.1080/17439761003791672.

Deffler, S. A., M. R. Leary, and R. H. Hoyle. 2016. "Knowing what you know: Intellectual humility and judgments of recognition memory." *Personality and Individual Differences*, *96*, 255–259. http://doi.org/10.1016/j.paid.2016.03.016.

Evans, J. S. B. T., and K. E. Stanovich. 2013. "Dual-process theories of higher cognition: Advancing the debate." *Perspectives on Psychological Science*, *8*(3), 223–241. https://doi.org/10.1177/1745691612460685.

Friedman, T. L. 2014. "How to get a job at Google." *New York Times*, February 22. http://www.nytimes.com/2014/02/23/opinion/sunday/friedman-how-to-get-a-job-at-google.html.

Gregg, A. P., and N. Mahadevan. 2014. "Intellectual arrogance and intellectual humility: An evolutionary-epistemological account." *Journal of Psychology and Theology*, 42(1), 7–18.

Gregg, A. P., N. Mahadevan, and C. Sedikides. 2016. "The SPOT effect: People spontaneously prefer their own theories." *Quarterly Journal of Experimental Psychology, 2006*, 1–15. http://doi.org/10.1080/17470218.2015.1099162

Haggard, M.C., W. C. Rowatt, J. Leman, B. Meagher, C. Moore, T. Fergus, D. Whitcomb, H. Battaly, J. Baehr, and D. Howard-Snyder, D. 2018. "Finding middle ground between intellectual arrogance and intellectual servility: Development and assessment of the limitations-owning intellectual humility scale." *Personality and Individual Differences, 124*, 184–193. https://doi.org/10.1016/j.paid.2017.12.014

Hill, P. C., E. K. Laney, and K. E. Edwards. 2014. Unpublished intellectual humility scale. Rosemead School of Psychology, Biola University, La Mirada, CA.

Hook, J. N., D. E. Davis, D. R. Van Tongeren, P. C. Hill, E. L. Worthington, J. E. Farrell, and P. Dieke. 2015. "Intellectual humility and forgiveness of religious leaders." *Journal of Positive Psychology, 0*(0), 1–8. http://doi.org/10.1080/17439760.2015.1004554.

Hoyle, R. H., E. K. Davisson, K. J. Diebels, and M. R. Leary. 2016. "Holding specific views with humility: Conceptualization and measurement of specific intellectual humility." *Personality and Individual Differences, 97*, 165–172. http://doi.org/10.1016/j.paid.2016.03.043.

Kahneman, D. 2011. *Thinking, Fast and Slow*. New York: Farrar, Straus, and Giroux.

Kruger, J., and D. Dunning. 1999. "Unskilled and unaware of it: How difficulties in recognizing one's own incompetence lead to inflated self-assessments." *Journal of Personality and Social Psychology*, 77(6), 1121–1134. https://doi.org/10.1037/0022-3514.77.6.1121.

Krumrei-Mancuso, E. J. 2017. "Intellectual humility and prosocial values: Direct and mediated effects." *Journal of Positive Psychology, 12*(1), 13–28. https://doi.org/10.1080/17439760.2016.1167938.

Krumrei-Mancuso, E. J., and S. V. Rouse. 2016. "The development and validation of the comprehensive intellectual humility scale." *Journal of Personality Assessment, 98*(2), 209–221. http://doi.org/10.1080/00223891.2015.1068174.

Leary, M. R., K. J. Diebels, E. K. Davisson, J. C. Isherwood, K. P. Jongman-Sereno, K. T. Raimi, S. A. Deffler, and R. H. Hoyle. 2017. "Cognitive and interpersonal features of intellectual humility." *Personality and Social Psychology Bulletin, 43*(6), 793–813. https://doi.org/10.1177/0146167217697695

McElroy, S. E., K. G. Rice, D. E. Davis, J. N. Hook, P. C. Hill, E. L. Worthington, and D. R. Van Tongeren. 2014. "Intellectual humility: Scale development and theoretical elaborations in the context of religious leadership." *Journal of Psychology and Theology, 42*(1), 19–30.

Owens, B. P., and D. R. Hekman. 2016. "How does leader humility influence team performance? Exploring the mechanisms of contagion and collective promotion focus." *Academy of Management Journal, 59*(3), 1088–1111. http://dx.doi.org/10.5465/amj.2013.0660

Peterson, C., and M. E. P. Seligman. 2004. *Character Strengths and Virtues: A Handbook and Classification*. Washington, DC, and New York: American Psychological Association.

Prime, J., and E. R. Salib. 2014. "Inclusive leadership: the view from six countries." Catalyst Report.

Roberts, R. C., and W. J. Wood. 2003 "Humility and epistemic goods." In *Intellectual Virtue: Perspectives from Ethics and Epistemology*, edited by L. Zagzebski and M. DePaul, 257–279. New York: Oxford University Press.

Roberts, R. C., and W. J. Wood. 2007. *Intellectual Virtues: An Essay in Regulative Epistemology*. New York: Clarendon Press; Oxford University Press.

Samuelson, P. L., M. J. Jarvinen, T. B. Paulus, I. M. Church, S. A. Hardy, and J. L. Barrett. 2014. "Implicit theories of intellectual virtues and vices: A focus on intellectual humility." *Journal of Positive Psychology, 0*(0), 1–18. http://doi.org/10.1080/17439760.2014.967802.

Sedikides, C., R. Meek, M. D. Alicke, and S. Taylor. 2014. "Behind bars but above the bar: Prisoners consider themselves more prosocial than non-prisoners." *British Journal of Social Psychology, 53*(2), 396–403.

Tangney, J. P. 2000. "Humility: Theoretical perspectives, empirical findings and directions for future research." *Journal of Social and Clinical Psychology, 19*(1), 70–82. http://doi.org/http://dx.doi.org/10.1521/jscp.2000.19.1.70.

Tangney, J. P. 2009. "Humility." In *Oxford Handbook of Positive Psychology*, edited by S. J. Lopez and C. R. Snyder, 2nd ed., 483–490. New York: Oxford University Press.

Whitcomb, D., H. Battaly, J. Baehr, and D. Howard-Snyder. 2015. "Intellectual humility: Owning our limitations." *Philosophy and Phenomenological Research, 94*(3), 509–539. https://doi.org/10.1111/phpr.12228.

Worthington, E. L. 2008. "Humility: The quiet virtue." *Journal of Psychology and Christianity*, 27(3), 270–273.

INDEX

INDEX